D0744571

DEDICATED TO:

Paulina,
Ty
and
Trevor

*From the
people of
Edmonton
and
hockey fans
everywhere.*

Wayne Gretzky, An Oiler Forever is a publication of *The Edmonton Sun* and is not associated with, endorsed by or sponsored by the Edmonton Oilers Hockey Club and Edmonton Investors Group Limited Partnership or any of their affiliates, the National Hockey League or any of its member teams or other affiliates, or the National Hockey League Players' Association.

ACKNOWLEDGMENTS

Publisher
Craig Martin

Creative Director
Terry Cowan

Photo Editors
Perry Mah
Terry Cowan

Editors
Laurie MacFayden
Shirley Taylor

Photo Reproduction
Brad Ray
Alex Wylie

Production
Will Stephani
Dru Warwick

Research
Darcy Anderson
John Sinclair

Stats/Graphics
Gary Logie

Marketing and Promotions
Bonnie Lopushinsky

Distribution
Larry Leclair

A special thank-you to Dick Chubey and all the
Edmonton Sun writers and photographers, past and
present, whose words and images helped
produce *An Oiler Forever*.

Thank you to Lyle Best, Robert Cameron, Mick Poliak,
Glen Zenith, Don Metz, Tom Braid, *The Toronto Sun*,
The Ottawa Sun and the Oilers Alumni Association for
their assistance and contributions.

Photographers
Gary Bartlett, Tom Braid, Perry Mah, Robert Taylor,
Dan Riedlhuber, Walter Tychnowicz, Christine Vanzella,
Brendon Dlouhy, Preston Brownschlaigle,
Dale MacMillan and Sean Connor.

Cover Photograph
Perry Mah

Cover Design
Terry Cowan

TABLE OF CONTENTS

Copyright The Edmonton Sun, 1999

All rights reserved. The use of any part of this publication reproduced, transmitted in any form or by any means, electronic, mechanical, recording or otherwise, or stored in a retrieval system, without the prior consent of the publisher, is an infringement of the copyright law. In the case of photocopying or other reprographic copying of the material, a licence must be obtained from the Canadian Copyright Licensing Agency (CANCOPY) before proceeding.

Printed by QUEBECOR JASPER PRINTING
A DIVISION OF QUEBECOR PRINTING INC.
Printed in Canada

Canadian Cataloguing in Publication Data

Jones, Terry, 1948-
Wayne Gretzky, An Oiler Forever

ISBN 0-9684526-1-2

1. Gretzky, Wayne, 1961- 2. Hockey players–Canada–
Biography. I. Title

GV848.5.G78J67 1999   796.962'092   C99-901361-0

ABOUT THE AUTHOR

Terry Jones, the highly respected sports columnist of *The Edmonton Sun*, has been in attendance at most major moments in Wayne Gretzky's career. The author of the original book *The Great Gretzky*, Jones also authored two subsequent Gretzky books early in his career.

Author of the highly acclaimed best-selling *Edmonton Sun* book *Edmonton's Hockey Knights, 79 to 99*, Jones has also written books on the Edmonton Oilers and Calgary Flames for the Creative Education series in the U.S., five CFL yearbooks, and was co-author of a book on the Edmonton Eskimos of the late '70s, *Decade Of Excellence*.

The Sun's exceptionally versatile and well-travelled sports columnist has a list of coverage credits which include 10 Olympic Games, more than a dozen other major international Games, eight World Figure Skating Championships and a long list of other major international sports events including World Cups of soccer and IAAF World Championships in Athletics. He's covered 27 Grey Cups, 19 Super Bowls and more than 100 World Series games. His hockey credits include all Canada Cups and similar events since the '74 Canada-Russia Series and more than 400 Stanley Cup playoff games.

A native of Lacombe, Alberta, with 32 years covering sports in Edmonton beginning at the *Journal* and on to his happy home at *The Sun*, Jones is a resident of Sherwood Park with his wife Linda, son Shane and twin daughters Trina and Nikki.

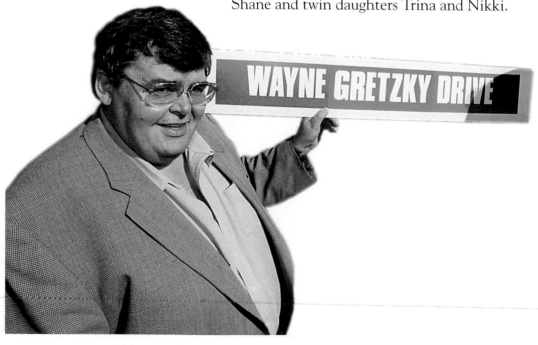

INTRODUCTION

It's sobering, sometimes, what you find in the files when you are researching a project such as this.

I found a column I'd written on March 30, 1981:

"It's the end of the 1998-99 National Hockey League season, Wayne Gretzky's final year with the Edmonton Oilers. Gordie Howe is 72 now. And how long has it been since Wayne Gretzky eclipsed Howe's old NHL assists record of 1,023 and his NHL points record of 1,809? Is that 3,000 points he's going for? How many times has he won the NHL scoring race? How many times has he won the Hart Trophy? How many times the Lady Byng?" the column began.

"How will we look back?" it continued.

"I'll remember that Edmonton was just a small city back then. I'll remember that the majority of people in the United States had never heard of the place. I believe I'll remember that Wayne Gretzky probably did as much to put Edmonton on the map as the Oilers, the Eskimos, the Drillers and the Commonwealth Games.

"I'll remember that I wrote a book on Gretzky after his first year in the NHL. I'll remember the last couple of paragraphs of the book. I couldn't sleep for nights after I'd sent it off to the publishers. I kept wondering if maybe I went overboard with the ending. I wondered if people in 1999 would laugh at what I'd written about a 'one-year wonder.' "

Scary. I don't remember writing any of that, but I did.

What I do remember writing was the dedication at the beginning of that book:

"To my son, Shane

"And to every father who had a sporting idol and every father's son in search of one."

Thank you, Gretz, for making me look good, especially on that last one.

I've dedicated this book to your kids because you told me it's the Edmonton years they always ask you questions about. Hopefully, when they peruse the following pages, they'll understand why you'll be "An Oiler Forever."

Terry Jones

Chapter

1

THE GREAT GOODBYE

On the night Wayne Gretzky played his last game at Skyreach Centre in Edmonton there was a plan in place to make a special presentation to him.

The nets.

They were going to give him both nets if he scored a goal.

"We thought it was a great idea," said Oilers general manager Glen Sather.

"He's put more pucks in 'em than anyone else.

"We thought it would be special for him. But it didn't happen."

Gretzky didn't get a goal. So he didn't get the nets.

Informed of the plan, Gretzky laughed.

"Both nets? I have a small apartment in New York."

Somewhere among the 17,099 fans on that night of Sunday, Feb. 21, 1999, there were probably a few fans who bought tickets to go to the game just in case it turned out to be the last game No. 99 ever played in Edmonton. But not many. Most were there to see him get a goal.

IT'S OVER:
Wayne Gretzky
waves goodbye
to fans at
Madison Square
Garden at the end
of an incredible
hockey career.

Retire? Gretzky had been averaging close to a point a game on a bad New York Rangers hockey team which was in a position, financially, to find him somebody with some goal-scoring talent to play with by the trade deadline. Gretzky went into the game that night 143 points short of 3,000 for his career. Who quits when they are 143 points shy of a number like that?

And remember, these were fans who had seen him run up 143 points before the end of the first period in Game 48 in 1982-83.

"I don't know," Gretzky told the media upon arrival in Edmonton. "Somebody told me the Rangers aren't coming here the next year."

GM Glen Sather said he hadn't seen a provisional schedule but scoffed at the suggestion.

"That won't happen," he said. "If next year is his last year, they'd want the Rangers to play here."

Nobody was grilling Gretzky on the subject of retirement this year.

"I'm not thinking this will be my last game here. I hope not," said Gretzky.

I'VE GOT A SECRET: The Great One started saying goodbye months before he made his retirement official.

we are again in Edmonton."

Almost a decade earlier Edmonton fans went to a game hoping he'd again make history against his old team.

It wasn't enough that Gretzky broke Gordie Howe's all-time points record of 1,850 that night, it was the way he did it. Nobody ever had a sense of stage, a sense of the moment like Wayne Gretzky. He waited until 5.3 seconds remained in the game to tie the game and then scored the winner in overtime.

"When it comes to Gretzky you don't question stuff like this," said ex-Oiler Craig MacTavish, a Rangers assistant coach. "He's always had a real flair for milestones. You come to expect it."

Gretzky was in no position to argue.

"It would be nice to do it here. So many of my great moments happened here. Most of my accomplishments came when I was a member of this team. At the time of that goal to break Gordie's record I was supposed to be the enemy. But Edmonton was happy it happened here. Edmonton wanted to be a part of it. Sure, it would be nice if it happened here."

It didn't.

Gretzky had one of the quietest games he'd ever had in the building. He discovered that night he wasn't just playing with a bad team, he was playing with a bad neck. After playing the next night in Calgary he would be out of the lineup for several weeks.

It was a forgettable game. But what Gretzky did after the game turned out to be worth remembering.

He signed some sticks.

None of the signatures were solicited. And the words he wrote on the blades of the Hesplers made every one of them special.

That said, he added that even if he knew, he wouldn't be telling the world at this stage of the season.

"I don't want it to get into a frenzy. The last thing John Muckler and the Rangers need is an extra distraction."

There was another quote he threw out:

"You have to get realistic in your life, too. I haven't made up my mind." Sather said he didn't see the day coming any time soon.

"I don't look forward to the year this league has to play without him, though."

But all the retirement stuff was on the second sports page. That wasn't the story. Getting the goal. That was the story.

The night before, the New York Rangers were playing the Penguins in Pittsburgh. It was late in the game. Gretzky was in alone with Adam Graves. No. 99 had half a net to shoot at and ... and he passed. Graves scored.

At that moment just about everybody in Edmonton thought the same thing. Gretzky had decided to save it. He was keeping goal No. 1,072 NHL/WHA regular season/post season – Gordie Howe's combined league record – for Edmonton.

"My dad always said my life was mapped out for me," said Gretzky when he arrived in town. "And here

One was for Sather. He signed several more for the Oilers' longtime equipment men and members of the training staff. He even autographed a couple for media members.

"He thanked me for what I'd done for him," said Sather. "It was pretty nostalgic. I hope it wasn't his way of saying, 'I'm quitting.'"

He handed me one after the game that night, too.

"*To Terry. Thanks for all the kind words and great support. Your friend, Wayne Gretzky. Feb. 21, 1999.*"

Problem was, I saw it as a stick, not a scoop.

Wayne's last game on April 18, 1999 was an emotional day for wife Janet, right, and their children Paulina, Ty and Trevor.

CROWNING GLORY: Wayne Gretzky addresses the media in New York on April 17, 1999, the day before his final NHL game.

All of a sudden it was the last week of the season. And suddenly there was smoke. And then there was retire.

Rangers colour commentator John Davidson, a regular on *Hockey Night In Canada*'s Satellite Hot Stove show, basically broke the story when he said there was an 80 per cent chance that Gretzky would retire. *The Toronto Sun* and the *New York Post* followed with sourced stories, "Gretzky's Gonsky" being the headline on the *Post* story.

"He wants us to be there on Sunday and I strongly anticipate that's the reason," Wayne's dad Walter told his home-town paper, the *Brantford Expositor*, of the Rangers' last game of the 1999 season in Madison Square Garden.

"I would strongly suspect that Sunday will be his final game," Walter phrased it for a Kitchener, Ont., radio station.

But Rangers GM Neil Smith insisted the Rangers were picking up his option for another year, saying, "Personally, I'd be surprised if he doesn't come back." And Gretzky's idol, Gordie Howe, and coach, John Muckler, were both trying to talk him out of it.

"I told him I'd like to see him score 1,000 goals," said Howe. "This is the time of the year when you are at your lowest. You don't make the play-offs and it's very discouraging. But one bad year does not make the end of a career. I'd like to see Wayne come back with a strong year. The show he put on at the all-star game, that last shift, my God, it looked like he could play until he was 60.

"He mentioned something about, 'This may be my last year,' " said

Howe. "I told him, 'Don't talk that way. Come training camp you're going to really get the itch again.' He's so talented he could get by on one skate."

Muckler worked hard until the last minute, trying to get Gretzky to change his mind.

"It would be a personal loss to me if he retires," he said. "We watched what that Oilers team accomplished over the years and for him to become the greatest player in the history of hockey ... well, just to be a part of that is a tremendous thing to have happen to you. I knew his mom and dad before they were married. Our families grew up together. My kids grew up with Wayne in Edmonton. It was a great association. I hope it goes a little further. I'm hoping the decision will be that he will stay. I don't want to think about the other.

"It's going to have a major effect if he retires. I don't know who takes over. Do I want him to stay? Damn right I want him to stay."

Gretzky wasn't saying much at this stage.

"I'm trying not to be an idiot about this. It's a lifetime decision. Once it's done, it's done – 100 per cent. I need to do what's best for myself. Nobody else has any bearing on this. Everybody I've talked to says, 'You've got to play next year,' and that part has been very difficult."

A total of 217 accredited members of the media headed for Ottawa for the Rangers-Senators game on Thursday, April 15.

Other than the various Gretzky sweaters fans were wearing and the signs they held up, it wasn't really a memory-making scene until there

Wayne Gretzky takes the opening faceoff against Ottawa Senators captain Alexei Yashin during his last game on Canadian soil.

was 4:43 to go.

That's when the crowd started chanting, "One More Year! One More Year! One More Year!"

The place went nuts as the scoreboard video screen began playing his highlights and listing his records to the sound of Carly Simon's *Nobody Does It Better*.

When the game ended, arena spotlights found Gretzky as he skated to the front of the Rangers bench. As he leaned on the boards, the Senators skated over and took turns shaking his hand. The Rangers banged their sticks on the ice as a salute to the Senators.

He was named the only star of the game.

Gretzky was clearly blown away by the crowd, which had given him an eight-minute standing ovation.

The Ottawa fans stood and cheered and chanted until Gretzky came out for a curtain call. Once more, this time having taken off his shoulder pads and obviously having put his sweater back on again, Gretzky came back to thank the Ottawa fans one last time for the moment.

As he left the ice, Wayne mouthed the words, "Thank you."

The chant "One More Year" had no effect. When it was over, Gretzky made it official: there would be just one more game.

On Canadian ice, it turned into The Great Goodbye. And when the Ottawa crowd and Gretzky were done exchanging love, The Great One couldn't stop himself. He said goodbye.

OK. Technically, he said 99 per cent; technically, he said barring a miracle.

But he did say goodbye. After an eight-minute ovation at the end of a 2-2 tie Gretzky finally let the world know that he was hanging them up and nobody was going to talk him out of it. He let the world see his eyes as he spoke from the heart and said the words, all the words except the actual "R" word. Then and there you could truly see that he was at ease with this.

There weren't 99 tears. There were none.

There were the sobs and red eyes from wife Janet and the kids, Paulina, Ty and young Trevor, whom she held in her arms. There was a lump in the throat of his dad Walter, who had driven 4½ hours from Brantford with his buddies Butch "The Doughnut Man" and Eddie "The Chip Man" to get to the game. But there was none of that on the surface from Wayne as he told the world that the last game of the season three days hence in New York would be his 1,486th and final game in the NHL.

"I didn't expect this response," said Gretzky. "That was an emotional experience I'll never forget tonight. The fans and the players, what they did tonight was something special. I was so happy my family was here tonight to see it.

"It was a fun day for me. I even talked to the prime minister (Jean Chretien). He tried to convince me to come back."

Jay Greenberg, columnist for the *New York Post*, put it best in his first paragraph the next morning:

"Most Canadians would rather see Quebec go than Wayne Gretzky."

Deep down, how long had Gretzky known he was going to come to this decision?

"You should know first-hand," he responded to my question at the press conference. "I was *this close* to telling people how I felt when I was in Edmonton, Feb. 21. I did everything but say it. But for the better of the club, I kept my mouth shut."

In the back of the room was wife Janet.

"I want him to be happy. But like everybody else I'm a fan, too," she said. "And I believe in miracles."

There wasn't one. The greatest player in the history of hockey was history.

Friday, April 16 in Madison Square Garden it was a fully accredited major event of the sporting century. Despite Gretzky having made the announcement on Canadian soil the night before, the city almost seemed to stop for his official, official retirement press conference. And Canada did stop.

Standing on a podium surrounded by what looked like bouquets of funeral flowers, Gretzky asked us to believe we were at a wedding. Dearly beloved, we are gathered here today to celebrate the joining of this man with his retirement.

The faces were long, conspiracy theories abounded in the background, but the greatest hockey player in history, the greatest ambassador in the history of the game – and arguably all of sport – pulled it off as spectacularly as any play he ever made.

Although there were a couple of close calls, not once were there tears and not once did he have to say, as he said on Aug. 9, 1988 in Edmonton, "I promised Mess I wouldn't do this."

As sports retirements go, this one went like The Great One's career. It was magic. It was memorable. It was classy. It was classic.

Held in the Paramount Theatre lobby in the Garden, the room featured 10 backlit pictures of No. 99 in his various uniforms, from Los Angeles Kings to St. Louis Blues to Canadian Olympic team, NHL All-Star, Canada Cup and even his Ninety-Niner team he took to Europe during the NHL lockout.

Dominating the room, on either side of the podium where Wayne, his wife Janet, sons Ty and Trevor sat with NHL commissioner Gary Bettman, were larger-than-life photos. One featured Gretzky in the Rangers' Statue of Liberty third uniform. The other featured him holding the Stanley Cup over his head in an Oilers jersey.

The NHL passed out special Gretzky retirement press kits featuring a picture of Gretzky in his first year – with long hair in an Edmonton uni-

The Great One holds court during a post-game media scrum.

Police officers escort Gretzky out of the Skyreach Centre after his final game in Edmonton on Feb. 21, 1999.

form – and one of him in a Rangers sweater.

He was introduced by Rangers broadcaster Davidson.

"Ladies and gentlemen, I'd like to introduce you to the greatest player who ever played. Wayne Gretzky."

We had, of course, the not-so-sneak preview of how this would go the night before in Ottawa. And Gretzky dodged the emotional moments like he avoided checkers in his prime. Watching him this day was as mesmerizing as watching him play.

"In life ... unfortunately, sometimes you go to funerals. And, fortunately, sometimes you get to go to weddings and fun parties," he began. "And to me this is a party. This is a celebration. I hope everyone understands that. I look upon these next few days as something to really enjoy."

Why now? If there was one question everybody who ever watched him play wanted him to answer, that was it. He was so close to those 3,000 points. He was so close to 2,000 assists. He was, some even believed, close enough to make it to 1,000 goals.

But Gretzky, who once scored 50 goals in 39 games, retired in a season when no one scored 50 goals in 82 games. And it turned out to be the first time in his pro career he registered fewer points than games played.

But still the question cried to be asked again and again from every which angle. Why? Why now?

"It's a gut feel," said Gretzky. "It's something I believe is right.

"My gut and my heart is telling me this is the right time. I'm at peace of mind. It's the right decision. This is the right time.

"It's not something I've decided in a week. I've thought about this for a long time. I kept it extremely quiet because we were in a playoff hunt and I didn't want to be a disruption to my teammates.

"I just started to feel the fatigue mentally and physically that I've never felt before. I started questioning myself about it.

"I went to Edmonton in February and I was about this close ...

"I spent a day with Janet when we got home from that trip and she said, 'Just wait' and I said, 'All right.'

"I kept it very quiet. It was between Janet and myself. I didn't even tell Michael until about three weeks ago," he said of his agent, Mike Barnett.

"I'm at peace of mind. I haven't wavered. I never budged. I just really know in my mind that I am making the right decision. I know in my heart I am making the right decision."

And then he said it. Two words.

"I'm done."

You don't say "I'm done" unless you know you're done.

"I'm done."

Those are harder words to say than "today I'm announcing my retirement."

Throughout his career, Gretzky showed an amazing ability to say and do the right thing at the right time and in the right place.

The headline in *The Edmonton Sun* the next morning said it all.

"NO RE-GRETZ!"

The New York newspapers went all out.

Newsday gave Gretzky both front and back covers. "The Greatest Ever" was the headline on the front page. "The Grace Gretzky" was the headline on the back page, the front page for the sports section.

Newsday gave him the first four pages.

The *Daily News* didn't even have a headline. Using a picture from the night before in Ottawa with Gretzky photographed from behind with his name and number on his back, waving goodbye to the crowd, it really was a picture worth more than 1,000 words. The *Daily News* gave him the first four pages.

The *Post* had Gretzky on the back cover and the first page and a half of the sports section.

It wasn't the sendoff Gretzky was getting in Edmonton or the send-

Wayne Gretzky has a chat with Aaron Moser, who was paralysed in a minor hockey game, during pre-game festivities in Edmonton on Feb. 21, 1999.

in Edmonton where I played with so many great players and championship teams and made so many friends," he said.

As was the case the night before in Ottawa, he offered special thanks to Glen Sather and John Muckler.

"Glen had me in Edmonton and he pushed me very hard to become the player I became. And then John came in and John kind of guided me to refine my tools and to kind of teach me to understand the concepts of the game itself."

He mentioned "Bruce McNall bringing me to L.A." but never once mentioned the name Peter Pocklington.

He thanked Oilers PR man Bill Tuele and the other PR men with whom he'd worked during his career.

Of all the people in the room Muckler took it the hardest and seemed to be the saddest.

"I guess I just didn't want to believe it," he said.

"This day wasn't any harder than that day 10 years ago," he added of the "99 Tears" day in Edmonton when Gretzky left the Oilers to go to the Los Angeles Kings.

"One of the reasons I took the job was because Wayne was here. I knew he was close to retirement, but I didn't think he was this close.

off Gretzky was getting in most Canadian newspapers. But the normally crass New York papers gave Gretzky the classy sendoff he deserved.

At the press conference, Gretzky had allowed himself to take a trip down memory lane. A few months earlier, in Edmonton, Kevin Lowe was asked the same question. It was the one that caused him to break down and cry. Gretzky didn't blink.

Which moment would he cherish the most when he looked back on his career?

"It's no comparison. My first Stanley Cup in Edmonton," he said.

"Every guy who is sitting here who lifted the Stanley Cup for the first time will tell you the same thing. We all loved our first goal. You loved it the first time the coach says you're going to play in your first NHL game. And that's boyhood dreams. But when you make it, there's no feeling like lifting that Stanley Cup. It's the greatest thrill in the world. I guess it's like your first-born child. It's something you don't forget. You always remember it like it was yesterday. It's very clear in your mind."

Gretzky thanked a lot of people, from teammates to family to people who had an influence on his career in minor hockey until the time he turned pro in Edmonton.

"Getting to play professionally and ending up

"Sad? Yeah, I'm sad.

"But after today, I have to admit it, I'm happy for Wayne. This is what he wanted. He has his reasons. I'm sure they are the proper reasons. I have to say that Wayne has always done the right thing. And I think, in the end, he's done the right thing again."

That didn't stop Muckler from trying to talk him out of it.

"Every time I came up with a point, he'd come up with a better one," said Muckler.

Doug Weight loses his helmet during Gretzky's last game in Edmonton, Feb. 21, 1999.

"I'm sure he'll miss it. He'll miss it terrible. But if he feels it's the right decision, then it's the right decision.

"I learned one thing through all of this. I shouldn't go into sales. I wasn't very convincing. He was."

Gretzky and his former coach and three former teammates who became assistant coaches under Muckler in New York experienced a plethora of emotions at his press conference. Craig MacTavish, Charlie Huddy and Keith Acton sat with the entire Rangers team, looking very much like they were at a funeral.

"Am I celebrating this like he wants us to?" said MacTavish. "No.

"He's trying to coach everybody through this emotional time, not just for himself but for everybody he touched in the game. But I feel par-

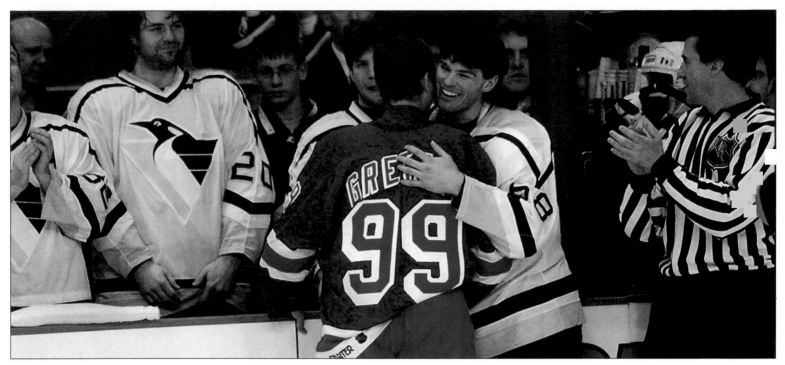

Wayne Gretzky gets a hug from Pittsburgh Penguins' Jaromir Jagr after his final game at Madison Square Garden.

ticularly good that he seems really confident with his decision. I didn't know how confident he was with his decision."

Acton said everybody Gretzky touched has to have mixed emotions.

"It's one of the highlights of my life that I got to play in Edmonton with Wayne," said Acton. "We didn't really know anything more than anybody else about Wayne's decision until we got to Ottawa. But I can see he's relieved by his decision. Like everybody else, I'd like to see him keep playing. But today I can look past that and see how content he seems, how comfortable he is with the decision. He's at ease with himself. You can see in his face that he's happy with his decision."

Huddy said he could see it, too.

"I'm happy for him."

Gretzky, when he returned from the April 15 game in Ottawa, phoned Mark Messier.

"We just talked about all the good times," said Gretzky. "He just basically said, 'Good for you. If that's your decision, good for you.' That was nice."

It was amazing the number of people Gretzky managed to think of and call in his spare moments during his retirement weekend.

Like Arnold Anderson.

He gave him the "scoop."

Anderson was the local Brantford sportscaster, the first person to conduct a radio interview with Gretzky. Wayne was 10.

Gretzky called to wish Anderson well as he battled cancer and to inform him of his retirement before he made the official announcement.

"That says something about the man that on a day like that day, he'd call," said Arnold's wife, Jean. "We were very moved. It was gracious for him to do that."

They both watched the New York proceedings on television.

"It was just an end of something that was decent and good," she said.

It was 6:35 p.m. Saturday, April 17, when the phone rang in my hotel room.

Gretzky chats with Rangers assistant coach and former Oilers teammate Craig MacTavish.

"Hi, Terry, it's Gretz. I had a couple of minutes when I had nothing to do and I wondered if you needed anything more from me today?"

Amazing. That one phone call will always be my example of the thoughtfulness of Gretzky. I set some sort of personal record for words written on that weekend – *The Sun* preparing a 32-page wraparound section for the Monday paper – and Gretzky was going out of his way to make sure I had everything I needed for the Sunday paper. How he found out in which hotel I was ensconced, I have no idea.

Gretzky told me of the Edmonton people he'd invited to his last game and told me of the things he had planned.

"After the game, I think it'll be the first time in history that a team which doesn't win the Stanley Cup, which doesn't make the playoffs, takes a team picture on the ice," he said.

The Rangers took a bunch of similar snapshots with Gretzky on the ice in the middle of the group after practice.

He talked about the second-last day in his career.

"It was kind of emotional," he said. "It was really emotional. And it was fun, too.

"Toward the end of practice, Muck called to me and said, 'OK, Gretzky, down and back, down and back, blueline and back, blueline and back, redline and back.'

"I looked at him and said, 'No way. I don't have to. I quit.' "

Gretzky said he had a "bit of a cry" in the dressing room.

"The team gave me some gifts. It was real emotional. I was a little teary-eyed. I had to go back in the training room for a couple of minutes."

One of the gifts from his teammates was a leather chair shaped like a baseball glove with a bronze plaque which read, "Thank you for your passion. From the 1998-99 New York Rangers, April 18, 1999."

Ex-Oiler Graves explained:

"He's a huge baseball fan. It's not so much the gift. We just wanted to let him know how we feel about him."

Gretzky thought it was terrific.

"It's a beautiful present," he said. "I guess a couple of the guys heard me talking one day a while back about how much I liked a chair in George Steinbrenner's office at Yankee Stadium," he said.

When they gave him that gift was when he went to the training room to have his little cry. When he came out, he went out of his way to let everybody know he wanted to paint a happy face on his last day of play.

"I don't think I've been in a situation like this. But I've been in all-star games, Canada Cups, a Game 7 of a Stanley Cup final. I always find a way to get through the game. I just told everybody to just enjoy the game. Have fun."

Yeah, right.

"I think everyone will slip Kleenex into their gloves," said Todd Harvey.

Gretzky's last day as a professional hockey player went off as if it had been planned for years, not hours. By the Rangers. By the NHL. By Gretzky himself.

There was so much thought involved. Even in the little things like going to the rink.

It was perfect, from the minute Wayne woke up until he went to bed.

"A good friend of ours came over in the morning," remembers Gretzky. "She brought over a bunch of coffee.

"A friend came over, a buddy of mine came over. We were organizing tickets for a good hour. I was trying to make sure everybody had tickets, that everybody got into the building.

"Then Mark Messier and Mario Lemieux called me. I talked to them a bit.

"Michael Jordan called me. I talked to him for a bit. Michael told me just because I'm retired now, don't think I'm going to become a better golfer.

"Janet was trying to get me to eat. The last thing Jordan said to me was, 'Make sure you eat.' So I went and had a quick bite to eat and I came down to the rink with my dad.

"I thought it would be nice to come to the arena with my dad.

"I'm the same as any kid, probably the same as you guys with your fathers. There's no relationship like father/son.

"My dad is a blue-collar man who worked eight to five every day, never missed a day of work and never made more than $35,000 a year. Everything he made he put into his kids and family.

"He almost died at one point and battled through it. And he's a good person. For people who know my dad, he'll do anything for anyone. He goes to hospitals. He visits kids. He's just a special man and he happens to be my father. I told him I get all the accolades and all the glory but he truly deserves it."

What followed was perfect.

It was, as advertised, The Great Goodbye.

Gretzky went so far as to say the day actually might end up as his all-time greatest memory. "Ask me in two months. Today's pretty thrilling."

It was a fully accredited great moment in sport long before the opening faceoff.

Fans were each handed "Thanks For The Memories 99" signs. Within minutes all the programs were gone. Members of the media were given special keepsake credentials.

Painted on the ice behind each net – Gretzky's office – was his number, 99.

The sign says it all ...

The jerseys changed, but the legend of 99 remains timeless.

The world's most famous sports arena was in darkness before game time as action highlights of Gretzky's career were projected onto the ice.

It began with what can only be called the opening ceremonies.

Rangers broadcaster John Davidson, as was the case at Gretzky's retirement press conference two afternoons earlier, was host. His first words set the scene perfectly.

"There have been times in this arena, Madison Square Garden, when you knew that you were witnessing history, when you knew that just being here was a privilege and honour that you would never forget. This is one of those times."

Then Gretzky skated onto the ice. The crowd chanted his name and the applause lasted so long, Gretzky got tired of waving and took a tour of the ice, stopping at the Pittsburgh bench to shake hands with a few of the guys he was about to play against.

His mom, wife and three kids were introduced, to cheers. NHL commissioner Gary Bettman and Rangers GM Neil Smith were introduced, to boos. And three Ranger players, ex-Oilers Adam Graves and Jeff Beukeboom and captain Brian Leetch were invited on the ice to represent the team.

"Also joining us, as a surprise to Wayne, is his first coach and general manager in the NHL, a former Ranger and now president of the Edmonton Oilers, Glen Sather," said Davidson.

Gretzky gave Slats a huge hug.

Next "the greatest player Wayne considers he ever played against ... Mario Lemieux."

And then "the player Wayne considers is the best he ever played with ... Mark Messier."

The place went crazy.

Presented with the official scoresheets from 30 of the games in which he broke a record, Gretzky also was given a 75-inch high-definition TV, and a new car – the 19th car of his career. His dad Walter was a passenger when the car was driven on the ice.

"I couldn't believe that," said Gretzky. "That was pretty classy. When they brought that car out, I almost fell over."

He'd given away most of the 19 cars he'd won in his career. This one he was keeping.

"Oh yeah," he laughed. "What was that line Jack Nicholson said? 'I think I earned it.'"

The highlight was Bettman confirming what had been rumoured for years would be the NHL's great gift to Gretzky.

"Appropriate in this, the millennium year of 1999 ... when you take off that sweater, your jersey, after today's game, you will be the last player in the NHL ever to wear 99."

Gretzky said he was moved.

"It's a great honour. Words can't describe it. When Muzz McPherson told me to wear the number in Sault Ste. Marie in 1977, I didn't expect that one day they wouldn't let anybody else wear it again."

Gretzky finished the ceremony by talking to the crowd.

There was hardly a dry eye in the house and the game hadn't started

THAT'S A WRAP: The Rangers call it a day ... and Gretzky calls it a career.

yet.

Brian Adams sang *O Canada*.

"O Canada, we stand on guard for thee. We're going to miss you, Wayne Gretzky," he sang.

John Amirante took a liberty with the *Star Spangled Banner*.

"In the land of Wayne Gretzkeeeeeee, and the home of the brave."

No. 99 loved it.

"The new words at the end ... Wow," said Gretzky. "I don't think those words are going to stick. But it was flattering."

Then there was the game.

In the seventh minute of the first period Gretzky set up Niklas Sundstrom but the left-winger fanned.

On the first shift of the second period he set up Sundstrom spectacularly and again Sundstrom failed to finish.

Twice in a mid-period shift he made magic on plays involving John MacLean, including creating a two-on-one, and both times MacLean messed them up.

Finally, with 29.9 seconds left in the period, Gretzky threw a classic breakout pass that his two wingers converted into a goal.

Assist No. 1,963. Point No. 2,857.

In the dressing room between the second and third periods, Gretzky got up and said something to the team.

"I gave a speech. People who know me and play with me know I don't give many speeches. It's not really my style. But after the second period, I called everybody in and said it's probably going to be crazy after the game, that I didn't know what to expect, what was going to happen. So what I did was I had the number 99 branded on the wood part of my blade and then with a silver marker, we put every guy's marker on it and the coaches and the trainers. I gave every guy who played with us this year and was there a signed stick as a gift from me for their friendships and for what they did for my game this year and just for the enjoyment of being around them."

Gretzky also found a few seconds to have a little chat with referee Bill McCreary before the puck dropped.

Wayne figured out fast that he wasn't going to get hit by anybody on the Penguins team, not this day. But just in case he got hauled down on a breakaway in the third period, he had a little

No. 99 celebrates his last National Hockey League point: an assist on Brian Leetch's second-period goal against Pittsburgh, April 18, 1999.

chat with McCreary on his way to the ice for the final period.

"I said, 'OK, one thing.'"

"He says, 'What?'"

"I said, 'Even if we're close, no penalty shot.' I said, 'Even if the guy tackles me, I don't want a penalty shot.'"

In the third, Gretzky kept creating and getting chances, including a glorious opportunity he created for himself late in the period.

The emotion was building.

When Natalie Cole's *Unforgettable* was played and Janet started to cry, that did it.

The tears came to No. 99's eyes.

Wayne Gretzky, An Oiler Forever

There was half-a-minute left in regulation time when John Muckler called a timeout.

At the time Gretzky was fighting with everything he had to control his emotions.

"That was the most emotional time," he said. "That's when it really hit me that I was done. I looked up and said, 'My goodness, I've got 30 seconds to go. That's when it hit me."

Muckler, when he called the time out, called Gretzky over.

"John kind of waved me over. He's got a daughter who was about to give birth in Edmonton and he called the timeout and I came over and he said, 'I got to tell you something.'

"I said, 'What?'

"He said, 'I just had a grandson today. And you've got to get the winner for him.'"

Gretzky looked around at the familiar faces in the interview room, the writers who had chronicled his amazing sense of stage, the ones who came to the rink believing he'd do something like he did when he went back to Edmonton as a Los Angeles King and tied the game and scored the winner in overtime to break Gordie Howe's all-time points record.

"I didn't get it for him today. And I know it's the right time."

During those final moments of the game Mark Messier and Paul Coffey stood beside the boards in the Zamboni entrance.

They, like those who have covered his career and watched Gretzky write storybook ending after storybook ending, were saying the stage was set for the guy again.

"He's gonna get the winner," they both thought.

"It seemed like everything in his career seemed to be like that," said Messier.

"He almost scored a goal toward the end of the game and Paul and I were sitting by the boards. We said, 'How many times did we see this happen? He came off the bench. The puck was on his stick. And he scored the goal.' And it almost happened again."

As storybook as this afternoon was, it didn't have the storybook ending.

Jaromir Jagr scored at 1:22 of overtime. The Pittsburgh Penguins beat the New York Rangers 2-1. In his last at-bat, the mighty Gretzky had struck out.

Well, not really. He played great.

Gretzky played like he did in the all-star game. Problem was the guys he was playing with in this game weren't all-stars, they were Rangers.

"I wish I could have been Michael Jordan, hitting that last shot to win

the championship. But that wasn't going to happen," said Gretzky.

"Maybe it was fitting that the best young player in the game scored the goal in overtime. Everyone always passes torches and all that stuff. He caught it. That's what I told him after the game."

There was a horrified look on Jagr's face when he scored. It was noticed that he didn't do his trademark salute.

I asked Gretzky if Jagr apologized to him.

He laughed.

"Yeah. He said he didn't mean to do that. That's what I used to say, I told him. People talk about passing the torch. Well, it's been passed."

The Garden crowd booed Jagr's goal. But only for a few seconds. Then they started chanting "Gretzky! Gretzky! Gretzky!"

No. 99 shook hands with all the Pittsburgh Penguins. The Penguins refused to leave the ice. When Gretzky took his first of several last laps around the rink they banged their sticks on the ice.

Gretzky did what he said he'd do the night before. He asked his teammates to come to centre ice and have a team picture taken together. Only Stanley Cup-winning teams normally do that. They've been doing that since Gretzky did it on the ice with the Oilers and their fourth Stanley Cup in the final game he'd ever play for Edmonton.

Eventually he went to the dressing room. The Garden went to black. On the video scoreboard a special career video of Gretzky's greatest moments, from his beginnings in Edmonton through to his Ranger game in Ottawa three nights earlier, was played for the crowd. It ended with the message: "99 Forever."

GETTING IT WRITE: The Great One speaks ... and The Large One (Edmonton Sun columnist Terry Jones) takes notes during a post-game media scrum.

Gretzky stepped back on the ice. He picked up a bouquet of flowers like he was Kurt Browning. Somebody threw out a New York Yankees hat. He wore that. Somebody threw out a Canadian Olympics hat. He wore that.

Gretzky cried. He had to cry. If he left the game dry-eyed, there would be something wrong.

"I wanted it to be a celebration. I didn't want everybody crying and all that stuff," he said.

It was a celebration. But eyes were wet throughout the rink. Even in the press box.

"My tears were tears of joy," said Gretzky. "I broke down a couple of times. They were tears of joy because I was kind of thinking of all the fun things, you know, the days of hard work together and ... tears of joy. No question."

When the tears had cleared and the most magical, mystical and memorable retirement celebration had been over for almost an hour, Gretzky walked into the interview room still wearing his full New York Rangers uniform.

He said he simply hadn't had time to take it off. No special reason. Then he thought about that for a second.

"Probably subconsciously I don't want to take it off. It's hard to take it off right now. I'm not going to put it on ever again.

"It's hard. It's hard to take it off right now. I have to be honest with you. I don't want to take it off."

But the freeze-frame we were all left with was at 6:13 p.m. on April 18, 1999 when Wayne Gretzky skated off the ice for the last time.

He'd made curtain call after curtain call and took lap after lap until he realized that the cheering wasn't going to stop.

He's Wayne Gretzky. The cheering will never stop.

A weary-looking Wayne rests his head against the microphone as he takes a question from a reporter after the April 15 game against the Ottawa Senators at the Corel Centre in Kanata, Ont.

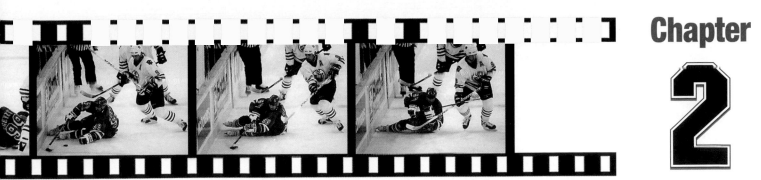

'I ALREADY HAVE A STATUE'

It was New York. The Big Apple. Manhattan. Madison Square Garden. Yet everywhere you looked there was Edmonton.

Gretzky retired a New York Ranger, but everywhere he turned, everywhere he went, were Edmonton Oilers.

Throughout "The Great Goodbye" weekend, the Oilers and Gretzky's past with the team was there. John Muckler. Craig MacTavish. Charlie Huddy. Keith Acton. Jeff Beukeboom. Mike Barnett. Eddie Mio. Glen Sather. Mark Messier. Paul Coffey. Glenn Anderson.

"After his last game, Gretz invited everybody to a party on top of the World Trade Centre," said Don Metz. "It was fabulous. He gave everybody sterling silver cigar holders with 99 engraved on the side. There were all sorts of famous people there. Jerry Seinfeld was there. Scott Hamilton, the figure skater, rented a private plane to get there from where he was performing. Mike Keenan showed up. Gretz made a speech. It was great.

"But what was kinda neat was that with all the people who were there, Gretz spent a lot of the night over in one corner. There was Slats, Muck, Mess, Coff, Andy, Charlie, MacT, Eddie Mio, all in the one corner just talking about the Edmonton days and the great times," said Don Metz.

Metz, head of Aquila Productions, the Edmonton outfit which has a world reputation in the video production field, goes way back with them all.

The newly retired Wayne Gretzky shakes hands with Oilers captain Kelly Buchberger after dropping the puck before Edmonton's playoff game against Dallas on April 27, 1999.

"Mike Barnett phoned from New York on the Saturday and asked, 'Are you coming?'

"I said, 'I guess I could get on the midnight flight.' "

Aquila, Metz denies, was not named after Gretzky. But he can see how you could come to that conclusion.

Metz was a cameraman for *The Boys On The Bus* video, filmed Gretzky's wedding and several other Gretzky projects including 28 of his Coca-Cola commercials.

But Metz swears he had no idea that Aquila was an ancient Italian city in the Abruzzi region famous for the number 99. It has 99 roads, 99 fountains, 99 arches and its identification with 99 goes back to Roman times. Nobody knows how it started. Metz swears when he started his company he named it Aquila after Mexican eagles.

Metz didn't take a camera crew to New York.

"I went strictly as a friend," he said.

Besides, it's not like he's lacking for Gretzky footage.

"We figure at our company, having worked with Gretz for over 15 years and with the Oilers off and on since 1979, in our library we have about 200 hours of Gretzky material alone."

He did concede, however, you could have put a terrific film together of Gretzky's last week, a *Boys On The Bus* production away from the cameras of the mainline media.

Like the 2½ hours Gretzky spent with Ranger assistant coaches MacTavish, Huddy and Acton the night of April 14 in Ottawa.

It was in Ottawa, when Gretzky made it 99 per cent official, that he threw out his first bouquets.

Sather and Muckler were the third and fourth names he mentioned.

"I became the person and the player that I became because of my mother and dad, Glen Sather and John Muckler. Those are the people who pushed me and patted me on the back. It's as simple as that," he said.

At his going-away press conference in New York, Gretzky made another statement:

"When Glen Sather had me in Edmonton, he pushed me. Then John Muckler came along and taught me to refine my tools."

Back in Edmonton, as the week progressed, Sather had put out the word that he didn't want anybody in the organization commenting on

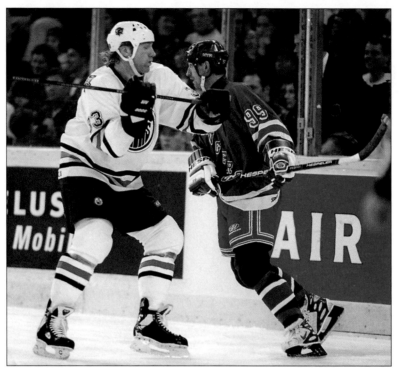

Gretzky the New Yorker squares off against his former teammates, including Marty McSorley (top).

Gretzky's retirement until he actually said the "R" word.

When he did, Sather held a press conference with Kevin Lowe, Dave Semenko and Marty McSorley.

Reaction to the Gretzky quotes about Sather was the first order of business.

"Care to take the stand in your own defence?" asked *The Sun*'s Dick Chubey of the "pushed me" and "refined my tools" quote.

"I dunno," said Sather. "I pushed Wayne. I pushed everybody because I could see the ability that they had. If we were going to get better, we needed someone who pushed hard."

As for the Ottawa quote, Chubey reported that Sather "gave it an aw gee, shucks, choirboy look."

"I think it's pretty special to have somebody like that make that comment," was Sather's response. "I tried not to treat Wayne any differently than Kevin, David or Marty. I think Wayne flatters me by saying that."

Lowe, an assistant coach with the Oilers, was making preparations for the playoffs and wouldn't be going to New York.

"It's the end of a time," he said. "But like all the old buildings that are now gone, it's a fact of life. His records and his accomplishments and, more importantly, his name, will never die."

One of Gretzky's phone calls the day before his final game was to Dave Semenko.

"He told me he appreciated our times on the bus, the time we spent off the ice and that he appreciated what I did for his career," said Semenko, now a scout for the Oilers. "He didn't have to say anything. He would have been just as successful without me. We all did our small part. We're the ones who owe him a lot."

Semenko cited his hat trick.

"When you played with him you had to keep your stick on the ice and he'd find you. It was a totally different game. I don't take anything away from the rest of my linemates, but playing with Wayne, you were excited. You knew you were going to play a lot and you knew he was going to find you."

Semenko said he was never told to act as Gretzky's bodyguard. He sort of figured that out on his own.

"Even when he first came here, nobody ever took me aside and said, 'Look at the size of that kid, you have to take care of him.' We all did it. We wanted to.

Gretzky has a huge hug for friend and former teammate Mark Messier.

"And it wasn't like every night I had to go and bail him out of something. There were just a couple of instances where somebody actually did something intentional to him and I reacted. Other than that, people left him alone. He was very tough to line up. You don't want to make yourself look foolish."

Gretzky, at the New York press conference, called Semenko "the funniest teammate I ever had."

Ron Low, at the end of his final regular season as Oilers head coach, said it was emotional for everybody in the Edmonton organization who had been an Oiler when Gretzky was an Oiler, or for any ex-Oiler wherever they might be.

"The hockey club that was here was as good as it was because he was on it," said Low, an Oilers goalie during Gretzky's early years in Edmonton.

"People rose to his level. I'm sure Mark Messier would have been a great player if he hadn't played with Wayne, but I don't know if he would have been as great as he is now. And I think there were a bunch of other guys on that team that you could say the same thing about. He was the guy who spearheaded it and a lot of people got better because of it."

Gretzky meant a great deal to a great many careers, not the least of which is that of his friend and agent, Mike Barnett.

After Gretzky left the stage at his official retirement press conference in New York, Barnett talked about his favourite times with No. 99. He talked about driving the long, dark road in the middle of the night from Calgary to Edmonton with Gretzky.

It was while travelling on Highway 2 when Barnett said he first realized just how special Gretzky was, not as a hockey player but as a person.

"Wayne hated to fly so we'd drive to the games in Calgary," said the former WHA hockey player and local bar owner who took over Gretzky's affairs, first out of Edmonton with his fledgling CorpSport International before he moved with him to Los Angeles to become almost as big in the hockey representation business as Gretzky had become in the hockey business.

"Joey Moss would come with us," said Barnett of the Oilers locker room attendant and special friend of Gretzky.

"Joey would be asleep before we pulled out of the parking lot."

Barnett would drive and Gretzky would talk on the way home.

"His comments were so profound, I'd look at the stars and say to myself, 'this has to be the second time around this planet for this guy. He can't be this profound. Not at this age. Not unless he's been around before.' He had it all figured out so early. He saw everything so clear, so early."

Barnett said he believed, finally, that Gretzky had done the right thing.

"I do, now, because of how positive he feels about it. He's listening to the same voice inside him that he listened to when he jumped in the hole or shot the puck. It's the same voice with the same clarity. He's been hearing that voice for the last three weeks."

Back in Edmonton, during the Oilers' 3-2 win over the Calgary Flames on Saturday, April 17, a capacity crowd viewed Metz's tribute to The Great One on the scoreboard above centre ice, a tribute he put together for John Shannon's *Hockey Night In Canada* production of

Gretzky with his longtime pal Joey Moss. Right, Gretzky gets off the plane in Ottawa prior to his last NHL game in Canada.

ing things happened. To be part of it, to be the same age and play all those years was something you'll never forget."

Wayne Douglas Gretzky and Mark Douglas Messier came into the world at the same time. They were born only eight days apart. They also came into the World Hockey Association at the same time.

And now, Messier suddenly realized, there was one.

"First Mike Gartner," said Messier. "Now Gretz. Leaves me."

Messier, that day, became the last of the WHA alumni left playing in the NHL.

Just over a decade earlier, it was Messier who made Gretzky promise him he wouldn't cry when he said his not-so-great goodbye on Aug. 9, 1988 in Edmonton. But, almost 11 years later, it was Messier trying not to cry.

In New York, Messier admitted it. He had to fight to hold back the tears as he watched his best friend complete his remarkable career.

"Just watching Wayne at the end of the game was really emotional. It was tremendously emotional for myself and for a lot of people Wayne had been in contact with over his career. I'd been pretty welled up with emotion for three or four days. I guess since Ottawa, when he first basically told the world about it. And just reflecting on the past 20 years and seeing Wayne and the whole thing, it was pretty sad to see it all come down."

Messier said it was a sad and happy occasion at the same time.

"I wouldn't have missed it for the world.

"It was kind of fun sitting in the crowd and just watching the whole show come down from a fan perspective.

"We don't often get that opportunity to sit in the stands with the people and hear the comments and that's what I really wanted to do tonight. It was hard because of all the things going on. But just to take it all in like a fan would and sit in the seats and watch the game and ... it was a great way to see him play his last game."

It wasn't just a hockey thing, said Messier.

"Wayne and I grew up together as 18-year-olds."

Messier was born on Jan. 18, 1961. Gretzky was born on Jan. 26, 1961.

"Going through the things we did in Edmonton obviously cemented a bond between us that is next to being brothers.

"I think because of that and because of the championships and because of the things we were able to do, not only on the ice but off the ice as well, but especially on the ice, when the pressure was on and we were able to find a way to win ... those friendships, I think, are really cemented via those occasions.

"Whether it's Kevin Lowe, who is one of my best friends, or Paul Coffey or whoever, all the guys, we've established a friendship, a bond, that's next to brotherhood and will be there forever."

Messier said while dozens of people tried to talk Gretzky out of retiring at that point, he wasn't one of them.

"I would never try to talk Wayne or anybody out of doing what they thought was right. Hockey is a tough game and it's a dangerous game. You need to be prepared and you need to be physically and mentally prepared to play. If you're not, it can get dangerous. And if you're second-guessing yourself about when you want to play or maybe you shouldn't be playing ... this is not the kind of game to be half in and half out. You are either completely consumed by it or you're out of it. And I think that's probably why he retired."

With that, Messier climbed down from the podium, took off the shades

Gretzky's last game.

"Everyone stood. Many dabbed tears from their eyes," reported Keith Gave of the *Dallas Morning News*, in Edmonton to preview the playoffs.

In New York, Messier was worried about the tear-dabbing when he arrived at Madison Square Garden, having been excused from a Vancouver Canucks team function in order to attend Gretzky's last game.

In what not long before had been Messier's town, Mark "The Messiah," the man who had delivered New York its first Stanley Cup in 54 years, showed up wearing dark sunglasses for his part in what was very much the Gretzky episode of *This Is Your Life*.

"I asked him about the glasses and he said, 'I had to wear them because if I started crying, I couldn't have everybody seeing this,' " tattled Rangers defenceman Brian Leetch.

"I've been fighting back the tears for four or five days now," admitted Messier. "Just reflecting on the past 20 years, it's pretty sad to see it all come down."

In the time between Gretzky's departure from the ice and his arrival in the interview room, Messier was asked to make an appearance in front of the media. He poured his heart out.

"Just watching Wayne at the end of the game ... I couldn't take it," he said.

"It was the ride. We were along for the same ride and a lot of amaz-

and headed for the party.

Coffey and Anderson managed to keep low profiles throughout the day. Sather didn't have a chance.

While they didn't bring him into the press conference room, Sather found himself in several media scrums.

"Wayne had a dramatic effect on the city of Edmonton and for all of us who live here," Sather told one gathering of reporters. "For Canadians he is the one person we can all look up to. He's been an inspiration to us all.

"My entire career was built around him. All the success I've had comes directly from Wayne."

Sather stood there and told them he believed Gretzky could have been greater.

"Unfortunately, I don't think he ever reached his peak," he said. "I always wonder how many Stanley Cups he'd have won if he'd stayed in Edmonton. He had just become a mature man when he left. He was just starting to mature as a player."

That, of course, was when Peter Pocklington sold him to Bruce McNall in Los Angeles.

Sather offered his impressions from back then as the sportswriters scribbled.

"Wayne was so much more intelligent than any other player. He was very articulate. He was an intelligent spokesman. He had a sense of humour about himself and a playfulness.

RANGER BLUE: Gretzky, right, lines up with New York teammates Adam Graves, left, and Brian Leetch.

"He is a wonderful human being. Think of all the cars he's given away to people. He always makes sure everyone gets everything they need. He never misses anyone. He's very compassionate. That's why he has so many friends throughout the game.

"As for the NHL, for anyone that's touched him, there's the realization that he has a special gift and we were all lucky to be around him. It's unfortunate that he's leaving. But he's leaving on his own terms.

"There are a million memories. For me most of the important ones came off the ice, not on it. I remember his laughter on the bus and at practice.

"I remember him going three-on-three after practice, fooling around with us like a father fooling around with his kids in the backyard and that's despite the fact these guys were professional hockey players.

"If you ever stop to talk to him about a game, he can remember every play. He could tell me not only where everybody on our team was on the ice at any time but he could tell me where everybody on the other team was on the ice. We didn't use videotapes. We had Wayne. He seemed to have total recall about what happened on the ice at any time.

"I don't think there was an awful lot you could teach somebody like Wayne. He has ability, a tremendous mind and he sees the ice differently than the rest of us. His ability to move laterally was the thing that impressed me the most.

"He was never late for practice. He wanted to be on the ice all the time. He was probably a coach's dream.

"Off the ice? Well, look at Joey Moss," he said of the Oilers locker room attendant who has Down's syndrome.

"It turned his life around. Here was something he could do to help a young guy. He turned the guy's life around. That was 17 or 18 years ago. That kid is still around and even signs autographs.

"If you think back over the years of incidents, situations and predicaments that hockey players get into, there hasn't been one problem that Wayne wasn't able to handle in a sophisticated, elegant and proper manner."

Metz, who is also the executive producer of the 12-part *100 Years Of Canadian Sport* series, had flown to New York with Sather, stayed at the same hotel, spent most of his time with him, went to the party with him and then took him to a few scheduled morning TV appearances.

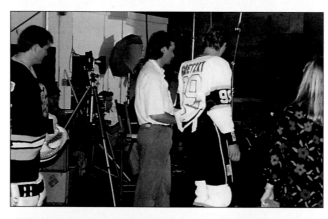

The Great One was in great demand making NHL commercials over the years, as these scenes from Don Metz/Aquila Productions shoots attest.

As soon as he got back to Edmonton, Metz sent a camera and an interviewer to tape some of Sather's even more revealing thoughts, the ones he'd heard Gretzky's old coach express away from the media that weekend in New York.

With Metz's camera rolling, Sather revealed the secret of the flushed cheeks.

"I always knew if I could get Wayne's cheeks to flush ... He had a certain blush in his face. When I got his face into that blush, I knew there was no stopping him. He never got tired. He could do what he wanted.

"I used to watch for that flush, that indication. That's when I knew he was on a whole different level than anybody else.

"There were nights when he could have scored nine or 10 points. And he would just back off because he didn't want to embarrass the team. But I used to keep playing him because I knew the opportunity was there for him to do something that nobody else could do."

The flushed cheeks made Sather use Gretzky in a great many ways he otherwise might not have considered.

"That's how we developed the situation how he started killing penalties.

"We used to do things on the ice to get him away from other players who would try to check him. We'd have him come in one door on the bench and run down and go out the other door. We'd have him go and stand beside somebody's best player.

"We had lots of fun because they were things nobody else did in hockey. The style of our team was so different. It was fun doing that because here you are sitting with the best hockey player in the world who was the most coachable and loved to play. It was a great time.

"What I'd probably do more than anything was double shift him. I'd let him sit on the bench for 10 or 15 seconds. I'd put him back out again. I'd get him into this second wind thing when he was young. And when he got into that then there was a flush on his face. It wasn't anything that probably anybody noticed except me and him. But I knew when he had it. There was a look about him. Then you couldn't stop the guy."

Sather said having Gretzky made innovations mandatory.

"The team was really built around Wayne," he admitted.

And so was the Oilers' freewheeling, firewagon, speed-kills, go-go game.

"I found the other game boring," said

Sather of the up-and-down-your-wing game played when Sather was an NHLer.

"I couldn't see Wayne spending his career playing boring hockey. And we couldn't play under the old way because Wayne wasn't a grind-y hockey player.

"We had too many guys who were free-spirited on our team. They needed something to keep their interest. They loved to come to practice. We did all kinds of things."

Sather said there was never a problem with Gretzky being bigger than the team, even if everywhere they went it was always "Wayne Gretzky and the Edmonton Oilers."

"It really was Wayne Gretzky and the Oilers," said Slats. "But he never put himself above the team.

"Wayne practised the same as the rest of the guys. He always had a roommate. He always travelled on the bus. He did the same things that everybody else did on this team because that's the way we ran the team. He never complained about anything. He never complained about practising. He practised harder than anyone."

Sather said Gretzky was better with the whole scene than his coach and general manager.

"The only time I really found it to be a pain in the neck was when we'd go into cities and reporters would know very little about Wayne and want to talk about him. They'd done no background work on him. They wouldn't know anything about him. And then they would expect me to explain everything to them, over and over again. I would get impatient and short-tempered with these guys. Whereas Wayne would do it. He would explain to them about everything they would want to know and do the interviews. Never was he short-tempered. He was a lot better with the press than I was. It was the same with the team. He was easy to deal with. But I think as an organization, sometimes, we got fed up with it, just because it was so redundant. You do it a million times, you get tired of it."

The Oilers boss said he was on the other side of the world when he knew for sure he wasn't dealing just with a great young hockey player, but a Canadian icon.

"I was in Africa one summer. We were on a photographic safari of Kenya, sitting in a little bar in a town south of Mombasa. It was the summer after we beat the Montreal Canadiens in the playoffs. We were sitting in that bar and there were two girls at the table next to us talking, not knowing we were Canadians. They were talking about how the upstart Edmonton Oilers had knocked off the legendary Canadiens. They were talking about this kid Gretzky.

"I think that night I kind of realized how important hockey was to Canadians because it touched everybody in this country. We don't really have any political heroes. Grassroots people, when they talk about

this country, they talk about weather and hockey. When you talk about the general concept about what we want to talk about, we want to talk about hockey. We love it. And Gretzky has been the main hockey hero in this country for the last two decades.

"There's no question. Wayne was the greatest as far as I'm concerned. Not from what he did but what he did for the sport. His image for the public has been one of purity. He has been a pure athletic hero. He's been unblemished."

Sather is reluctant to suggest there won't be anybody who will come along and approach the greatness of Gretzky. He rather hopes somebody will. But he's convinced nobody will get half of Gretzky's records.

"They're going to be very, very hard to break. There's probably 30 records that are unbreakable."

Sather said maybe once he was Gretzky's father figure. But that was a long time ago.

"I think I'm more of a friend than a father. We've sort of passed that stage where you are a father image. It disappears and you become a friend. With Wayne it might have been like that when we were young. It's flattering for me to hear him say that. We went through some pretty good times and some pretty rotten times. But there wasn't anything we could do about it. We adjusted. The friendship has endured and probably always will, like it will with a lot of those guys on that team."

Maybe, Sather suggests, he could become a grandfather figure for Gretzky's kids.

"I went to lunch with Mike Barnett, his kids and Wayne's kids in a restaurant in Central Park in New York. Michael's wife was there and my wife was there. But Wayne wasn't there. We were sitting there and Michael and I were talking about hockey players' numbers in the league and who wears what number. We got to Dominik Hasek's number. We were trying to think how many guys in the league wear Hasek's number. Mike and I were stuck. We could think of one or two

Wayne and Janet share a quiet moment. Below, Wayne's dad Walter poses for a picture with Janet, Trevor, Paulina and Ty.

guys. Guess who had the answers? Gretzky's son Ty had the answers. He was just like Wayne. That's when I realized here's a whole new evolution coming on. This torch is being passed from Wayne to his son now. His son is just like Wayne. I don't know if he can play hockey or not. I haven't seen him skate. But he has the same kind of mind Wayne has. It was just bang, like that, he had the answer. That's the way Wayne used to be when he was young. So that was the moment I realized he had retired and his son is now carrying the Gretzky name. It'll be interesting for me to watch what happens with his family."

Sather said he knew for days he would be in New York for Gretzky's last game.

"I knew he was going to retire when Neil Smith phoned me and asked me to come to New York as a surprise for Wayne," he said of the Rangers GM. "He asked me to keep it quiet, so I didn't tell anybody.

"Then a couple of days later Wayne phoned me in the press box at one of our last games of the regular season. He asked me if I would come to New York. He said he'd like me to come as his guest for his retirement. I couldn't very well lie to him. I told him I'd already been invited and I was going to come and that I was going to be there and it was supposed to be a surprise. He was pretty excited and said, 'Well, I'll act surprised.' "

Despite the fact he already knew, Sather said when Wayne gave him the call was when it happened, when he was overcome with nostalgia.

"I think when somebody tells you he's retiring, your mind starts to race on to all the things that have happened and the years you spent together and all the fun moments and closeness that you had. There's a million things that go through your head.

"It was sad. It was emotional. But it was typical Wayne. He put a spin on it so that it's not a negative deal that he retired. It was a graduation for him. It was something to celebrate. He chose to do it on his terms. He did it the right way. It was the year 1999. I mean how more perfect could it be? It was like he orchestrated it all.

"It was pretty classy the way things happened. The party was great, being on the ice with those guys was tremendous. It's like the first Stanley Cup we won. You remember that. It was a very emotional time."

At some stage of the party at the top of the World Trade Centre, as the clock ticked towards midnight, Sather mentioned something to Gretzky about him coming to Edmonton to drop the puck at an Oilers playoff game so he could wave goodbye to Edmonton fans, too. It was one of those things you say half-kidding, half-serious and then forget, not expecting it to happen.

Gretzky showed up on April 27 for Game 4 of the Oilers playoff series against Dallas, totally unannounced, to take Sather up on his, er, invitation, nine days earlier in New York.

Down three games to none and facing elimination, the Oilers were inspired to play the second-longest overtime playoff game in franchise history that night.

Gretzky, who had left the Oilers before Petr Klima's winner 55:13 into OT in the 1990 Stanley Cup final, was gone for this one, too, leaving after the second overtime to catch a flight back to New York so his pilot could make clearance for a flight the next day.

The Great One's visit will be remembered, almost certainly, longer than the long game which Dallas coach Ken Hitchcock declared to be the greatest game of the entire Stanley Cup playoffs, won by his Stars two months later.

It was classic Gretzky.

He walked on the red carpet as fans waved their white towels and made as much noise for him as he'd ever heard in the building before.

For two minutes the crowd poured its love down on the man who did more than anybody to put Edmonton on the map. If he was wearing skates, he could have taken as many laps as he did after that last game in New York and the crowd would have stood and cheered as long as he remained in sight.

But Gretzky, consistent to the end of his career, didn't want to take

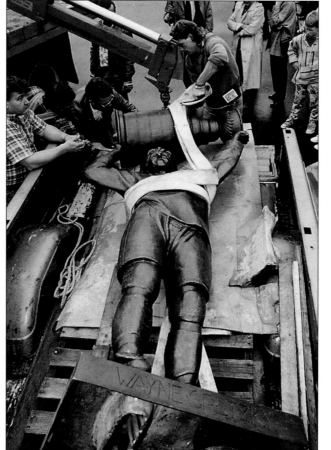

Workers get ready to install the Gretzky statue in front of Edmonton's Skyreach Centre.

anything away from a playoff game, and finally dropped the puck, shook hands with Kelly Buchberger and Joe Nieuwendyk, accepted handshakes from Brett Hull and Mike Modano and said play hockey.

It was perfect. It wasn't the big Wayne Gretzky Night to match the one he had in New York. That one would come in the fall. But it told us once again just what a classy, classy guy he has been, and will continue to be, for the game.

"I knew Wayne wanted to do something here for the crowd and that he wanted to come here. And I knew it would be a classy, subtle thing between him, the team and the city," said Sather in his press box bunker that night.

No. 99's former coach and GM swore he didn't know Gretzky was going to be there until he was there.

"At 3 p.m. I got the call.

" 'It's Wayne,' he said.

" 'I'm here.'

" 'Surprise.'

"We had a big laugh. It was great."

Sather then called Jim Hole and Bruce Saville of the Oilers ownership group. NHL commissioner Gary Bettman was also in town. Along with Sather's wife Ann and Sather's two sons, Gretzky's agent Mike Barnett and the retired legend occupied the Oilers' suite during the game.

"It was a wonderful gesture on his part. He did it for the fans of Edmonton."

Sather said the idea was something much more immediate than visiting here for his big day in the fall.

In the dressing room Gretzky made a short speech to the home team.

"He shook hands with every player, went into the training room and shook hands with everybody in there and gave Teddy Green a great big hug. Just that fact he was in there was inspiration," said Sather.

It was quite a night for Gretzky, too.

No. 99 confessed he did something that night he'd never done before.

He said he had never before looked at his statue in front of Skyreach Centre until he went to the rink for this game. He said he'd always closed his eyes or looked the other way. That night he finally felt like he wanted to see it out there. It was OK. He was an Edmonton Oiler again. For life.

"That's the first time I saw my statue outside. I didn't want to look at it. I'd always avoid looking at it when the bus would drive up to the rink," Gretzky revealed.

"I hated coming back to Edmonton to play. I say that in the best possible way. You know how I hated coming back to play in there. It was really hard. I never liked it. I was never comfortable. I always felt so much a part of the team and so much a part of the city. I dreaded it."

He said for all the years it was almost impossible to look anywhere in the stands and not see a familiar face in Edmonton.

Going to visit his statue was part of the Edmonton exorcism.

"When we drove up to the rink, it was the first thing we did. Mike Barnett and I walked by my statue and I took a real good look at it out there."

Once Gretzky walked inside, he knew it would be a joy returning to town from now into the future.

"It was overwhelming," he said of the two-minute standing ovation he cut short when he dropped the puck between Buchberger and Nieuwendyk.

Lightning lights up the night sky behind the statue of the NHL superstar who 'did more than anyone to put Edmonton on the map.'

"It felt like Game 7 of the final against Philadelphia to me.

"And what a great game!

"I went down to the Oilers dressing room late in the third period," he said, adding it was at the request of the police who were worried about a security problem when the game ended, not figuring that would be about three hours later.

"It was kind of crazy. I spent the better part of three overtime periods watching the game on TV in the dressing room. I flew all the way to Edmonton to watch close to 60 minutes of hockey on TV. But that was great, too. Dave Semenko and Esa Tikkanen watched it down there with me."

Gretzky said it was a fun, fun night, but the best part might have been phoning Sather when he arrived in town at 3 p.m.

"Slats mentioned the idea to me at that party we had in New York. I didn't want anybody to know I was coming, not even Slats. So I waited until we got to Edmonton to phone him.

"When he answered the phone, I said, 'Hi, Slats, this is Gretz. I wonder if you could get me a couple tickets for tonight's game?"

"He said, 'Sure. No problem. Whose name should I leave them in?'

"I said, 'Mine.'

"We both had a good laugh.

"I was glad to be back. I wanted to go back for the fans. I think it was fitting for me to go back for Glen, for the team and for the fans. I feel like such a part of the history and tradition of this team.

"It was nice to be in the dressing room with the players and to talk to Kevin, Marty and Bucky," he said of Lowe, McSorley and Buchberger.

"It was nice to see everybody.

"It was nice to be in that dressing room again. I'd been in the back a couple of times to visit Sparky Kulchinsky and Barry Stafford and the gang. But I hadn't been in the actual dressing room. It was great to look at all the pictures and everything again."

No. 99 said he couldn't wait to come back for the Oilers Alumni golf tournament in the summer and for his Edmonton tribute night in the fall.

"I don't want anything overwhelming," he said. "Whatever they are going to do for me, I know I'm going to be thrilled with it. I already have a statue."

WAYNE'S HOCKEY ASSOCIATION

It wasn't the greatest moment in Edmonton's aviation history. There were all those heroic deeds and landings and takeoffs by the Blatchford Field bush pilots: Wop May, Punch Dickins, Leigh Brintnell, Grant McConachie, Matt Berry, Walter Gilbert and the like.

But when Wayne Gretzky landed in a Learjet at the same airport in the wee hours of Nov. 1, 1978, it was the most significant date in Edmonton hockey history.

Gretzky, of course, wasn't the pilot. While he would go on to spend a great many future flights up in the cockpit, he was basically in baggage for this one. He didn't even get one of the passenger seats. Eddie Mio and Peter Driscoll claimed those.

"Because Wayne was the smallest and the youngest of the three of us, we felt it was only right that he be the one to be stuck in the jump seat in the back of the plane," Driscoll laughs today.

"A little while later we found out he was petrified of flying. We kind of wondered why Wayne surrounded himself with hockey sticks like that on the trip. It was kind of like he was hugging all the hockey sticks we'd brought along. I think he thought they would protect him."

Today Mio says it's all a warm, fuzzy memory, but it was traumatic when it happened.

Eddie Mio, Peter Driscoll and a teenager named Wayne Gretzky arrive in Edmonton in November 1978.

"We were told after practice. And they couldn't tell us where we were going. Either Winnipeg or Edmonton.

"They told us to grab as much stuff as we could and bring it to the plane. So we did. We had a lot of stuff. And I had my goalie bag. That takes up a lot of room by itself.

"There was a bar on that plane, like in a limousine. Driscoll and I drank a lot. Wayne didn't drink anything.

"We didn't know how to feel. We didn't even know where we were going. We didn't know whether to be excited or not.

"I remember getting on the plane and the pilot turning around and asking us who was paying for the flight. Gretzky was the guy making all the money, but he didn't have any and didn't even own a credit card. Peter and I had a house together and I knew he didn't have a credit card and probably wasn't walking around with a lot of cash either. I had my Toronto-Dominion Bank credit card. It had a $500 limit. I was hoping they didn't phone to find out that was my limit.

"When we got to Minnesota, we found out we were going to Edmonton.

"But when we got there, we landed at the International airport. We were supposed to have gone to the Municipal airport downtown because everybody was waiting at the hotel for the press conference.

"The pilot wanted more money to fly from one airport to the other. He took another swipe at my credit card.

"The most important thing to me when we landed was to make sure the Oilers put the flight on their credit card. To this day I wish I'd kept that receipt. But I had them rip it up, right on the spot. I should have kept that. That would have been a great souvenir."

Gretzky laughs: "Eddie always jokes that I was a throw-in on that deal."

The Legend of Ninety-Nine begins with Hockey Night In Canning and little Wayne Douglas Gretzky, at age one, sliding on stocking feet and shooting a little ball with one of those souvenir-stand mini-sticks at his grandma, the goalie. It involves the pylons at the world's most famous backyard rink at 42 Veradi in Brantford, Ont. It involves the nine-year-old kid who scored 378 goals in 85 games with Lenny Hachborn, Jimmy Burton, Greg Stefan and the rest of the kids on the Nadrofsky Steelers in 1971-72.

It is that of a young man signing autographs, appearing on *Hockey Night In Canada* and being interviewed by *Sports Illustrated* at age 10. It conjures up images of the kid who faced such jealousy as a young player that he moved away from Brantford to play. It involves Muzz McPherson suggesting he wear No. 99 during his one year in major-junior hockey with the Sault Ste. Marie Greyhounds because the number 9 was already taken. But in Edmonton, the Legend of Ninety-Nine begins with that famous flight.

The chartered Learjet, including the short hop from one Edmonton airport to the other, cost Oilers owner Peter Pocklington $7,900.

For Driscoll it's become a claim to fame.

"That's what people remember about my hockey career, that I was in

The contract with which Nelson Skalbania signed Wayne Gretzky over to Peter Pocklington.

that trade and on that plane with him," says Driscoll. "People ask about that all the time."

Driscoll married a girl from Indianapolis. He now works in the city where Gretzky's career began, and he coaches kids' hockey there.

"It's a big thing to the kids that I used to play with Gretzky," he says. "I guess it's a big thing to me, too."

Mio would go on to have a different claim to fame.

A decade later he'd be Gretzky's best man.

When the three arrived at the late-evening press conference, Mio and Driscoll headed straight for the food laid out for the media. They hadn't had anything to eat all day, and left Gretzky to talk about suddenly becoming an Oiler.

"In Nelson's eyes, I think he feels like he's doing us a favour. He said Edmonton is the best city in North America so I guess we'll have to wait and see," said Gretzky upon arrival.

"It's funny, really. Here I am, only 17 with a three-year head start on most guys, and already I've been traded."

HAPPY BIRTHDAY KID: Teammates help Wayne Gretzky celebrate his 18th birthday in January 1979.

Gretzky may or may not have noticed it at the time. But there was a short sidebar which was part of the coverage in the paper the next morning. A local Tier 2 junior player by the name of Mark Messier, also a 17-year-old, was headed to Indianapolis to begin his WHA career, filling a place in the lineup left by Gretzky.

"Lots happened since then. That was a long, long time ago. But it still seems like yesterday," Messier said of Nov. 1, 1978.

"Gretz was flying into town and I was flying out of town. Our careers kind of intermingled a bit since then."

An Edmonton native, Messier was then playing for the St. Albert Saints in the Alberta Junior Hockey League.

"I'd heard of him as a kid growing up and I'd heard of some of his exploits, like everybody else, but I hadn't met him."

Neither could have guessed what they'd do together on the same team in the NHL.

If there ever was a move that had NHL or Bust written all over it, the Gretzky signing was it for the Oilers. The $825,000 deal was a steal of a deal for owner Peter Pocklington. He not only got Gretzky, Mio and Driscoll, the deal absolved the half-million-dollar payment to former Oiler ownership partner Skalbania in the event the franchise made it to merger with the NHL.

"I hope you agree that we've taken a step toward improving the hockey future of the Oilers, either in the WHA or the NHL," was the last paragraph of Pocklington's prepared statement which arrived at the press conference hours before Gretzky, Mio and Driscoll did.

"Maybe Nelson should have left me here in June," said Gretzky upon arrival.

It all was a classic case of deja vu, the arrival of Gretzky, Mio and Driscoll to become Oilers on that now historic flight.

Gretzky had returned to the same airport where Skalbania had landed back in June to announce he'd signed Gretzky.

When that happened, it was swift and sudden, not the long, soap-opera scenario involved when Bobby Hull jumped to the World Hockey Association to give the league instant credibility in the beginning.

It was 4 p.m. on Sunday, July 11, 1978 when Skalbania parked his private jet at Edmonton's Municipal airport.

Skalbania wasn't all that subtle about it. He decided to land in Edmonton to announce the story then and there because he wanted the news to get out then and there. He wanted the NHL owners to swallow their cigars at their draft and meetings in Montreal. And, having previously been a part-owner of the Oilers with Pocklington, he knew the reporters in town.

The signing was completed on the flight between Edmonton and Vancouver. On board were Skalbania, Gretzky, his mom Phyllis, dad Walter and agent Gus Badali.

Skalbania gave Gretzky a $250,000 signing bonus, $100,000 for the first year, $150,000 for the second and third and $175,000 for the fourth.

And the timing was perfect.

The governors were meeting in Montreal. And 24 hours earlier an 18-year-old jockey by the name of Steve Cauthen had just won the Triple Crown riding Affirmed in the Belmont Stakes. Skalbania was quick to make the point that nobody was suggesting Steve Cauthen should still be riding for $75 a week in a major-junior jockey league or some such. And Bobby Orr had been an underage junior. Gordie Howe had been an underage junior. Why not Wayne Gretzky?

"It was really wild," Gretzky remembers today. "I didn't know where I was going but I went to Vancouver. I was told by Gus that 'the guy who owns a team wants to sign you.' But at the time, believe it or not, it was Houston or Indianapolis. When I wrote the contract out on the plane, it had 'Houston or Indianapolis' on the contract. At the time Nelson was negotiating to buy Houston. Gus was pushing big time for it to be Houston."

Before the flight and the mid-air contract signing, Gretzky said Skalbania took him aside.

"He asked me, 'Do you think you can play pro hockey?'" Gretzky remembers today. "I told him, 'If I didn't think I could, I wouldn't be here.'"

Skalbania, a noted jogger, wondered if he was dizzy for thinking of doing such a deal. So before he did it, after flying Badali and the Gretzkys to his home in Vancouver, he decided to take Wayne out for a little run

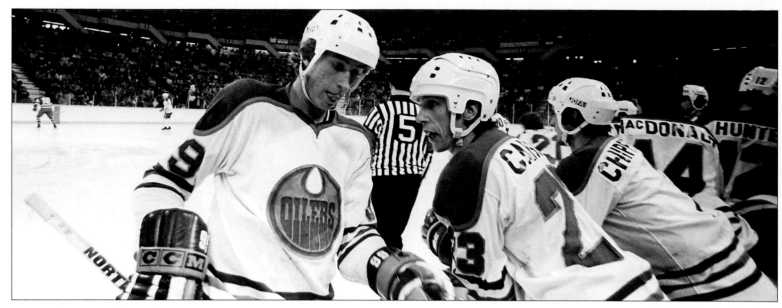

Wayne Gretzky's first two pro goals as an Indianapolis Racer were against the Edmonton Oilers, but he soon switched jerseys.

to check him out. It turned out to be a six-mile mini-marathon.

"Nelson was a big burner and liked to run," Gretzky remembers now. "He made me run six miles with him. I think he was surprised I was able to run the whole six miles. The rest is history."

Gretzky's sister Kim, before an injury, was considered a good bet to become a Canadian Olympian in track. And Gretzky had run some. He didn't just get his name in papers as a hockey player when he was a kid. He earned mentions at Ontario high school meets in the 800- and 1,500-metre events as well as cross-country competitions. He passed with flying colours.

"He didn't know, but I loved to run," said Gretzky.

Looking back, there's one part of the proceedings that Gretzky laughs at now.

"We're going from his place to the airport and his Rolls-Royce breaks down. So he gets another Rolls-Royce sent out and it breaks down, too.

"The most my dad ever made was $32,000 a year and Nelson says to him, 'Walter, never buy a Rolls-Royce.' "

There Gretzky sat, that afternoon in June, in a crowded private jet fingering a cheque for $50,000 – a mere down payment on a four-year personal-services contract with a three-year option worth as much as $1.75 million.

"I don't know if this will kill any talk of merger between the two leagues or not," said Skalbania at the time. "But I do know I didn't like going on my hands and knees begging to get into the NHL last year. Who knows, maybe they'll call a truce now and say enough is enough. This situation now is just ridiculous."

Gretzky, for his part, was saying the right things.

"A lot of people will think I was foolish not to be thinking of playing sometime in the Stanley Cup playoffs. But right now the NHL is just going on prestige. It's good. But who is to say it's better than the WHA? I think the WHA has proved to be of equal calibre to the NHL.

"I guess the master plan worked," said Gretzky that day at his official-signing pit-stop press conference. "The dream's come true."

The summer before, Gretzky was earning $5 an hour fixing potholes on a road gang.

It was a personal-services contract and if it didn't work out, Skalbania joked that Gretzky could end up doing odd jobs for him.

"Who knows," Skalbania laughed. "He could end up as a deckhand on my boat in the Mediterranean or the most expensive racquetball partner in history."

Skalbania made Gretzky scribble out the details of the contract.

"I had to write it," said Gretzky at the airport that day. "I was handed a crumpled sheet of paper. Gus was talking, my dad was too nervous and Skalbania said he couldn't write it because the figure made him dizzy," said Gretzky.

"I still find it hard to believe," said Walter six months after Gretzky had signed the deal. "I've worked 22 years for Bell Canada and I've never been able to save much money. Now, at 17, look how much Wayne has."

Whether or not they swallowed their cigars in Montreal was open to some debate.

New York Post hockey writer Larry Brooks tells the story of how it went down at the other end.

"It was June 15, 1978 and what was then called the NHL amateur draft had concluded at the Queen Elizabeth Hotel in Montreal. I was sharing a cab to Dorval Airport with Islanders GM Bill Torrey, who had heard the news that the Indianapolis Racers had announced the signing of a 17-year-old named Wayne Gretzky.

"A publicity stunt," Torrey told me. "He certainly couldn't play in our league. He'd get killed."

Torrey and the Islanders, of course, would become very familiar with Mr. Gretzky in the not-too-distant future.

Later Torrey would marvel.

"Everybody kept saying, 'Wait till he gets hit.' Hell, he never got hit."

So Gretzky was an Indianapolis Racer.

Skalbania would later look back and make fun of his idea that No. 99 was going to be the sizzle to sell the steak in Indy.

"Season ticket sales soared," he said. "They went from about 2,100 to 2,200."

Maybe the signing didn't cause them to go nuts in Hoosier country. But in hoser country ...

"All summer long people kept asking me if I'd met Wayne Gretzky yet," said Mio. "They knew I'd be playing with him and there'd been so much hoopla about his signing for so much money. It was all I heard. Gretzky! Gretzky! Gretzky!"

Mio wasn't sure what he was going to make of this kid everybody was talking about.

"I met him. And I talked with him. And I liked him!

"I realized, as did everybody else, I guess, that all the talk was not his fault. Right from the day I met him he was a real personable and likable kid."

Driscoll said it worked the same with everybody.

"He didn't look like much the first time I saw him, but the first time I saw him on the ice I knew he was something special. In the first practice we gave him the puck and he wouldn't give it back."

"When he came in it was obvious he was going to do something. He had that ability to read ice we'd never seen before. We all felt it was going to be nice to watch this kid grow up. He was pleasant, polite, showed a lot of respect for the veterans that were around. He was a class act from start to finish."

Driscoll and Mio will always treasure the idea that they were the guys with Gretzky in that trade and on that fateful flight. And one of the top NHL referees today likes the idea that he has one to tell his grandchildren, too.

"I played against him in his first game in the WHA when he was in Indianapolis," says Paul Stewart. "How many guys can say that? I remember asking him if he had a note to be out so late because he looked so young."

Gretzky didn't last long as an Indianapolis Racer. But he was there long enough to be photographed for a hockey card.

Gretzky owns the world's only signed Indianapolis Racers rookie card.

He signed one years ago, put it in a vault at the time as a hedge against financial disaster, and has since never signed another one.

Gretzky also lasted long enough in Indianapolis to create one of the greatest hockey trivia questions of all time.

Question: Against which team did Wayne Gretzky score his first goal as a professional hockey player?

Answer: The Edmonton Oilers.

"My first two goals were against Edmonton," Gretzky remembers today of that night playing for the Racers with linemates Kevin Nugent and Angie Moretto.

"They were both against Edmonton and they were both against Dave Dryden. Twenty years later somebody sent me a tape of my first two goals against Edmonton and I'm looking at them with my kids, and my young boys were laughing at me. They said I looked like I was a little kid."

After eight games – three goals, three assists and six points – Gretzky was off to become an Edmonton Oiler.

He almost became a Winnipeg Jet.

"Crazy Nelson," remembers former Jets owner Michael Gobuty of Skalbania. "Nelson wanted to play backgammon for Gretzky against a one-third ownership of the Jets. It was the day before Nelson sold him to Edmonton.

"To my chagrin, I didn't agree to the backgammon game. I found out later that I could have beat him. Nelson, I discovered, really wasn't that good of a backgammon player."

Pocklington tells the story of how he could have had him earlier.

"I almost had him without knowing it in the summer," said the man they were referring to fondly as Peter Puck back in those days.

"Gretzky's lawyers in Toronto at the time happened to be my lawyers. I told them I'd love to bring this kid to Edmonton. They told me he was too young. But a few months later, Birmingham Bulls owner John Bassett was talking to Badali about him. The price was too high for Bassett but he told them to get hold of either Skalbania or Pocklington. He'd just been on the phone talking to Skalbania so he suggested Badali should phone him. If he'd been on the phone talking to me …"

When Pocklington's turn did come, he said it was simple.

"When Nelson sold me the Oilers, the deal was I'd have to pay him a half-million if the Oilers got into the NHL," said the now ex-Oilers owner way back when. "I gave him $300,000 cash and we ripped up the agreement for the half-million. It was that simple. That's my philosophy.

Keep 'em simple. And keep 'em big. The whole thing took about five minutes on the phone to finish off. Nelson needed the money right away."

Gretzky was unaware of most of that at the time.

"Nelson told me I could go to Winnipeg or Edmonton," Gretzky recalls today. "He told me I had my choice. Winnipeg or Edmonton.

"Gus Badali was a real big believer in Edmonton. He told me if any team in the WHA makes it into the NHL, Edmonton would have the best chance."

Skalbania looks back on it now and laughs.

"In those days, I hit big on some things and lost big on some other things. But the worst was when I sold Gretzky to Peter Pocklington. It was crazy for me to do it. And Winnipeg could have had Wayne but they thought it was too much money to pay for a 17-year-old player."

Glen Sather took one look and he was a big believer in Gretzky.

OK, two looks.

Sather was asked by Pocklington when the Oilers were in Indianapolis to play the Racers to take a look at Gretzky because there might be a chance to get the kid.

"The morning skate was kind of a relaxed atmosphere," remembers Sather.

"There was a little kid out there skating. I thought he was one of the players' kids. I was looking for this phenom Gretzky and I couldn't find him."

That night he scored the two goals and Sather got an eyeful.

Gretzky was the first to admit he was more effective on the ice than in the kitchen.

"Wayne was playing with a couple of guys who didn't really complement him, but he was light-years ahead of everybody on the ice," Sather recalls. "It took me about two seconds after the game to call Peter and tell him to make the deal."

Gretzky stayed his first three weeks in Edmonton with Glen and Ann Sather and family.

"The thing I remember most about living with Sather is one night him telling me that one day real soon Edmonton would be in the NHL, that one day I'd be captain of the team in the NHL and one day we'd win the Stanley Cup. And I believed him, too," Gretzky remembers today.

No. 99 also remembers how he almost let Sather convince him to wear No. 14 for the Oilers.

"That's the number he had made up for me. He said it would put a lot less pressure on me than if I wore No. 99. I told him, 'It doesn't matter what number I'm wearing, I'm going to have a lot of pressure. And I like No. 99. By game time I had No. 99 again."

Gretzky was in Grade 11 at the time. And he was a teenager.

"Gus had me on a weekly allowance. Not much more than your average 17-year-old would get," Gretzky explained.

It was weird. One day Gretzky went into the lounge at the Northlands Coliseum after practice with his teammates. They ordered beer. He ordered ginger ale. The lounge manager was embarrassed at having to ask the rink's biggest drawing card and the No. 1 bringer-of-business to his establishment to leave. Under Alberta's liquor laws, he wasn't even permitted to be in the place.

The manager offered to buy Gretzky a drink on his 18th birthday. And No. 99 showed up to take him up on the offer. But he took a sip, made one of those faces a kid makes when he's forced to eat his liver, and offered the rest of the drink to someone else sitting at the table.

He was something, on and off the ice. But it was on the ice that the old pros on the Oilers WHA team couldn't believe.

"We'd heard all those things about him," said Al Hamilton. "But it didn't take long to realize he had something special. I remember I came in from the point, all of a sudden the puck is on my stick and the goaltender is out of the play. I missed the net by 20 feet. That's how shocked I was."

Gretzky scored in his first game as an Oiler. So did Driscoll. And 11,762 fans liked what they watched for openers in the 4-3 win over the Winnipeg Jets.

So did Sather.

"He made some fine plays and showed that remarkable instinct he has," said the coach. "He seems to see everybody on the ice."

Gretzky's first goal as an Oiler wasn't a typical Gretzky goal by any stretch.

It was a 50-foot blast.

"I don't know where I got that power from," he said.

One of the most unforgettable nights in Gretzky's career was Dec. 13, 1978. And not because he broke any record. He broke a lot of records over the years. But on Dec. 13, 1978, hockey fans in Cincinnati watched something you just don't get to see. That was the night he was benched.

Gretzky would never be known as a two-way player. But Sather, in a game against the Stingers, benched Gretzky that night for "not helping out enough on defence" generally, and specifically for "screwing up" defensively on a goal which put the Oilers down 2-1.

No. 99 responded to the symbolic spanking by his coach by coming off the bench to score his first pro hat trick in the final 40 minutes.

He scored his 13th and 14th pro goals in that game on plays made from what would become known as "his office" behind the net. He finished off the hat trick with a blast from 40 feet.

Gretzky said it wasn't the first time in his life he'd been benched.

"It happened last year in Sault Ste. Marie," he said of his junior season. "I can't remember who we were playing, but I think I got seven points, four of them goals, in the last two periods."

Sather said he was slightly miffed by Gretzky's minus-six rating in the first four games of a road trip.

"He could have sulked," said Sather on the time. "But Wayne got mad instead. The smoke was coming out of his ears."

Years later Sather would look back at that episode and smirk.

"I think that game made Wayne Gretzky a hockey player," he said. "That night he stuck it to me and carried us to a win."

By the end of December, they weren't calling Wayne "Brinks" any more in Edmonton. He was The Great Gretzky. Definitely doubts still existed around the rest of the hockey world, especially in NHL circles, but the hockey fans of Edmonton had seen enough.

He'd only been an Oiler for a couple of months and it was quite clear. He was the most exciting thing to happen to Edmonton since they discovered oil at Leduc No. 1.

For the first six seasons in the WHA, the Oilers hadn't really been worth watching, although Edmonton led the league in attendance. But suddenly they were watching something special and they knew it.

Gretzky made it into the top 10 of WHA scoring despite the weights Sather had tied to his wings. And any doubts there were in his own dressing room had completely disappeared.

Goaltender Dave Dryden said it for everybody after a game one night.

"Personality-wise, he's incredibly mature. He's thoughtful. He's not the least bit spoiled. And the thing I like best is that he's not self-satisfied. He stays out late after practice. He wants to be as good as he can possibly be. And he's not a follower, he's a leader.

"Talent-wise, his biggest asset is his ability to control the puck and himself. He has the rare ability to wait for somebody to make a little mistake and take advantage of it for everything it's worth. Most players have preconceived notions of what they're going to do. I'm convinced he doesn't.

"You can't compare him to anybody. He's unique.

"With his talent and with the personality he's shown us so far, the sky is the limit. I've seen a lot of guys with talent who didn't put it to good use. But I'm convinced this is one kid who has all sorts of talent and is going to use it all."

That said, Gretzky was still a 17-year-old kid. And once in a while it showed.

The day before he turned 18, his teammates had a little fun with him.

First they bought him a cake for his birthday. Then they shoved his face into the icing while a newspaper photographer snapped pictures.

This was followed by a special one-man Happy Birthday comedy skit by Steve Carlson, who starred in the movie *Slapshot!* as one of the Hansen Brothers.

Carlson did an impression of Gretzky from the night before in a game against the New England Whalers.

THE SKY'S THE LIMIT: With the arrival of Wayne Gretzky, the WHA Oilers were suddenly worth watching.

Gretzky, during the game, had been nailed by Gordie Roberts. It was a bone-jarring check. Gretzky hit the ice and threw his stick and one glove in a temper tantrum.

Carlson copied him perfectly, although with some exaggeration.

A red-faced Gretzky watched and got the message. It was his final temper tantrum.

By his 18th birthday, Gretzky had exceeded everybody's expectations. He had 23 goals and 46 points in 39 games and was uncontested as the Oilers' scoring leader.

"I remember him telling me he'd be happy with 20 goals and 40 assists before the season started," said Badali. "The last time I talked to him he thought he might score 50."

Gretzky said the WHA required adjustments.

"The biggest thing is that pro goaltenders are quick learners," he said. "You can't beat them with the same moves you used in junior."

Ah, yes. Junior. He still had 2½ years of junior eligibility remaining. And back in Brantford, his parents were still collecting family allowance cheques for him.

"I can hardly wait for my birthday," he said often that winter. "I'm tired of reading '17-year-old Wayne Gretzky' all the time."

On Jan. 26, 1979, he turned 18. And there was no pushing his face into the cake in the shape of No. 99 which they wheeled out to centre ice. There was a bottle of baby champagne from his teammates. And the Oilers made it a surprise party for Wayne by flying in his parents, brothers Keith, Glen and Brent and his sister Kim.

The on-ice birthday party was advertised, but not what came next.

Gretzky signed a contract which, according to everybody, would

'Wild' Bill Hunter, who brought the WHA to Edmonton, and Gretzky share a laugh during Reunion 99 festivities on Aug. 25, 1999.

make No. 99 an Edmonton Oiler until 1999.

"There's no out," said agent Badali.

"There's a renegotiation clause after 10 years but there is no out," said Pocklington, who swore that night he would not give up Gretzky as a price for merger.

Gretzky looks back at that now and takes great delight in the whole deal.

"I signed until 1999. This is the year."

Watching him play in the first 10 minutes of the game that night, it was hard to believe he'd make it all the way to 1999. Gretzky couldn't possibly have played any worse.

"I couldn't make a pass. Heck, I could barely write my name on the contract."

How could that be when he had been as cool as a cucumber playing on the same line with Gordie Howe in the WHA All-Star Series against the Soviet Union only a couple of weeks earlier?

"I had Gordie to settle me down in that game. I didn't have him tonight," he said.

Looking back two decades later, Gretzky enjoys telling the story.

"My dad told me I should sign it. He said you never know if you're going to get injured. He said, 'You love it here, sign it.' I had a lot of people telling me it was for too long and not to sign it. But my dad said, 'Take the security.' It worked out."

Well, there was a moment of hesitation.

One person telling him not to sign was a teammate.

"I told him I had to sign it. I told him about the big signing ceremony they were having before the game.

"He told me to sign Bob Smith.

"You know, I actually started to make the 'B' for Bob ... but I couldn't. But that's one weird looking 'W' on Wayne where I signed."

In the dressing room after the game, Gretzky seemed cool about it all despite the fact one of his naked teammates had decided to, er, leave an impression by sitting on his cake.

"Looks like I'm here for life," he said. "I've played in four different cities in the last three years. I don't need to go move again. Everything is great here. There's no sense to leaving."

With the Oilers 61 games into the season, Gretzky rang up his 80th point. In his last 17 games he had 32 points, just under two points per game. And he'd moved into fifth place in the scoring race.

On April 10, Gretzky scored his 39th, 40th and 41st goals and registered his 58th assist. That gave him 99 points.

Considering his goal of 20 goals and 40 assists, 99 points was a nice number. But he closed with 110 points to finish third in WHA scoring, won WHA Rookie of the Year honours and led the Oilers to their only first-place finish in their WHA history. The Oilers made it to the Avco Cup Final that year but lost out to the Winnipeg Jets.

Today, Gretzky says people may not believe it, but he owes a lot to the WHA.

"I don't know where my career would have gone if I hadn't played in the WHA," he says.

"I would have played that year in junior. I might have been hurt. I could have got messed up or gone to the NHL in a bad situation.

"I'm very grateful the WHA was around and that I became a part of it."

IMAGES OF GREATNESS: Over the years, Wayne Gretzky made lookin' good look incredibly easy – both on and off the ice .

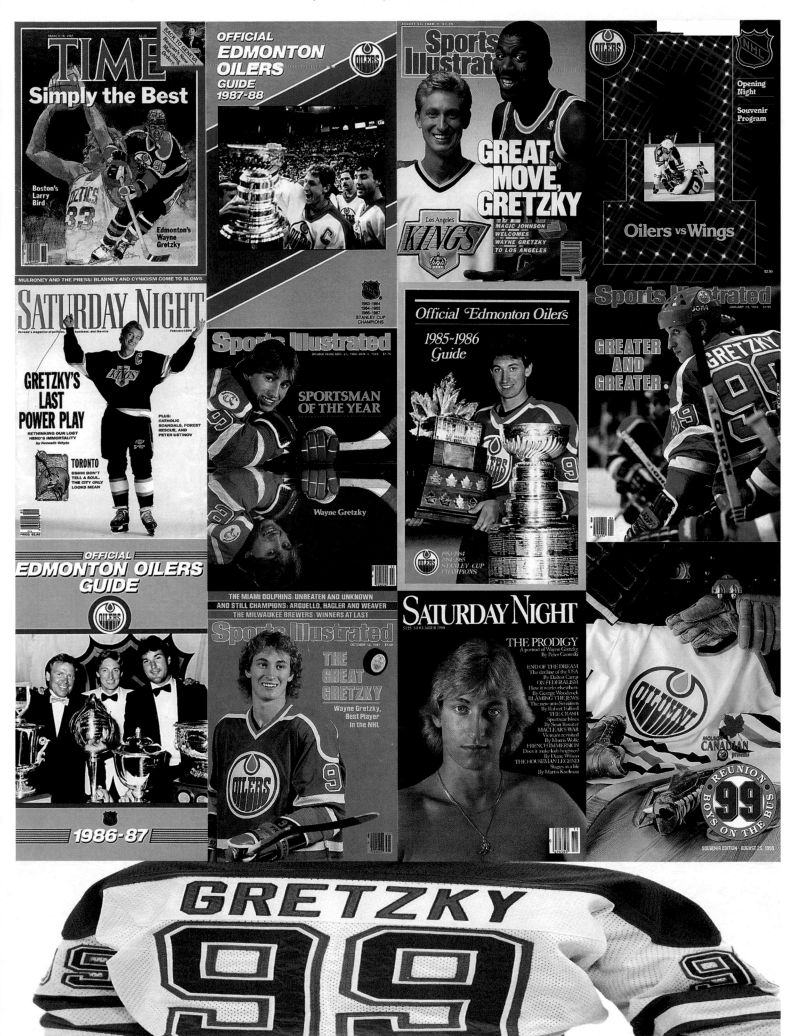

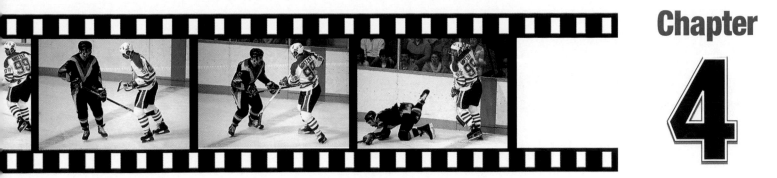

Chapter
4

A FINE HOW-DO-YOU-DO

the Seven Years War was over. The Edmonton Oilers were in the NHL. And Wayne Gretzky may have looked great in that other league, but this was the NHL, yadda, yadda, yadda, yadda.

Gretzky heard the talk.

"I'm going into my fifth year as a rookie," said No. 99. "Each year I've had to prove myself. Each year they told me the checking would be tighter. Each year they told me I'd get hit more. Each year they told me I wouldn't score. Each year I've been told I'm going to get run out of the rink. I'm going into the NHL at 18, just like Gordie Howe and Bobby Orr. There's going to be a lot of pressure. But I plan to prove myself."

With those words, Gretzky approached his first NHL hockey season.

The Kid had an interesting off-season, participating in *Superstars* and *Showdown*, a couple of TV competitions, signing endorsement deals with Titan sticks and Perfecta blades, participating in almost every pro-am golf tournament and charity softball game there was.

When it came time to set up residence in Edmonton again, you wondered if he'd show up as a different kid.

He didn't.

A very young Wayne Gretzky took the pressure of moving from the WHA to the NHL in stride ... and spent the next two decades proving his naysayers wrong.

TRULY CANADIAN, EH? Shinny on an outdoor rink is the epitome of the game for hockey's purists.

Despite the money he was making, he was on an allowance established by his parents and administered by agent Gus Badali.

"I didn't really spend much money this summer," he said when he hit town. "My agent keeps a pretty good eye on it. I'm still going to take out only as much money as I need for a month. I mean, if I see a shirt I want to buy, I want to have enough money in my pocket to buy it."

Gretzky didn't change. But he sure did notice people changing around him.

"People reacted a bit different to me at home in Brantford," he said. "I'd walk down the street and see people I used to know and they'd be a bit edgy. I think they wondered if I'd still talk to them or something dumb like that. It's a funny feeling."

And everywhere he went he heard about next year and how Gretzky wasn't going to be as great now that he was in the big time.

"That's all I heard all summer," said The Kid. "As the summer went on, I heard more talk about how it's going to be a different story this year. Every year people have told me how I'm going to be in trouble at a higher level. I heard more of that talk this summer than I heard all my life.

"I knew I'd hear all that stuff again. Different guys told me how everybody is going to try to run me in the NHL. One guy bragged that it took him 10 years to run Bobby Orr but he finally did it. Some of it was a psych job. But most of it was serious. A lot of guys I met want

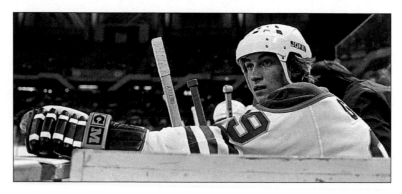

me to be prepared."

Gretzky said there was one refreshing change.

"Not as many people questioned my skating and hockey ability like they did before," he laughed.

The Kid made a prediction.

"I'm pretty confident. I don't think it will be that big of an adjustment."

The Edmonton Oilers had been able to protect Gretzky as part of the merger terms. And the first-year franchise dazzled at the draft, picking Kevin Lowe in the first round, Mark Messier in the second and Glenn Anderson in the third.

Sather managed to steal Lee Fogolin from Buffalo and to work out a deal that brought Dave Semenko, lost in the merger draft, back to Edmonton without him ever having actually left. Al Hamilton, Dave Dryden and Bill (Cowboy) Flett were old pros who had joined the WHA and were returning to the NHL for one last lap around the league. Eddie Mio and Peter Driscoll remained from their famous flight from Indianapolis. Doug Hicks, Colin Campbell, Ron Chipperfield, Risto Siltanen, Dave Hunter, Blair MacDonald, Brett Callighen, Dave Lumley, Stan Weir and Pat Price were other guys who headed to camp as original NHL Oilers.

Fogolin was kind of looking forward to camp and meeting the kid he'd heard so much about.

"I'd been looking forward to seeing this young phenom named Wayne Gretzky," Fogolin tells the

THREE AMIGOS: Gretz is flanked in the dressing room by goaltender Dave Dryden and Brett Callighen.

story all these years later.

"I was disappointed to learn he wouldn't be there. I was told he had a high school classes. I thought to myself, 'High school?' I'm thinking, 'What gives here?' But it didn't take long to realize what a great talent he was. And we all know what happened that year. It was mind-boggling.

"He was so much better than everybody else. Right from the beginning. I remember one goal where he came out from behind the net, then scored on a backhander in the opposite side of the net. For any other player, to score a goal like that would be like winning the 6/49."

Gretzky was enrolled at Ross Sheppard composite high school.

At the time he figured he could pull it off, play in the NHL and finish off his high school diploma.

"I promised my parents that I'd complete Grade 12," he said as he went back to school when the other pros were headed to Edmonton to go back to camp.

"I think going to school will keep my mind thinking. Keep me sharper. And it'll give me something to do on road trips. You can't read *The Hockey News* all day. I need Canadian history and English. My classes are in the afternoon. We practise in the morning. With two classes I should have no problems with road trips."

The strangest sight as the Oilers first NHL training camp began was Gretzky sitting in the stands watching "rookie camp."

"It's a funny feeling when you're 18 and you don't have to attend rookie camp," said the WHA's last rookie of the year.

"Everybody out there is older than I am."

Gretzky loved the pre-season, playing against NHL players. And in the pre-season he looked every bit as good as he had in the WHA.

If the jury was out on him, some of the members of that jury didn't take long to register their votes. He had some early converts. Like Phil Esposito.

The kid scored five points in 21 minutes against the New York Rangers in one of the games.

"He's the greatest young player I've seen since Bobby Orr," Esposito declared after that game.

The pre-season flew by for these guys and everybody on the Oilers' first road trip, en route to playing their first NHL game, was flying higher than the 35,000 feet the pilot's altimeter suggested. And nobody was flying higher than No. 99.

"You've got to be a man to play hockey but you have to have a lot of boy in you, too," he said on the plane to Chicago where the Oilers would open against the Blackhawks.

"The boy is really coming out in everybody right now. I was really pumped going into last year in the WHA. But I could feel it in those exhibition games. The crowds seemed more excited. This may sound dumb, but every time you score a goal, it's more exciting in the NHL."

The scene won't be forgotten by anybody who was on that team.

"Hoo boy," said Gretzky in the basement of the old Chicago Stadium as he horsed around with his teammates before that game.

"I can't believe this is happening.

"When they play the national anthems, I know I'm going to get butterflies."

History would record that Lowe scored the Oilers' first goal at 9:49 of the first period, assisted by Gretzky and Callighen, although that goal would come into some question 20 years later. Gretzky was named the third star of the game that the Oilers lost 4-2.

"I've never been that nervous before a game in my life," Gretzky said when it was over.

The Kid had another assist in his home opener, a 3-3 tie against Detroit. The next night, at home against Vancouver, he scored his first NHL goal. It was a backhand through the pads of Canucks goalie Glen Hanlon with 1:09 left to secure a 4-4 tie.

"That's five years in a row that I've scored my first goal on a backhand. Last year it was on Dave," Gretzky said of goalie Dryden.

Hanlon didn't go around boasting of having the claim to fame of giving up the first Gretzky goal in NHL history. He usually avoided talking about it. Even on the day Gretzky announced his retirement he was reluctant to talk about it.

"Out of respect for Gretzky, OK, I'll talk about it," Hanlon finally agreed when nagged by West Coast reporters. "But I don't enjoy it.

"He came down and went around the net and it looked like he was going for the wraparound. I went down and instead of going short side, he stuck it over top of me. It was a typical Gretzky goal. The goalie was on his back and he was still standing."

Gretzky's great adventure had begun.

As a 17-year-old, he had spent his WHA season in a room-and-board situation with Ray Bodner and family and debated about staying there another year or getting an apartment. The apartment won out when

Away from the ice, Gretzky always had time for charity events like this wheelchair basketball game.

Kevin Lowe offered to be his roomie.

"He was a lot older than me," Gretzky laughed in later years. "He was 19."

They were Felix Lowe and Oscar Gretzky.

"I wouldn't say Gretz is a terrible cook," said Lowe, when I decided to check in on the Odd Couple early in the season. "It's just that I'm a better cook than he is."

The two worked out a deal with the 14-year-old girl across the hall. She vacuumed their apartment in trade for hockey tickets.

Gretzky was in awe of Lowe's cooking.

"He's amazing," he reported. "Kevin cooks roast! He bakes lasagna! Cherry cheesecake!"

Lowe laughed.

"I can't be that good. I can't get him fattened up."

Lowe recalled the night before they caught that plane for Chicago and the first game of the season.

"We'd moved in," he said of their south-side apartment. "But we hadn't assembled our beds yet. The night before we were leaving we scrambled around trying to put those beds together."

Waterbeds.

"We ended up waiting up half the night until the mattresses were filled."

It was a terrific time for those two kids in those first few weeks. They didn't even try to be cool. And Lowe, even if he had to be chief cook and bottle washer, loved being with his new roomie. He said he figured some of the good things about Gretzky were rubbing off on him.

"He's unaffected. A lot of guys would have blown the situation Gretz is in. He's younger than I am, but it doesn't feel that way.

"We're getting on great as roommates," Lowe said in the middle of that

LET'S GO, GUYS: Gretzky and Co. have a pep talk with the home-team goalies during a pre-game warmup.

FLOWER POWER: The Oilers' budding superstar is followed up the ice by Montreal Canadiens legend Guy Lafleur.

domestic scene that day. "We think a lot alike. We're both shooting for the same sort of thing. I know I'm not going to be content to be a fringe Oiler. I want to be a star. Gretz already is a star. But he wants to be the calibre of somebody like Guy Lafleur. I think we're both the kind of guys who are going to work every night to be as good as we can possibly become."

Lowe added one more thing.

"I don't know if I should be saying it, but Gretz isn't doing too much homework so far. I'm going to have to get on him about that."

By now there weren't many places No. 99 could go in Edmonton and not be recognized. But it hardly turned him into a recluse.

"I still find it kind of neat to walk down the street and have someone know who I am and want my autograph," he discussed the subject quite candidly back then.

"I guess I even take a bit of pride in that because it means I've done something people like."

Gretzky's regular linemates that first season were Blair MacDonald and Brett Callighen.

By Nov. 2, Gretzky had played nine games and scored two goals and added eight assists.

He celebrated his first anniversary as an Oiler that night in Edmonton against the New York Islanders. The Oilers won 7-5. And Gretzky, for the first time in the NHL, skated onto the ice as the game's first star.

The Kid put on his greatest perfor-

LITTLE BIG FAN: Fido seems unimpressed as Gretzky demonstrates stickhandling techniques to WHA Oiler Garnet (Ace) Bailey and his son.

mance in the NHL to that point. And it wasn't just the two goals and an assist. If his linemates had converted even a decent percentage of their chances, he would have had at least double that.

It was his first game back after missing a game and two-thirds because of tonsillitis.

"Gretzky made me look like a donkey," Islander goalie Glenn (Chico) Resch said quite candidly about it in the visitors dressing room.

Sather said Gretzky's game that night said something about him.

"The Islanders scored in the second minute of the game and their goal was Wayne's fault. It was his mistake. And he knew it. He looked at me on the bench and I knew by his expression that he knew it. He wanted to get out there and get it right back."

Gretzky scored on the Oilers' first shot on goal 21 seconds later.

"That's the hardest shot I've ever taken in my life," he reported in the Oilers bathhouse after the game. "But to be honest, I was shooting at the other side of the net."

MacDonald raved that night.

"Things just happen when he's out there. "It's unbelievable how much he's matured as a playmaker. Last year, in the WHA, he'd often get to the blueline and shoot. But he learns fast. Now he gets to the blueline and waits for his three or four options."

Sather, on the night of Gretzky's first anniversary as an Oiler, made a statement.

"I'll tell you one thing. I wouldn't trade him for four New York Rangers and Barry Beck. Oops! You know what I just did – I just compared him to somebody. That's the first time I ever compared Wayne to anybody. I promised him when I came here I wouldn't put any pressure on him by doing that."

On Nov. 21, the Oilers made their first trip to Toronto to play at Maple Leaf Gardens. They'd beaten the Leafs at home earlier in the month. This time Gretzky had two goals and two assists in a 2-2 tie in Toronto.

He was inspired.

He'd read a story on himself printed in the Maple Leafs program.

"It was all about what a good year I had last year in the WHA and it was really complimentary and everything," he mentioned a couple of months later. "It predicted I'd probably do OK in the NHL. But the last line of the article said I'd finished third in scoring in the WHA but, of course, there was no way I'd finish third in the NHL."

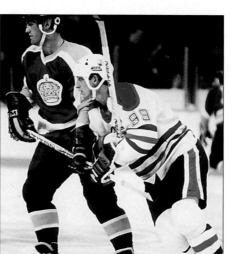

Witnesses saw him throw the program across the dressing room and declare: "I'm going to have to finish no worse than third."

THE SPORT OF KINGS: Marcel Dionne (16) and the L.A. Kings were regular thorns in Gretzky's side.

And so began the tradition of Gretzky using negative media mentions as major motivation.

It wasn't, you should understand, a Leaf policy to be negative about Gretzky.

The next day King Clancy, a Hall of Famer and Leafs executive, was holding court in the Hot Stove Lounge.

"Cripes, guys have been telling me he can't skate. Damn rights he can skate! And he skates down in the ice. He doesn't skate on top of it. He's like a good horse pulling a wagon. He digs in."

And Lee Fogolin tells of another conversation.

"Harold Ballard came up to me and remarked, 'Lee, you know what? I would deal my whole team for him. We'd probably win more games.' "

While the Leafs had nothing personal against Gretzky, the league did.

CRUNCH TIME: Gretzky sandwich, anyone?

It quietly put in a Gretzky rule before the season.

The Calder Trophy for rookie of the year had a definition change.

Previously it was defined in the NHL rulebook as: "To the player selected as the most proficient in his first season of competition in the National Hockey League."

A few words were added going into Gretzky's rookie year.

Those words were "in any major professional league."

The NHL had refused to concede the WHA was a major professional league throughout its existence. And now it was? Yet it refused to list a WHA statistic of any player in league material?

Gretzky was clearly the most amazing first-year player in NHL history. But he was banned from winning the Calder.

Ah, there were other trophies. And in a way, to this young team, the Montreal Canadiens were a trophy. Being in the NHL was one thing. But the night of Dec. 14 was special on the first-year schedule. It was the night the most storied squad in NHL history would skate on Edmonton ice.

What happened just wasn't supposed to happen. The Oilers beat the Canadiens. It had never happened before. Never. A first-year team had never managed to beat the Canadiens while playing their first game against Montreal.

Gretzky had a goal and an assist in the 5-3 win and led the team off the ice to a standing ovation. His goal and assist weren't what people were talking about that night. The fans saw something they'd never seen before from Gretzky. He played a two-way game that night.

"How can you help but get yourself more up than for any other game you've ever played?" he said. "The fans were cheering for us in warmup."

You're on the other side of something like that and the last thing in the world you are expecting is for the star of the show to ask you for your autograph.

"He called me Mr. Lafleur," said Guy in horror. "And then he asked me for a couple of autographs."

Gretzky seemed a trifle embarrassed to hear that The Flower had ratted on him.

"Aw, come on," said The Kid. "I have a lot of respect for Mr. Lafleur. But the autographs were for my brothers."

Gretzky kept referring to him as Mr. Lafleur throughout the entire interview.

Like this quote:

"Let's be honest, who wouldn't like to beat Mr. Lafleur in the scoring race."

When I went back to Lafleur with that reaction he shook his head.

"Wayne is a nice kid, but I wish he wouldn't call me Mr. Lafleur. He makes me feel old already."

Lafleur said he'd seen enough of Gretzky already to know how his career was going to go.

"I don't think there's much to say about Wayne that hasn't already been said. He's going to be a star. And the game needs another star."

Gretzky, in his first stop in most cities in the league, was greeted by major spreads in the local newspapers.

Lowe, who also roomed with Gretzky on the road, said he could tell when Gretzky was going to have a good game on the road just by the volume of ink in the papers.

No. 99 said there might actually be some truth in that.

"It puts extra pressure on me. When the press is building me up, it promotes hockey and helps put people in the building. I guess I get out there and try especially hard to make sure I do as well as the press says I can do. Then, of course, there are the people who are coming to see me flop. That's the other side of the coin."

EYES ON THE PRIZE: Wayne Gretzky swoops in on an opponent.

By Jan. 24, in preparing to play a game against the Maple Leafs in Edmonton, Gretzky had played 45 games, scored 26 goals and 43 points for 69 points in his rookie NHL campaign. He was ahead of his pace from the year before in the WHA and had passed Charlie Simmer to move into a tie for fourth place in NHL scoring with Dave Taylor.

Gretzky had just played his 125th game as a pro. He had 112 games plus playoffs to play before he'd use up his eligibility as a junior hockey player. Between the WHA and NHL he had 176 points.

Gretzky had managed at least one point in 36 of those first 45 NHL games. He'd had two four-point games, six three-point games and 15 two-point games. And the night before, in a 4-3 win over Pittsburgh, Gretzky scored his fifth winning goal of the season, his first winner at home,

the other four having come on the road. The number of road wins was significant because the Oilers had exactly four wins on the road.

That day, on the first anniversary of the signing of his 21-year deal at centre ice, Gretzky was asked if he could win the NHL scoring race in his rookie season.

"You mean beat Jesus and God?"

He meant Marcel Dionne and Guy Lafleur, two guys he was prepared to admit were better. But the rest of the best?

"I'm as good as they are," he said that day. "The key is to keep telling myself that I'm as good as they are."

And now he was willing to remind people of all the things that had been said and written back when they lifted the lid on the season.

"At the start of the season there were a lot of people who were still saying I couldn't play in the NHL," he said, taking on the subject he hadn't touched since the year began.

He said the toughest thing was getting it through his head not to be in awe of the other players, other than Lafleur and Dionne.

"Three years ago I was in the stands watching Gilbert Perreault and I was thinking he was the greatest. Now I have to go on the same ice with him and convince myself that I am as good as he is," said Gretzky, admitting at the same time that he was enjoying the challenge of playing against the NHL stars, especially in their rinks. Indeed. Gretzky had more goals on the road than at home.

And Gretzky was making other statements which spoke volumes about his maturity.

The Oilers were well out of a playoff position when he said it, but it was the beginning of Gretzky speaking and his teammates listening.

"If we don't make the playoffs, we've wasted the year," he said. "If we don't make the playoffs, we'll go to camp next year and more or less be starting from scratch again. The whole thing about this year is to gain experience, to develop character as a team. If we do make the playoffs, then we'll be going into the future with a winning attitude. That's what we need. That attitude is everything. A lot is riding on this."

With 28 games to go, Gretzky had already passed Bryan Trottier's record rookie total of 95 points, not to mention Dionne's first-year total of 77 points and the 74 that the next three on the list, Perreault, Richard Martin and Bobby Smith, all managed in their first years.

On Feb. 16, Edmonton fans were in for another game they'd remember for ages when Gretzky tied Billy Taylor's record for seven assists in a game as the Oilers crushed Taylor's former employers, the Washington Capitals, 8-2. Taylor, who had been a Caps scout, had held the record since March 16, 1947.

"I've only been watching him since peewee," said Capitals coach Gary Green. "Nothing he does surprises me. He's smart as a whip and so quick. When he's playing a team that was as slow as we were ... he just walks around us."

Gretzky said he came to the rink with a premonition.

"I just had a feeling I might explode," he said.

Veteran Al Hamilton was kicking himself for costing Gretzky the record outright.

FLYIN' HIGH: Gretzky takes flight during a game against the Philadelphia Flyers.

"I blew it," said the old defenceman of yet another teed-up Gretzky setup. "If I'd scored he'd have been in the record book alone. Hey. That's showbiz."

Green said the Capitals spent the night watching Gretzky.

Dave Hunter said so did the Oilers.

"Tonight we just sat back and watched. Was this Gretzky's night or what?"

Hamilton said it was impossible not to become a spectator at times.

"It's kind of fun to watch him, isn't it?"

Gretzky was getting fresh questioning this night.

"What did you eat for breakfast?" someone asked.

"Breakfast? Aw, nothing special."

One writer laughed.

"Just blew a heck of an endorsement from Wheaties, kid," he said of the Breakfast of Champions.

"Hey, I'm still in a fog," Gretzky recovered nicely. "Yeah, it was Wheaties. Definitely Wheaties!"

Sather used Gretzky to centre two lines during the game, taking a regular shift with Callighen and MacDonald and centring a makeshift line with Bobby Schmautz and Dave Semenko.

"I heard a lot of people say my endurance is bad, that my durability is bad," said No. 99. "That's crap! The more I play the better I play."

Gretzky pokes one past the Broad Street Bullies.

Schmautz enjoyed the night. He'd been on one a lot like it a few years earlier.

"The last time I saw a guy have a night like this was when Darryl Sittler piled up 10 points against us when I was with the Bruins. And with Wayne, there wasn't a cheap one in the bunch," said Schmautz. "Before he's done he'll rewrite all the record books. It's too bad they don't con-

sider him a rookie."

Much mention was being made of the Calder Trophy after Gretzky's seven-assist night.

"It would be nice to win that trophy," said Gretzky when asked about being the best first-year player in the league. "I'd really be proud to win it. But they've ruled that I can't because I played in the WHA last year, so there isn't much I can do about it, is there?"

Gretzky hadn't even played a full season yet and he was already becoming the most popular player in the league. Well, not with everybody. Not with the custodians of the cord cottages. He wasn't making any friends with the goalies.

Ron Low, who would one day go on to coach the Oilers, tells the story of the first time he faced No. 99.

"I thought, what's the big deal? There was a big fuss about him, but he didn't look like much to me. I remember one situation where I went out to the faceoff circle to take away his angle. I've got him taken care of. He has no shot. But all of a sudden he got it to Blair MacDonald and it's in the net. There was no play there. But he made it."

Low was swapped by the Quebec Nordiques to the Oilers on trade deadline day, March 12. Edmonton just happened to be in Quebec City.

"I remember walking into the dressing room in Quebec City and saying, 'That can't be the guy scoring all those points.' He was just a skinny little runt. I mean, he was really skinny at that time. I looked at him and I was sure you could break him in half with a bodycheck. But like a lot of people said, you went to hit him and it was like hitting a pillow. He just disappeared on you all the time."

Darryl Sutter would tell the story about the first time he played against Gretzky in Edmonton that year with his parents in the crowd and his dad, Louis, wondering why in heck his son wasn't hitting that Gretzky kid.

"Dad, I'm trying, I'm trying," said Darryl.

Low, two weeks after he joined the Oilers, would see there was something inside this kid, too.

"It was a night in Atlanta. They had the guy who was goaltender for the U.S. gold medal win at the Winter Olympics in Lake Placid," he said of Jim Craig. "He didn't face the Canadian flag during the anthem. Gretz didn't like that. He said it on the bench: 'This guy is done.' Wayne just lit him up like a candle in that game."

Gretzky had two goals and two assists in a 5-4 win in that game.

Gretzky and the Oilers were on a tear, trying to make it into the 16th and final playoff position.

With Low standing on his head in goal and Gretzky stepping up to another plateau, the story virtually every night was the same. Gretzky and goaltending.

They won 6-3 in Quebec the day Low was traded and five of six through Atlanta. A 5-2 win in Detroit made it six of seven as Gretzky visited Brantford to accept what, amazingly, was his first hometown athlete of the year award between games as the Oilers prepared for a huge game against the Leafs on *Hockey Night In Canada*.

That night No. 99 played his greatest game yet. He scored two goals and added four assists for a six-point night as the Oilers won 8-3. In his last eight games, seven of which the Oilers had won, Gretzky had scored 10 goals. He went into that game with 127 points, six behind Dionne. Suddenly he was tied for the lead in the scoring race with three Oiler games remaining in the season. And the Oilers were in position, with their next game, to clinch their playoff position.

That next game was in Vancouver. And the Canucks assigned Jerry Butler to check Gretzky and keep him off the scoresheet. The playoff party was on hold.

Back in Edmonton to finish off the schedule, Gretzky scored against Minnesota in a 1-1 tie.

That was goal No. 50.

In his first season in the NHL, Gretzky had scored 50 goals. That made him the youngest player ever to score 50.

No. 99 made it 51 and added two assists for a 137-point year in a 6-1 win over the Colorado Rockies to end the regular-season schedule, the Oilers finishing 16th with 28 wins, 39 losses and 13 ties.

Of all the goals and assists from that first year, Gretzky would remember one he didn't score, the one that would have given him the Art Ross Trophy outright.

It was in that last game of the season.

"I had a great chance in the final few seconds," he remembers now. "I had the whole net to shoot at. And I put it over the net."

After the final regular-season game Gretzky could hardly talk. He'd lost

Gretzky, centre, had two goals and an assist in the Oilers' first post-season matchup against the Flyers. Philly swept the best-of-five series with the youngsters, 3-0.

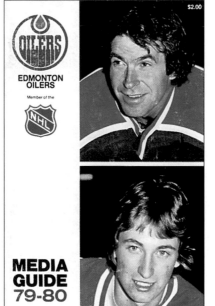

11 pounds in the game that night. Weak from the tonsillitis he'd battled to overcome all year, he'd scored 12 goals and 12 assists in the final 11 games and was clearly more driven to get into the playoffs than to win the scoring title.

"I should have had my tonsils out that year, but I didn't want to miss any games," said Gretzky, who managed to miss only one. "That whole year I was weak. And there were times when I had a fever and my throat was so bad ... well, I lived on more than Kevin's cooking that year. I lived on Aspirin and penicillin, too."

Dionne had a game to go, managed two assists, and they ended up tied at 137 points. Dionne had 53 goals and Gretzky had 51 and there was a provision with the Art Ross that goals would settle any ties.

Dionne had only one thing to say about winning the Art Ross.

"I'm just polishing it for Wayne."

How true those words turned out to be.

"It would have been nice if Marcel had beaten me by even one point," said Gretzky. "It's a little discouraging to tie for a scoring title and still lose."

Gretzky won the Hart Trophy as the league's MVP in his first season in the league. And they gave him the Lady Byng Trophy, too. But being ruled ineligible for the Calder (which was given to Peter Stastny, a veteran of a great deal of international competition) and losing the Art Ross Trophy because he had fewer goals left a lot of people thinking he'd been cheated.

He could have had the Grand Slam!

In his rookie season!

At the time there were only six trophies awarded in the NHL. The other two were the Norris for defencemen and the Vezina for goaltending. Gretzky could have won all the trophies for which he was eligible.

He liked the two he had.

"One is just as nice as the other," he said.

"Maybe someday we'll win a Stanley Cup to put between the two."

It wouldn't be this year. But, without managing to win a game, Gretzky and the Oilers managed to make a mark in the Stanley Cup playoffs, too.

The Oilers played the Philadelphia Flyers in a best-of-five series. The Flyers had finished first overall.

Game 1 went to overtime. Game 3, the first-ever Stanley Cup playoff game in Edmonton, went into double overtime.

Gretzky had two goals and an assist in the series, swept 3-0 by Philadelphia.

"Let's face it, the series could have gone either way" said Bobby Clarke when it was over. "There's no way they'll be a 16th-place team next year."

Bill Barber bottom-lined it.

"Now they've got the experience of a playoff drive and a playoff series," he said.

"And, of course, they've got Gretzky."

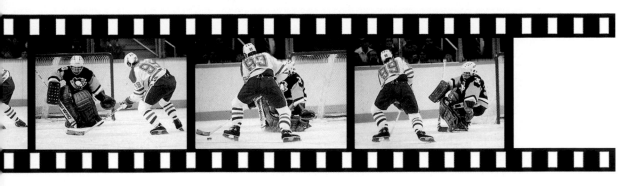

NO PAIN, NO GAIN

It was to a small hospital in Paris, Ont., that Wayne Gretzky went to avoid the madding crowd of well-wishers and have his tonsils removed in the summer of 1980.

Having your tonsils taken out is generally not news. With anybody. But it was with Gretzky. Was he really that weak in his first NHL season and still able to accomplish what he'd accomplished?

If this were true, think what he could accomplish in his second season if he were healthy. Heck, if that was true, he'd probably go and break Bobby Orr's and Phil Esposito's single-season records.

Gretzky, after he'd had the tonsils out, had been barely able to talk or eat for a week.

"I couldn't even eat ice cream for the first few days," the patient reported. "I lived on popsicles. But now I'm eating popsicles, ice cream and drinking 7-Up," he said, throwing in a plug for his new soft drink endorsement deal.

"My tonsils were bothering me so much last year, I saw four different doctors in Brantford and Edmonton. And it got worse, a lot worse, toward the end of the season.

"In the two years I've played pro hockey, every game my throat has bothered me."

Wayne Gretzky celebrates an Edmonton goal with Kevin Lowe.

SIMPLY THE BEST: Paul Coffey, Wayne Gretzky and Mark Messier were many a hockey pool player's dream.

Coach and GM Glen Sather said the public didn't know the half of it. Gretzky was taken to hospital one night in St. Louis and they didn't tell anybody.

"There were a lot of nights he should have been in bed. But that's part of what makes him great. To him, being sick was just part of the challenge."

Removing the tonsils was an early summer procedure. Gretzky was back in action not long later. He played 18 games for Brantford in the Inter-County Baseball League that summer, including the final – a 9-5 Brantford win in which he scored three runs, had six RBI and ended the season with a .492 batting average. Toronto Blue Jays scouts liked what they saw and offered him a tryout with the possibility of him being sent to their Pioneer League team in Medicine Hat the following summer. He said he'd spend the winter thinking about that.

The Kid had another amazing summer.

He went to Sweden for two weeks for hockey schools and participated in both the Canadian and American *Superstars* competitions, finishing third in Canada and sixth in the U.S. He made a tour of Canadian armed services bases, signing autographs. And he added to his ever-lengthening list of endorsement deals. He now had 7-Up, Titan, Perfecta, Jofa, GWG, Bic ... and attended a Big press conference when he signed on with Neilson's chocolate bars.

Why a chocolate bar company would sign up a 19-year-old kid with pimples, nobody was too sure. But it was big money, the contract was printed on a huge slab of chocolate and Gretzky signed the deal with icing for the Mr. Big photo-op.

"I really didn't skate much," he said of his summer. "But it sure was a pleasure when I did get out there. I feel a lot stronger now that my tonsils are out. When I go all out my throat doesn't hurt like it has the last couple of years. I'm refreshed."

And so it was that Gretzky came to camp.

GRETZKY AND THE JETS: The Oilers' playoff road almost always went through Winnipeg.

There were still disbelievers. Seems Dionne added his name to the list.

"He was quoted in *The Hockey News* as saying I won't have proved myself until I've been in the league for five years," said Gretzky.

Gretzky thus declared his one goal for his second season in the NHL.

"To score one more goal than Marcel Dionne," he said.

Gretzky read everything. He knew every sportswriter and sportscaster in the league by this time and what they were writing and saying about him.

"Apparently, I still have to prove myself to media people like Stan Fischler and Dick Beddoes," he said of the highest-profile Gretzky bashers.

"I'm helping them make bigger names for themselves, I guess, but they still claim I'm not that good."

Fischler suggested that Gretzky ran up the big numbers in his first year because he was playing for a team that barely made the playoffs. He suggested he wouldn't have those numbers if he were on a winning team.

Oilers boss Glen Sather reacted to that one.

"When you're on a losing club, there aren't as many guys helping you. Gretzky doesn't have Bobby Orr passing him the puck like Phil Esposito."

Funny, Sather chose to mention Orr and Esposito. They would indeed be the theme for Gretzky's dream second season.

How do you top finishing tied for the scoring lead and winning the Hart and Lady Byng trophies in your first year in the NHL? Orr and Esposito were the correct answers.

HOME BOYS: Gretzky and gang gave the Coliseum crowd plenty to cheer about.

Neilson's Mr. Big spokesman receives 20th birthday greetings in the form of a huge chocolate bar.

Gretzky wasn't concerned that he'd set the bar so high in his first season.

"I'm really looking forward to this year. I think we have a lot better team now. And I have a lot more desire to get going now than I ever had. And I can't tell you how much stronger I feel now that I've had my tonsils out."

The team the Oilers iced for their second season was even younger than the first. The oldest player was now 28-year-old Stan Weir. Their No. 1 draft pick was a kid by the name of Paul Coffey. They also picked a kid by the name of Jari Kurri in the third round and a goalie by the name of Andy Moog in the fourth. Gretzky, Mark Messier and Coffey were 19, Kurri, Glenn Anderson and Kevin Lowe were 20 and Risto Siltanen and Dave Hunter were 22. The average age of the team was 23.5 years.

Anderson, drafted in the third round the year before, chose to play for Canada in the 1980 Olympic Winter Games in Lake Placid. Everybody had a good laugh when the Oilers fact book came out and the 20-year-old Anderson listed his boyhood idol as the 19-year-old Gretzky.

As the season started, GM Sather temporarily surrendered coaching duties to Brian (Bugsy) Watson. And Sather said it was pretty obvious what Job 1 was for him.

"Every day my No. 1 priority is to find a goal scorer for Gretzky," said Slats. "We have to have somebody on that line who can score and score every night. If I could find somebody, either in a trade or through the draft, who could score 50 or 60 goals …

"The only thing that I worry about until I find him is that I'm going to burn him out."

It was during this season that morning radio sportscasters were forced to give more than just the score of Oiler games; they had to include how many points Gretzky got the previous night. In Canada, "How many did Gretzky get last night?" was the first thing you wanted to know when you got up in the morning, if you didn't manage to find out before you went to bed.

Keeping track of Gretzky's statistics became a national obsession. And for Dick Chubey, *The Edmonton Sun*'s hockey beat writer, they became the meat and potatoes of his job.

Chubey, in his game stories, would always manage to find some statistic. Like the day he reported Gretzky had broken Glen Sather's record.

"Manager-coach Glen Sather required 10 seasons and 658 games to account for 193 career points," wrote Ice Chubes. "Gretzky has vaulted past that in his 115th game."

Then he quoted Sather:

"I knew I shouldn't have played him tonight."

At the start of the season there were seven times before Christmas Gretzky had the hole in the doughnut. Mostly he was having two- and three-point nights, although he did manage five against Chicago and Quebec, and four-point outings against the Rangers and Washington.

With a year to work on it, teams were going out of their way to develop strategies to stop Gretzky. Some had success. Others ...

Ryan Walter tells about the great plan to stop Gretzky in the aforementioned game against Washington.

Capitals coach Gary Green came up with a strategy.

" 'You follow Gretzky all over the ice. If he sits on the bench, you come on our bench. Just stay with him, got it?' he told Walter.

"I told him, 'Yeah, I think I can do that.' "

For the first two periods the Caps captain shut Gretzky down.

Somehow, and Walter is still a little fuzzy on the subject, he looked up to where Gretzky was supposed to be early in the third period and there stood Dave Semenko.

"I have to fight Semenko and then I have to leave the ice and go to the penalty box and serve a fighting major," said Walter. "As I was skating to the box, I looked at the Edmonton bench and at Bugsy Watson and Bugsy had this big smile on his face.

"Gretzky got it going and the Oilers won the game."

In the first half of the year, some were saying Gretzky wasn't having the year he had the year before. As if 17 goals and 39 assists for 56 points in 35 games was chopped liver. But Gretzky had asked for that kind of reaction and expected it.

"You know, when you score two goals, they expect three," was how he put it.

A trade for a guy to be Gretzky's triggerman turned out to not be necessary. Sather found a guy. Right

Mark Messier and Wayne Gretzky.

under his nose. Jari Kurri.

And about Gretzky having not as good a season as the year before? Suddenly, it was quite obvious he was having a season like no one had ever had before in history.

The Oilers were in Quebec City when they completed the first half of their schedule. A five-point night from Gretzky lifted the Oilers to a 6-3 win over the Nordiques and this was deja vu all over again.

"Why do I think I've been here before?" said No. 99.

The five points left him tied with Marcel Dionne. But Dionne had 10 more goals and won the $500 prize the NHL used to give for the half-season scoring race.

"After 120 games, I have the same number of points as Dionne, yet I've lost two scoring titles," said Gretzky.

A few games later and it was obvious to even Dionne that this would not be the case after 160 games.

The first clue came the night the Oilers beat the Montreal Canadiens 9-1.

"I don't think it has ever happened that we've been beaten worse," said Guy Lafleur. "I've never seen so many goals scored against us."

Gretzky had a hand in five of them, scoring one and setting up four. Kurri had three of the goals. And Sather was definitely calling off his search for Gretzky's go-to guy.

"It was the thrill of a lifetime to beat Montreal 5-3 last year," said Gretzky. "From a fan's point of view, that's the biggest win we've ever had."

Three goals and three assists in a 10-4 win over Winnipeg on Feb. 6 pushed Gretzky passed Dionne. And that's when it suddenly occurred to everybody, including all the "One-Year Wonder" doubters from the start of the season. Good God, the kid had a shot at Bobby Orr, the kid had a shot at Phil Esposito.

In 1970-71, Orr set the NHL record for assists with 102. At his current pace, Gretzky would end up with 104.

That same season, Esposito set the record for points with 152. Projected, Gretzky would end up with 151.

Outspoken during the pre-season, Gretzky had gone out of his way to not comment on the scoring race through the season to this point. But after the six points against Winnipeg, he decided to

Dave Semenko cruises over to join a goal celebration.

remove his muzzle.

The Orr record, he said, was the one that most fascinated him.

"If I'm going to break a record, that would be the one I'd want. I consider myself a playmaker more than a scorer. I don't consider myself a natural scorer."

As for the scoring race ...

"It will be different from here on," Gretzky offered. "Last year I played catch-up all the way in the scoring race. Now that I'm ahead, I think it will be easier on me."

Orr and Esposito weren't the only angles as the season progressed. There was also Liut.

Would Gretzky win the Hart Trophy again? By Feb. 18, when the St. Louis Blues hit town, it was totally obvious the battle for the Hart Trophy was down to two. Wayne Gretzky. And Mike Liut.

That made for a big buildup before that game. And with Gretzky's already well-developed sense of stage ...

You got it.

Five goals!

And two assists.

That was the night Gretzky began rewriting the record book.

While he set Oiler records for most goals in a game, fastest two, three, four and five goals in a game, Gretzky tied the NHL record for most goals in a single period with four.

The record was previously the exclusive property of one Harvey (Busher) Jackson.

"Busher Jackson?" asked the now 20-year-old Gretzky. "Who is that? He must have broken in before Gordie Howe, eh? I never heard of 'The Busher.'"

Jackson was a Toronto Maple Leaf from the Charlie Conacher era. He was a member of the famed "Kid Line" that won the 1932 Stanley Cup the same year he won the Art Ross Trophy.

The Busher died in 1966. But still around and watching the game that night was former Blues netminder Glenn Hall, the legendary Hockey Hall of Fame goalie.

"Wayne Gretzky is the greatest player I've ever seen," said Hall as the seconds clicked off the clock. "Some year he is going to get 250 points in a season. He'll score 100 and get 150 assists."

Gretzky was only one goal shy of equalling the NHL record of six goals in a game. If he had done it, he would have done it in front of the man who had set

QUICK ON THE DRAW: One thing the Oilers had plenty of was speed.

OILER STAR VS. NORTH STAR: Gretz has a run-in with Minnesota's Curt Giles.

the record, St. Louis coach-of-the-moment Red Berenson.

He'd heard of him.

"I remember Berenson getting that record," said Gretzky.

"I was eight that year.

"I was playing novice hockey.

"But I remember that."

The Oilers beat St. Louis 9-2 that night and Gretzky's seven points gave him a seven-point lead on Dionne.

With 23 games to play, Gretzky needed 40 points to equal Esposito's record and 28 assists to tie Orr's.

"It's going to be close," said No. 99.

There was now no stopping Gretzky from being the storyline for the rest of the season. And the story took a strange and controversial twist in Hartford on the night of March 25.

Gretzky's statistical line on the game – one goal and three assists in a 7-2 win over the Whalers – is one of those "no room for a story on the back of a scorecard" deals.

What happened was something out of *The Twilight Zone.*

The Whalers were almost out of life for a playoff position and decided to gamble by pulling their goalie. Normally this is a one-minute-to-play thing when a team is down a goal. And normally when the puck goes into the empty net, that's the end of it.

Not this night.

The Oilers scored three empty-net goals. Three!

The Whalers had managed to restrict Gretzky to a single assist playing normal hockey. But No. 99 scored once and drew assists on two others when Whalers coach Larry Pleau made his moves.

The four-point night left Gretzky one point back of Esposito with 151 points. Five games remained.

In Boston, Bruins GM Harry Sinden called it "a farce."

Sinden didn't make the statement because Esposito and Orr were Bruins.

"I hope it doesn't detract from young Gretzky's accomplishment," he said.

Espo shrugged.

"Big deal," he said. "He's going to get the record anyway. Over the course of a season, things even out. These sort of things happen a lot."

Gretzky was now scoring at an unprecedented clip of 2.01 points a game. And the first "Great Gretzky Watch"

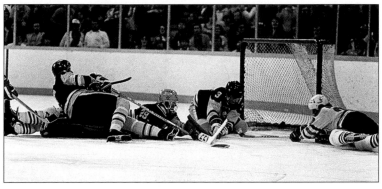

POETRY IN MOTION: 99's moves never failed to amaze his fans and opponents.

was under way as members of the media scrambled to Detroit to watch him break it.

"I've got three tickets," said Gretzky. "One for my mom. One for my dad. And one for my little brother. But I know a lot of other people are driving down from Brantford to see the game."

He didn't break it. He tied it.

Gretzky could "only" manage one assist with a pass to Risto Siltanen in a 4-2 win.

It was point No. 152. It was registered at 1:52 of the third period. And the time, back in Edmonton, was exactly 1:52 p.m.

Walter Gretzky always said his son's life had been planned out for him. But that was ridiculous.

Walter jumped up in the stands when his son made that pass and Siltanen scored that goal.

"I normally would never jump up," he sheepishly admitted later. "I generally just sit and watch. But I was so satisfied by it all ... I think it's the first time I've ever jumped up to cheer."

Gretzky broke the record the following night in Pittsburgh, assisting on goals by Messier, Callighen and Kurri in a 5-2 win. The three assists gave him 155 points, but also gave him 102 assists. That tied Orr!

"I'm happy to get it over with," said Gretzky of the Espo record that he broke as a result of a 24-point spree (four goals and 20 assists) in a 10-game span.

While Gretzky had said his only goal for the season was to beat Dionne, he confessed that he actually had another one.

"I wanted two points per game if I could get it because no one has ever done that before."

Esposito said when he broke the record he figured he might have it forever.

"When I did that, I thought nobody would ever get that total," Esposito, who had retired that year, reacted at the time.

"I remember when I did it, some people were bitter. They wanted to cheapen it because it was now a 12-team league instead of a six-team league. I don't want to be like all the other old fogies in sports. We can't stop progress, so why try. Gretzky has far more ability than I have ... had. I'm still having trouble with that past-tense stuff."

Esposito said the biggest difference between him and Gretzky at the

time of their reaching the record was significant.

"I got my points because I was with one hell of a hockey team. Gretzky gets his because he *is* the Edmonton Oilers."

Walter Gretzky, who had driven to Detroit, returned home after the game, and made the 4½-hour drive to Pittsburgh, jumped out of his seat again.

"I've only jumped out of my seat twice over something Wayne did," he said. "The first time was in Detroit and now I've done it again. This tops it. This is the proudest moment of my life. I never dreamed this would happen."

Wayne gave the record stick to his dad.

"He didn't remember to save his stick after his 100th goal in Philadelphia," said Walter. "He gave it away to a kid. Can you believe that? Sticks and pucks are part of the memories which will mean a lot in 10 or 15 years."

Gretzky's assist on the Orr record equaller was, appropriately, his 99th of the season.

Messier scored it. Glenn Anderson had the other assist.

"Knowing Wayne, he'll never forget that three 20-year-olds were in on that goal," said Walter.

It was Game 78 when the once supposedly impossible-to-break Orr record fell in a 4-4 tie with Colorado as Gretzky set up Kurri for two goals in the game to do it.

Orr played 78 games in Boston in 1970-71 to establish the record. Gretzky required the same number of games. He'd registered 22 assists in his last nine games to do it.

"I really wanted to do it tonight so nobody could complain that I did it in more games," said Gretzky after the game.

Gretzky had one more record to set that regular season. The one that belonged to Bill Cowley.

Unlike Orr and Esposito, Cowley wasn't planning on sending Gretzky a telegram or making any personal phone call.

Cowley owned the "highest-points-per-game, one-season" NHL record as a result of a 1.97 average, scoring 71 points in 36 games with the Boston Bruins in 1943-44.

"Two points over an 80-game schedule," said Cowley. "That would be something."

Gretzky was on pace to do just that.

"I never thought I'd see the day when a player did that. I always thought that would be impossible."

Old Bill Cowley wasn't having trouble letting go of his record or anything like that.

"They forgot old Bill Cowley a long time ago but they'll never forget Wayne Gretzky," he said.

So why no telegram? Why no phone call?

"To be honest about it, I don't think much of my record," he said. "Heck, I didn't even know I had a record until 10 years after I finished my career. And even then it was my son who found it in a program at some game he was at in some town.

"A week or so ago my wife said the phone would start ringing from reporters, but I said nobody would notice and if they did they wouldn't make much of it. Until you called, I was right."

Cowley wasn't putting down Gretzky's accomplishment. Or the record category.

"For someone to average two points a game over an 80-game schedule, well, that's about as impressive a mark as you can make in hockey as far as I'm concerned. It's just that I never felt that my name should have been in the book. I only played 36 games that year. I don't think 36 games should have rated that record. I've been waiting for the day when the NHL would whitewash my record out of the book. I've been waiting for the day when the NHL would say, 'Let's get rid of that Cowley record because he didn't play enough games.' "

The Oilers finished off the season with a pair of 7-2 wins against Vancouver and Winnipeg, respectively, with Gretzky adding two more goals and five more assists. The Oilers finished in 14th place overall with a 29-35-16 record and Gretzky ended up with 55 goals, 109 assists and 164 points – 12 more points than Esposito and seven more assists than Orr. His points-per-game average worked out to 2.05. Dionne was 19 points back.

The youngest player before Gretzky to win the scoring title and the Art Ross Trophy was that Busher Jackson guy who won it at the age of 21 in 1931-32. Busher, that year, had 28 goals and 25 assists for 53 points.

Gretzky earned 94 points in the second half of the season, surpassing the record of 87 set by Stan Mikita of the Chicago Blackhawks in 1967-68, the season the NHL went from six to 12 teams.

Heck of a year. But there was more memory-making coming up. The Oilers were in the playoffs. And first up was the Montreal Canadiens.

The Oilers had only lost one of their last dozen games going into that series. But this was Montreal. These were the Canadiens and they'd lost only three of their last 26 and only one of their last 27 at home. And this was the Forum, the Taj Mahal of hockey.

When the bus pulled up to "the cathedral," as Gretzky called it, the Oilers all took time to look at the marquee. "Stanley Cup Playoffs. Canadiens vs. Edmonton."

They'd already looked at the papers. And in one of them Montreal goalie Richard Sevigny had predicted Guy Lafleur would "put Gretzky in his back pocket."

Didn't work out that way.

Edmonton won Game 1 by the eyebrow-raising score of 6-3. Gretzky had five assists. And when he skated behind the Montreal goal after his fifth assist he patted the back of his hockey pants where his hip pocket would be.

When the siren sounded on Game 1, the great debate was if the hockey

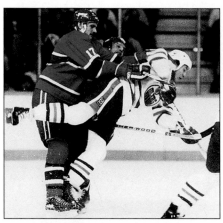

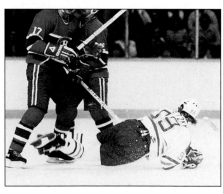

UPSY-DAISY: Gretzky gets airlifted courtesy the Montreal Canadiens.

world had just watched Gretzky's greatest game. (There had already been so many and he had only been in the league for two years, so it made for a good discussion.)

To anybody who thought that made Gretzky the story, he pointed to the corner of the dressing room and correctly labelled Andy Moog as the story.

Coach Sather had taken a gamble and decided to start Moog in goal. Ron Low, who played so well against Philadelphia the year before, was out with a broken thumb. And Eddie Mio was out with a broken finger.

That left journeyman Gary Edwards and Moog, a kid who had played for the junior Billings Bighorns a year earlier. Sather went with the kid and Moog was wonderful.

"Honestly," said Gretzky, "Andy Moog is the most confident 20-year-old I've ever met."

Maybe. Other than that kid he met in the mirror every morning.

The Oilers weren't the first team in Stanley Cup history to score a shocking first-game win in the playoffs. But when they won the next one 3-1 ...

Whoa. What was happening here? The Oilers were kids. Didn't they realize who they were playing?

"This is *Fantasy Island*," said Paul Coffey.

"Do you think anybody in the NHL believes this?" said Gretzky, who set up the winning goal and the insurance marker.

"We told ourselves that they have all the pressure," said Gretzky. "So why get uptight? We made up our minds to just give it everything we could give it."

The Oilers had not been intimidated. Not by the Forum. Not by the history. Not by the uniform. Not by anything.

"They play with no nerves," said Canadiens coach Claude Ruel, whose team had finished third overall in the regular season.

I flew with the Canadiens back to Edmonton as they tried to figure out how it was they found themselves in such a jam.

"Gretzky," offered Yvon Lambert.

"All we've been doing is panicking whenever Gretzky is on the ice," said Keith Acton.

Gretzky said that was great if that's how they had it figured. But he figured otherwise.

"The key to this whole series is not how I play but how Dave Hunter, Dave Lumley and Stan Weir are able to contain Guy Lafleur," said No. 99 of The Flower, who had been held to two shots in two games.

It was hard to imagine what the scene was going to be like back in Edmonton for Game 3 of the best-of-five series. The fans were so numb from pinching themselves, you had to wonder if they were going to be able to sit down in their seats.

Suddenly there was the suggestion that the pressure would now all be on the Oilers.

"I don't think so," said Gretzky. "Edmonton has been waiting 80 years for this sort of thing. It's going to be great."

The scene was everything you would have expected and more. On one side of Northlands Coliseum hung a sign that read, "We Believe In Miracles." On the other sign sat a fan in a Montreal Canadiens jacket with a bag over his head.

The Oilers swept. You had to go back to 1952 to find the last time Montreal was swept in a playoff series. And that was the Stanley Cup final and the guys on the other side of the ice were named Gordie Howe, Terry Sawchuk, Ted Lindsay, Red Kelly, Marcel Pronovost, Sid Abel, etc.

Mind you, on the other side of the ice this night was Wayne Gretzky. He had three goals and an assist.

It was one of the greatest upsets in hockey history against the greatest franchise in the history of hockey.

And that's exactly what Gretzky said after the game that clinched the series sweep.

"We beat the best team in hockey. Who knows what we can do?" said the 20-year-old who had three goals and eight assists in three games. "Any time you beat the Montreal Canadiens in the playoffs that tops anything in hockey. It's the next biggest thing to winning the Stanley Cup."

Somehow, the New York Islanders, who had one pennant hanging from their rafters as opposed to 22 for the Canadiens, managed to take that personally.

When the Oilers arrived in New York and picked up a copy of the *New York Post*, they were met by headlines.

"Isles Hope To Make Gretzky Eat His Words."

"That ticks me off," Island Bob Nystrom was quoted by the *Post*. "If he considers Montreal the best team in hockey, we'll just have to go out there and prove him wrong."

There was also a quote from Stephan Persson.

"The Canadiens *were* the greatest team in hockey but not now. I think Gretzky's got it backwards."

Gretzky didn't know what to say when he saw the headlines.

"I guess we had better beat them now. That's all I have to say."

The defending-champion Islanders did a pretty decent job of proving their point, if Gretzky managed to be bewildered by it. They won the first two games of the series, 6-3 and 8-2.

Back home on Easter Sunday, a 5-2 Oilers win, and Gretzky suggested it was Edmonton's day of official confirmation.

"With the Montreal series and so far in this series, I'd say we have matured by at least a full year as a hockey team in the last three weeks."

Matured?

Mature wasn't the right word for the events that happened back at the Nassau County Coliseum.

Ken Morrow's overtime goal won Game 4 for the Islanders in Edmonton and the Stanley Cup champs had a good grip on the series again. But back on Long Island, the Edmonton Boys Choir had been formed.

With four minutes remaining in Game 5, the Oilers were sitting on their bench singing.

Gretzky watches from his 'office' while Islanders Denis Potvin (5) and goaltender Billy Smith pounce on the puck.

Butch Goring (91) embraces Gretzky after the Isles' playoff triumph.

There's no singing on the bench in hockey.

But that's what the Oilers were doing.

"Here we go, Oilers, here we go!

"Here we go, Oilers, here we go!

"Here we go, Oilers, here we go!"

Even Glen Sather, who was pretty much prepared to believe anything, couldn't believe that.

"Every time we got in trouble, we started singing," he testified.

"Teenagers," marvelled assistant coach Billy Harris.

Apparently the singing started in the dressing room between the second and third periods.

"I think it was Mark Messier who started it," reported Paul Coffey.

"We don't know how to be goody-goodies yet. We're a young team. We don't know how to sit there and take it all in stride.

"What it comes down to," said Gretzky, who set up two more goals for his 19th and 20th points in eight playoff games, "is that we're too young to know what pressure is. We're the youngest team in the NHL. We're just a bunch of kids. What we're saying to ourselves is, 'Let's give it our best shot.' It's wrong to say we're going to beat them. All we're saying is that we've got nothing to lose."

As Gretzky spoke, from out of the showers came the song again:

"Here we go, Oilers, here we go!"

Gretzky didn't sing along. He'd already proved on a television show that year that he couldn't sing. But he did have a conversation with the guys from Styx, the band that showed up in the Oilers dressing room.

They were tentatively scheduled for a concert in Nassau County Coliseum on the same date that would be Game 7 if it was necessary.

"Are you guys going to be here Sunday or are we?" he asked.

Styx had their concert.

The Oilers returned home and lost Game 6 as the Islanders made damned sure they didn't have to take this team to a Game 7.

Gretzky, who ended up with seven goals and 14 assists for 21 points in nine playoff games – the highest total of any player who didn't make it to the Stanley Cup final – put it all in perspective that night in the Oilers dressing room.

"The most important thing we did was to create a winning attitude. Now, when a player comes to this team he'll have to adopt the attitude which is here."

The words came easy as I wrote my column that night.

"The song may be over, but the melody will linger on. You are tempted to write 'The End' to the Impossible Dream today. But, really, it's the beginning. And from now on you have to believe that all things are possible."

Chapter

6

FIFTY IN THIRTY-NINE

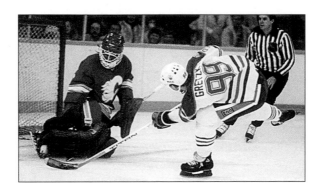

It was the 1944-45 season and as the Allied forces invaded France after storming the beaches of Normandy, Maurice (Rocket) Richard was helping take people's minds off the Second World War.

The year before he'd scored 32 goals in the NHL's 50-game season of the time. There were skeptics suggesting he wouldn't be able to do it again the following season. But Montreal Canadiens coach Dick Irvin wasn't one of them.

"He'll be a star," said Irvin. "Not only will he be a star, he'll be the biggest star in hockey."

Irvin had the Rocket, nicknamed by sportswriter Baz O'Meara, on a line with Elmer Lach and Toe Blake that became known as the Punch Line.

By the 19th game of the '44-45 season Richard had 19 goals and the talk began. Could he score 50 in 50?

On Feb. 10, Richard scored twice against Detroit, his 42nd and 43rd goals of the season, one short of the record owned by Joe Malone. On Feb. 25, against the Leafs, he broke the record. It took until the final game of the season, at the Boston Garden, for Richard to score his 50th.

In the spring of the 1961 season, just as Roger Maris and Mickey Mantle were going for Babe Ruth's single-season home run record, both Frank Mahovlich of Toronto and Montreal's Bernie (Boom Boom) Geoffrion took runs at the Rocket's record.

MY BODYGUARD: Wayne Gretzky and Oilers enforcer Dave Semenko.

AIR SAMMY: Tough guy Dave Semenko (27), known more for his fists than his grace, takes flight in front of the Vancouver crease.

Mahovlich had 37 by mid-season but finished with 48. And Geoffrion, who missed six games, made it to 50 – but not until the Canadiens' 68th game of the season.

Bobby Hull became the third player to score 50 in a season and did it often, but never did it inside 50 games. It wasn't until Mike Bossy, in the season previous, that anybody matched the Rocket's 50 in 50.

But this year would be different. Wayne Gretzky wouldn't just give the Rocket's record a run; he wouldn't merely equal it, he would smash it beyond belief.

Gretzky didn't go into his third season in the NHL thinking Rocket Richard. But as he went into the 1981-82 season, he did call his shot.

"I think it's time I started shooting more," he said during training camp.

"I think it's time for me to go for more goals. The teams are starting to get wise to me. They figure that nine times out of 10 I'm going to pass."

Gretzky won the scoring championship outright in his second season but Bossy, Marcel Dionne and Charlie Simmer all scored more goals. But Gretzky could read the statistics. He was 17th in the league in shots on goal and had scored 55 goals. If he started to shoot more ...

"I must have learned something from watching Guy Lafleur for five weeks during the Canada Cup," said Gretzky after he went through the pre-season, scoring two goals for every assist.

"My shot seems to be harder. My release is quicker. The goals are going in."

Supposedly a slow starter, Gretzky – who had faced failure in the

Canada Cup prior to camp – rocketed, if you'll excuse the expression, into the season.

He scored seven goals in his first 10 games, two against the New York Rangers on the road in Game 12, four against the Quebec Nordiques at home in Game 13 and two against the Toronto Maple Leafs at home in Game 14.

That was 15 goals in 14 games.

That was 10 more goals than at the same stage of his first season and seven more goals than at the same stage of his second season.

And he'd picked himself up off the mat to do what he did in those three games. The night before the Rangers game, the Oilers were back in Long Island and at 7:17 of the second period, Islanders netminder Billy Smith swung his stick and left Gretzky crumpled on the ice. He tried to return for a couple of shifts, but it was obvious he was hurt. He did not return for the third period.

Gretzky scored the two goals against the Rangers playing hurt.

"My dad always told me that pros are paid to play," he said. "I'm making good money and even though the injury was an aggravating one, I felt I had to try to play. I had to sleep with my leg bent, a string tied to the leg to keep it in position. I skated in the morning but went back to the hotel and put more ice on the knee. Then I came to the rink at about 4:30 for more treatment."

Gretzky had to wear a girdle in the game.

The bruise from Battlin' Billy's goal stick was on the muscle part of his knee and had to be protected by a heavy bandage and a girdle.

"I figured if Joe Namath can wear pantyhose, I can wear a girdle," he said as the New York writers scribbled the quote.

After those three games, Rocket Richard and 50 in 50 was the hockey storyline.

As predicted by Gretzky, the Oilers after their playoff success were taking a large leap toward their future. By Nov. 4, they had as many points in the standings as they had on Dec. 20 of the previous season. They were a full two months ahead of their 1980-81 pace in the win column. The team was a story in itself.

But 50 in 50 was the focus throughout the hockey world and Gretzky didn't know what to say.

"It's a little early to say I'm shooting for it. But I'm scoring more than I normally do."

Gretzky kept referring to his pre-season statements.

"I was right about the other teams figuring I was going to pass 90 per cent of the time. That goal I scored against Bunny Larocque the other night was a perfect example. Two guys went with Jari Kurri. So I just walked in. There didn't seem to be any sense passing."

Sather said Gretzky was changing his game slightly, possibly temporarily, in other areas.

Gretzky and Paul Coffey swarm the crease.

"He isn't behind the net as much," observed Sather. "Everybody knows that's his style and guys are hammering him back there. So he's moving in front more."

St. Louis Blues netminder Mike Liut offered an interesting observation.

"Bossy," he said, "can score on you with a half-dozen different deliveries. Gretzky isn't like that. And Wayne's shot doesn't overpower you. It's just that it never hits the middle of the net. Just the corners."

All of a sudden charts, graphs, thermometers and other special scorekeeping boxes started showing up on the sports pages of newspapers around the league.

Two goals in Hartford, one each against the Rangers and Islanders on a second trip to New York, two in St. Louis, two more at home against Vancouver and another at home against Detroit, left Gretzky one ahead of the Rocket's pace. He had 24 goals in 23 games.

Next up, on Nov. 25, the Los Angeles Kings.

Led by Gretzky's second four-goal performance of the season, the Oilers equalled a club record for most goals in one season with an 11-4 win over L.A.

"This game is never easy, but some nights it's a little easier than other nights," said No. 99.

He now had 28 in 24 games.

Two against Chicago in the next game and one against Winnipeg the following outing, and Gretzky was two months ahead of his goal-scoring pace from the previous season. It had taken him until Game 55, on Feb. 13, to be exact.

Gretzky failed to score in four consecutive games, one against Montreal, one against Quebec and a pair with Vancouver before he stopped the "slump" with one goal in a 5-5 tie with Vancouver. Then, in Game 32, he scored Goal 33 with 1:02 remaining against the Islanders. It was the winner against the team the Oilers had made their measuring stick.

"That's probably the happiest I've been after a goal," said Gretzky that night.

Fifty In 50 was still the storyline. But with Gretzky there was always a new plot. And plenty of subplots.

Gretzky was now two points shy of averaging two points per game in his entire NHL career. He now had 490 major-league points (including his year in the WHA). And it now looked like he would achieve his start-of-the-season "long shot" goal of scoring 500 major-league points before his 20th Christmas.

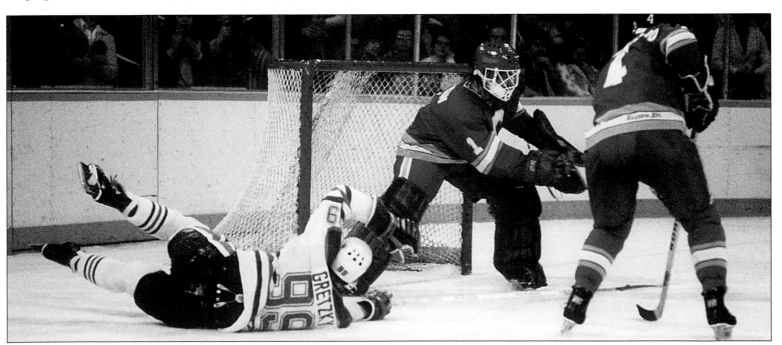
No. 99 didn't have to be vertical to be dangerous in front of the net – especially if the opposition was the dreaded Calgary Flames.

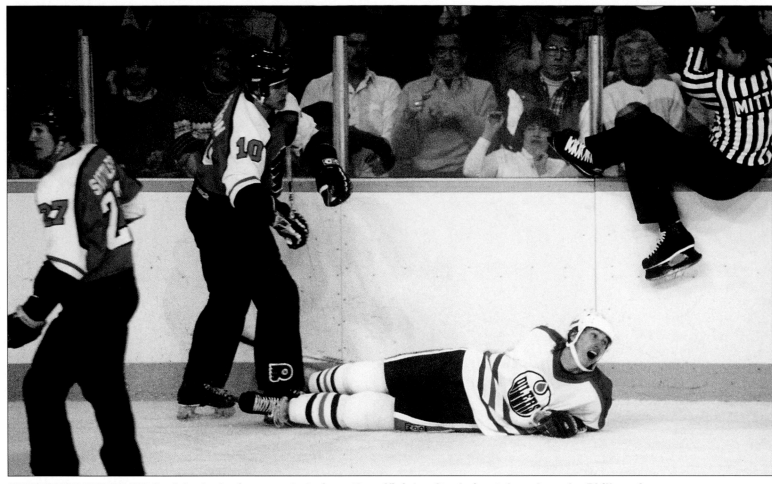

DIDN'T YOU SEE THAT? Gretzky looks for some help from the officials after being taken down by Philly enforcers.

And this with a collection of "fire hydrants" on his line. (Glen Sather, referring to Blair MacDonald's season with Gretzky, had said: "A fire hydrant could score 40 with Gretzky."

No. 99 had gone the early part of the season with Jari Kurri and Brett Callighen or Pat Hughes on his wings. But through early December he was largely teamed up with Dave Lumley and Dave Semenko.

Could anybody score 50 in 50 with Dave Semenko on his wing?

But just as that question was being asked, Lumley became the subplot to himself.

And Gretzky stopped scoring. It was like he called a time out. He went four games without a goal, but had 10 assists in those games, as he stopped shooting and started passing again trying to get Lumley his record.

"I'd really like Lummer to break the record," said Gretzky in the middle of his temporary mate's unlikely run to break Charlie Simmer's record of 13 consecutive games with a goal.

"I'm certainly going to do everything I can to give him every opportunity to do so. This thing has kind of changed Lummer's whole life. Not only on the ice, but off. Everybody knows, now, about the attitude problem he used to have. What he is accomplishing has given him a great new attitude and he has a new confidence in himself on and off the ice that I think he is going to keep for a long, long time."

"Most of the thrill isn't the streak so much as it is just a chance to play with Wayne," said Lumley as he narrowed in on the record, feeling a little guilty that Gretzky was now losing pace on Richard.

"I can't help but wonder what the other players in the NHL are thinking. 'How in hell can Dave Lumley score goals in 10 straight games?' I'm still not comfortable in this role. I'm not a goal scorer. I'm Dave Lumley, the guy who went 16 games without scoring for the Nova Scotia Voyageurs in the American Hockey League. I'm the guy who spent 13 straight games in the press box earlier this year and who needed two right wingers to get hurt to get into the lineup."

With a goal in the next game, Lumley had another quote.

"It's almost embarrassing," he added as he got real close. "It's like one of those quiz items. Which of the following names doesn't belong on this list: (a) Bobby Hull, (b) Andy Bathgate, (c) Mike Bossy, (d) Dave Lumley. Those are the three guys I passed to make it 11 straight games. I have to be everybody's choice as the guy who doesn't belong."

Lumley suggested if he should happen to break Simmer's record it should probably be listed with all the other records Gretzky was beginning to accumulate.

"It's the kind of unselfish guy Gretz is," he said. "I've thought about the possibility that this record might be completely due to him. On one hand, I tell myself it can't be because he's only assisted on half the goals. But at the same time, he's been on the ice for them all. When he hasn't had assists, he's been drawing guys away from me. I can't say for sure, but I really get the feeling he's going out of his way to try and feed me because of this. Especially early in the game. I'm getting a lot of chances early in the game. I think he wants me to get my goal early so he can go back to his regular game. All I know is that I head for the empty spaces and I can count on the puck ending up on my stick. Playing with him you are guaranteed at least two great chances every game. I love playing with him. I don't know how to describe it. More than anything, I guess, it's fun."

Lumley didn't get it. He fell one game short of the 13 consecutive games record held by Simmer. And with the end of Lumley's streak, things started to change. Every winger on the team was getting a chance to play with Gretzky because he was being long-shifted and double-shifted.

"It's given me maybe six to eight more minutes ice time a game than I had last year," Gretzky figured. "All I know is that I seem to thrive on extra ice time and longer shifts. For some reason, and I don't know why, when my body gets tired I seem to do a lot better."

After going four straight games without a goal, Gretzky went four straight games – away against Los Angeles, Colorado and Calgary and home against the Islanders – getting one goal each night.

Then he hit big again. A hat trick at home against Minnesota.

He also assisted on four others and that night reached the two-points-per-game plateau.

"I really haven't had any big nights until this year, until this game," said Gretzky.

Gretzky's idea of a big game wasn't the same as most. He'd had four five-point nights and three five-pointers.

The night put him three goals ahead of the 50-in-50 pace again. They were goals 36, 37 and 38 in game No. 35.

By this point, people weren't trying to figure out 'if'; they were trying to figure out when.

The date circled on a lot of calendars was Jan. 16. The Oilers would be in Maple Leaf Gardens that night to play Game 47 against the Leafs.

Gretzky himself, his dad Walter and his then agent Gus Badali all said that's when they figured No. 50 would come.

On Dec. 20, in a 7-5 loss at home against the Flames, Gretzky scored two more.

His 39th was a tip-in of a Risto Siltanen shot. His 40th was also a tip-in of a shot from the stick of Callighen.

No. 99 added one more in a four-point win at home against Vancouver on Dec. 23.

So it was that Gretzky hit Christmas with 41 goals in 37 games. The projection to that Toronto game still seemed about right.

Wrong.

The Los Angeles Kings were the first holiday visitors to Northlands Coliseum on Dec. 27. And if the record seemed three weeks away when they arrived, it seemed a whole lot closer when they departed.

Gretzky, for the second time against the Kings and for the third time in the still-young season, had a four-goal game.

"It's like he's trying to throw a blanket over a ghost," said Kings coach Parker Mac-Donald.

Two of Gretzky's goals had come short-handed. On one he undressed Kings blue-liner Jay Wells. On the other he scored on a breakaway.

His even-strength goals came on a bee-line from behind the net and on a rebound from the top of the crease.

The explosion gave Gretzky 45. And it gave him a record.

That night he shattered the existing NHL record for the fastest 100 points established by Phil Esposito 11 years earlier. Esposito took 51 games to hit 100 and Gretzky had 102 in 36. The accomplishment barely rated

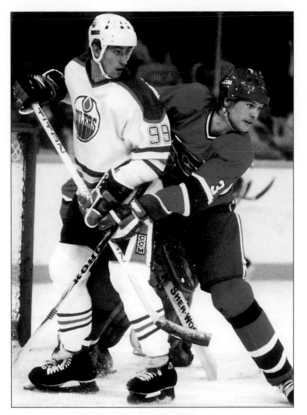

TIE & TANGLE: Gretzky is handcuffed by Montreal (top), Calgary and Boston opponents.

a paragraph in most dispatches that night.

So much for all the projections of Toronto and Maple Leaf Gardens for No. 50 – unless Gretzky went into a stall or wanted to try to get Dave Lumley another run at a record.

"I sure hope it's before then," said Oilers assistant coach Billy Harris, a former Leaf. "I want to get tickets in Toronto and right now I hear they are scalping them for $200 each."

The Oilers schedule had them at home to Philadelphia on Dec. 30, in Vancouver for New Year's Eve, then back at home against Boston, Colorado and Calgary.

Speculation began that Gretzky could get 50 in 40.

"I've got a long way to go to get that," he said. "We've got two defensive-minded hockey teams to play in the next two games," he said of the visit to Edmonton by the Flyers and a New Year's Eve game in Vancouver.

"It would be nice to do it, but if I don't I won't worry about it."

Gretzky was projecting maybe Boston back in Edmonton on Jan. 2.

"It would be nice to get it in Edmonton," he said of the challenge of breaking the record against the Bruins, and particularly checker Steve Kasper, who was winning fame as a Gretzky stopper.

"I've been watching films of the Bruins for the last two weeks," he said.

Whatever, all of a sudden it was time to determine how the Rocket was taking all this. Now there was absolutely no doubt that his record would fall. I tracked him down.

"It's hard to believe," he said. "I started thinking about my record being equalled when the first expansion came. But I never thought it would be surpassed. And he's probably going to do it before his 42nd game!

"Every time he scores a goal it looks easy. Everything he does looks easy. He plays everywhere. He's all over the place so he's impossible to check."

The Rocket did have some reservations.

"The game has changed," he said. "All the players think of now is shooting the puck and skating after it. They don't hold onto it any more. There are too many weak players on defence, too. That's why Gretzky is having so much fun now. The game is all offence.

"I think in a six-team league like there was 20 years ago, Gretzky, in spite of everything, would be the top scorer," the Rocket added.

Richard said maybe it was a case of everything that goes around comes around. He

Wayne Gretzky bested Rocket Richard with 39 goals in 50 games, thanks to a five-goal outburst against the Flyers.

said he is a thing of the past in the present.

"He's playing the kind of hockey I grew up with," said the Canadiens' No. 9.

"He's great. There's no doubt about it. There's no way anyone will stop him from becoming the greatest star in hockey."

Mike Bossy said the heck with 50 in 50.

"Gretzky isn't just anybody," said the New York Islander who had tied Richard's feat the year before. "And this isn't the first record he'll break. He seems on course for a 100-goal season. I think he can do it."

The Flyers came to Edmonton with 22 wins, 12 losses and a tie and one of the better goals-against records in the league.

And you know what happened next.

As I wrote it the next day, the Rocket's red glare became a mere flick of a Bic. The not-yet-turned-21-year-old who was already being referred to as the greatest player in hockey history, broke the greatest record in hockey by playing the latest greatest game in his career.

Five goals in one night!

Nine goals in two games!

50 in 39!

It wasn't the first five-goal game of Gretzky's career. He'd fired five against St. Louis in his second season. But this was against Philadelphia and this was with the hockey world watching and the Rocket's record on the line.

"We take a lot of pride that we can force other teams to play our game ... that we can control a big guy like that with our zone defence. But I

don't think anybody is going to stop him," said Flyers defenceman Jim Watson after the game.

Gretzky scored the first one on a five-footer from the edge of the crease at 7:47 of the first period.

The second one came on a drive from 35 feet at 10:12 of the opening stanza.

The third was on a breakaway at 3:52 of the second period. The shot was from 25 feet out and went in off goalie Pete Peeters' chest.

You could read the determination on his face from the top of the blues as the crowd played every shift with Gretzky. When he scored his fourth goal of the game – No. 49 – on a 30-footer over Peeters' shoulder at 5:13 of the third, the crowd reacted like never before.

Strange. The Coliseum crowd had chanted, "Guy! Guy! Guy!" for Guy Lafleur in Edmonton at the Canada Cup and "Andy! Andy! Andy!" for goaltender Andy Moog in the playoff series against the Montreal Canadiens, but Gretzky had never before heard his name in a chant. Until that moment.

"Gretzky! Gretzky! Gretzky!"

Goal No. 50 came with three seconds to play and Peeters pulled for an extra attacker. It went into an empty net.

"What he did was absolutely amazing," said Peeters, an Edmontonian.

Doug Hicks remembers it like yesterday and treasures the game summary.

"We all piled onto the ice to congratulate Gretz and our team got a bench minor," remembers Hicks.

"I served the penalty. I got on the scoresheet.

"Nine goals in two games? Score nine for the season today and you get a million-dollar contract."

The Flyers marvelled at what they'd watched happen against them.

"Any superlatives I might offer would be inadequate," said Flyers coach Pat Quinn when he met the media after that game.

"This is absolutely crazy," said Flyers captain Bobby Clarke in the dressing room. "At least with Bobby Orr, you'd see him wind up in his own end and you could try to set up some kind of defence to stop him. Gretzky ... he comes out of nowhere. It's scary."

Ignored that night was the fact Gretzky had just scored his 198th, 199th, 200th, 201st and 202nd goals since turning pro in the WHA less than 3½ years earlier.

Gretzky had scored on 15 of his last 32 shots.

"Last year I would have passed on three of the goals I scored tonight," said Gretzky in the Oilers room.

Two Oilers said they saw it coming.

"Things like this aren't supposed to happen, yet when he sets a goal for himself, he gets it," said Paul Coffey. "He wanted to do it before the 40th game. You could bet $1 million against him doing it but I knew he would."

Gretzky's roommate Kevin Lowe also expected the explosion when the two were having bacon and eggs, cooked by Wayne, on game day.

"He doesn't really say much about his goals, but he said at breakfast there was no reason he couldn't score five against the Flyers."

Gretzky himself didn't know exactly what to say at the time.

"I wasn't born in 1944-45. I can't remember seeing any six-team NHL games on television. But I did see the Rocket on a between-periods interview once.

"All I can say is I believe hockey is better now than it was 15 years ago. I think today's players are bigger and better. And 15 years from now, I think they will be bigger and better than we are. Everything improves."

He wasn't going to play down the accomplishment, though. This was hockey's greatest record. And he smashed it to smithereens.

"I guess I'm more delighted with this than anything," he said, and then asked if he might be excused for a few minutes.

What he did on the ice that night was one thing. What he did off the ice that night was just as impressive.

"I was sitting at home listening to the radio and the station was keeping us right up to date," said Walter Gretzky the next day.

"First they said he had 47 goals , then 48, then 49 ... I was really excited.

"Then he scored No. 50 and ...

"Well, right after the game, Wayne called us from the dressing room. He said he just wanted to let us know what happened. I want to tell you, when Wayne called, that accomplishment of 50 goals in 39 games meant absolutely nothing – nothing at all compared to that phone call. Heck, he's a 20-year-old. He's busy with all sorts of friends and plenty of things to do. There aren't many 20-year-olds who would take the time."

Walter, after his son's last game that afternoon in New York, said it was his favourite memory and he wasn't even there.

"There are two hours time difference between Edmonton and Brantford but I was up late. The phone rang. It was Wayne. He said, 'I just wanted to let you know that I did it.' I said, 'Did what?' He said, 'Fifty in 39 games.' I was joking, of course. I said, 'What took you so long? Then he told me he needed to get back, that he'd excused himself for a minute from the press, and said, 'I just thought I'd call you and mom.' "

Glen Sather made the observation that night.

"People are now going to have to re-evaluate their stars of the century. And I still don't think we've seen the best of Gretzky yet."

But the few words Bobby Clarke said to Gretzky that night said it all:

"I know everything that's been written about you. I think none of it is adequate."

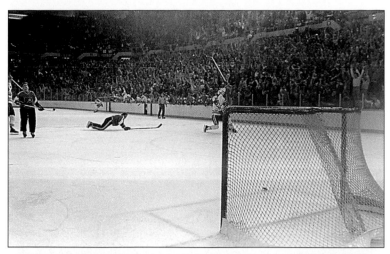

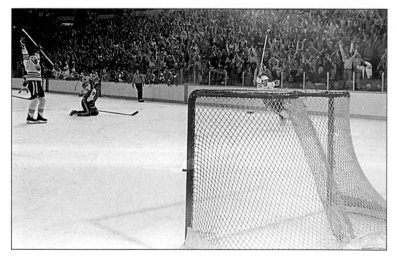

MIRACLE MILESTONE: Gretzky's historic empty-netter.

A SEASON OF SEASONS

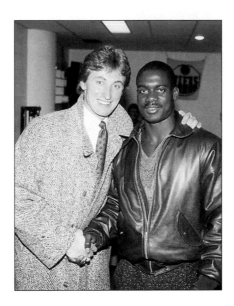

halfway through his third season in the NHL, Wayne Gretzky was receiving thousands of pieces of fan mail per day.

Some were addressed only "To Wayne Gretzky, Canada."

"Like writing to Santa Claus," said Oilers coach and GM Glen Sather.

One fan, from Finland, addressed a letter to "The King Of Ice Hockey, Wayne Greatsky, Canada."

"I don't have enough time to read all my own mail," said Gretzky. "I read as much as I can. But the thing I'm most surprised with is most of the mail I get is so sincere. Mrs. Moss handles most of my mail. And I'm sure she feels the same way about how sincere 95 per cent of it is."

Sophie Moss is the mother of Wayne's girlfriend at the time, Vikki.

"One day he told Vikki that he had so much mail he didn't know what he was going to do. He had a couple of green garbage bags full of mail. He told Vikki, 'I've got to get someone to help me.'

"Vikki volunteered me. She said, 'My mom will!'"

Sophie Moss surrounded by Wayne Gretzky's fan mail.

Sophie hadn't even met the young man.

"They'd only been dating a few weeks, perhaps. He didn't know me. He hadn't met Joey yet.

"My husband had passed away. It gave me something to do. I got the job. And I loved it. I absolutely loved it."

She did it until a month or two after Gretzky left Edmonton, long after his daughter stopped dating No. 99.

She just wished she'd kept score. It would have been one of Gretzky's greatest statistics.

"There were just thousands and thousands and thousands," she said.

"And so many of the cards and letters were just wonderful. They were just beautifully written words on how much they admired Wayne and wanted an autograph. Everyone wanted an autograph. Wayne would sign thousands of them on pictures and we'd send them out.

"I'd keep the business ones and the ones that really struck me and make sure Wayne saw them. There were so many beautiful cards for his birthday and a lot of the Christmas cards were really special. I sent a lot of those to his mom and dad.

"There was too much mail for me to handle by myself. I had friends help me, addressing envelopes and that end of it. A dear, dear person who helped me an awful lot was Sister Antonio. I'd take loads of mail to the convent. She'd sit and help me for hours."

Sophie Moss won't talk about any specific piece of mail. She feels that's not her place. She does admit there were several proposals of marriage and sex.

"I wouldn't tell you because you'd print it. But there were some funny ones.

"But the ones I remember best, and by far the majority of them, were the beautiful ones. So many people worshipped Wayne, just worshipped him."

She admits she's one of them herself.

"He's kept in touch. I still see him once a year or so.

"I'm grateful to have known someone like Wayne. I'm grateful I had a chance to work for him with the mail. I met a lot of wonderful people through him. My life has been enriched.

"And I'm truly grateful, I'm sure I don't have to say, that Wayne introduced Joey to the Oilers. He gave him a reason to get up in the morning. Because of Wayne, Joey matured and became a real part of society."

She didn't become his mother-in-law. But he's long been like a relation.

"He was like one of my sons. He's always been like family."

Gretzky went from being famous to an icon that year, from The Great

Gretzky's endorsement deals included GWG jeans and (opposite) Mr. Big bars.

Gretzky to The Great One.

He was invited on *The Tonight Show* by Johnny Carson. He and the team visited the set of *M*A*S*H*. He left hockey tickets for actresses such as Morgan Fairchild to watch him play in Los Angeles. He was trying to sing on one TV show and act on another. He met Ronald Reagan, the president of the United States. And he kept putting up the numbers like he was playing pinball.

One night in early November, Gretzky showed up at practice and found out he had a new winger.

Mary Campbell.

She was a 25-year-old Ottawa recreation department worker. She was Gretzky's winger for 15 minutes at the Oilers workout. It was for a CTV show, *Thrill Of A Lifetime*.

"I've never skated with a girl before," said Gretzky.

"You've never done anything with a girl before," kidded Paul Coffey.

Gretzky's impact on the game was everywhere. Like Christmas. There had never been a Christmas like it before in Canada.

Under Canadian Christmas trees on Christmas morning there are traditionally many sets of skates and much hockey equipment. And mostly there are Montreal Canadiens and Toronto Maple Leafs sweaters. That year it was Edmonton Oilers sweaters. And most of them had to have No. 99 on the back.

"The term is probably 'phenomenal,'" said Jerry Sabourin, an executive with Grant emblems, the licensed manufacturer of NHL crests for Sandow hockey jerseys.

"The Oilers are outselling the Canadiens and Leafs combined at least two to one. I've never seen a demand for any one team even remotely close to the demand for the Oilers. For every one Oiler crest that goes out, there's only one from all the other NHL teams combined."

Sabourin estimated the split was "about 60 per cent Gretzky and 40 per cent Oilers."

Gretzky was swamped with endorsement offers.

He'd come a long way in a hurry. Wasn't it just yesterday he signed his first endorsement contract, pitching Rafino pizza in Edmonton?

"One thing a lot of people forgot," said Gretzky. "In my first year in the NHL there were a lot of people debating this and that about me. But the one thing they all seemed to agree upon was that it was such a shame I was playing in Edmonton instead of New York or Toronto.

"They said I wouldn't get as much publicity because of where I played and it would certainly restrict the amount of endorsements and stuff like that.

FORGET THE WHEATIES: Gretzky ultimately ended up flogging his own cereal, Pro Stars.

"After experiencing everything I've experienced so far this year, I feel more than ever that Edmonton is the perfect place to play. I've proved from a contract point of view, from a publicity point of view and from an endorsement point of view that Edmonton hasn't hurt a bit.

"As for the publicity, I didn't think it was possible for a Canadian athlete to get this much publicity. Everybody dreams of doing something that hasn't been done before. Everybody dreams of being on the cover of *Sports Illustrated* and all the rest of it. I guess you figure if you did something that's never been done before you'd get a lot of that. But I didn't expect a Canadian hockey player could get that much, regardless.

"In the first two years, I could go to a U.S. city and hide in places like Pittsburgh, St. Louis and Minnesota. It was easy to be one of the guys. Now I can't go out with the guys without worrying about it getting hectic. The recognition has a lot of disadvantages when it comes to being one of the guys but, still, it's worth it. I'm not complaining."

Michael Barnett had come into Gretzky's world, working for agent Gus Badali on the sports marketing end of things, and had set up a strategy.

"We're trying to attach him to items we consider to be of proven quality," said Barnett. "We're trying to match him with companies which are as significant in their world as Wayne is in his world."

The idea was to up the numbers and lower the time involved on Wayne's part.

"This year Wayne will make probably one-fifth the appearances he did last year, do one-third the company endorsements, but for about six times the financial reward.

"We try not to lose sight of the fact he's 20 years old and that he has the zest for things that 20-year-olds do. So if an endorsement comes along that can take him to Hawaii or the Bahamas, chances are he'll go for it. But I think he's at a point where there's not much a company can offer him that's new. The first two years, maybe, it was exciting. But now it's

more of a job and one that should, at best, be a part-time job.

"A considerable number of people want a piece of him. The fan mail is a big thing. Six out of every 10 letters are from outside of Canada, one in 10 is from Europe and right now in our offices there are something like 25,000 to be answered."

Hence the need for the services of Mrs. Moss.

"We use a postage machine and order glossy pictures of Wayne 20,000 at a time," Barnett reported.

And it was all just getting going.

The Oilers, in early January, headed out on a five-game road trip to Calgary, Washington, Philadelphia, Toronto and Detroit. It was the road trip where everybody figured Gretzky would get his 50th goal after it became obvious he was going to do it inside of 50 games.

When the Oilers hit the eastern seaboard there were 132 requests to interview Gretzky in Toronto. And they'd just landed in Washington for a game on a Wednesday, to be followed by a game Thursday and then the Saturday night *Hockey Night In Canada* stop in Toronto against the Maple Leafs.

Upon arrival in Washington, Gretzky had to handle interviews from a horde of media men and women, including an advance party of sportswriters from Toronto who were basically chronicling "The Road to Toronto."

After finishing with everybody, Gretzky jumped in a limo with NHL president John Ziegler and took a tour of the local TV and radio stations, on a previously planned promotional run around town to promote the NHL All-Star Game scheduled a few weeks later in Washington.

Gretzky had become a walking, talking, one-man media event.

He had a film crew attached to him, too, filming *A Day in the Life of Wayne Gretzky*.

Despite the distractions, Gretzky had a goal and two assists in a 6-6 tie against the Caps.

There were more media members waiting the next day in Philadelphia and now so many interview requests for Friday and Saturday in Toronto that Oilers media relations man Bill Tuele had to call a special press conference.

Gretzky was happy with that.

"We've decided to have a two-hour press conference after the practice in Toronto," Gretzky announced to the "Road to Toronto" travellers. "I'm going to sneak home and see my parents after that. I would have been interviewed in Toronto from just about the moment we landed until we took the ice."

Gretzky managed one goal in Philadelphia but the Oilers were awful and lost 8-2.

This trip was taking its toll.

Gretzky was bigger than Pavarotti when he hit Toronto, in that Pavarotti tickets were $150 and tickets for the Gretzky game were said to be going for $250.

All week Gretzky had been a media event. Every time he stepped off a plane, bus or train (the Oilers used those three forms of transportation on the tour), there was at least one television

Wayne was on hand for the opening of a Speedy Muffler shop in Edmonton ...

... and signed autographs at an Edmonton Sun carriers breakfast.

crew waiting to record the momentous event. But Washington and Philadelphia were nothing compared to Toronto.

Veteran Toronto observers suggested that never in the history of Canadian sport had there been such a reception for a Canadian athlete, including those coming home with gold medals from Olympic Games.

One, Peter Smith, the manager of the Westin Hotel, said it could only compare to a royal visit.

"The only time I've seen anything that came close to this was when I was the manager of the Edmonton Plaza Hotel in 1978 and we had Queen Elizabeth and Prince Philip in the hotel for the Commonwealth Games."

The Gretzky press conference was massive, with more writers and broadcasters in one room than normally cover the Stanley Cup. The scene became the story. Gretzky had little new to say, but answered every question and did over an hour of one-on-ones with electronic media outlets.

"This scene is absolutely unbelievable," said Oilers owner Peter Pocklington. "If you weren't convinced before, you have to be convinced now

that Wayne has done more to put Edmonton on the map than all of the other citizens of Edmonton combined."

Sather surveyed the scene with his trademark smirk.

"How can I complain?" he said. "Wayne deserves this. Wayne just proved again what a classy young gentleman he is. The kids today need somebody to idolize. I think it's better that they choose to idolize Wayne Gretzky than Mick Jagger."

Gretzky, when he was done, marvelled at the scene himself.

"I guess what happened here this afternoon is just about the biggest compliment ever paid to me," he said.

One specific scene said it all.

After the game in Toronto, in order to get No. 99 safely from the dressing room to the team bus, Dave Semenko and a couple of others had to act as bodyguards. The doors to Maple Leaf Gardens and the team bus were surrounded by a mob of teenaged girls screaming with delight just to get a glimpse of Gretzky – and ecstatic if they actually managed to touch him.

"I feel like the Beatles," said Gretzky in an embarrassed sort of way as he worked his way down the aisle to his usual seat at the back of the bus.

There was nothing to scream about for Oilers fans in that game either, although Gretzky did get another goal. Even goaltender Grant Fuhr, who had a 23-game winning streak going and found himself being interviewed by *Ebony* magazine on this trip, couldn't help. The Oilers lost 7-1.

Twenty-four hours later, in front of a crowd of 20,628 in Detroit, the Oilers managed a 4-4 tie with Gretzky collecting a pair of assists. But these weren't the same Oilers returning home as the players that had left. Nor the same Gretzky.

One thing Gretzky and the gang were willing to admit as they headed home: playing in Edmonton certainly had its advantages.

"Edmonton is a blessing," said Gretzky. "I can find time for myself when I'm at home. I doubt if it would be like that in places like New York or Toronto."

But it wasn't just Gretzky. It was the whole team. This wasn't a one-man show any more.

"In the past, even at the start of this season, all the media were there for Wayne and only Wayne," said Glen Sather. "But now other players are getting used to the idea that the people are becoming interested in them, too. Right now Grant Fuhr, Paul Coffey, Kevin Lowe, Glenn Anderson and Mark Messier – Dave Lumley when he was on that scoring streak – are all drawing people who want to talk to them. To some extent, everybody is getting a taste of it."

On Jan. 26, Wayne Gretzky turned 21 and celebrated it with a goal and an assist in St. Louis as the Oilers got themselves going again and put together a four-game winning streak. But Gretzky didn't sound like

Wayne Gretzky ended up becoming friends with music producer David Foster.

he was enjoying the idea of becoming an actual adult.

"I can't go to a ball game and have a beer and a hotdog and be just like anybody else any more," he said on his 21st birthday. "I can't be myself now. I can go to all sorts of private boxes, but I can't go sit in the stands and have a hotdog and a beer."

It had become clear that he was not just a household name in Canada, but pretty much everywhere.

"I've seen the change in the last year. Heck, in the last month," he said. "In the last month alone it's a bigger change than I've seen in the last 20 years.

"In a lot of ways, the change is nice. I still enjoy being recognized and having people ask me for my autograph. But there's so much of it. It's also frustrating."

He also felt his fear of flying was getting worse.

"I admit it. I get scared on planes. I don't know what it is. There have been a few close calls in the last couple of years. Now I'm the happiest guy in the world when the plane finally lands. It doesn't bother me as much when I'm in a group, but when I'm flying around every day to fulfil my commitments in the summer, it really bothers me."

He was also developing a fear of crowds.

"You never know what can happen," he said as he contemplated the idea of going from Superkid to Superman. "You never know who is out there. When they start shooting at the Pope, you start worrying."

Gretzky's "childhood" stats were complete.

He had 167 goals, 270 assists and 437 NHL points prior to turning 21. Include his WHA season and he had 213 goals, 334 assists and 547 points as a pro.

"I guess what he does now is shoot for consistency, maturity and leadership," said Sather.

Just as you started to worry that Gretzky might be losing that gee-whiz

appeal, he went to the NHL All-Star Game in Washington, D.C. And, gee whiz ...

"I'm certainly not going to forget this," said No. 99 of the day before the game.

"I met the president of the United States and Bob Hope. I was in a fog all day. I couldn't believe it was me sitting there at the White House with them. Even just being able to go inside the White House was a big thrill.

"I think that's the biggest thrill I've had, for me to sit beside the president of the U.S.A., one of the most powerful men in the world. And all the people I've met in show business this year. It's been something. Like when Kevin, Mark and I met Goldie Hawn and Burt Reynolds. I'm sure to them I was just another person passing through, but for Mark, Kevin and I to meet them, well, I'm sure we got a bigger thrill meeting them that they had meeting us.

"And being friends with people like Alan Thicke has exposed me to some interesting things. I really enjoyed being on the *Paul Anka Special* even though I can't sing, and this summer I'm going on *The Beachcombers*."

He was invited on *The Tonight Show* with Johnny Carson, but weather led to travel problems for Gretzky to get from a game the night before in Quebec City to California, so he had to cancel.

"You can put that down as my biggest disappointment of the year," said No. 99. "But the thing that disappointed me most was that my parents brought me up to live up to my promises. I had never missed an appearance in my life for anything that way. When I say I'll be there, I'll be there. There are a lot of times I can't do something and I'll say no. But if I say yes, you can count on me. And then I don't make it for the biggest one of them all? I really felt bad."

The White House made up for that.

If there was any idea that Gretzky was getting used to rubbing shoul-

Boxers Craig Payne and Lennox Lewis pay a visit to the Oilers dressing room.

ders with the rich and famous, it went out the White House window.

"I kept looking at Gordie Howe and doing exactly what he was doing," said No. 99.

"I told Wayne, 'Just pretend the president is not there, finish your meal and don't look up," said No. 9.

Howe claimed the only reason he was invited to tag along was so Reagan would have somebody his own age to relate to.

"He told me his dad took him to watch me play when he was a kid," laughed Gordie.

Gretzky was the only player mentioned in the president's speech.

"One of the latest sports heroes in this country is a modest young man named Wayne Gretzky," said Reagan. "We know that just north of the border there are so many fine people like him and we are happy to have them as neighbours and friends. That's what hockey and sportsmanship are all about."

The president also said that the Washington Capitals should give up two draft choices and the state of Texas to get Gretzky.

When Gretzky came off the all-star game the countdown to Phil Esposito's single-season record of 76 goals began.

Twenty-seven games remained. Gretzky already had 69 goals (not to mention 83 assists and 152 points).

He'd scored 61 goals in his first 50 games, if you wanted to work the Rocket's record the other way.

Again there was a plot in place.

The Oilers were in Vancouver for Game 50 and Richard Brodeur had drawn the short straw and was in goal for the Canucks.

This was the same Richard Brodeur who a month earlier had gone on the record as saying Gretzky was "arrogant, a whiner and a crybaby."

Gretzky whacked a 15-foot shot past him with 6½ minutes to play to give the Oilers a 4-3 win.

There was an amazing amount of pressure on Gretzky now. He was on the cover of *Sports Illustrated* for the second time in a season, unheard of

for a hockey player. And it looked to some, including one of the Oilers coaches, like he was getting tired.

"As soon as he gets goal No. 80, I'd send him away for eight or 10 days," said assistant coach Billy Harris after Gretzky's two-goal game – Nos. 71 and 72 in a 7-4 win over Minnesota on Feb. 17.

"It's not my decision but I know how I'd handle it. I'd get him away. We've been kind of concerned the last few games how tired he's been looking. Until the second period tonight, he looked pretty tired to us. What he did in the last two periods was the sensational stuff you almost come to expect from Wayne. We haven't seen him like that for a while."

From the outside this had to seem rather ridiculous. After 61 games the Boy Wonder had 72 goals, 89 assists and 161 points, had already broken Rocket Richard's record and was about to break Phil Esposito's, and there were people out there asking, "What's Wrong With Wayne?"

"People expect me to get four goals every game," said Gretzky.

"I'm not tired. I'm frustrated. I just don't think I've played up to my abilities in the last couple of weeks, that's all."

Owner Pocklington went so far as to suggest that he and Sather had actually asked Gretzky to take a break and not give the world of sport the full-meal deal and find out just how many goals, assists and points it was possible for a player to get in one season.

"We both went to him," said Pocklington. "But he says there's no way he'll do it. He doesn't think it would be fair to the team."

The team? How about hockey? How about the fans? How about himself?

Gretzky registered goals 71 and 72 in a 7-4 win Feb. 17 over the Minnesota North Stars. It was his first multi-goal game since a Jan. 31 hat trick against Philadelphia.

As much as there was another Gretzky Countdown going, Messier also had one going for a 50-goal season and the Oilers as a team were on pace to set a record for the most goals scored in a season.

Gretzky was hoping to get Esposito's record at home and almost apologized when he didn't do it.

It was a game against the Hartford Whalers, and guess who was putting expectations on whom to get four goals in a game?

Gretzky needed four against the Whalers to tie Esposito's record at home. He didn't do it. He scored three.

The Oilers were heading off on an eight-game road trip and the record was going to be long gone by the time Gretzky got back.

"We play our last two games of the year at home," said No. 99 almost apologetically. "If I score in either of those games, that's the one the fans will remember. That will be the real record."

Gretzky only getting three that night was quite all right with goalie Greg Millen.

The previous season Gretzky chose Millen to score his historic 153rd point against to break Esposito's single-season points record.

Another Espo record on the line and Millen in goal again? No fair. Millen was Gretzky's junior teammate in the Soo.

"Greg used to pick me up in the car and take me to practice every day," Gretzky remembered. "It's a small world after all, isn't it?"

Millen had two words for Gretzky.

"Too small," he said.

"I'm just glad he stopped at three."

First stop on the road trip, Detroit. And guess who was there waiting for them when they walked into their hotel lobby?

John Ziegler. And Phil Esposito.

The NHL president informed Gretzky the two would be travelling with him until he tied and then broke Espo's record.

"Our instructions to Wayne are to go out and get a bunch of assists and no goals," assistant coach Harris said to Esposito. "We thought it would be nice if you could accompany us at least as far as Pittsburgh," Harris said of the third game on the trip.

"Pittsburgh?" said Esposito. "I don't even want to go to Buffalo."

The next morning a Detroit sportswriter predicted Gretzky wouldn't get a goal against the Red Wings.

"I think he'd prefer to wait and score it against a real NHL team," scribbled the scribe. The Red Wings were being called the Dead Things at the time.

Gretzky got one.

Tied the record.

Glenn Anderson set him up to beat Bob Sauve at 16:34 of the third period.

One stat was fascinating. Gretkzy had tied the record on 293 shots. Esposito took 550 shots to set it.

Esposito claimed to be delighted.

"I wanted to be here, and I want to be wherever it is that he breaks it," he said after the game that nobody seemed to notice was Gretzky's third straight five-point outing.

"When I broke Bobby Hull's record of 58, I wished he could have been there to see it. I was coming here whether the NHL asked me to come or not. It's great what Wayne is doing for the game."

The entire entourage shuffled off to Buffalo. Game 64.

Strange scene. The Gretzky convention of media men had reassembled. But there was no Gretzky.

He went home to visit his grandmother, to go to school with his kid brother and to see other brother Keith play a game.

The press people would report a day later that Gretzky ate cabbage rolls and borscht at his grandmother's, that he sat in on brother Brent's Grade 5 class with the same teacher, Mrs. Chiu, that he'd had when he was 10 years old.

"A couple of kids in class did speeches on me," he said, somewhat embarrassed.

Keith, who was appearing in a TV commercial with his famous brother at the time, had two shorthanded assists, No. 99 reported of the

The Oilers superstar met a lot of famous people, including actor Kirk Douglas, as his own celebrity status grew.

kid who refused to wear the same number.

"It was the first time I'd watched Keith play in three years and he was great," said Wayne.

Gretzky said having Esposito around made him a bit uncomfortable.

"He's got to get back to work," he said.

No problem.

Gretzky got his goal.

That was No. 77, ironically the number Esposito wore on his back at the end of his career. His 77th goal came in Gretzky's 64th game, 14 fewer than Esposito had required 11 years earlier.

Gretzky also scored Nos. 78 and No. 79 that night as he played 28 minutes in the game and took 10 shots to up his total to 303, 247 fewer than Esposito fired to get his record.

And again nobody noticed. But he'd registered a fifth straight five-point night.

Don Edwards made a couple of great saves on Gretzky before he scored the record goal.

It was a 20-footer at 13:24 of the third period.

Esposito had been saving an anecdote for the moment.

As guests of hockey fan Jamie Farr, the Oilers made a splash visiting the set of the hit television show M*A*S*H.

Seven years earlier, he said, he'd received a long-distance call from his dad in Sault Ste. Marie.

" 'Phil, there's a boy who will break all your records one day. He's 14 years old and he's playing junior in the Soo. His name is Gretzky. Wayne Gretzky.' I remember saying, 'That's great, dad. But he's only 14. Let's wait and see.' "

Esposito said he enjoyed the experience of watching Gretzky break his record.

"I had goosebumps for him."

Gretzky went on to set a record for setting records. He even "forgot" one of them.

With his second goal of his hat trick in Game 74 against Pittsburgh in Edmonton, Gretzky broke Mike Bossy's record of 85 for most goals in a season, including playoffs.

There wasn't even time to properly hype that one. And Gretzky forgot to collect the historic puck.

"I forgot all about it," he said. "When it went on the PA that I'd broke the record, they'd already dropped the puck for the faceoff. I could have got it after the first whistle but I thought, 'The heck with it.' "

Eventually somebody in the stands ended up with one heck of a souvenir.

The hat trick was Gretzky's 10th of the season. That was good for another record. Another Bossy record. The New York Islander held the record with nine. That night Gretzky also passed his own record of 109 assists in a season with his 110th. And, of course, every time he scored or got a point, he was breaking his own single-season records as well.

Agent Gus Badali made an interesting statement as the record went down and Gretzky had four consecutive five-point nights in the process.

"Wayne really has played cautious hockey for two years. Only this year has he played up to his capabilities. In the past he was afraid to make a mistake with the team fighting for the playoffs. I feel this is the first year he's played comfortably. He's doing things now and taking chances like he did when he was a kid. I think one of Wayne's fears was that he didn't want to be called a hotdog in the NHL. And you could be assured if he was doing in his first two years what he's doing this season, there would have been people calling him a hotdog."

The price of a hotdog went up in Edmonton. And you had to give the Oilers credit for timing. No sooner had Gretzky managed to break the record than they announced a ticket price increase of more than $3 a seat per game ($24 instead of $18 for the best seats). They were reworking Gretzky's contract so he'd be making $700,000 a season.

Nobody complained about the cost. They were watching the Greatest Show On Ice and they knew it.

A week later in Calgary, Gretzky reached a milestone with his 200th (not to mention 201st, 202nd and 203rd) regular-season points. It was Game 76.

Wayne had flown his dad in for that game.

"I'll admit it," said Walter. "Most of the things he's done, I thought he would do. All the other records, I expected him to get. But this is something else. Two hundred points? No way! I'm like anybody else. I thought I'd never see the day."

Funny. While Walter was saying that outside the dressing room, Wayne was saying something else again inside the room.

"It was my dad who suggested the possibility to me," he said.

The thing that made the night was that it was Calgary. Hated rival. And the fans in Calgary made it wonderful.

Nobody ever thought they'd see the day when an athlete wearing an Edmonton uniform would get a standing ovation in Calgary, but it happened on the night of March 25, 1982.

They came to boo Gretzky, as always. And they did boo, too.

"It's different here than anywhere else in the league," said Gretzky. "I've been booed before but here they boo like they really mean it."

When it happened, when he fed Pat Hughes a perfect pass for a goal at 9:16 of the first period, there was a chorus of boos.

But then, one by one, the same people who had begun to boo realized they'd witnessed history and, one by one, they started cheering.

"It surprised me," said Gretzky. "I thought this was the last place this would ever happen to me. Because of the ovation they gave me, this means a little more than what happened in Buffalo when I broke Phil Esposito's record. I think it shows when a Canadian does something special, they'll drop everything to stand behind him and show their appreciation as fellow Canadians."

Gretzky, who all but guaranteed the Edmonton fans a goal at home in the last two games of the season, didn't get one.

But he did get 92 for the season. Ninety-two!

It boggled the mind then. It boggles the mind still.

Ninety-two goals, 120 assists and 212 points.

It was the greatest single season in hockey history.

Chapter

8

FINAL JEOPARDY

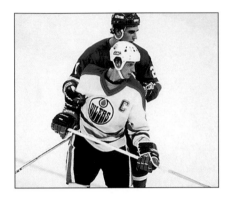

It had been such a wonderful year. And it ended up such a waste.

Wayne Gretzky went to camp the year after the Miracle On Manchester, the mother of all first-round playoff upsets, knowing that everything would be different for him from now on. And for his teammates, too. Their *Fantasy Island* days were over.

"That's when I knew I couldn't be satisfied without a Stanley Cup," said Gretzky of what happened in the playoffs after his most marvellous of seasons – when he won the scoring race by 65 points, averaged 2.6 points a game, scored a league-leading 12 winning goals, recorded the fastest 500 points in NHL history, set an NHL record for 10 hat tricks, set an NHL record of two shorthanded goals in a span of 27 seconds ... and, oh yes, scored 50 goals in 39 games to break Rocket Richard's record, and 79 goals in 66 games to break Phil Esposito's record of 79 goals in 78 games.

"What happened has given me a challenge for the future. If you're playing for the Edmonton Oilers, Team Canada or street hockey, you're playing for a team and you're playing to win. I had a great season, but in the end, because of the way everything turned out, it didn't mean that much. I know now that I won't be satisfied with much until I have a Stanley Cup ring on my finger."

Pesky Flame Doug Risebrough puts the squeeze on Wayne Gretzky. The longtime Calgary forward went on to become Edmonton's vice-president of hockey operations.

Gretzky ended up a "weak-kneed wimp," playing in Europe for Canada at the World Hockey Championships.

In Finland, he stayed up late, talking with roommate Kevin Lowe about what had happened.

"We talked about how impossible it seemed that teams like Vancouver and Los Angeles and Chicago, who had so many problems all year, were there and we weren't," he said. "You can analyse it up and down, like Kevin and I did in our room over in Finland those first few nights, and what it all comes down to is maturity. If we don't learn our lesson there, if we don't come back next year as a much more mature team, then the same thing will happen to us again next year. If we're going to get better, we're going to have to get straightened out. I guess we got carried away with who we thought we were."

They were weak-kneed wimps. That was the phrase I chose to use in a paragraph that would take on a life of its own for years:

"From today until they've won a playoff series again, they are weak-kneed wimps who thought they were God's gift to the National Hockey League but who found out they were nothing but adolescent, front-running, good-time Charlies who couldn't handle adversity."

Several years later in his book *Gretzky* by Wayne Gretzky with Rick Reilly (Harper-Collins), Chapter 4 was titled "The Weak-Kneed Wimp Years."

"Terry Jones of *The Edmonton Sun* said it was the biggest choke job in Stanley Cup history and that we were all 'weak-kneed wimps.' I really objected to that. My knees are fine," Gretzky wrote in the book. He also wrote, "We were young and obnoxious" and it was "the pie in the face" which was "the best thing that ever happened to us."

Game 1 of that series pretty much telegraphed what was to follow.

The Oilers grabbed a 4-1 lead in that game in the Coliseum. And then they gave the game away. Final score: 10-8.

But the game everybody will remember is the one the Oilers led 5-0 in the Forum in Los Angeles. That was the Miracle On Manchester. The entire Oilers bench was booing the Kings' power play. That's what turned it. The Oilers ended up losing that game and that best-of-five series.

Would these young Oilers learn from it all? Would Gretzky go the me-me-me or we-we-we route at the crossroads of his still-young career?

They were fair questions as the summer turned into fall.

Gretzky unloaded a $36,000 Ferrari off the train in Edmonton that summer. He sat with Hollywood stars at the Holmes-Cooney fight in Las Vegas and was pointed out by Howard Cosell. In the off-season. That summer there were stories about him saying he wanted to become a Hollywood actor. He bought his own junior hockey team. He took a trip to the Soviet Union to visit Vladislav Tretiak. He did commercial after

commercial. He received offers for cameo appearances on *Three's Company* and *The Love Boat*. There were offers from David Letterman and Merv Griffin and there was the raincheck from the previous year with Johnny Carson.

Regardless of what had happened to the Oilers in the playoffs, there was no question what had happened with Wayne Gretzky. He had graduated from sports star to sports icon. At this time the previous year he wasn't getting telegrams from people like Mick Jagger after throwing out the ceremonial pitch for an Expos baseball game.

I addressed that subject in a Sept. 15 column in *The Sun*:

"Let's not pull any punches here. I know what you've been thinking. You've been thinking it all summer. You're thinking that it's amazing it hasn't happened yet but you are becoming more and more convinced that success is going to spoil The Great Gretzky. You believe that the timing is finally ripe for Wayne Gretzky to get carried away with being Wayne Gretzky. I've heard it from fans all summer. So why not confront him with it?"

I did.

"I think more and more people are expecting it to work out that way," he said. "And I think that's natural. But it's not getting to me.

"I enjoy doing the things that I've been able to do recently. I enjoy being in Vegas for a big fight and all the other things. I enjoy the TV shows and everything. I'm not going to pretend I don't love it. I'm 21 years old and I'd rather do those sort of things than sit home and go fishing for three months in the off-season like some of the older players.

"But I'm not stupid. If anything, all those other things remind me that I can't get carried away with anything.

"I know I get to go to all these places and do all these things because I'm Wayne Gretzky. If I don't keep on being Wayne Gretzky, all that stuff will go away. I'm not allowing myself to pretend it's any other way. I've seen a lot of professional athletes have a couple of great years and forget. When that

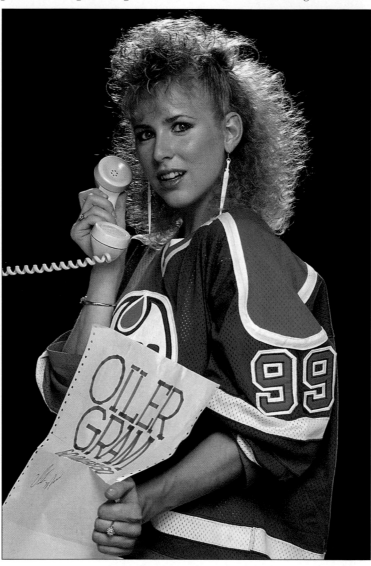

Wayne's former girlfriend Vikki Moss poses with a Sun 'Oiler-gram,' sent to wish the players well on their playoff run.

happens, everything goes away. I've told everybody, including my teammates, if they think I'm stepping out of line or putting myself above the team or anything like that, to tell me. I trust that they would tell me."

Gretzky went to camp saying the Oilers couldn't go through the motions for the first 50 games and then dial it up for the playoffs now that they had realized unsuccessful playoffs are all anybody remembers.

"We have to try to win as many games as last year. We have to try to score as many goals. Matter of fact, I believe the first several games are going to be very critical and crucial to this club because of what happened to us in the playoffs. It's important that we start like a house on fire. If we lost a bunch at the start, it could really affect us psychologically after what happened to us in the playoffs. This is the most crucial year we've had.

"The bottom line, I hope, is that I'm not stupid. I know I can't score 212 points every year. The most important thing I have to do is work as hard as I can on every shift and play every game to the best of my ability. The thing that separates the real professionals from the average players is consistency. I still have to prove that I can consistently play like I've played. That's my goal."

And so it was, with his head still screwed on straight, Wayne Gretzky and the Edmonton Oilers went into the next season.

The Oilers did not blast out of the gate as Gretzky had hoped. After their first 10 games they had five losses and two ties.

But Gretzky was on the scoresheet every night and had three points in half of those games. He didn't miss a beat. If anything, he took some of the focus off the early season struggles.

It started with a pre-season game in Toronto when Gretzky scored a goal that was considered by many to be his ultimate masterpiece.

"It was the most incredible goal I've ever seen him score," said Mark Messier at the time.

"He lost the puck, got it back, then beat three guys who had him cut off. I don't think they should feel ashamed, either. He's made fools out of the best players in the NHL."

Gretzky started the season on the same pace he produced throughout the previous season as he scored his 200th and 201st goals in his 242nd game.

By November the hockey world was beginning to take note that there was a different theme for the 21-year-old magic man this season.

Sun scribe Dick Chubey took note, as always, exceptionally early.

Gretzky, he wrote, was going after Guy Lafleur's record for registering points in 28 consecutive games. And as Gretzky began closing in on the mark, Ice Chubes decided it was time to interview The Great One on the subject.

"The Silent One" was *The Sun's* headline on Chubey's story the next day.

"I'm silent on this one," Gretzky had told him. "I haven't talked about it until now and I'm not going to start. I'll talk about the weather, I'll talk about the Eskimos' fifth Grey Cup in a row, I'll talk about anything you want, but ..."

In Montreal, Lafleur was saying he treasured this record the most but wasn't expecting to keep it.

On Dec. 5, Gretzky matched The Flower's record and owner Peter Pocklington said the heck with 28.

"Eighty!" he said of No. 99 scoring a point a game throughout the entire schedule.

"Eighty. No question. I think he's going to do it. I think he's capable of coming up with a point in every game during the regular-season schedule."

Glen Sather didn't roll his eyes.

"Eighty sounds good to me. I don't know what he can do. He's Wayne Gretzky."

And Gretzky?

"Eighty is a lot of games," he said.

"All I could think of was stopping short at 27. That would have been really discouraging. Now I've got it. Now it takes the pressure off. Now I can talk about it."

The point of the point streak, he said, was part of proving he could be consistent.

"More than anything I wanted to be consistent this year," he said. "I wanted to be more consistent instead of scoring in bunches. A prominent general manager in this league said I wasn't a consistent hockey player. I wanted to prove him wrong.

"It's my fifth year in the league and people are still saying things. It's actually kind of funny. They say, 'Ah, but he can't skate like Orr' or 'He can't shoot like Hull' or 'He's not as tough as Howe.' "

On the night he broke Lafleur's record I showed him a list of names in the dressing room. Milt Schmidt. Eric Nesterenko. Jim Pappin. Dick Duff. Bill Gadsby. Ross Lonsberry. Ted Kennedy. Peter Stemkowski. Bill Cowley. Max Bentley. Doug Bentley. Gary Dornhoefer. Bill Goldsworthy. Bill Mosienko. Doug Harvey. Danny Grant. Ken Warram. Guy Charron. Ron Stewart. Syd Howe. Camile Henry. Toe Blake. And Tim Horton.

"What do they have to do with me?" asked Gretzky.

I explained. At the start of the season, Gretzky was 101st on the all-time NHL points chart. Career!

Those were the names of the non-active players he'd already passed this season. He'd already gone from 101st to 60-something.

"I've passed all those guys? That's very surprising. I'd never even thought about that. Makes me think, though. If Nelson Skalbania hadn't signed me when I was 17 ... and for sure if I'd come along in some other era, I'd prob-

NEVER A DULL MOMENT: Even when he appeared to be on cruise control, Gretzky was a joy to watch.

ably be in my first year in the league."

The Gretzky point streak ended at 30 on Dec. 9 in Los Angeles against a rookie goalie by the name of Gary Laskoski. It would be his claim to fame.

As the season hit the halfway point, Gretzky was one point ahead of his pace from the previous season. And that's when it happened.

Gretzky turned into a goon.

On the night of Dec. 22 at the Coliseum, nobody was talking about his goal and two assists to reach the 600-point plateau.

OK, it wasn't a classic bout.

"He should have got two minutes for delaying the game," said Dave Semenko.

"It wasn't much of a fight," admitted Neal Broeten, the Minnesota North Star who made the match.

Wayne Gretzky, An Oiler Forever

"I just got tired of people asking me when my last fight was," said Gretzky. "At least now Doug Lecuyer is out as a trivia question. He's now not the only guy I've ever fought in the NHL.

"I can hear the buzz around the league when they read the game summary," he laughed. "Gretzky ... a minor for roughing and a MAJOR!?!"

The Oilers were having fun again and Gretzky was getting two or three points every night, five in Winnipeg on Jan. 5 and six in Minnesota on Jan. 15, five at home against Montreal on Feb. 4. There were scores of 10-4 in back-to-back games, 9-4, 8-6, 7-4 in back-to-back games, followed by 7-3 in back-to-back games with another 7-3 a game later when ... the Oilers were in Pittsburgh. Final score, 10-7.

"That was street hockey," said Gretzky who scored his 49th and 50th of the season, the latter being the winner on a breakaway.

"I thought we were going to have to score 15 to win. It was such a stupid game. I know we won, but who's kidding who? That was ridiculous."

When the Oilers returned to Edmonton, Gretzky started it. By now the whole world knew that the 'O' in Oilers did not stand for zero. But as the team sat in their dressing room prior to a game against the Winnipeg Jets, Gretzky started the chant:

"Shutout! Shutout! Shutout!"

The team took up the chant.

"I figured if everybody saw me talking shutout ... I figured if I started thinking that way, maybe everybody would. So I said, 'This is the game.' Shutout! Shutout! Shutout!

"I mean, let's face it. We won a game 10-7 in Pittsburgh. It's not funny any more."

It was a called-shot shutout. The Oilers won 3-0. It had been 279 games between Oilers shutouts –1,176 days since Eddie Mio accomplished the only other shutout in Oilers regular-season history. Andy Moog got it. But Gretzky called it. When the Oilers recorded their last shutout, Gretzky's career NHL stats were 11 goals, 26 assists and 37 points.

Three assists in the Oilers' last road game, in Vancouver, pushed Gretzky to the 700-point plateau and erased his own NHL assists record of 120 set the previous season.

"It's a little bit different kind of feeling than breaking a record by Bobby Orr or Phil Esposito, but it's a record," said

Gretzky vs. the Chicago Blackhawks.

A sombre Edmonton dressing room.

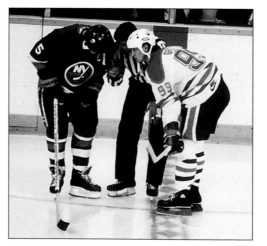
Isles' Denis Potvin (5) and Gretzky get the official word.

Gretzky who flew his grandmother in for the game.

Gretzky ended the season with 71 goals and 125 assists for 196 points, 74 more than second-place Peter Stastny of Quebec. The Oilers were 47-21-12 for a 106-point season. They were first in the Smythe Division and third overall.

To the casual fan, this season didn't compare to 1981-82. There was far less excitement involved. Last year they were the Amazing Oilers, catching the imagination of the nation with Gretzky under the spotlight from start to finish. Not this year. This year the real spotlight wasn't going to be turned on until the playoffs.

"Last season," said Gretzky, "we were a Cinderella story. We went through the league like a whirlwind and everybody wondered if we were for real. Maybe, in a way, we weren't for real. But this year we were. Teams were much better prepared to play us. This year I think we're much more intelligent. The big difference is that we realize we can be beat."

As the Oilers headed into the playoffs in their fourth season in the NHL, it had become a cliche. Gretzky & Goaltending. That was the magic combination. There hadn't been an exception to that rule, regular season or playoffs. And No. 99 wasn't arguing against the theory. He just believed the billing was wrong. He went on record as suggesting it should be Goaltending & Gretzky.

"One forward can't win the Stanley Cup," he said. "No team wins the Stanley Cup without top, top goaltending.

"I realize what my job is on this team. Definitely I want to have an entire playoff similar to the series I had against Montreal two years ago. If I do, I know what it can mean to the team.

"I think this will be the first year when they can't just watch myself and my line. I'm rested, physically and mentally and I'm excited. I think I'm fresher mentally this year than I was last year simply because I haven't had the media attention I had last year. And I'm more excited about these playoffs than any I've ever played in."

In retrospect, Gretzky said he was glad the Oilers lost in the first round the year before instead of losing later.

"One thing I know about sports and that's nobody remembers who fin-

ished second. If we had made it to the semifinal or the final I'm not sure we would have learned our lessons. We learned a lot more by losing the first round. We grew up faster."

It didn't really look like Gretzky was saving it for the playoffs. Until the playoffs.

The Oilers won Game 1 against Winnipeg 6-3 with four goals and an assist from Gretzky.

"What can you say about him?" said Lee Fogolin of the fact Gretzky tied two Stanley Cup playoff records in the game. He tied one for most goals in a period, with three. That was shared by 13 others. And he tied another for two shorthanded goals in one game. Only Dave Keon and Bryan Trottier had turned that trick before. No one knew if four goals – all on breakaways – was a record.

"It's the thrill of every young goalie to face Wayne Gretzky on four breakaways," said Jets GM John Ferguson.

MILES OF ISLES: Gretzky goes up against New York's Denis Potvin (5) and Bryan Trottier (19).

Gretzky said in that first game somewhere was his major motivation personally for these playoffs. He went into this Stanley Cup season hearing about the two knocks people still were putting on him: He doesn't do it in the clutch. And he can't score on breakaways.

"I think I prepare a lot more when there's criticism about something

I've done," said Gretzky. "I don't know what makes me like that, but when somebody says I can't...

"If I'm more mentally prepared for these playoffs than ever, it's because of what people said last year. Last year the team took a lot of abuse because of what happened. And maybe I took a little more criticism than the other guys. People said I was tired and anemic and ...

"If there's one thing I want to do this year in the playoffs it's to make sure people can't say any of those kind of things about me. If I'm more mentally prepared, that's where it comes in. I was hyped up tonight, no question. I was just ready tonight, that's all."

Oh, one other thing about the start of this playoff season, Gretzky said that night.

"For everybody who confronted me in the off-season about what happened last year in the playoffs, there was somebody who told me he was disappointed because he had me in the Stanley Cup pool and I let them down," he said.

Gretzky added two assists in Game 2 and another in Game 3 as the Oilers swept the series with the Jets.

Next up for Edmonton was Calgary. The Battle of Alberta. And the

TAKE IT EASY, FELLOWS: Tempers flare as the Oilers and Islanders mix it up during playoff action.

Oilers won the first two games at home without much help from No. 99. He didn't get a point in the 6-3 win in Game 1 and had merely two assists in the 5-1 win in Game 2.

"I've always said it takes 20 guys to win," laughed Gretzky. "Now, 19."

Gretzky joined the series in Game 3.

Seven points. Four goals. Three assists. The Oilers won 10-2 in Calgary. It was another record for Gretzky. Most points in a single Stanley Cup playoff game, breaking Dickie Moore's record of six. Gretzky also tied playoff records for most hat tricks in one playoff year, most short-handed goals in one game and one year, most goals in one period and the fastest goal from the start of a period other than the first – and the Oilers were only six games into the playoffs and 6-0.

"When things go wrong Gretzky is like a scavenger," said Calgary coach Bob Johnson. "He senses every mistake and just eats you up."

Glen Sather said he had no problem with Gretzky when he wasn't getting goals.

"I know people were asking where Gretzky was. But he was plus-nine

Gretzky tries to wrap one around goalie Billy Smith.

going into the game. And I don't really give a *@#$!*% about records. Wayne had a chance to tie Rocket Richard's record for five goals in one game but he passed the puck to Mark Messier instead of shooting. That's a sign of guys playing for a team."

The Oilers lost the fourth game of the series to the Flames 6-5 but put them away 9-1 in Game 5 back home.

Bring on the Chicago Blackhawks!

"We're playing the best, most complete hockey the Edmonton Oilers have ever played," said Gretzky. "But we can't ignore the facts. The teams we beat to this point weren't in the top 10. The teams we play from here on in are in the top four."

Having said that, they swept the Chicago Blackhawks 8-4, 8-2, 3-2 and 6-3.

Wayne Gretzky & Gang were in the Stanley Cup final!

"The dressing room before the game was really something," said Gretzky of the last giant step toward the dreams of their childhood.

"I've never seen our hockey club like that. Glen usually comes in

GREAT MOVE, GREAT ONE! Gretzky dekes out New York Islanders goalie Billy Smith (31) and Butch Goring.

and gives us a speech before the game but he didn't even bother to come in. He knew we were so ready.

"We'd keep seeing that clock up there and it seemed like it was ticking so slow. 'Come on, clock,' I felt like yelling. 'Tick!'

"It was crazy. I think we were all more nervous when the score was 5-1 than we were when it was 0-0."

Four years in the National Hockey League and Wayne Gretzky and the Edmonton Oilers were in the Stanley Cup final.

"We grew up as kids in Canada thinking maybe one day we'd be able to have our name on that trophy," rasped Gretzky as he went into the series with laryngitis.

"We'd watch the Stanley Cup finals as we were growing up. It would be the biggest thing that ever happened to me if I had a chance to put my name on the Stanley Cup."

This was the chance.

The series opened in Edmonton and the Islanders won the opener 2-0. Gretzky didn't get a point.

In Game 2, Andy Moog had a tough night and the Oilers lost 6-3. Gretzky had two assists.

On the Island, the three-in-a-row Stanley Cup champs moved within a win of four straight with a 5-1 win. Gretzky had an assist.

The Islanders had effectively managed to contain No. 99.

"I don't think we can get better mileage out of Wayne," said Sather. "Maybe a lot of other people, but not Wayne. He's giving it 100 per cent and if anybody criticizes Wayne Gretzky that person isn't playing with a full deck."

Gretzky saw it more as a slump.

"I'm paid to put the puck in the net and I'm not. I'd be concerned if I wasn't getting the chances, but I am. Billy Smith is either stopping them or they are hitting the post."

Gretzky had but one assist as the Islanders swept the series with a 4-2 win in Game 4.

And Gretzky knew, despite the fact that he'd led the Stanley Cup playoffs in scoring with 12 goals and 26 assists for 38 points, and completed his season and

post-season with 37 NHL records, there would be people pointing fingers again.

"I can take the roses when we're winning and the heat when we're losing. I have to score. I didn't get a goal in the series.

"As a team we learned from what happened to us last year. Now we have to learn some more.

"We're so young, I think all the excitement got to us a little bit," he said of being in the finals for the first time.

"We got frustrated. We have to handle frustration better. We played very well in the first game and couldn't score. We allowed that to set the stage for the whole series.

"To sum it all up, the Washington Capitals have been in the league for 10 years and they just made the playoffs for the first time. We've been in the league for four years and, over the last two, we've had the best record in hockey. In our fourth year in the NHL and we were in the Stanley Cup final. We didn't win. But everything in life is built around learning from your mistakes.

"I don't think losing four straight to a team winning their fourth straight Stanley Cup is going to leave any scars. Hopefully we now know what it takes to play in the Stanley Cup Final. I don't think we knew that when this series started. But I think we know that now."

Gretzky & Gang learned maybe their biggest lesson before they left the rink that night.

When it was all over, Gretzky and Kevin Lowe, who left the Oilers dressing room together, were left with an indelible impression of the New York Islanders and why they were the Stanley Cup champions for a fourth consecutive year. They walked by the Islanders dressing room. The doors were open.

"Those celebrating were management, executives, wives and everybody like that" said Gretzky. "Not the players.

"The players were so exhausted, so tired, wearing ice packs ...

"We got on the bus and I remember Kevin saying, 'That's the difference. They won and they're wounded. We lost and we're fine.'"

Gretzky was held to just one assist as the Islanders swept the 1983 Stanley Cup final series 4-0.

THE CAPTAIN AND THE CUP

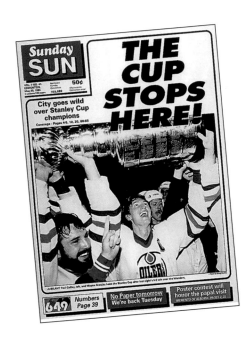

the Edmonton Oilers dressing room has traditionally been the most media-friendly in the entire league. But after practice on Oct. 4, 1983, captain Lee Fogolin kicked every press card-carrying, pencil-packing person out.

Fogolin, in his final official act as captain, then conducted a private ceremony, handing Wayne Gretzky a new jersey with the captain's 'C' sewn on the front.

"I'd talked with Glen Sather for some time," said Fogolin after he let the media back in the room. "Maybe little changes like this will help us win a Stanley Cup.

"Not that I'm saying it would have made a heck of a lot of difference if we had won the Cup last spring. We probably still would have made the change.

"Some people may look at this as a demotion on my part, but that's not the case," said Fogolin. "I've played 10 years now and the most important thing is to win a Stanley Cup."

Sather said it was time for the move for a lot of reasons, some that the average fan might not consider.

Wayne Gretzky happily hoists the Stanley Cup during the Oilers' victory parade.

The Great One holds the Stanley Cup close to his chest while police officers escort him past hordes of screaming fans.

"A change of direction might do us some good, give us a different point of view," said Sather. "Fogie is a little older and we have so many young guys on our team. Wayne's their age and could have a big influence on off-ice situations."

The Sun's Dick Chubey could read between the lines.

"Roughly translated: When the captain vacates the speakeasy, the sheep should follow," wrote Ice Chubes.

Gretzky wore his new 'C' into the new season coming off quite a summer.

He umpired a John McEnroe exhibition tennis match at a celebrity event.

"That was a ball," he said. "John and I got into this little thing for about 20 seconds or so. We were just fooling around. He was yelling at me and I was yelling right back."

Gretzky, during the summer, also rubbed shoulders with the likes of Burt Reynolds, Jack Lemmon, Linda Evans, Sammy Davis Jr., Barbra Streisand and Jack Nicholson.

He also made an appearance on a TV show called Dance Fever.

"I had to come out and dance, all by myself. It was the most embarrassing 10 seconds of my life," he said. "They wanted me to do something,

spin around or something, at the end of the little dance. I just jumped up in the air and told them it was my Mark Messier move."

Gretzky also kept busy with his growing empire of endorsements, adding a cereal called Pro*Stars with other items such as lunch boxes, wallpaper and the like to the list.

But the, uh, highlight, was filming an episode of his favourite TV soap opera, The Young and the Restless.

"That was great. I played a bad guy," said Gretzky.

Actually, it wasn't so great, Gretzky.

"He shoots. He misses!" was Lucinda Chodan's first-paragraph review in The Sun of his appearance on the soap.

"No. 99 shot wide with such lacklustre lines as 'Call me Wayne, everybody does.'

"And though his introduction – as 'Wayne from our Edmonton operation' – brought a thrill to every loyal Edmontonian, even the most faithful Gretz fan had to groan when he leered unconvincingly at one of the sudser's heroines and winked."

If nothing else, it brought Gretzky's focus back to hockey in a hurry as training camp opened. And if that didn't do it, there was that 'C' on his sweater.

Paul Coffey, Wayne Gretzky and Dave Lumley get a grip on hockey's Holy Grail.

"After going to the finals last year, this is the first year we can realistically say we've got a chance to win it," said the new Oilers captain as the team prepared for its fifth year in the NHL.

"If we don't get to the finals again, then management will start making trades. And as far as I'm concerned, personally, I know I can't be mediocre."

Gretzky always had a fear of flying but it was obvious on a couple of pre-season flights that it was getting worse.

"I'd like to be able to do what John Madden does," said Gretzky in Bloomington, Minnesota, that September. "I'd like to get a Winnebago and just drive to games. I'm getting worse on planes, I really am. I may be the only guy in the NHL who wants to go back to the days of the six-team NHL. Remember, they rode trains."

Coach Glen Sather said he noticed it, too.

"We're going to have to get him some more help," said Slats.

Gretzky, wearing his new 'C,' led the Oilers to a great start, winning their first seven games of the season. No. 99 had at least two points in every one of those games, three three-point games and a five-point game.

Chubey managed to come up with yet another new statistic on Gretzky when No. 99 scored a goal and an assist in his first game as Oilers captain. Gretzky had managed at least a point in every game, home and away, against the Toronto Maple Leafs, Quebec Nordiques, Detroit Red Wings and Pittsburgh Penguins, to this point of his career.

When the Oilers blew out the Washington Capitals 11-3 and Gretzky had enjoyed another five-point night, he climbed up on a soapbox after the game and informed the world that the Oilers were not really 10-2-1 as the standings suggested.

"We're 3-0," he said.

Gretzky said the Oilers had decided they were playing in two different leagues this year.

"Out-of-division games are designated games," he said, noting that the NHL would award home-ice advantage throughout the playoffs to the team with the best record against its other conference clubs.

"We get a lot of criticism that we have so many points in the standings because we play in a weak division," he said. "It's like we're being made fun of because we play in such a weak division. It's not our fault we're 30 points ahead of the teams in our division by Jan. 1.

"Heck, it's tough for us. It's tough to get up in the morning and look at the standings. Edmonton fans are lucky we have the kind of makeup we have on this club. It's still so much fun for our team that we show up and go for it every night. The bottom line is entertainment and I think Edmontonians get their money's worth in entertainment."

Fans on the road got their money's worth, too. Like the night in Winnipeg in early November when a leather-lunged fan who had paid to see Gretzky seemed displeased by the fact the home-town Jets were leading 3-0.

"Come on Gretzky, do something!" the guy screamed. Ever accommodating, Gretzky scored a shorthanded goal 71 seconds later and ended up having the most productive night of his career on the road, scoring four goals and adding three assists to lead the Oilers to an 8-5 come-from-behind win.

"I did hear some catcalls, some uncomplimentary criticism," said Gretzky of the shouts from the stands.

Jets GM John Ferguson shook his head.

"Ken Linseman gets hurt and the trouble with that is that so-and-so gets to play more," he said of Gretzky. "The guy is just bleeping amazing."

Sather agreed.

"Tonight Wayne Gretzky was the eighth wonder of the world," said the Oilers coach and GM.

"That was the greatest single performance of any athlete I've ever seen.

Edmontonians turned out in droves to celebrate the Oilers' Stanley Cup victory.

That was a good hard hockey game and he just refused to be denied. He didn't seem to get tired. He just seemed to get stronger every shift. He'd come to the bench and he wouldn't even be panting. It seemed to be fun for him. He was out having a good time."

It was the fourth seven-point game for Gretzky. The others came on home ice.

The next big game for No. 99 would make bigger news.

On Nov. 19 the Oilers beat the New Jersey Devils 13-4. Gretzky had his first eight-point night in the NHL and Jari Kurri scored five. After the game *The Sun*'s Dick Chubey asked a question that pushed the wrong button. Gretzky called the Devils "Mickey Mouse."

It was a strange night. Ron Low was in goal for the Devils for most of the long night. And Gretzky found it no fun at all running up the score against his old friend.

"It got to the point where it wasn't even funny," Gretzky told Chubey.

"How long has it been for them? Three years? Five? Seven? Probably closer to nine. Well, it's about time they got their act together. They're ruining the whole league. They better stop running a Mickey Mouse organization and put somebody on the ice. I feel damn sorry for Ron Low and Chico Resch."

Gretzky didn't make many mistakes in his career. But if he could take back two words they'd probably be Mickey and Mouse.

"The Devils Made Me Do It" was the headline in *The Sun* the next day. Gretzky telegraphed an apology to the Devils.

"In the apology, basically what I said was that I regretted the statements I made," said No. 99. "It's not my business to say anything like that."

Billy MacMillan had been fired as Devils coach after that game, the 18th loss in 20 games for the Devils. He was replaced by Tommy McVie. And the first thing McVie did when he took over was defend Gretzky.

"The reason Wayne took a shot at the Devils was that he has a close friend in Ron Low and when he saw his good friend having all those goals scored against him, he said something he normally wouldn't say. He's a class young man."

Gretzky kept the point streak going through Dec. 18 in Winnipeg when he scored two goals and two assists in a 7-5 win. In his 34th game, it was his 100th point of the season. Even when No. 99 scored 212 points in 1981-82, he didn't get his 100th point until his 39th game. It was the earliest anybody had ever hit the century figure.

As we entered the new year, I decided to take a new tack on covering No. 99:

"A wise man once wrote that you can't measure Wayne Gretzky on the same chart as other hockey players; you have to compare him to the all-time greats in other sports. So the question today:

"Can Gretzky catch Pete Rose?

"Can Gretzky catch Joe DiMaggio?

"Rose has the National League record for consecutive games with at least one hit – 44. DiMaggio has the major-league record at 56. So far this year Gretzky has managed to register at least one point in 41 consecutive games.

"The wise man who made the first comparison to other sports was Dave Anderson of the *New York Times*. When Gretzky had scored 50 goals in 39 games and was en route to scoring 212 points, including 92 goals, Anderson wrote there were really only three occasions in sports history where you could come up with comparisons to what Gretzky had done that year. One was 1921. Babe Ruth hit 59 home runs that year and began the obsession with the long ball in baseball. The next closest hitter to him had 24. In baseball, again, there was Rogers Hornsby in 1924 when he batted .414 and the next best was .375. And there was the year in basketball when Wilt Chamberlain averaged 50.4 points per game compared to 31.6 by the next closest.

"But it's like that every year with Gretzky, who, one game into the second half of the season, has 47 goals and 125 points. And now, as he mounts what has the makings of his greatest year yet, every which way you look at it, the comparisons are certainly long gone from any hockey player who ever played.

"Gretzky is already hockey's Babe Ruth.

"But is he Pete Rose *and* Joe DiMaggio?

" 'I don't know,' said Gretzky. 'I don't think so. It seems to happen more in baseball and I can't explain why it hasn't happened in hockey. I can't explain why nobody has ever come close to a streak like this one I have right now, when all those baseball players had long ones. Logic says it's tougher to do in baseball. I have more than four or five shifts a game to get my points. A baseball player is going to get four or five times at bat and he could get walked every time. Really, I have to think it's tougher in baseball.'

"Gretzky said guys like Rose and DiMaggio had to go through more, as well, because they became a media event with their streaks. Gretzky has had very little of that. He's been a media event before. But it's not working like that with this one.

" 'I have no pressure at all,' he said. 'The biggest thing about this streak is that it doesn't bother me. When I set the record on the streak the first time it was 28. I thought about it a lot. There was a lot of pressure for me to get it. And when it finally ended, it was a big relief. I don't feel like that about it this year. I've gone more than a half a season and most of the time I'm not even thinking about the streak.' "

Famous last words.

Gretzky, who had yet to even go into the third period without a point, was about to enter as intense a media watch as he'd ever experienced. The U.S. writers, particularly the ones on the eastern seaboard, picked up on my DiMaggio angle and played it for all it was worth.

There was so much focus on the streak that nobody paid much notice when Gretzky scored three goals in Hartford on Jan. 7, other than to note that the streak had reached 42 games.

What he'd also done was score 50 goals in 42 games.

If his 50 goals in 39 games was regarded as the most incredible accomplishment in the history of hockey, then you'd figure 50 in 42 would be the second most incredible accomplishment.

"The second-fastest 50 of all time and there's no hoopla," said assistant coach John Muckler. "It's taken for granted. I guess that shows how great he is."

Gretzky said it's just the way the world works.

"It's nice to get 50 in 42. But it's not 50 in 39," he said.

"Fifty in 39 is tough to break. I was right on target after 37 games. But I scored four and five goals in my last two games to get the 50 in 39 and I didn't get four and five in those two games this year."

The streak was the story.

"We'd been in the West since the middle of December and it was kind of quiet about the streak out there," said Gretzky when the Oilers hit Detroit on Jan. 9.

"I didn't realize how much publicity the streak was getting back East.

Now I'm starting to think about it."

Two nights later the Oilers were in Chicago and that's when Gretzky and his streak became The Streak for the entire world of sport.

Gretzky came within two seconds of having it stopped at 43 games but stripped the puck off Blackhawks' Troy Murray and scored into an empty net. Two seconds.

"It was the flukiest one I'll ever get," said Gretzky. "I knew there were seven seconds left, that I had time, but I was lucky to tip the puck."

Gretzky had hit a post and been robbed by Chicago goalie Tony Esposito earlier in the game.

Gretzky made reference to DiMaggio.

"I guess you can call this one a broken-bat single," he said.

With the DiMaggio baseball hitting streak record comparisons now a full-fledged storyline, I found myself headed to the Super Bowl from where I filed the following column:

"TAMPA BAY, Florida — I must live right.

"After two weeks of unsuccessful attempts at reaching the man by telephone – the man notorious for not granting interviews – there I was sitting beside him on Northwest Flight 735 from Chicago to Tampa Bay yesterday.

"Joe DiMaggio!

"There I was, sitting at Gate 6 at Chicago's O'Hare Airport talking to Jim Murray, a 21-year-old employee of Modern Architectural Specialties Ltd. of Edmonton, bound for the Super Bowl.

"Suddenly the young Mr. Murray gave me the elbow. 'Look!' he said. 'Mr. Coffee! Mr. Coffee!'

"Joe DiMaggio. The Yankee Clipper. The man who was once married to Marilyn Monroe. The man who hit safely in 56 consecutive games in the major leagues. The man whose name is being mentioned every day as Wayne Gretzky continues his consecutive games point-scoring streak.

" 'I don't know if I'm going to be much help to you,' said DiMaggio,

Lee Fogolin hands over the 'C' to the new Oilers captain.

who not only agreed to be interviewed, but insisted we do it on the plane in the first-class section where he happened to have an empty seat beside him.

"DiMaggio said he'd noticed his name in the papers regarding Gretzky's point-scoring streak.

" 'Correct me if I'm wrong, but as I understand it, nobody in hockey has ever had a streak like this and my baseball streak is the only one to compare him to,' he said.

" 'Where's he at now?'

" 'Forty-six,' I replied. 'One shy of your baseball record of 56 if you count the last nine games from last year.'

" 'You can't count the ones from last year,' needled DiMaggio. 'They don't count games from last year in baseball.'

"DiMaggio said he couldn't relate to what Gretzky is accomplishing on ice, 'but I think I can relate to what he's going through off the ice.

" 'I had a lot of pressure. I'm sure the pressure on him is beginning to get greater and greater. Fans get kind of crazy when something like this happens in sports. I was getting people knocking on my hotel room at 4 a.m. looking for autographs.

" 'And there's all that media coverage. I'm sure he is dealing with different things than I dealt with. He has all those TV guys. At least I didn't have to worry about them. But when I had my streak there were 12 newspapers in New York. Now there are only three. I guess that balances it out.

" 'I don't know how it is for him right now but I found out one thing was really good for me. During the streak, I'd go to the ballpark two or three hours earlier than normal. I had to get away from the adulation and the demands. I discovered the dressing room was the safest place to go. The most privacy I had was in the dressing room. That was the only place I could relax.'

"Surprisingly, DiMaggio said he experienced relief when his streak ended.

" 'Let's put it this way. I didn't make any intentional outs to get it over with. And when it ended, there wasn't any joy in Mudville.'

"He also said he has trouble comparing the two sports.

" 'I have no idea if a period in a hockey game is the equivalent of a time-at-bat or anything like that. I do know that Gretzky won't have to worry about one thing I had to worry about. He doesn't have to worry about the hockey game getting rained out in the middle of the second period. My streak was getting up there pretty good. Maybe 35 or 40 games. High 30s, I think. I'd already been to bat two times and failed to get a hit. In the top of the sixth I managed to get a scratch single. Then it began to pour. The other team was barely able to get in their time at bat in the bottom half of the inning. If they'd called the game before the end of the complete inning, my time at bat in the top of the sixth wouldn't have counted and the streak would have been stopped.'

"I informed DiMaggio that when I first brought up his streak in relation to Gretzky's streak that Wayne told me he considered the streak in baseball much more difficult to maintain than one in hockey.

" 'If that's true, then how is it nobody else in hockey ever had a streak like he's had?' asked DiMaggio.

" 'Maybe it's different now, but I remember when hockey games were all 1-0 and 2-1 and 3-2. Even if they score more goals these days, I've read a few stories about it and I've read a few stories about him. I think his streak is remarkable. And I think he's remarkable.'

"Does DiMaggio have any advice for Gretzky?

" 'From what I can gather, he doesn't need any. He knows how to carry on.' "

And carry on he did.

Gretzky had three assists in Game 45 in Buffalo and suddenly he was in New Jersey for Game 46. And it was Mickey Mouse Night. Fans showed up wearing Mickey Mouse ears.

"If somebody was smart he'd bring in 20,000 sets of Mickey Mouse ears from Disney World," said Oiler winger Pat Hughes. "You could make a fortune."

Phil Russell, the former Edmonton Oil King, humourously suggested there had been improvement since Gretzky last played the Devils.

George Vecsey in the New York Times asked the question:

"To mouse or not to mouse?

"That was the question posed by top officials of the New Jersey Devils for the visit by Wayne Gretzky and the Edmonton Oilers."

It was the one night people were going to the rink with other questions on their mind than whether Gretzky could continue his point streak.

"If we were playing like Mickey Mouse then, maybe we're like Donald Duck now," he said.

"I might get a standing boo," said Gretzky, expecting the worst.

It turned out to be a terrific game, the Oilers winning 5-4 and Gretzky adding three more assists. But it was a long night for him. There were hundreds of signs in the stands and plenty of catcalls for the man that called mouse. He even laughed at some of the signs. His favorite was the one which read "Gretzky is Goofy."

"I kind of felt my way through the game," said No. 99. "I learned something from all this. I'm 22 going on 23 and I made a mistake."

Goalie Ron Low, who would one day go on to be coach of the Oilers, had something to say that night, too.

"He's got a pretty flawless record and if that's the only mistake of his lifetime, he'll be a pretty lucky guy."

Gretzky went from Mickey Mouse Night to the cover of Sports Illustrated again, this one with the heading "Greater And Greater."

At this point, people were wondering what the odds were of Gretzky going an entire season managing to get at least a point a game. I decided to find out.

"Five hundred to one," said Sonny Reisner, the most flamboyant and well-known oddsmaker in Las Vegas at the time.

Then the manager of the sports book at the Castaways, Reisner's biggest claim to fame (other than posting lines on the Academy Awards and even on the Dallas 'Who Shot J.R.?' episode) was being the first to hang up numbers on dozens of incidentals in the Super Bowl, from the number of fumbles and interceptions to who would win the coin toss.

"Wayne Gretzky is capable of being the highest scorer in the NHL, NFL and NBA combined," said Reisner. "I've never hung up a number on anything like this unusual streak before. But even as great as Gretzky is, somewhere along the line, it's inevitable that the streak has to be

Randy Gregg and Wayne Gretzky ride together in a Stanley Cup parade.

stopped. That's why I have to make the Edmonton wizard 500-to-1 to go the full season with the streak intact."

Nobody got rich.

The streak ended at 51.

Gretzky, performing for the fourth straight game with a bruised right shoulder, and despite having four shots on goal, failed to get a goal or an assist in a 4-2 loss to the Los Angeles Kings at home.

"I guess I won't win the 500-to-1 odds," said Gretzky.

The best chance to keep the streak alive came when Gretzky set up Charlie Huddy, who missed a wide-open net in the first period.

"I said to Gretz, 'Hey, what can I say? I had an open net and I screwed up. That's the way it goes. I don't think I'm going out shopping when I get home. My wife is on her own."

Gretzky said it was amazing how much emotion took over as it all built.

"I'm disappointed that it's over. But it's a relief, too. It's been hectic for me and for the whole club. Of all the records I've chased in the past, there's been nothing like this. I'm disappointed it's over but in a way I'm glad. The thing for us now is to get back in gear as a hockey club."

That they'd have to try to do without Gretzky. He missed the next six games with what turned out to be a slightly separated shoulder. The Oilers won the first one, against Calgary, 10-5 without Gretzky. But they lost the next five.

Gretzky was shut out on two other occasions as he finished the remainder of the season. He ended up with 87 goals, 118 assists and 205 points. The Oilers finished first overall with 119 points, scoring a mind-boggling 440 goals.

It was time for the real season to begin.

The Oilers swept the Winnipeg Jets for openers. But the Calgary Flames pushed the Oilers to the limit in a Battle of Alberta playoff series to savour.

And the southern rivals weren't giving Gretzky any kid-glove treatment after he scored two and added two assists to give the Oilers a 5-2 win in Game 1.

"They must have cranked me eight or nine times," said Gretzky of his rough ride in

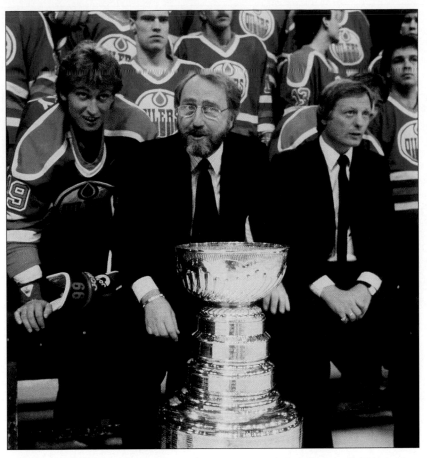

A popular fellow by the name of Stanley started showing up in Edmonton Oilers team pictures in the mid-'80s.

Game 4, a 5-3 win in Calgary that gave the Oilers a 3-1 series lead.

Sather used the word "maimed."

"Where does it say you can't hit Wayne Gretzky?" asked Flames coach (Badger) Bob Johnson.

Gretzky was shut out in Game 5 as the Flames won 5-4 in Edmonton and he had two assists as the Flames took the series to the limit with a 5-4 win in Game 6.

There was more than a little soul-searching done by the Oilers going into Game 7, much of it by Gretzky.

"I spent the whole day thinking about it," said No. 99. "All I thought about were the questions. Where was I? Why didn't I perform? I thought about the other series like the Islanders last year and I told myself, 'No way do I want all those questions this summer.'

"This was the most critical game of my career. I was sweating yesterday and today. For whatever reasons, I wasn't doing my job. I had the flu and a few nagging injuries. But I wasn't doing my job. And I knew I had to make sure I went out there and had the game of my life. I knew this was going to be the biggest game of my career and the biggest game in the history of the organization."

Gretzky had a goal and two assists to lead the Oilers to a 7-4 win to take the series.

"We sat in this dressing room before the game and told ourselves this was our 100th game and if we lost it, everything we'd done in the regular season, the 440 goals and the 199 points in the standings wouldn't mean anything," said Gretzky.

"We sat in here and said, 'We're a hell of a team. Let's prove it.' Maybe we found out a bit about what it takes now. To win the Stanley Cup, you have to work your ass off as a team."

Gretzky also knew that something happened in this series that was going to stay around for a while.

"There's going to be a rivalry now for sure," he said.

The Oilers swept the Minnesota North Stars with Gretzky scoring 10

points in the series. The difference was night and day from the dressing-room scene of a year earlier when they'd won their way to the Stanley Cup final.

"All of a sudden, after the game, the room went hush," said Gretzky. "All of a sudden our attitude was that we hadn't won anything yet. Last year we thought we'd won a whole lot. We discovered in a hurry that we'd won nothing. Last year we couldn't believe it. This year we can believe it."

The final series opened in Long Island with the NHL having adopted a 2-3-2 World Series format.

It was The Drive For Five vs. The Run For One. It was also Billy vs. The Kid – Billy Smith vs. Wayne Gretzky, Part 2.

The Islanders went into the series still owning the Oilers. Despite making the Islanders their designated credibility games, they didn't beat them once.

There aren't many games when Gretzky doesn't get a point that the Oilers win. But the ultimate was the Oilers' 1-0 win in Game 1 with Grant Fuhr playing a great game in goal and Kevin McClelland scoring the only goal.

Gretzky was shut out again as the Islanders bounced back to win Game 2 6-1 and he had two assists as the Oilers won Game 3 by a score of 7-2 back home. Gretzky scored twice, however, in Game 4, to end a 10-game streak of not scoring a goal against the Islanders. And he added two more as the Oilers won Game 5 by a score of 5-2 to take the series four games to one.

"I feel like retiring right now," said Gretzky as the Oilers and the Northlands Coliseum crowd went crazy.

"I've been in the NHL for five years and all the time you pick up the papers and read, 'Well, they haven't won the Stanley Cup yet, so they're not that good.' Well, we'll never have to hear that again. We've proved that an offensive team can win."

Years later, Gretzky and most of his teammates would call winning that first Stanley Cup in May 1984 their all-time favourite moment in the game.

The sight of Gretzky hoisting his first Stanley Cup in the air is definitely one of John Muckler's favourite Gretzky memories.

"I'll never forget it because when Wayne picked it up, he had trouble holding it in the air," said Muckler. "It was almost like he was afraid he'd fall over backwards."

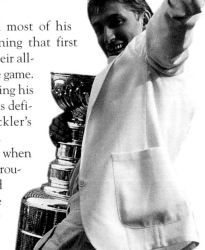

Chapter 10

THE STANLEY FUN RUN

Wayne Gretzky had barely put the Stanley Cup down when he was taking another tour of the ice, still trying not to cry, with another cargo in his arms.

The scene in the Coliseum the night the Edmonton Oilers won their first Stanley Cup was incredible. The fans swarmed the team on the ice and the players recognized a lot of their faces. Gretzky recognized one in particular. His brother, Brent, had managed to get over the glass and onto the ice with the other fans. Gretzky skated around the ice with his kid brother on his shoulders.

"I feel like retiring right now," said Gretzky when he reached the dressing room after winning the Cup he would later declare to be his favourite because of the "wonderfulness" of that whole scene, "a whole city winning it with us like that." The way the players shared the Cup with Edmonton after they won it established a tradition which led to the expression and belief to this day: Stanley had more fun in Edmonton.

"I've been in the NHL for five years and all I've heard about this team is, 'They haven't won a Cup yet, so they're not that good.' Well, we'll never have to hear that again," said Gretzky. "We've proved that an offensive team can win. We've won it now! Oh, what a feeling!"

Wayne Gretzky enjoys a Stanley Cup moment with his father, Walter.

The Oilers left the dressing room and went into the off-season to carry on in and around Edmonton for weeks, taking the Cup with them, unannounced, from watering hole to watering hole.

Edmonton went crazy. The Oil Capital of Canada became the Oilers capital of Canada, the hockey capital of Canada.

A crowd estimated to be about 200,000 attended the biggest parade ever held in Edmonton and just about every citizen visited Valley Zoo that summer to see the 36 Long Island ducks then Mayor Laurence Decore won in one of those bets mayors make.

"I always said that it's great to win individual awards but it would be better to win the Stanley Cup," said Gretzky halfway through the summer. "But I don't think I understood the extent of it. There's not even a comparison.

"I'll admit it. I've spent all summer gloating. And the best part of all was sharing it with everybody in Edmonton. We kept taking the Cup out to different restaurants and bars and we got a fantastic response. People in Edmonton had seen the Stanley Cup from a distance on television all those years when it was something the Montreal Canadiens used to win. To take it around, sort of unannounced, every night for a couple of weeks, and to let hundreds of people drink from it ... that was probably the biggest kick of all.

"Part of how great our summer has been came down to not having to answer questions like, 'What happened?' We had a lot of those to answer after we lost the first round to Los Angeles and when we lost four straight to the Islanders.

"I can't wait for that first game in Edmonton when they raise the banner in the Coliseum and we're presented with the rings."

Not everybody in the world was thrilled that the Stanley Cup was residing in Edmonton, Alberta, Canada. And hockey author, columnist and broadcaster Stan Fischler, who seemed to take the Oilers' win personally, gave Gretzky and gang plenty of inspiration for the following season.

Writing in the *Village Voice*, Fischler called the Coliseum "an oversized igloo," Edmonton "one of the bushest towns this side of Peoria," and "glitzy" Gretzky the "Pinocchio of the tundra."

Fischler, in *Inside Sports* under a title "It's Only A One Year Dynasty For Gretzky And Team Arrogance," wrote that "Edmonton should fervently embrace Lord Stanley's mug for the next 11 months for it will reside elsewhere in 1985."

When the celebrating stopped, what kind of champions would the Oilers be?

Would they develop a pride and tradition like the Montreal Canadiens?

Was this the beginning of a dynasty or a one-year wonderful?

Which way would Gretzky and the Stanley Cup-champion Edmonton Oilers go now that their greatness had been confirmed with a championship?

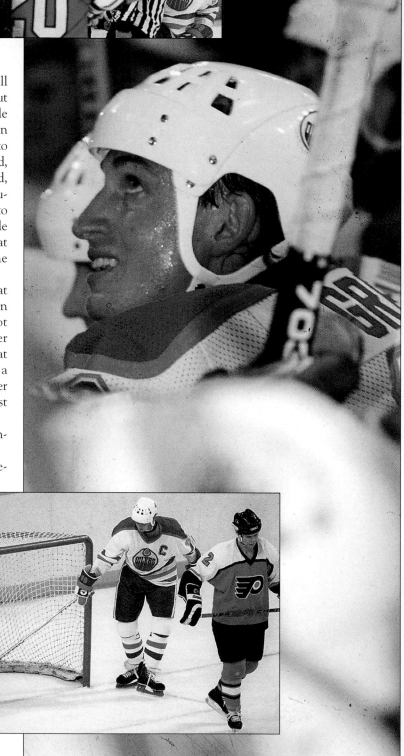

Playing against the 'Broad Street Bullies' was always a battle.

Those were fair questions as Gretzky and the Oilers went into their sixth season.

After a 2-2 tie in Los Angeles to open the 1984-85 season, Gretzky & Co. came home for the magic moment.

We Are The Champions became their theme song that night with the smoke and the spotlights and the raising of their first Stanley Cup banner.

The Oilers had gone from the hunters to the hunted. And they didn't miss a beat.

They won 5-1 against St. Louis that night, their first of six wins in a row followed by a tie, four wins in a row, another tie and two more wins in a row.

The defending Stanley Cup champions set a record out of the gate. Longest undefeated streak from the start of a season. Fifteen games. It broke a record set 41 years earlier by the 1943-44 Montreal Canadiens.

Toe Blake, the legendary Montreal coach who played for that club, said he wasn't worried about losing that record. "I'm more concerned about them beating our record of winning five Stanley Cups in a row."

Gretzky had a six-point night in an 8-5 win to help make it happen.

Gretzky and Jari Kurri were both going great. They finally had a left-winger.

"This is the first time in six years there hasn't been talk of finding a left-winger for our line," said No. 99 of the trade Glen Sather made to acquire Mike Krushelnyski.

Gretzky in his first 21 games had 17 goals and 30 assists for 47 points before he was shut out by the Montreal Canadiens. And he was loving the whole scene of taking the lap around the league as Stanley Cup champs.

"The first thing you notice is that the crowds are much louder when you are Stanley Cup champions," he said. "It's like when the Islanders came to Edmonton. It was almost like a playoff game. It's like that for us now as we go to other cities. And that's great. It gives us a push. It'll make us a better team."

So what would Gretzky use to amuse himself and amaze the hockey world this year?

For starters, at age 23, there was the countdown to 1,000.

On Dec. 5 it went 983, 984, 985, 986, 987. Five points against the New York Islanders in a 7-6 Oilers win over the team they couldn't beat until they beat them in the Stanley Cup final.

Gretzky, with the five-point night, moved past Dave Keon (986) into 13th place on the all-time NHL scoring chart. And while he was at it, Gretzky also accumulated his 606th assist, moving him past Islander veteran Denis Potvin and into 20th place, all time. No. 99 also pulled into a tie for 28th place with Reggie Leach with 381 career goals. But the 1,000 figure had a ring all its own and was good enough for the latest Great Gretzky Watch, except this was called The "Grand" Gretzky watch.

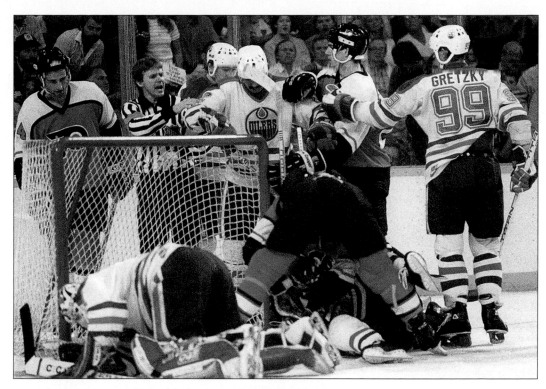

BOYS WILL BE BOYS: Gretzky keeps his cool while all around him tempers flare.

Even on one leg, Gretzky made it look easy.

Gretzky went into the season in 23rd place on the all-time points-production list. The previous year he'd passed such notables as Yvan Cournoyer, Ted Lindsay, Bernie Geoffrion, Mike Bossy and many more. He started off the Oilers' sixth NHL season by knocking off Bobby Orr, Bryan Trottier, Rocket Richard, Andy Bathgate and now Keon. Orr played 657 games, Trottier 701, Richard 978, Bathgate 1,069 and Keon 1,296. It was Gretzky's 418th game.

One by one he was having fun knocking off the most famous names in the game as the hockey world waited for Gretzky to get around to the big one – Gordie Howe's 1,850 points in 26 NHL seasons.

He'd just won his first Stanley Cup and all the greatest career records in the book, it was obvious already, were there for him to break in far less time than they were set.

"Gordie was as great a player as there ever was," he said. "He's the greatest I ever met in my life. I've got a few more years left. And I'm going to get a lot more points. But I'll be entirely satisfied if I end up being second to him."

Gretzky admitted as the countdown to 1,000 continued that he'd been thinking a lot about retirement lately. While that sounded ridiculous coming from a 23-year-old who was still being referred to in print as The Kid, it was Gretzky talking and you had to listen.

"I'm more and more involved in looking after my own affairs and my own businesses," he said. "With the Flower having retired the other day, I'm more and more conscious of the fact that every time I step on the ice now, it's one less time I have in hockey. It's a long way away because every time I step on the ice now is more fun than the time before. But I'm definitely thinking now about what I want to do when I'm finished. Hopefully it won't be for four or five more years.

"I'm not trying to make predictions. But I was thinking the other day. The Flower played for 14 seasons and he was kind of frustrated in his last three. Fourteen seasons. I'm in my seventh as a pro. That's halfway.

"Guy Lafleur was put on a pedestal. When he stopped scoring, despite how he was playing other parts of the game, people viewed him as playing poorly. When you are used to going to the rink from the time you are five until you are 30 and when you are used to scoring ... when it stops, it takes the fun out of it.

"I know right now that I won't hang on for a record. If I finish second to Gordie, to me that will be finishing first."

He also said he'd done some thinking about where he'd reside when his career was over.

"Edmonton is home for me and that's where I'd like to be when my career is finished. It's a nice city with a small-town atmosphere. I have a lot of opportunities in Edmonton and they've always treated me first-class. I see no reason why I'd go anywhere else. But it's not as if I have a no-trade or a no-sell clause in my contract. I hope I never get traded, but that's part of the game."

Gretzky found out a few days later that when he became an ex-hockey player he could at least compete with an ex-president.

The Oilers had a couple of days off in mid-December and owner Peter Pocklington had set up a golf day with ex-U.S. president Gerald Ford. Gretzky was put in the same foursome as the fearsome (he was legendary for beaning spectators) Ford.

"Was I nervous?" Gretzky gasped after shooting a 93, the same as partner Ford at the Thunderbird Golf & Country Club in Rancho Mirage, California

"I knew I was in trouble when I went triple, triple, triple the first three holes.

"With two holes to go we were down two strokes and we ended up winning when I got my act together and parred the last hole. Mr. Ford asked me if we should start pressing. I told him, 'You're better at finances than me.' He was very gracious about the whole thing."

Gretzky said he hadn't been that nervous since he was 17 playing with Gordie Howe.

"But even then, it was nothing like today. I guess I'm lucky. I had lunch with one president (Ronald Reagan) and played golf with another."

In St. Louis on Dec. 15, the day after his game of golf, Gretzky scored five goals and added an assist in an 8-2 win over the Blues to move within two points of the 1,000 figure.

The first three goals were his 31st hat trick, one short of the NHL record shared by Phil Esposito and Mike Bossy.

"What we saw tonight wasn't just the greatest hockey player but one of the greatest athletes in the world," said Blues coach Jacques Demers that night. "He's like Jimmy Connors, Muhammad

Gretzky never got tired of supporting Stanley.

Gretzky vs. Lanny MacDonald (right) and the Flames...

... and vs. Doug Gilmour and the St. Louis Blues.

Ali and Reggie Jackson the way he performs for a crowd. People come just to see him play, and when does he ever disappoint them?"

Gretzky had scored five against St. Louis in Feb. 18, 1981. And, of course, there were the five goals against Philadelphia when he scored 50 in 39.

He was still one short of equalling the record shared by Sid Howe, Darryl Sittler and Red Berenson.

"I was in the building the night they gave Red a car and replayed all six of his goals," said Oilers assistant coach John Muckler, who coached Minnesota in 1968.

"Gretzky toyed with us," said Demers. "It was unbelievable. I've never seen anything like it in 13 years, that one spinarama backhand goal he scored. How do you check him? It's impossible. I remember one game with him here last year when we were all over him and he still got five assists. Tonight, as an opposing coach, I had to be careful not to start enjoying him myself."

Sather had seen so much by this point that he chose only the more amazing Gretzky nights to rave about No. 99. This was one of them.

"He scored every which way," said Slats. "The whirl-around goal was like one you see in shinny, on the road, where a guy's fooling around with no goalie in the net. What a goal. And the last one, the way he stripped the puck off Craig Levie for a breakaway ... who else could have done that?"

Gretzky said all the stars and moons and planets seemed to be aligned this night.

"Everywhere I seemed to go, the puck was there. It was one of those nights. I honestly thought I'd get the 1,000 points tonight. The goals? Well, maybe I was due," said Gretzky, who had scored three in the previous six games. "I've had a lot more chances than the year when I scored 92."

Gretzky now had 32 goals and 84 points, 29 games into the season.

He went into New Jersey for the next one telling the people back home that he really wanted to save the record for Edmonton.

"Maybe I'll get it here, but hopefully I won't," he said. "Maybe it doesn't mean a lot now but years from now I'd like to sit back and say I got my 1,000th point in Edmonton.

"I'm excited about this one. Seven seasons ago when I turned pro, who would have ever thought I'd have 1,000 points by Christmas 1984? Not me, that's for sure.

"I'm looking forward to this for a couple of reasons. I play on a great team with great players. And when I came into the league there were people who doubted me as a player. Even when I scored 137 points my first year, there were people who said I wouldn't do it again. Well, 1,000 points is a mark of consistency. It shows I've come to play every night. Barring injury, I should be able to reach 1,500. But who knows? Maybe I'll get a lot more, maybe I won't. But of all the records and accomplishments, getting 1,000 points seems to have a nice ring to it."

Gretzky had one assist – point No. 999 – in New Jersey and headed home for a game against the Los Angeles Kings to manufacture the milestone.

Howe checked in with some thoughts on the eve of Gretzky's grand night.

"There's only one record he's not going to get," said Gordie. "He's not going to play with his two sons for six years.

"My 1,850 points? I kissed that one goodbye a long time ago. It shouldn't take him long. Maybe four more years.

"I'm not surprised at Wayne saying he wouldn't touch that record. He's just trying to be nice. He's a respectable young man. He's a perfectionist. Yet he downgrades with everything he does. He's done that with all the records he's set.

"With him one point away from 1,000 at his age, it really makes you stop and think. He's really done something. It scares me to think what he'll end up with."

Howe said he hopes Gretzky, deep down, wants his record as much as he's ever wanted anything.

"Erasing the name ... it motivated me. I erased Rocket Richard's name. He helped me. I hope erasing my name can help Wayne."

Howe said he knew right then Gretzky would smash his records to smithereens.

"What you have to look at is that nobody else even comes close to him. There are 100 great players and nobody is anywhere near being equal to him."

Gretzky, of course, registered No. 1,000 against the Kings. And Nos. 1,001, 1,002, 1,003, 1,004 and 1,005. He scored his 33rd and 34th goals of the season in a 7-3 win.

Again Sather offered a thought.

"What makes Wayne the best is that over his career so far I don't think I've seen him take two or three games off. Every game, there's guys trying to check him but he has more determination than anybody. That's what makes him great. That's what makes him cook."

On Dec. 30 Gretzky prepared to celebrate New Year's Eve by celebrating his sixth 100-point season. His three-goal, three-assist perfor-

A familiar scene on Coliseum ice during the '80s.

Gretzky shares a laugh with Oilers owner Peter Pocklington, centre, and coach Glen Sather.

mance led the Oilers to a 6-3 win over the Detroit Red Wings.

"He could have had 10 points if things had gone his way," said Darryl Sittler, the former Toronto Maple Leaf who enjoyed a 10-point night in 1976 against Boston. "Some night he'll probably beat that record."

That hat trick moved Gretzky into a tie with Esposito and Bossy for that category.

Back when Gretzky was fashioning his 50-goals-in-39-games season, I remember talking with Boston sportswriters who had covered Bobby Orr. They said it may seem like fun writing about Gretzky now, but wait till later. With Orr, they said, they became very frustrated with trying to write about greatness every game. They said the time would come when there was nothing left to write about Gretzky.

Bobby Orr didn't have the same scriptwriter as Gretzky.

A night in late January 1985 was the perfect example of the way it would be throughout Gretzky's entire career.

It was the night he scored his 50th goal in 49 games. Ho-hum, right? How can you get excited about that when the guy scored 50 in 39?

When it happened it just happened to be his birthday.

It just happened to be the day when one assist would vault him past Orr in the last statistical category in which he hadn't already passed him.

And he just happened to also score Nos. 51 and 52 of the season, which gave him his 33rd hat trick of his career to break the record shared with Phil Esposito and Mike Bossy.

"I guess I'd been kind of ho-hum about it all year," said Gretzky. "I really didn't think about it. But when I got up in the morning, I got kinda excited.

"It was my birthday and my mother came in for it, so it kind of reminded me of the first birthday I had here when I signed the contract at centre ice. And I knew I had a shot at it and I decided I didn't want to come up short. I realized I'd be awfully disappointed if I had a shot at it and didn't get it.

"I didn't want it to be 50 in 50. I wanted to do it in under 50. I'd have been disappointed if I didn't get it tonight and had to wait until Monday to get it," he said.

In the three games in which he'd hit the 50-goal mark in fewer than 50 games, he'd never had less than a hat trick. The first time it was five against Philadelphia and the second time it was three against Hartford.

"I think I know what it is," said Gretzky. "It's the emotional excitement. When I'm emotionally excited, when I have a smile on my face and I'm pumped for something ... I play a lot of this game on emotion."

Gretzky's next milestone was 1,100 points. But when you've just hit 1,000, how are you going to make news at 1,100?

When Gretzky did it, it was against the Los Angeles Kings. He made the Kings the first team he'd get 100 points against. He had 100 against L.A. and 1,000 against the rest of the league.

"I play well against L.A. because we have a little history," said Gretzky

HE SHOOTS, HE PARS! Wayne Gretzky watches *Edmonton Sun* hockey writer Dick Chubey stickhandle around the green.

of listening to "Gretzky Sucks!" chants in the Forum, of losing a scoring title to Marcel Dionne and of the Miracle on Manchester.

"When we go to L.A. it seems I have a lot of friends who come to the games and there are a lot of people who like to cheer against me in L.A. That really gets me into the games."

And guess who the Oilers drew in the first round of the playoffs? Los Angeles.

Gretzky ended the season with 73 goals, 135 assists and 208 points. The Oilers finished first in the Smythe Division and second overall with a 49-20-11 record. And he added five more points to his points total against the Kings as the Oilers swept the best-of-five first-round series.

With a goal in each game, including the winner in Game 3, Gretzky also led the Oilers to three straight wins over the Winnipeg Jets in the Smythe Division final.

It was in the fourth and final game of that series when something strange happened.

Winnipeg became Waynerpeg.

The Winnipeg crowd that had adapted that old "Gretzky

Paul Coffey, Wayne Gretzky and Kevin Lowe frolic with Stanley.

Sucks!" Los Angeles chant, finally waved the white flag in the third period of an 8-3 Oilers win in which Gretzky had three goals and four assists for a seven-point night and gave him his due.

"Gretzky! Gretzky! Gretzky!" they cheered for him instead of against him.

"My dad once told me not to get mad about the things fans chant," said Gretzky. "He said, 'Don't get mad, get even.' I think I got even."

Gretzky tied his own Stanley Cup record for most points in a playoff game with seven.

"The thing about me is that people expect me to score three or four points a night in the playoffs. The playoffs are really tough on me that

way. I'm judged on goals and assists and I know that. I also know there are some nights when I get five points when I haven't played that well and some nights when I don't get many points when I've played the solid style of game a team has to play to win in the playoffs," said Gretzky.

No. 99 went to the rink thinking something special might happen that night.

"I couldn't believe how fresh I felt. I not only had my second wind, I had a third wind. I really had jump."

Gretzky, who hit two goal-posts and failed to score on a breakaway, was taken off the ice with 42 seconds left, depriving Waynerpeg of watching The Gr-eight Gretzky.

Why didn't he stay out there?

"I was just too pooped to play any more," he said.

The extra time off between series that a team receives when it sweeps a series resulted in an 11-2 whupping of the Chicago Blackhawks in the next round. That was followed by a 7-3 win over the Blackhawks on Edmonton ice, as Gretzky had four- and three-point games and the Oilers won their first nine playoff games.

People were beginning to wonder if the Oilers could sweep the Stanley Cup. But Gretzky was kept off the scoresheet in Game 3 at Chicago Stadium and the 'Hawks won 5-2. In the end, it turned out to be a tough enough six-game series. Still, Gretzky managed 18 points.

The Oilers were back in the Stanley Cup final and No. 99 was trying to sell the Oilers as underdogs because the Philadelphia Flyers had more points, finishing first overall in the final standings. Nobody was buying it until Gretzky not only was shut out in Game 1 in Philadelphia, he didn't manage a single shot on goal as the Flyers took the series lead with a 4-1 win.

Gretzky gave the Oilers a 1-0 lead in Game 2 that the Oilers rode to

Oiler teammates and Joey Moss, centre front, help The Great One celebrate his 24th birthday.

a 3-1 win. And, as was the case the year before, the Oilers came back to play games 3, 4 and 5 at home, won them all and watched the NHL bring in another Oilers rule and go back to a 2-2-1-1-1 playoff format.

Gretzky scored four goals and added an assist in the 4-3 win in Game 3, scored two within 15 seconds in a 5-3 win in Game 4 and then scored his 18th goal and 28th, 29th and 30th assists in the playoffs as the Oilers won 8-3 to capture the Cup.

This time Gretzky was selected the winner of the Conn Smythe Trophy, although he always maintained that Paul Coffey deserved to win it, and if not him then Grant Fuhr.

"It was probably the toughest one ever picked," he said at the time. "But who cares who gets their name on the Conn Smythe. We all get our names on the Stanley Cup again. That's the only Cup that counts. It's like all the records we set. Who cares? We won the Stanley Cup. Who cares about anything else?"

Again it was a sensational scene in the Coliseum as the crowd chanted, "The Cup Stays Here! The Cup Stays Here!" while the minutes ticked off the clock.

The Oilers had won all 10 playoff games at home and, combined with their last six from the year before, broke another Montreal Canadiens' Stanley Cup playoff record.

This time they celebrated at Commonwealth Stadium and again they took the Stanley Cup to places it hadn't been before as Edmonton

DOIN' THE WAVE: Gretz and Peter Puck, in happier times.

enjoyed another summer with Stanley.

And while they celebrated, Edmonton, the Oilers and Wayne Gretzky began to wonder just how wonderful this fun run with Stanley was going to be.

How many Stanley Cup rings would they collect?

"The ring's the thing," said Gretzky. "You can't carry the Stanley Cup around forever. You can only see the trophy once in a while. The most treasured thing is the ring. Carrying the Cup around the ice may be the greatest thrill of your life. But you wear the ring and every time you look at it, you see something different. You see the good times and the bad, the success and the sweat. To me, having the ring is more valuable than having your name on the Cup. If I had to make a choice, I'd take the ring."

How many more Cups and rings would they win?

"If we stick together and keep improving, there's no reason we can't win again next year and again the next year and give ourselves a chance at a fifth in a row," said Gretzky.

"As silly as it sounds, things are getting a little easier for me. Our guys are all getting better. Jari Kurri. Paul Coffey. Mark Messier. They've all improved so much, it makes it easier for me to play.

"We've got to be rated as good as any team that ever won two in a row," bubbled Gretzky. "All I know is that 15 years from now I'm going to say, 'Gawd, I played on a great hockey team.'"

Chapter
11

STILL THE GREAT ONE

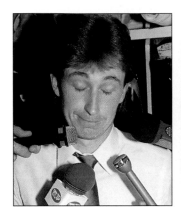 

If you can't beat 'em on the ice, beat 'em in the alley. That was Conn Smythe's idea. But they couldn't beat Wayne Gretzky and the Edmonton Oilers on the ice or in the alley. That left the boardroom.

Gretzky sounded off that summer when the NHL voted in a new rule. He said the NHL was legislating against him and his back-to-back Stanley Cup-champion teammates. He identified Cliff Fletcher and the Calgary Flames as having done the dirty deed.

The league had decreed that when coincidental minor penalties occurred, teams would continue to play with five skaters instead of the traditional four.

"I don't think there was any question the rule was brought in because of our hockey team," said Gretzky. "Calgary is the instigator. They've built a very physical, tough hockey team."

Fletcher, the Flames GM, denied it.

"First of all, we weren't the instigators of the rule. The head of officials for the NHL and the league hierarchy thought it was in the best interests of the game. We're the ones who moved its approval. But 16 other teams voted for it, too, remember.

"Wayne is entitled to his opinion. With all deference to him, I think fans want full-strength hockey – five skaters against five. Calgary is not trying to undermine Edmonton."

HOW SWEET IT IS:
Gretzky and Paul
Coffey hoist the
hardware after
knocking off the
Flyers in 1987.

Gretzky said the Oilers would overcome.

"I think people believe that because there's no more 4-on-4s, the Oilers aren't going to win the Stanley Cup. Well, we can skate with anybody 5-on-5, too. But we worked on the 4-on-4s. We worked on it 10, 15, 20 minutes every day. And because we worked at it and became good at it, 17 teams said, 'You can't do that any more.' The fans pay $20-$25 a ticket, and that's an exciting part of the game. You have to entertain people. I think this rule change is going to take away a lot of excitement."

With 73 goals and an NHL-record 135 assists the previous year to go with his second Stanley Cup and first Conn Smythe Trophy, Gretzky swore the rule change wouldn't cut back his production.

And speaking of production ...

The other big story of the summer came with the publishing of *Martina* by Martina Navratilova. The lesbian tennis star wrote that she'd like to bear a Gretzky child.

"One of the nicest men I know, and one of the best looking, too, is Wayne Gretzky, the greatest scorer in the history of hockey. Can you imagine the genes Wayne and I could put together?" Navratilova wrote.

Gretzky, who had met Navratilova on several occasions, and even invited her out to the bar with teammates when they were in the same city, said he considered her a good friend.

"But I'm happily attached," he said of his continuing relationship with Vikki Moss.

Gretzky, who had spent many of his previous summers with a back-breaking appearance and endorsement schedule, spent almost the entire off-season in Edmonton.

"This is the first year I've worked out in the summer," he said of the hour a day he spent at the Centre Club.

He bought a junior hockey club in Hull, Que. But what would he do to amuse himself that winter in Edmonton? He was running out of records to set.

The Oilers won their first five, eight of their first nine, 14 of their first 20 with two ties ... and Gretzky had points in every game but one.

On Dec. 11 in Chicago, in a 12-9 win, Gretzky managed seven assists again to tie his record and the one Billy Taylor set with the Detroit Red Wings in 1947 in that very same building. But the next time the Oilers played in Chicago, on Jan. 27, was the beginning of something Gretzky had never really experienced – over the long haul, at least: a slump.

He was still getting his points. Three against St. Louis. Four against Calgary. Three against Calgary. Three against New Jersey. Two against Washington. One against Buffalo. One against Detroit ... but no goals. Gretzky hadn't scored a goal in nearly three weeks.

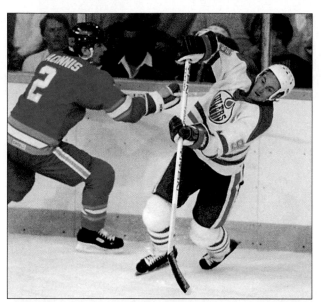

Gretzky takes a shot from Calgary's Al McInnis (top), and poses with Kent Nilsson (above).

"I'm not concerned," said Gretzky. "I'm not saying I wouldn't take one off my rear end, though. Maybe if I don't get one soon, they'll be bringing a cake for me."

That reference was to the cake the Oilers presented to Kevin Lowe on the one-year anniversary of his last goal.

"It bugs Wayne that he hasn't scored," said Lowe. "But I think he's at that stage in his career when it upsets him a lot less than before. These things are going to happen. In the past when he hasn't scored, he would overexaggerate and shoot from everywhere until they went in."

Jari Kurri had scored in six straight games and was leading the league in goals with 41 when the Oilers came home to play Quebec and Gretzky made it nine straight games without a goal – and had another seven-assist game.

Gretzky said OK, maybe he would never find the net again.

"I've still got a good chance at beating 212 points and 135 assists. I'm getting two assists a game. If I get 160 assists, that would be high. But so much for scoring 100 goals this season. Maybe that's why I have so many assists. I'm not getting the open ice. They're sending two people at me, a forward and a defenceman, and that leaves a guy open."

In February I broke a story under the headline "Megabuck Mess," subheaded "Gretzky Suing Money Managers."

Gretzky claimed to have lost more than half-a-million dollars in an investment deal.

Gretzky's association with Gus Badali as his agent ended that year. Ian Barrigan of Edmonton and Mike Barnett took over his representation.

"It was an education in business which was costly and very unnecessary," said Gretzky.

"Fortunately, I'm able to separate hockey from personal business. I don't think it's had any effect on my play, as witnessed by my personal statistics. Unfortunately, it has bothered my father an awful lot," he said of Walter, who was instrumental in choosing most of the people Gretzky had surrounded himself with and was now taking legal action against.

Gretzky started scoring goals again. But the Gretzky Watch was now strictly on assists. The year before, when he upped the record to 135, there wasn't much notice. But he was really rewriting it this time.

With 135 assists already in the bag in early March, Gretzky was now out to register more single-season assists than anybody – other than himself – had previously managed total points.

"He's going to do it," said Dave Lumley. "He's going to get more assists than anybody has points. These things keep coming out of the woodwork with Wayne. You think he has no more records to go for and ..."

Other than Gretzky, only Bobby Orr (102) had ever managed to hit the century mark in assists.

"Sometimes you sit around and wonder what's going to happen," said No. 99. "I got to thinking about assists when I hit the 100 area (101 after 52 games). I knew I could average two assists a game."

Gretzky was going for both his assists and his points record as the 1985-86 season went down the home stretch.

In Game 65, against Vancouver, he equalled the 135 assists mark with four assists against the Canucks.

Wayne Gretzky gets into the spirit while shooting a commercial with Joey Moss (left).

With seven games to go, he had 148 assists and was now 15 points back of the 212 mark.

"When I got to 200 the first time, it seemed out of this world," said Gretzky. "I remember I flew my mom and dad in for the game in Calgary. It was something special."

Calgary vs. Edmonton is as good a sports rivalry situation as there is anywhere in sport, and it was getting real good in hockey all of a sudden. And Gretzky was in the middle of it with his accusations against Cliff Fletcher and the Flames for changing the rules at the start of the season.

With two games to go, Gretzky needed two points to break the record of 212. And the Oilers were in Calgary.

"I don't expect to be cheered," said No. 99.

He wasn't. And the bad blood between the two teams boiled over that night.

The Flames refused to acknowledge, in any way, shape or form, the fact that Gretzky equalled and then broke the NHL's all-time single-season points record.

"Wayne set an all-time NHL record and the Flames didn't even have the class to announce it over the PA system," a livid Glen Sather ranted after the game.

"If Lanny McDonald had set a record in our building, you can be damned sure we'd announce it. Even if Calgary had beat us 25 times in a row. I think the game is bigger than the two teams and bigger than the people who come to watch the two teams. It's unfortunate people don't have minds big enough to

understand some of that stuff."

With three assists that night and one back at home in the last game of the regular season, Gretzky ended up with 215 points, 163 of them assists. He scored his 37th hat trick. In the entire season he was held pointless only three times and recorded 61 multiple-point games. His NHL record count was now up to 41. The Oilers, despite the end of 4-on-4, matched their best year with 56 wins and 199 points to finish first overall by a dozen points. They scored 426 goals. And they took care of the Vancouver Canucks, who had finished 60 points back, in three straight.

And that made the match. Edmonton-Calgary. And the Flames had done their homework.

A 4-1 win in Edmonton to open the series was followed by a 6-5 win the Oilers admitted they were fortunate to pull off. The Flames won Game 3 in Calgary by a 3-2 count and Gretzky was having a quiet series.

In Game 4, a pair of nines beat everything.

Gretzky took this once-again bloody Battle of Alberta into his own hands and parted the red sea personally, scoring three goals and two assists in a 7-4 win.

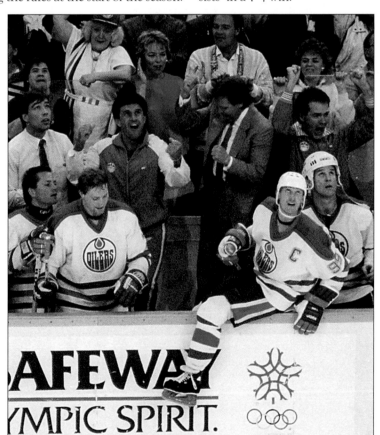

Oilers and fans watch the clock tick down on another victory.

"Wayne had one of those games you can only dream about," said Sather.

"Wayne took it upon himself to win this game for us and he did," said Craig MacTavish.

Gretzky couldn't move in Calgary without being verbally assaulted.

He couldn't even get away from it when he went to the racetrack between games.

He sat in the clubhouse. The people at the next table started chanting: "Whiner! Whiner! Whiner!"

Signs were everywhere.

"I brought the cheese, who has the whine?" read one.

"Keep the Cup shiny, whiney," read another.

The most popular joke in Calgary was: "What do you call a basement full of Gretzkys? A whine cellar."

"One thing about good players is that sooner or later they're going to play good," said Gretzky, who had

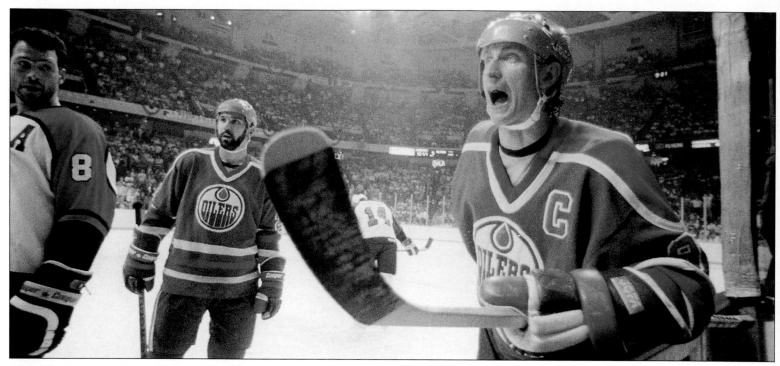

Gretzky gives an official an earful during the 1987 Stanley Cup playoffs in Philadelphia.

one goal and three assists in the first three games playing with Kurri, who was struggling against Calgary coach Bob Johnson's game plan.

"Jari has been having a little trouble but he got a goal tonight and maybe this will bring him out of it," said No. 99. "Maybe it'll bring us all out of it. We were down two games to one and it could have been 3-0 if we hadn't put together a good third period in Game 2 and won it in overtime. What happened tonight was a result of grinding it out. It was one of our gutsier games. We had a good talk and came to the conclusion that they were hungrier than we were."

The Oilers lost 4-1 back at home in Game 5, with Gretzky scoring the only goal. They "gutted it out," as Gretzky put it, to win Game 6 by a 5-2 score in Calgary.

That produced Game 7, a game which would remain as indelible a memory for fans in both cities as any of the five Stanley Cups won in Edmonton or the one won in Calgary during the eight-year run when the final was held in Alberta.

Steve Smith, a rookie, scored on his own net on his birthday. The Flames won 3-2.

The Edmonton era was interrupted.

Gretzky's dream of winning five Cups in a row was over.

The Oilers were out of the playoffs. There was no Stanley Cup to take from bar to bar to bar.

"I think five in a row is special and now it's not going to happen," said Gretzky, adjusting to the reality weeks later.

"I feel like I let myself down and other people down."

He had a strange summer.

"We were done four weeks early. I was off for four weeks without any commitments," he said.

Gretzky even went skating.

"It's the first time I've ever skated in summer," he said.

"The summer was so long that I went skating. I never do that."

He said this one wasn't like losing to Los Angeles in the Miracle on Manchester.

"We were young then. That's what makes this loss so disappointing and frustrating. We didn't win when we were supposed to win. We had the best record over the regular season. We had the talent. And we had won before."

And it wasn't like being swept in the final by the Islanders.

"Realistically, the Islanders were a better team," he said.

Gretzky said it would be interesting to see how the Oilers would go into their next season.

"You'd like to win every year, but sometimes it's good to lose.

"If you win every year, loyalty sets in and guys might not be moved like they should. Not that we need major, major changes, because our nucleus is still young. But maybe this will wake players up, because a sense of complacency does set in."

Gretzky, when he returned from a Pacific cruise with entertainer David Foster, had thought some more about it. And one thing he said he and his teammates had better begin to admit to themselves was that the Flames, who won three games in Edmonton and outplayed the Oilers in a fourth, were worthy winners.

"The Flames won fair and square," he said. "They prepared all year for us. When we beat the Islanders, we spent the whole year preparing for them."

Gretzky said he spent his summer vacation "reminding myself what a great feeling it is when you *win* the Cup."

Not winning the Cup would make the regular season longer than if they'd won it, said Gretzky. They'd had another month off in the summer. Getting the next season started wasn't the idea, he said.

"If there's anything we're anxious about it's to start the playoffs, not the regular season. The playoffs are what it's all about," he said as the Oilers prepared to open the season in Philadelphia. "We're not anxious to get the season started. We're anxious to get it over with. We know we're going to finish in a playoff spot in our division. We're anxious to get right back into the playoffs."

The Oilers lost their opener and Gretzky didn't get a point. And the Oilers started slowly. They lost their first four games against the Flames and coach Glen Sather, although his team managed to win a few more than it lost, said one thing was becoming obvious.

"We don't seem to have the emotion of the past, that burning desire."

Gretzky said at the start of the season that he'd have to have another 200-point season to win another scoring race – and this year it was a race. A dozen games into the season, Gretzky was off to a good enough start. He had 30 points. But Mario Lemieux had 29.

"It's going to be a race," said No. 99. "Maybe the incentive will be good for me. It's been locked up in January the last few years."

Gretzky, as he spoke, had 490 career goals.

The countdown for 500 was under way. Like 3,000 hits and 300 wins

The Great One wasn't above honing his shooting skills against the 'shooter tutor.'

in baseball, 500 goals is THE number in hockey. But Gretzky wasn't making much of the countdown.

"Five hundred goals is something, but 800, that's something else," he said, making it quite clear that Gordie Howe's 801 was his magic number.

"To me, 500 isn't that different from 400. It's a nice plateau. But it's a long, long way from 800."

Only 12 players had scored 500 goals in their careers to that point.

When it came, of course, Gretzky made the night more than memorable. He always did.

On Nov. 22, with Troy Gamble in the Vancouver net, Gretzky scored Nos. 498, 499 and 500 as the Oilers won 5-2 over the Canucks in Edmonton.

No. 500, like the 50-in-39 goal, was into an empty net, the 21st empty-net goal of Gretzky's career.

It came in Gretzky's 575th NHL game. The previous fastest 500 had been scored by Mike Bossy in 689 games. It was also Gretzky's 39th career hat trick.

"I guess being that close to scoring a goal a game excites me more than the actual 500th," said Gretzky.

Again, the goal became a bigger deal on the day than it did along the way.

"I wanted to get it at home," said Gretzky, noting the next game was in Calgary.

"They're not fond of me in Calgary. I was really hoping to get it tonight. Glen Sather double-shifted me in the last few minutes."

Sather said it wasn't hard to read it in Gretzky when he came to the rink.

"I could see early that this was going to be the night," said Slats. "I told him, 'Quit screwing around and get it over with.' When he saw that empty net he was like a male dog in heat."

At least Gamble didn't have the goal on his record. It was his first game in the NHL.

"I was pretty awestruck," said Gamble.

Gretzky was still leading the scoring race, but other than the 500-point plateau he wasn't making much news that year, nor were the Oilers as they skated through the season waiting for the playoffs to come around.

If the Oilers had found out in the spring that their loss to Calgary was popular in a lot of places outside the city limits of Edmonton, Gretzky was finding out the same thing personally.

In fan balloting for Rendez-Vous '87, Mario Lemieux was getting all the first-place votes and Gretzky was in third place.

That fans were beginning to overdose on Gretzky's greatness was the diagnosis by many. And Gretzky didn't disagree.

"I've won it too many times," he said of the scoring race. "When I came into the league, I came under a lot of heat and fire for my early success. It seemed they wanted to protect the players who held the old records and nobody wanted to see a new guy take over. They would say I didn't play on a good team, and, 'Sure, but he hasn't won a Stanley Cup.' Now it seems like they want somebody else to take over."

Gretzky said he knew the way it was.

"Let's say I ended up with 160 points. Would I get the Hart

Trophy? Definitely not. Nobody else has ever managed to get more than 160 but that's the way it would be," said Gretzky, who had totals of 215, 212, 208, 205, 196 and 164.

No. 99 was in no danger of losing this race to Lemieux, who was 21 points behind at the time. But he also was well aware that sometime soon big No. 66 was going to have a big year and the Art Ross and Hart trophies Gretzky was winning every year were someday going to have Lemieux's name on them.

"It's probably beneficial to me that I have to prove myself every night. It motivates me more than anything," Gretzky said.

After the slow start, the Oilers found their game again. They even got around to figuring out the Calgary Flames. And Sather made moves that Gretzky had kind of telegraphed to expect at the start of the season. The two biggest were the acquisition of Kent Nilsson and Rexi Ruotsalainen.

"I don't think I've ever felt this team as excited as we've been the last few days," said Gretzky at the trade deadline that year. "There was real excitement when Kent and Rexi showed up. It's such a positive feeling here. I don't think I've ever felt it this excited."

The Oilers' longest season turned out to be an unqualified success as they finished first overall again, winning 50 and losing 24. Their 106-point season was six better than the Philadelphia Flyers.

While Gretzky didn't finish strong – he scored one goal in his final eight games – he ended up with 62 goals and 121 assists for 183 points. Kurri nosed into second place with 54 goals and 54 assists for 108 points, with Mark Messier and Lemieux tied for third at 107.

If Gretzky's numbers were down, it was for a good reason.

"When you are being checked, you have to make sure you are not being outplayed," said Sather.

The Oilers opened against the Los Angeles Kings and, after the long wait to

Wayne and Janet pose with Santa during the Oilers' Christmas skate; below, Gretzky shows off the puck from his milestone 500th goal.

off rematch. But Winnipeg knocked off the Flames.

"Edmonton just won the Stanley Cup," declared Calgary GM Cliff Fletcher.

The Oilers' road to the Cup always went through Winnipeg and, while the games were great, the result was a four-game sweep as Gretzky added six more points to increase his playoff total to 21.

The playoff poolsters who had Gretzky were happy – until the Oilers played the Red Wings in the third round.

The Oilers took the series in five games, but Gretzky had a grand total of two assists. And, as he hit the Stanley Cup final against the Philadelphia Flyers, the storyline was "Gretzky In Slump."

ESPN led off a sportscast saying Gretzky was upset with his ice time. And there was even one suggestion in print that Gretzky was depressed by the loss of Vikki Moss as his girlfriend.

"Wayne will sacrifice a lot for his team if that's what it takes to win," explained Sather before the start of the Stanley Cup finals. "That's why he is such a great champion."

Gretzky said winning is what it is all about.

"When you are losing there are a lot of fingers pointed. But we're winning. It's like what you do as an individual doesn't mean anything when you're winning. Likewise, you can get all the points you want, but if you're losing it's hardly worthwhile."

Kurri had one goal in six games and Esa Tikkanen one in nine on his line. Gretzky hadn't managed a goal in the entire Detroit series and had but three in the entire playoffs.

Gretzky scored and assisted on another in Game 1 as the Oilers won 4-2.

"The guy for us was Gretzky," said Sather in the post-game interview room.

"Wayne showed us why he's the greatest player in the world. There was pressure mounting on him. He heard so much conversation about only scoring three goals in the playoffs."

get back into the playoffs, stunned the Coliseum crowd by losing 5-2. But they went from awful to awesome in winning Game 2 by the not-too-Stanley-Cup-like score of 13-3. Gretzky had a goal and six assists for seven points and the Oilers' new post-season theme song, *Still The One*, was played over and over again with goal after goal after goal.

Gretzky's first assist that night set a Stanley Cup record. It was his 177th playoff point and it broke Jean Beliveau's all-time playoff record.

The Oilers scored a 6-5 win in Game 3 in Los Angeles. Game 4 belonged to Gretzky with a goal and four assists in a 6-3 win. Back home, the Oilers put the Kings away 5-4 in their first best-of-seven first-round series.

The hockey world had been waiting for the Calgary-Edmonton play-

Gretzky enjoyed the media interviews in the dressing room that night.

"I thought I had forgotten where the net was," he said.

Gretzky set up Kurri for the winner in overtime in Game 2 as the Oilers grabbed the series by the throat at home.

Gretzky picked up four assists as the Oilers and Flyers split in Philadelphia, and the Oilers headed home with every intention of carrying the Cup.

The series looked over when the Oilers led Game 5 by a 3-0 score. But they blew it.

"That Stanley Cup was hanging up in the middle of the building and everybody saw it and everybody was too anxious," said Sather.

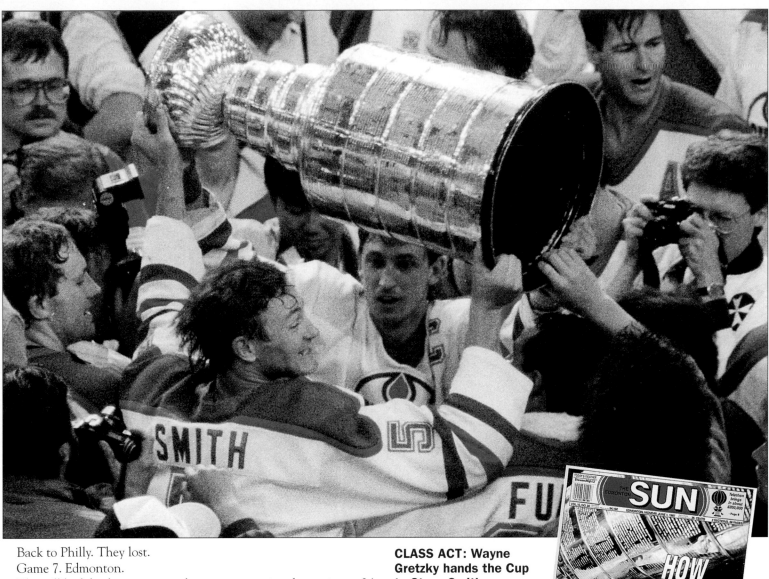

Back to Philly. They lost.

Game 7. Edmonton.

They all look back on it now as being an exceptional experience. It's always Game 7 in the Stanley Cup finals whether you're playing on the road, the pond or the backyard rink at 42 Veradi in Brantford, Ont.

The Oilers won it 3-1 and for Gretzky and gang it was their 17th playoff series win against five losses, but statistics like that didn't matter much as the streamers fell from the roof and *Still The One* reverberated around the Coliseum.

Ron Hextall, the Flyers goaltender, won the Conn Smythe Trophy and there was no controversy about that.

Gretzky carried the Stanley Cup for the third time and there was no controversy about that, either.

"The greatest rush in my life is when I pick up that Stanley Cup," he said. "And this one was the sweetest.

"It's every boy's dream to win the Stanley Cup, and being on a Stanley Cup winner is such a tremendous feeling. This was the hardest Cup to win.

"It was such a long summer.

"And this was the biggest game I've ever played because there was no in-between. It was either going to be the greatest summer of my life or the longest summer of my life," Gretzky continued.

"It's going to be the greatest.

"It really was the hardest Cup we ever won. We started off against Los Angeles and we lost. And we roared back and won four straight. Everybody thought we walked through that. But we played four tough games to win.

"Then we had Winnipeg. They beat Calgary. They're a good team. We beat them. We played four strong games. Then Detroit beat us in the first game and we roared back.

CLASS ACT: Wayne Gretzky hands the Cup to Steve Smith.

"Then we're up 3-1 with these guys and everyone is saying, 'Well, when's the parade?' Then it's 3-3.

"And then we go from heroes – maybe the best team ever, one of the best teams people can ever remember watching – to maybe goats.

"Everybody rebounded, came back, played the game of their lives.

"It wasn't easy living down last year. Last year was such a tough year for us because we were expected to win a third straight Stanley Cup, and then when you lose the way we lost ... it was worth the wait. It's a great feeling. Believe me."

The freeze-frame memory from the Oilers' third Stanley Cup wasn't a goal or a play or a celebration on the ice or downtown.

When Gretzky accepted the Cup, he looked around and found Steve Smith.

The kid who was a rookie the year before. The kid who had scored on his own net on his birthday. The kid who would be remembered as the guy who cost the Edmonton Oilers five in a row. Gretzky went out of his way to find Smith and make sure he handed him the Stanley Cup to hold high and carry first.

Wayne Gretzky did a lot of classy things in his career. But handing the Cup to Steve Smith was as classy an act as you'll ever see in sport.

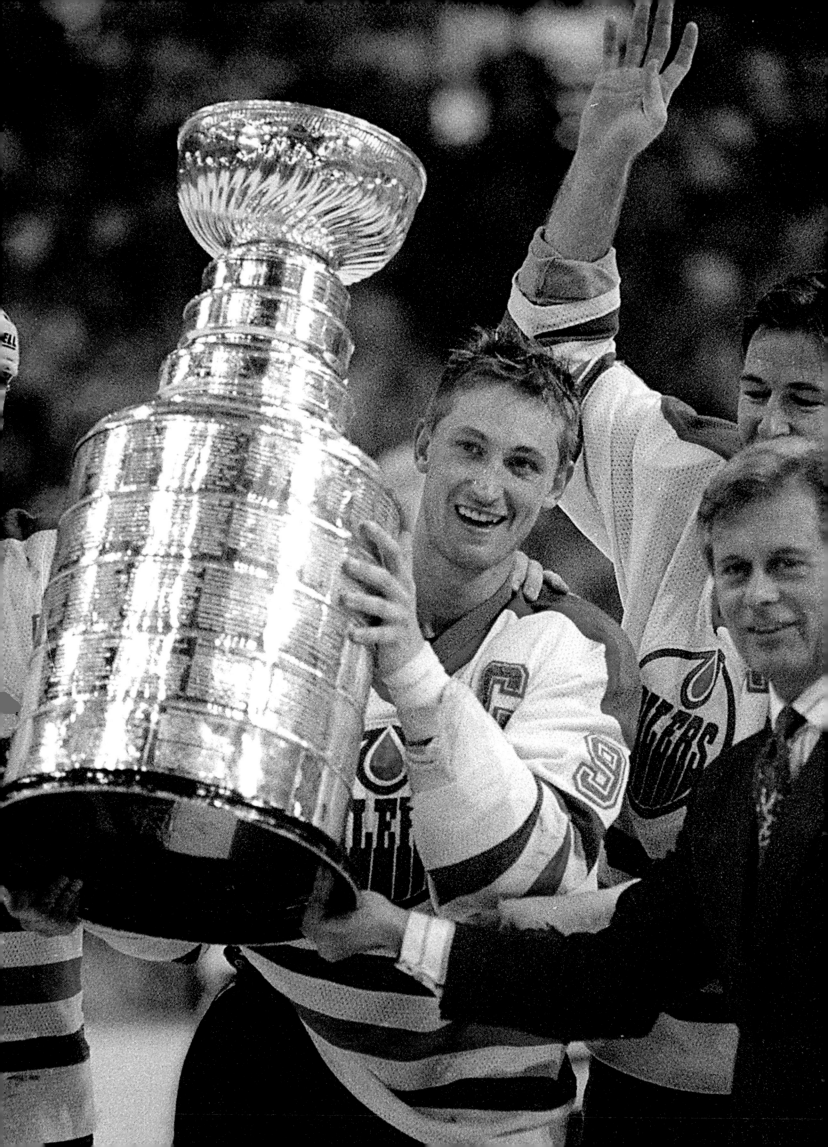

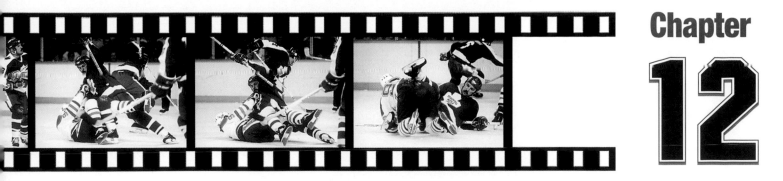

THE LAST HURRAH

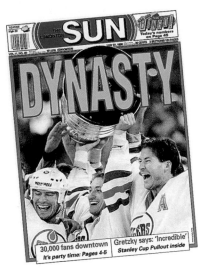

the greatest player in the history of hockey had already played eight years in the NHL, scored 543 goals and 977 assists for 1,520 points in the regular season plus 69 goals, 140 assists and 209 points in the playoffs, won eight straight Hart Trophies and seven Art Ross Trophies, just carried the Stanley Cup for the third time and owned a total of 44 NHL records. And it took until June 16, 1987 for Gretzky to have the paycheque to prove it.

"Today," said Gretzky's new financial adviser Ian Barrigan of Edmonton, "Wayne Gretzky is the highest-paid player in hockey."

He'd been making less than Dave Taylor in Los Angeles.

Going into his ninth year in Edmonton, would No. 99 finally make a million?

"For the first time in his career, yes," said Barrigan.

The 1999 contract had been ripped up. Gretzky had signed a three-year deal.

"I believe it's fair," said Barrigan. "Wayne feels it's fair. Nobody held a gun to anybody's head."

Coming off a Canada Cup win for the ages, to go with the 1987 Stanley Cup victory, Gretzky declared the Oilers still the one to beat as the NHL's regular season got ready to go.

"We're still the team to beat, no question about that," said Gretzky on the eve of the Stanley Cup banner-raising opener.

Wayne Gretzky accepts the Stanley Cup from NHL president John Ziegler in 1988. It was Gretzky's fourth – and final – Cup victory.

"We're still the team everyone is trying to knock off.

"The key thing is to make sure that we finish first overall. We won a Stanley Cup last year because of that. Because we do so much more travel than the other clubs, it's important to have that home-ice advantage and save the playoff travel."

The season wasn't very old when Gretzky realized he'd moved into a new dimension that had nothing to do with his new contract.

"It's different now," he said as he posed with the puck that represented the turning point in his career.

"Things change for me now. It used to be games and seasons. From now on, it's milestones and longevity."

One thousand assists.

As with any other major moment in his career, Gretzky had the table set for a story.

He wasn't merely getting his 1,000th assist. He was in a race with Marcel Dionne, the veteran he battled in his rookie year for the scoring championship, to see who could get to 1,000 first.

Guess who the Oilers were playing? Uh-huh. Marcel Dionne and his new New York Rangers teammates.

Guess how many points Dionne had at the end of the game? Uh-huh. Nine-hundred-and-ninety-nine.

Gretzky didn't just get one point, either. He registered his 42nd career hat trick and his 18th five-point night.

"This is special because only one other guy has been there and he's the greatest," said Gretzky that night of Gordie Howe, who held the NHL record at 1,049.

"No. 1,050 is going to be very special," he said, looking down the road a couple of months.

Gretzky reached the mark in his 645th game. Dionne was playing in his 1,258th.

Gretzky said he hoped Dionne got it the next night.

AIN'T IT GRAND: The puck marking Gretzky's 1,000th assist.

"The game is changing again," he said.

"You have to be in a very special situation to have those kinds of records. I've been very fortunate to be with a team, and in a time, when team speed, passing and offensive hockey has been the name of the game. The game is going in the opposite direction now. It's going in the direction of defence."

Gretzky had been saying it for some time but he made the point with extra emphasis that night.

"Assists have always meant more to me. Assists say something about not being selfish. Kids grow up thinking goals are everything. If a kid gets three assists in a game, he's not happy. If he gets three goals, he's happy. If I've done anything in my career so far, maybe it's to show kids that setting up a goal should be as satisfying as scoring a goal."

He also used the moment to dedicate the milestone and the season to his grandmother, the 86-year-old lady fighting leukemia who used to volunteer her legs as the toddler's goalposts.

"Everything I do now is for her," he said. "She means the world to me. When I do something, it perks her up. It's a boost she needs at this time."

At the next home game, assistant captains Kevin Lowe and Mark Messier presented Gretzky with a silver stick in a pre-game ceremony to commemorate his becoming only the second player in NHL history to accumulate 1,000 assists. Gretzky was visibly pleased.

"There's a tradition in baseball that the player with the highest batting average always got a gold bat," said Lowe. "Gretz always admired that. He's seen George Brett's and he really admired it."

It was engraved with the names of all the players he played with to get the 1,000 assists.

That night Gretzky scored two goals to pass Edmonton native Johnny Bucyk, the Boston Bruins

"He plays his next game in Los Angeles, where he spent most of his career. That's where he deserves to get it. Maybe it worked out best for both of us."

If Gretzky hadn't reached the milestone marker this night, guess where the Oilers were to play the next night?

Yup. Calgary.

"I had a tough time getting one point tonight," said Dionne. "He got five.

"He has too much power. He has too much going for him. He's a scoring machine. He makes plays that are incredible. He's going to get all of Gordie Howe's records. I'm not going to go down on the same page as those two guys. Wayne Gretzky and Gordie Howe will go down in history in a special category together."

Gretzky told me that night that he agreed with that. And it wasn't his ego talking.

Hall of Famer, and move into sixth place in the all-time scoring tables with 556 goals.

On Dec. 6, against the Minnesota North Stars in the Coliseum, Gretzky had another one of those "I was there" games. He scored five goals. And if they had "gone upstairs" for video replay in those days, chances are it would have been six and Gretzky would have tied the record shared by Syd Howe, Red Berenson and Darryl Sittler.

Television replays showed that Gretzky had batted the puck into the net nine minutes into the third period, for what would have been his fifth goal en route to scoring six and equalling the record.

Rookie ref Paul Stewart waved it off despite the fact the goal light had been turned on.

"They tell me that it was in," said No. 99. "That makes me disappointed because it was a record. You don't get too many chances at it. I know how hard I worked tonight to get five."

Oilers co-coach John Muckler raved.

"Wayne was special tonight. He's had a lot of great games but this has to rate with the best of them."

If Gretzky had been given credit for the other goal it would have moved him into a tie with Phil Esposito on the career scoring charts. He tied it the next time out against Winnipeg and broke it two nights later against Vancouver.

It was Game 661 in his ninth season for Gretzky. Espo needed 1,282 games over 18 seasons.

Gretzky, at the end of the calendar year, had played 38 games. He had 29 goals and 57 assists for 86 points.

But he was not on the ice for the new year. For the first time in his career Gretzky had suffered a major injury. Surgery wasn't required but he was, Dr. Gordon Cameron insisted, going to be out for three weeks to a month.

Late in a game against Philadelphia on Dec. 30, after having scored a goal and added three assists in a 6-0 win over the Flyers, defenceman Kjell Samuelsson fell on him.

"I knew when I went down that it was bad," said Gretzky of his sprained right knee.

"But I thought it was bad in a maybe-I'll-miss-a-couple-of-games way," said Gretzky, who was projected to be back for his 27th birthday on Jan. 26.

Mark Messier presents Wayne Gretzky with a commemorative stick from the Oilers in honour of The Great One's 1,000th assist.

By this time of year, Gretzky always had his scoring titles in the bag. Not this time. When he came back on Nov. 29 in Calgary he would have to hunt down Mario Lemieux for the title.

"I'll probably be 25 points behind him when I get back," said Gretzky.

"It's hard to score in Hartford from my couch in Edmonton.

"I'll have a lot of ground to make up when I get back. But if I get back in time, it should be good for hockey. If I get back in time it looks like we'll have a *real* scoring race. It's supposed to be a scoring *race*. It's supposed to be something for the fans to talk about. It's supposed to be fun."

When Gretzky got back he was 19 points back of Lemieux's 105.

He was 15 points back at the end of the evening, thanks to assisting on all four goals in a 5-4 loss to the Flames.

There was a feeling from the fans when he came back, an electricity in the air that Gretzky said he hadn't really felt since the 50-in-39 season.

"It's very noticeable," he said after a three-point night against New Jersey to increase his point total to 10 in his first three games back.

"I can really feel it. Just from the way the fans react to everything. I can feel everybody reacting around it. I can feel it with the fans and I can feel it with my teammates. Everybody is really into it.

"I don't know if I can catch him, but I'm off to a pretty good start," added Gretzky, now freely admitting that he'd accepted the challenge.

"My teammates are being very unselfish. I can already see they are trying to do everything they can to help me. I think we're going to have to be careful not to put it ahead of winning.

"I just have to chip away and chip away. I still think I'm going to need a couple of six-point nights to do it. Mario is a talented player. He's going to get two or three points most nights."

In his first seven games after the injury Gretzky had three-, three-, two-, four-, three-, three- and three-point outings.

Pittsburgh at Edmonton on Feb. 17 was a game with a real buzz around it.

Gretzky, in the three-point game against Toronto which preceded it, had two assists. That moved him into a tie with Howe. He had 1,049 assists. Forget Lemieux, Gretzky could break Gordie Howe's career record in front of Lemieux.

It didn't work out that way.

Gretzky vs. Lemieux didn't come off.

And Howe would hold a share of his record for a while longer.

Gretzky went down at 4:45 with an eye injury.

Lemieux left the game not long later with a broken nose.

Gretzky's injury was frightening.

"It's extremely disappointing. I guess injuries are a part of the game, but when you're leading 5 -0 and there's just a minute to go in a game ..."

Dr. Cameron said it was amazing Gretzky had only missed seven games – one because of tonsillitis and the other six with a sore shoulder – in 9½ seasons as a pro player.

"He's had remarkably few injuries, especially considering the amount of time he logs on the ice," said Cameron.

"I don't take the body a lot," Gretzky laughed in response.

But it wasn't a laughing matter for the Oilers.

"We've got a chance for a run at first place overall," said Gretzky. "Hopefully the guys can keep winning."

And the guys didn't include Mark Messier. He was out with a hip-flexor.

While they had a five-game streak in there where they didn't win a game, the Oilers went 5-4-4 while he was out.

When he returned, there was a whole new Gretzky Watch.

"The Race & The Chase," as the headline on my column had it.

The race?

With Gretzky back the Oilers could re-enter the great race for first place overall. It had been years since there was a race for first place like this one. Calgary, Boston and Montreal were all in it with the Oilers.

The chase.

AWWWW-RIGHT! Few things were sweeter than scoring against the hated Calgary Flames.

"It was at the exact same spot on the ice where Brett Callighen got hit – right at the blueline," said Gretzky of his former linemate who never played another game after taking a stick in the eye.

"I kind of fell into the stick," he said of Jari Kurri's lumber. "It got me in the middle of the eye. It was a scary thing. I couldn't see for a while. I got my vision back in the dressing room."

The Oilers left Gretzky at home to recover while they took a three-game road trip to Winnipeg, St. Louis and Chicago.

When Gretzky got back, he did it.

At age 27, Wayne Gretzky broke Gordie Howe's assist record of 1,049 in his 681st game – 1,086 fewer than Howe required to establish it – on a goal by Kurri.

Gretzky. From his office behind the net. Out front to Kurri. Scores!

"I thought about who'd score it," said Wayne. "It was only right Jari should score it."

It wasn't perfect. His idol wasn't there. His fiancee wasn't there. His mom wasn't there. His owner wasn't there. And there were even, believe it or not, 887 fans who weren't there.

Other than that it was perfect.

A tape-recorded message from Howe was played on the PA system.

"Hello, Wayne, this is Gordie Howe. I'm sorry that I couldn't be there tonight but I'm awful happy and it's my pleasure to join with the fans there at home to congratulate you on such a wonderful feat. Thank you for allowing me to carry the record for a while. There's no one on Earth that I'd rather see break it than yourself and, well, there's another kid in Philadelphia, but he's way behind," he said of his son Mark.

"Congratulation to the king of all assists!"

His fiancee, Janet Jones, wasn't there.

She left Edmonton on a 6 a.m. flight to Los Angeles where she had a casting call.

His mom – in Edmonton to see Wayne get the record against Pittsburgh and ending up in the hospital with her son when he suffered the abrasion to the cornea in his left eye – was at home in Brantford.

She phoned to find the satellite co-ordinates to watch the game on TV. But the game wasn't on TV.

Owner Peter Pocklington wasn't there.

His plane had been delayed in Toronto. He listened to the record-breaking point as called by Rod Phillips on radio driving in from the airport.

NHL president John Ziegler had meetings all week and sent Brian O'Neill to follow Gretzky until he registered the assist.

No. 99 was given a Tiffany mantel clock by O'Neill on behalf of the NHL.

The Oilers gave him a gold hockey stick engraved with the words: "March 1, 1988. Kurri (32) (Gretzky-Tikkanen) 12:44. Edmonton vs. Los Angeles. Northlands Coliseum. 1,050 assists. NHL record."

The Oiler players gave him a $50,000 bond to be given to his first-born on the occasion of the child's 21st birthday.

To most hockey fans, Gretzky's greatness had been confirmed a long time ago. To Gretzky it was confirmed this night.

"It's No. 1," he said. "It's No. 1 because it's one of those records people say may never be broken. A

KEEPING UP WITH JONES: Wayne follows girlfriend Janet Jones out of the Coliseum.

Wayne and teammates gather around the Clarence Campbell trophy after winning the 1988 conference title.

lot of records are for games and seasons. This is a record for consistency.

"A lot of people said a lot of things early in my career. They said, 'Let's see him do it over time. Let's see him do it over 10 or 11 years.' I think when you accomplish something like this it throws all the doubts out the window.

"This is the record which says it doesn't matter who scored the goal, the one which shows the kids that an assist is as important as a goal.

"And I think it shows you can be 170 pounds and under six feet tall and still excel in a sport. I think it shows that brains are a part of playing a game."

He claimed not to be upset that Howe didn't show up for the occasion.

"Gordie called me. He had a couple of charity functions. He told me if I really wanted him there, he'd change his schedule. The phone call meant more. I was grateful for the phone call."

Gretzky said he felt a little sad for Howe as he listened to the tape on the PA system.

"He did it in a different era. It was such a different game when he played. There's a big part of me which believes what he did, nobody should touch."

Gretzky said his injuries made him appreciate his accomplishment even more.

"When I was injured and missed a month, I guess somebody up there was saying I needed a break and needed a rest. When I injured the eye, on the very edge of breaking the record, that's when I started to tell myself how thankful I am that I haven't been hurt."

Missing 16 games cost Gretzky the scoring crown. Lemieux, playing 77 games, ended up with 168 points. Gretzky, playing 64, ended up with 149.

The Oilers were 44-25-11, finishing second in the Smythe Division to the Calgary Flames and third overall.

Those standings suggested to many that Stanley wasn't going to be staying in Edmonton for another year. But Gretzky made a few points prior to the playoffs.

"I think we're good enough," he said. "I also think three or four other teams are capable of winning it. But one thing I can tell you is that I'm going into the playoffs more rested than ever before.

"I've played a lot of hockey in the last few years," he said, listing four Stanley Cup playoffs through to the finals, two Canada Cups and Rendez-Vous '87.

"I've also played pretty much every exhibition game over the last nine years. I was worn down. But the '87 Canada Cup rejuvenated me. I really had a great time at the Canada Cup."

Then there was the injury time.

"It marked the first time I'd really got away from the game for any length of time," Gretzky explained. "That time off probably helped my career in the long run. It'll make things better for me going into the playoffs."

There was another thing. The Oilers were playing Winnipeg in the first round. Winnipeg was a staple for every Oilers' Stanley Cup season.

Without a "Drive For Five" storyline, thanks to Steve Smith, it was Hugh Campbell, the Eskimos GM, who gave the hockey team their calling card for the playoffs.

"The Double Double" he called the idea of going for two two-in-a-row Cup seasons.

The Oilers won the series in five. Gretzky managed only one goal in the series but had 11 assists.

That brought on the Calgary Flames for the Smythe Division Finals. And, for the first time ever, an Edmonton-Calgary Stanley Cup playoff series opened in Calgary.

Gretzky figured that could work to the Oilers' advantage.

"There's pressure on them they've never experienced before," he said. "This is the first time they've played with the expectation to win. They'll be expected to win that first game."

They didn't.

Edmonton 3, Calgary 1.

When it was over, Gretzky, sounding a lot like Wild Bill Hunter back in the Edmonton Oil Kings junior days, called it the biggest win in Oilers' history.

"I don't think we've ever had a bigger one."

JUST HANGIN' OUT: Joey Moss, centre, shares a dressing room moment with Wayne and Janet.

Gretzky, fuelled by the Calgary fans, sank the Flames in overtime of Game 2.

"They do get me going," said No. 99 after he scored the winner at 7:54 of overtime.

"They're more worried about me than their own team," he said after the 5-4 win.

The shot Gretzky ripped for the winner would be talked about for ages.

"If Wayne ever shot the puck harder, I don't think I've ever seen it," said co-coach John Muckler of the guy who brought the Oilers back from a 3-0 deficit in the game and sent them home to Edmonton with a 2-0 series lead.

When the Oilers won 4-2 and 6-4 back home, *The Edmonton Sun's* headline said it all.

"How Sweep It Is."

Jacques Demers had guaranteed "No Sweep" before the Oilers played his Detroit Red Wings in the Campbell Conference Finals. And Demers' team did win a game. But he was betrayed by several players on his team, and refused to play them in Game 5 after they missed curfew at an Edmonton nightclub.

Gretzky had three three-point nights and two two-point nights in the series.

For the fifth time in six years, Gretzky and the Oilers were in the Stanley Cup Finals. After two finals against both the New York Islanders and the Philadelphia Flyers, the Oilers had somebody new to play for the prize – the Boston Bruins.

This was not considered a match made in heaven for either Gretzky or his teammates. The Oilers had a worse record in the Boston Garden than anywhere else in the league. And Gretzky had more trouble with Kasper, the Not-So-Friendly Ghost, than anybody else.

Steve Kasper had made a name for himself when it came to shutting down Gretzky. It was his specialty.

Gretzky said he wasn't afraid of no ghosts.

"If he can play 32 minutes, he's going to see me a lot," said No. 99.

"It's different when you play league games, basically four lines, at 19 or 20 minutes a game. In the playoffs guys often get double-shifted. And if we get up one or two goals, it'll be pretty tough for them to have a guy following me around. Hopefully, we can get the jump early and they'll have to change their style a little bit."

And as for 10 losses and two ties in the Boston Garden by the Oilers in 14 visits over the years, Gretzky had an answer for that, too.

"I think what people always tend to forget is that the West is the most difficult place in the league to play, at least until the playoffs. We always go into the Boston Garden as part of a five- or six-game road trip. By the time we get to Boston, guys are usually mentally and physically tired. We're not at our best.

"It's like Philadelphia. We didn't have a very good record in the Spectrum either. But we won two Stanley Cups against the Flyers. It's tough to go in there during the season. But when we went in there during the playoffs, we did fine. This time we're going to charter into Boston and we'll be fresh."

The Oilers made sure they took care of business at home.

Going against ex-Oiler Andy Moog in goal, Gretzky scored the first goal and Keith Acton the winner in a 2-1 opener.

Gretzky led the Oilers to a 4-2 win in Game 2 but the story seemed to be his ultra-short haircut.

"I saw that haircut and did a double take," said his brother Glen. "He looks like k.d. lang."

"Who cares," said Peter Pocklington after Gretzky scored and set up

Glenn Anderson and Mark Messier for goals in the game that sent the Oilers to Boston with a 2-0 series lead.

The series, to many, was over then and there. In essence that was true. But plenty was to happen before Gretzky carried the Stanley Cup for the fourth time.

Like the Larry Bird and Wayne Gretzky double-dip in Boston.

Because of a scheduling problem, the Boston Celtics played a playoff game in the afternoon and the Bruins in the evening in the old building. It was a once-in-a-lifetime special day in sport that transcended two sports.

If you had tickets to both, you would have framed them. Larry Bird in the seventh game of an NBA playoff series. Wayne Gretzky in the third game of a Stanley Cup final. The two greatest players on the two greatest teams. Bird for lunch. Gretzky for supper.

Bird was brilliant.

"That was the greatest individual performance I've ever seen," said Danny Ainge as Bird scored 20 points in the fourth quarter to lead Boston to a 118-116 win over Atlanta.

"The second half was just awesome," said Celtics coach K.C. Jones. "I have never seen two players go head to head like that, not like Larry Bird and Dominique Wilkins did today. Kevin McHale said it was the best basketball game he'd ever seen in his life and he was in it."

Gretzky and the Oilers' 6-3 win didn't have the drama. But Gretzky gave it a go to match Bird's game. He had four assists.

"I think I was kind of lucky tonight," said Gretzky. "The puck just seemed to be bouncing for me tonight."

As memorable as the Bird-Gretzky double-header was, what followed was absolutely unforgettable. It was one of the most bizarre nights in all of hockey history.

Game 4 was, as *The Edmonton Sun* headline read the next morning, "The Game That Never Was."

The night the lights were supposed to go out on the Boston Bruins, they went out in the Boston Garden. Left in the dark with the teams tied 3-3, the league found some rule which insisted the game didn't happen but that all the stats counted (Gretzky had two assists) and that Game

5 would be played in Edmonton.

The Oilers won Game 5 by a 6-3 score. Gretzky had a goal and two assists. *Sun* hockey scribe Dick Chubey called it "an unprecedented 4.67-game sweep."

The Oilers won 16 games in the playoffs and went 11-0 at home, including 3-0 in a four-game final.

Gretzky had scored a point in each of 12 straight final games going back to the 1987 series with Philadelphia. He led all Stanley Cup scorers in the playoffs with 12 goals and 31 assists for 43 points and led all point-getters in the final with three goals and 10 assists for 13 points.

THEIR CUP RUNNETH OVER: Lovebirds Wayne and Janet embrace Stanley.

He won his second Conn Smythe Trophy. Only Bobby Orr and Bernie Parent had won the trophy twice. And this time there was no debate about somebody else on the Oilers deserving it. Except as Gretzky saw it.

Gretzky said there's one great thing about the Smythe.

"Only one guy gets it."

He also said there's also only one thing wrong with it.

"Only one guy gets it.

"Mark Messier and Grant Fuhr could have won it just as easily. I feel kind of bad that they didn't win it."

Sather raved that Stanley Cup-winning night.

"I've been watching Wayne play since he was 17. He has a mystique. There's no one like him. He's been great for this franchise, great for this team and great for this city. He's a good example for every kid in this country. As long as we've known him, he's never had a hair out of place."

The Oilers had found a new way to win the Stanley Cup that year. And after they carried it, they found a new way to celebrate it.

The highlight of the night was the picture of the entire team, on the ice, with the Stanley Cup. That scene has been repeated by every Stanley Cup winner since.

"The picture made it perfect," said Sather. "It was done for everybody, the players and the people who have been behind this team for so long. They were all a part of the picture. Nobody has ever done something like this before. It was a great idea. It was Wayne's idea."

It was the last time in his career he'd win the Stanley Cup. It was the last time in his career he'd wear an Edmonton Oilers uniform.

THE ROYAL WEDDING

the phone rang in the radio station newsroom sometime in the early morning in the middle of January, 1988.

The tape began recording.

Wayne Gretzky, the caller breathlessly announced, had been at Earl's Tin Palace after the game the night before and had announced the news to his teammates: He was getting married to Janet Jones.

I was working a three-year gig for that No. 1-rated radio station as a member of the Morning Crew with Rob Christie, Audie Lynds and Janet From Another Planet, and arrived at 5 a.m. to be met by legendary local newsman Bob Layton, who informed me what 630 CHED's cash-for-news-tips line had produced overnight from somebody looking to earn the $1,000 prize.

I checked out the tip. It was the goods. I had a scoop. And I had to scoop myself. I had to break it on the air, not in *The Sun*.

Having the jump on the story, however, made all the difference in the next day's coverage.

"She said yes," said Wayne. "It's definite. We're getting married. We were meant to spend our lives together. She's a tremendous lady, a great person."

Gretzky revealed the details.

He said he'd proposed to her by phone to South Carolina where she was on location shooting a movie. Then he phoned his mom and dad. Then he went out and played.

LOOK WAAAAAY UP: The groom-to-be has a private moment in St. Joseph's Basilica.

At the Tin Palace after the game, he broke the news to the boys, buying a few bottles of Dom Perignon to celebrate.

"My last words to everybody were, 'Let's keep this quiet for a while.' I guess it kept quiet for about four hours."

Gretzky's agent Mike Barnett said Wayne had laughed when he heard it on the radio in the morning.

"He said, 'I should have phoned the radio station myself and made the $1,000,' " said Barnett.

Janet was on the set in South Carolina. She wouldn't reveal the exact nature of Wayne's proposal when I tracked her down there.

"That's between Wayne and myself," she said. "We can't tell you everything. All I can say is that he proposed in a very special way. I'll never forget it for the rest of my life. It was very special," said the future Mrs. Gretzky, adding that it was "wonderfully romantic."

Gretzky had kept her up all night with phone call after phone call.

"After the game he kept calling me all night, getting friends and players on the phone. It sure sounded like they were really celebrating up there. But the nicest part was that he called my mother first. My family was thrilled."

While Janet was from St. Louis and Gretzky from Brantford, Ont., they both said there was not one single solitary second of discussion on where the wedding would be. It would be in Edmonton.

And from the second that was known, there was no question. It would be the social event of the season. Within hours it was being referred to as Canada's Royal Wedding.

It was at the Canada Cup training camp in Banff that reports surfaced of Gretzky holding hands and escorting a girl who wasn't Vikki Moss.

And when the event locale switched to Hamilton, Gretzky admitted it.

"I haven't been seeing Vikki since early summer. I don't want to say much because Vikki's family is in Edmonton and I don't want to hurt them."

Gretzky said he'd met Janet in St. Louis about five years earlier. He said they started seeing each other again that summer of '87.

In early January, under the headline "On Cloud 99," Gretzky admitted more. He was in love.

"She's a great lady. It's definitely serious. But we haven't talked about marriage," he said.

He told the story of how they first met. It was on the set of Dance Fever. She was a featured dancer. He was a celebrity judge. Both were involved with other people then, Gretzky with Vikki Moss and Jones with tennis star Vitas Gerulaitis.

"He remembers the first encounter better than I do. But, gosh, he was a nice guy," said Janet. "I never had it in the back of my mind that we'd be married one day." What brought them together was meeting again at a Boston Celtics-Los Angeles Lakers basketball game in L.A. when both were freshly uninvolved.

"We were both getting on with our lives and we just happened to meet each other," said Jones. "We'd met before and we hit it off right away. We make each other laugh. We genuinely like each other.

"We are very much in love and very happy, but marriage, you know, is in the future," said the actress who had appeared in films such as The Flamingo Kid, A Chorus Line, American Anthem and Police Academy, appeared on the covers of Life and Harper's Bazaar and in commercials for Wrangler, Shasta Cola and Kodak.

She also talked about appearing semi-nude in Playboy, saying she didn't regret it at all except for the publicity it received in Canada once she started dating Wayne.

"In the States it was like, 'Wow, she didn't show enough. In Canada it was like, 'She's a Playmate!' I wasn't ashamed of any of the pictures but I was most concerned about Wayne and his family. In the newspapers, all the pictures they're using of me are from Playboy, not from Vogue or Harper's Bazaar.

"They were very suggestive shots but I don't think Wayne was bothered by it. The thing that bothers us is how it has been used."

Mom Gretzky said she had no problem with the Playboy pictorial.

"She's a nice girl," said Phyllis Gretzky of his son's choice for his bride. "It doesn't bother Wayne so it doesn't bother me."

Janet said they were both kind of hurt about the newspapers trying to make something of their previous relationships.

Mr. and Mrs. Wayne Gretzky wave to onlookers after coming out of the church on July 16, 1988.

Wayne points out a familiar face in the Edmonton crowd to his new bride.

"It's not true that Wayne's the reason I split up with Vitas or that I'm the reason he split up with Vikki."

Other than that, the rest of their world together was wonderful.

They both said being actress and athlete left them with plenty in common.

"I think we understand each other's pressures," said Wayne. "There's a lot of pressure being a professional athlete. She's been a big help taking the pressure off."

Jones said she was a pretty good sports fan but not much of a hockey fan before meeting Wayne.

"Wayne changed my mind about it. He was really good about explaining it to me."

Everybody was thrilled when they officially became engaged.

Mark Messier and Kevin Lowe claimed to be most thrilled.

"We win the bet!" said Messier.

"Gretz will have a new bride. Walter and Phyllis will have a new daughter. And Kevin and I get $1,000 each."

Messier explained that the three had made the bet when they were all 18 years old, as to which of them would end up at the altar first.

The groom walks down the aisle accompanied by proud parents Walter and Phyllis Gretzky.

But there was some dispute about that.

"That's the story and we're sticking to it," said Lowe. "We're telling him that now. He claims the bet was that the last guy to stay single was supposed to get $1,000 from the other two guys. We did make the bet when Gretz and Mess had serious girlfriends and I was telling them they'd be first. I'll win either way. I figure I roomed with Gretz for three years and then with Mark for three years so that makes Mark next."

Messier said no way.

"I won't be getting married for 10 years."

Messier wasn't one of the players at the Tin Palace when Gretzky ordered the champagne. He said he'd found out in the wee hours of the morning.

"There was a knock on the door. Gretz came over. I've never seen him happier."

Gretzky called home, too, of course. Dad Walter answered the phone.

"Walter talked to him first. I was in bed," said mom Phyllis. "Then I got on the other line and we were all talking. We were all really happy for him."

Phyllis said she wasn't surprised it happened but was shocked by the speed of it all.

"I just thought it was kind of quick," she said that day. "It was just such a long time with Vikki and all that this seemed kind of sudden."

Brent Gretzky, Wayne's youngest brother, said his mother told him just before he left for school.

"I couldn't believe it," he said. "I told all my pals at school. They couldn't believe it either."

Brent added that when the family first met Janet she "knew nothing at all about hockey."

He added, "That's when me and my brothers taught her all about hockey."

There was one other guy Gretzky called that night: Eddie Mio.

"He called me late at night. He said, 'Eddie, I'm getting married.'

"I said, 'Wayne, that's just super.'

"We didn't really talk very long. I just told him how happy I was for him. He said a few things. And we hung up.

"About three minutes later he called me back.

"He said, 'I just wanted to ask you that if I asked you to be my best man, would you not ask me to be your best man?'" Mio laughed.

"I was shocked. I was honoured just to be one of the people he thought of calling that night, much less for him to call back and ask me to be his best man.

"With Mess, Kevin and Coff, maybe I was the easy choice," he said.

"I don't think it meant I was his best friend and confidant. I was just glad to be involved. Today, sometimes, I think I'm better known as Wayne Gretzky's best man than for the 10 years I played."

Not long after the wedding date had been set and the plans began to take shape, Janet announced she wanted children and wouldn't be waiting long.

And not just one.

"We plan on having kids right away. I don't think we'll stop at one. I come from a family of seven. Wayne comes from a family of five. I think that says it right there."

Wayne said his dad couldn't wait to become a grandfather.

"Dad is happy as can be that she's tall," he laughed. "He says that means we'll have tall athletes. That's the thing my dad worries about."

Gretzky, who during the previous couple of years had been throwing out a lot of quotes about how early in his career he might retire, had suddenly changed his tune dramatically.

"She's added years to his career," I wrote in the middle of the playoffs. Gretzky said he was beginning to look at his career from a different per-

SHOOTING THE STARS: Hundreds of media representatives were on hand for the nuptials.

Video wizard Don Metz of Aquila Productions was honoured to shoot Canada's version of the Royal Wedding.

spective as he contemplated walking down the aisle.

"I think I want to practise with my kids," Gretzky was suddenly telling me.

"I see Charlie Huddy out practising with his kids and that looks great to me. It's great to see them skate with their dad. Now I'm looking forward to that. When I was nine I used to skate with Doug Jarvis. That was great."

On the other hand, there was one voice that suggested he could think of a couple of reasons the Oilers might not beat the Calgary Flames in the playoffs.

"Grant Fuhr is tired and Wayne Gretzky is getting married," said owner Peter Pocklington.

Janet said she couldn't believe that.

"It hurt my feelings," she said. "I don't want to sound sour about it. I don't think he meant to hurt me. But Wayne saw it right off. He saw that it hurt my feelings. A lot of people I expect to say a lot of things but I don't expect to hear those things from some people. It threw me for a little bit of a loop."

Gretzky said his bride-to-be was getting a pretty good preview of what it was going to be like being married to him.

That said, No. 99 offered the thought that a good playoff performance was not only important to his career but important to his marriage.

"The wedding added a lot of pressure – unfair pressure. It's so silly. But Janet has been put under a lot of pressure. She handles it well. But when I scored the winner in overtime in Game 2 in Calgary, she was pretty happy. It took a lot of pressure off her. I don't know who was happier after I scored that goal in Game 2, me or her."

Gretzky, in the same interview, said the two hadn't talked much hockey yet.

"So far she hasn't asked me why I don't backcheck more," he laughed.

"She asks a lot of questions but we don't go into detail about it."

Wayne said she'd already been a big influence on his career.

"This is the first year I faced any adversity. She was there telling me this was the best thing to happen to me."

Janet said the whole year of hockey had been good for them as a couple.

"My first season has been a long season – and a great season. From the Canada Cup to the Stanley Cup playoffs, I've seen a lot of good hockey. I've also seen the way Wayne has reacted to a lot of things. I think the

WE'RE OUTTA HERE: The newlyweds make their getaway in a limousine.

time off for the injury really helped him appreciate what it would be like if he retired too soon. He had a chance to watch from the outside. Having gone through the year together, I know I'm going to be totally supportive. I know he's got to be doing his thing to be happy."

The Great One admitted that there had been so much hype about the wedding that they actually thought of eloping.

"We've both been blown away so far with all the publicity for the wedding. We just felt like two kids in love with each other who were going to get married, two normal people who were going to get married. The Royal Wedding aspect and the media event it is bound to be was totally unexpected."

One big story out of Vancouver had Gretzky spending $250,000 on the wedding ring. He had to create another story by denying it cost anywhere near that.

Every tidbit of information was a headline.

Playboy publisher Hugh Hefner declining an invitation to the wedding was a story.

Plans for an exotic Caribbean honeymoon aboard a private yacht was a headline.

Gretzky giving his wife a Rolls-Royce convertible for a wedding present was big news.

Vladislav Tretiak and his wife Tatania accepting their invitation and flying in all the way from Moscow was big international news.

There were huge stories on her $40,000 wedding dress with detachable train, and even one on her "pastel-toned" lingerie for the occasion.

Gretzky giving Mio and the other Oilers in his wedding party custommade black tuxedos made by Sam Abouhassan of Edmonton was news.

Designer Pari Malek was interviewed about the 1,500 hours in the making of Janet's wedding dress.

The Lincolns, the band hired to play at the reception, received plenty of press.

"Bachelor Bash Quiet" was a big headline.

The Gretz Grannies were celebrities and interviewed upon arrival.

The rehearsal and dinner party were well covered.

You get the idea. It was nothing less than Canada's Royal Wedding.

It was an event. And when the big day finally arrived it had the kind of coverage of a Royal Wedding.

The coverage in *The Sun* was so extensive it was hard to envision any Gretzky event in the future that could possibly occupy more pages of the paper, although one would come along in short order.

The guest list included virtually the entire Oilers family, Hollywood's Alan Thicke, David Foster and Tim Feehan; hockey's hierarchy including John Ziegler, Alan Eagleson, Mike Keenan, Tretiak and Gordie Howe. Jackie Parker and several members of the CFL's Edmonton Eskimos family were invited. And, yes, even a small number of media, including hockey writer Chubey and columnist Jones.

The hype became so huge that the day before the wedding Gretzky was worried there'd be a letdown.

"I hope they aren't disappointed," he said. "There are not going to be 50 or 60 Hollywood or sports celebrities here. Obviously, because of the careers both Janet and I happen to have, there are going to be a few celebrities. But by far, the majority of people are our friends – plain ordinary people from Brantford, St. Louis and Edmonton. I'm thrilled that Edmonton is so excited about the wedding but I don't want them to think it's going to be something it isn't."

I wrote that story at Gretzky's request. He was worried. But it didn't make anybody less excited about the event. And it didn't make it any less of an event.

I mean, how do you downplay something when the prime minister is invited?

"I guess that's the problem," he laughed. "We know the prime minister."

The Sun produced a special section full of wedding-day coverage. The lead story of the section, with an '*Edmonton Sun* Staff Writers' byline:

"Edmonton's favourite son Wayne Douglas Gretzky took Janet Marie Jones for his wife in a colourful ceremony full of style and elegance.

"The bride, dressed in a magnificent white satin gown rumoured to have cost $40,000, and Wayne, looking slightly nervous throughout in his traditional black tuxedo, exchanged vows before more than 650 selected guests at St. Joseph's Basilica.

"While 3,000 well-wishers waited outside, the hushed audience inside listened as Wayne and Janet repeated their vows in unison.

"Each confidently answered 'I do' when asked during the 40-minute ecumenical service, conducted by retired minister Canon John Munro, they kissed and hugged, then smiled at each other and kissed and hugged again.

"Janet had earlier caused a stir by arriving two hours before the ceremony to dress in the church, disappointing crowds outside who had hoped to catch a glimpse of the radiant bride in her wedding gown.

"Wayne arrived 30 minutes before the service was to begin, accompanied by his best man, Eddie Mio.

"Groomsmen were Mark Messier, Kevin Lowe, Paul Coffey, brothers Glen, Brent and Keith Gretzky ...

"When he walked down the aisle it was at the side of his parents, Walter and Phyllis Gretzky, while members of the Edmonton Symphony Orchestra played *Trumpet Voluntary*.

"As he walked past his grandmother, 84-year-old Mary Gretzky, Wayne gave her a wink and a thumbs-up sign.

"Local rock star Tim Feehan sang Beethoven's *Ode To Joy*.

"While Feehan sang, Janet stood with her arm behind Wayne's back and gave him a playful tickle.

"When the pair left the church following the ceremony they were welcomed warmly by the crowd.

"Wayne looked relieved while his bride appeared overjoyed as they posed and kissed on the steps of St. Joseph's, much to the delight of cheering onlookers."

Nobody was disappointed.

Sun fashion writer Anne Alexander, who died of cancer two months before this book was published, filled a page with a story on Janet's wedding dress and an interview with wedding co-ordinator Connie Duguid.

The happy couple head out on their honeymoon.

Alexander and Kerry Diotte filled another page with reaction from the bride. ("It was everything I hoped for and more. No one could be happier than I am today.") David Quigley and Richard Watts covered the reception. ("The only person not too happy with the wedding reception was the chef. He had to keep the food warm as the meal was delayed more than an hour while each of the guests personally congratulated the newlyweds.") Diotte interviewed the relatives. ("Wayne told me he's happier than when he won any of the Stanley Cups," said brother Brett.) Gord Bannerman covered the crowd outside. ("I love Wayne Gretzky and I wanted to see Janet's dress.") Chubey and Jones took the day off work to attend the wedding and the reception and build up a multitude of points with their wives Gail and Linda.

Unlike Chubey and the author, one guy invited to the wedding ended up working it. Big time.

"I was shooting practice for TSN," said Don Metz of the Stanley Cup final the Oilers won over the Boston Bruins.

"Wayne came up to me and asked if I was interested in coming to his wedding. I told him I'd be honoured.

"He said, 'I was hoping you could bring a camera and maybe grab a couple of shots for me. I've hired a couple of still photographers but I'd kinda like a couple of video shots if you could get them.'

"I said, 'Why don't you just tell Mike Barnett that you've given me the video rights,' " Metz laughed.

Gretzky said why not.

"We shot the wedding with six cameras and a crew of 12. We sent out 68 different packages of the wedding around the world. All the networks. Germany. Japan. Everywhere. We had three edit suites in the basement of the Basilica.

"We were offered a lot of money to make that video for sale commercially," said Metz. "Wayne wanted it to be private. It's stayed private."

The reception was a lot of fun.

Alan Thicke noted that the Gretzky wedding had been compared to the Royal Wedding of Lady Diana and Prince Charles, and said that was why Gretzky had his hair cut.

"So his ears would look bigger."

Thicke added another line:

"Mark Messier was always referred to as having the best body in hockey. Now that has to be Janet. She's kind of Messier with speed bumps."

He had another zinger:

"We all have warm memories of this wedding, such as Peter Pocklington being outside scalping the last few tickets to the wedding."

Mio thanked Wayne "for having me as his best man. I've had more press in the last 11 days than in the last 11 years."

It was a wonderful wedding. And it looked for all the world as if Wayne, Janet and Edmonton would live happily ever after.

THE SALE OF THE CENTURY

It was Wayne Gretzky's wedding day. Eddie Mio was doing his duty as best man, getting the groom to the church on time.

"We were on the way to the church when Wayne looked at me," said Mio.

" 'Eddie, I'm getting traded out of here. I'm not going to be here,' Wayne told me. On the way to the church."

Mio looked at Gretzky and played it perfectly, considering the situation.

" 'Wayne, you're getting married. Don't even think about it. Enjoy the day,' I told him.

"I didn't believe it. I didn't think it was possible to take Wayne away from Edmonton. I just didn't think anything like that could happen. No way."

Don Metz, the now high-profile Edmonton video maker who filmed their wedding, couldn't believe his ears either.

"A few days after their wedding I drove Wayne and Janet to the airport. They were in the back seat in my Suburban," said Metz.

"I was chatting with Wayne, looking at him in the rear-view mirror.

" 'When do I see you again?' I asked.

" 'How does Oct. 5 sound?' said Gretzky.

"Oct. 5? What about training camp?"

" 'I don't think so,' said Wayne, looking out the window.

"I asked him who he'd play for. He kept looking out the window. For those four or five seconds it felt like time stopped. And I knew better than to ask again."

99 TEARS: Wayne Gretzky couldn't hold back his emotions at the Edmonton press conference where it was confirmed he was heading to L.A.

A DONE DEAL: Peter Pocklington, left, and Wayne Gretzky face the media at Molson House on Aug. 9, 1988.

Gretzky's dad Walter said it was all telegraphed to him.

"I knew Wayne was getting traded days before he did because Nelson Skalbania phoned me and asked, 'How much does Wayne make?' I said, 'Why?' He said because Peter's shopping him to the highest bidder. I said, 'No, he's not.' He said, 'Yes, he is.' That was during the 1988 Stanley Cup finals.

"Then a couple of days after they won, Wayne said, 'You know, dad, I'm going to shop around for a house in Edmonton.' And I told him, 'You better forget that, they're shopping you.

"He said no they're not. I said yes they are."

It wasn't as if the idea had never come up before, though.

The first time the subject of selling Gretzky came up was after his first year in the league. Just days earlier he'd won his first Hart Trophy.

"He ain't for sale," said Pocklington that day. "I've had huge offers from U.S. teams for Wayne. It doesn't matter. You can't put a price tag on him. He isn't for sale. He's Edmonton property and hopefully the longevity of his career will match Gordie Howe."

Howe had retired a week earlier at age 52.

The story went away for another day.

The year Gretzky won his first Stanley Cup it was out there again.

The headline over my column that day was "Broadway Wayne?"

"Wayne Gretzky to the New York Rangers for $18 million, so Peter Pocklington can save Fidelity Trust? That's the rumour. Repeat, rumour.

"Gus Badali, Gretzky's agent, was tipped on it from a source in Calgary who called his Toronto office. Badali reacted by putting in a call to Pocklington.

"Mike Barnett of the Sierra Sports Group, which manages Gretzky's

endorsements, says he's heard it 'six or eight times' in the last 48 hours."

Pocklington, at the time, was running for the leadership of the Progressive Conservative party in an attempt to become prime minister of Canada.

"Nonsense," screamed Pocklington at the rumour reports.

"Wayne is more valuable to me than the family jewels. I'd never sell him. Never is a long time in my life but I'd never sell him. It's absolutely false. I promised Edmonton on Day 1 that Wayne Gretzky would be here for 20 years and nothing has changed. Trade Gretzky to New York for $18 million, eh? If I traded Gretzky out of Canada, nobody would vote for me."

Pocklington said it was political dirty tricks.

"Who started the rumour? Joe Clark? Or the Calgary Flames? If I were a betting man, I'd bet it was Joe Clark's people. But if it was the Flames, that's just as bad."

Gretzky handled that rumour like any other curve ball thrown his way.

"It doesn't bother me," he said. "When you are in the public eye, there are always going to be rumours like this.

"All I know is that for five years I've worked hard and did the best I could for the Edmonton Oilers and I honestly believe they'd tell me before they'd trade me. It doesn't bother me. It won't affect me in the playoffs."

The story went away for yet another day.

It came back again a few days after Gretzky hit the 1,000-point mark.

This time it came from Harold Ballard, the owner of the Toronto Maple Leafs.

"I asked how much Gretzky would cost and I was told $18 million,"

NO MORE DENYING IT: Oilers general manager Glen Sather had trouble believing the Gretzky trade rumours had become reality.

Ballard told me for publication in *The Edmonton Sun.*

"I know they tried New York. Pocklington will deny it. But I know they tried New York. And he asked me once."

Pocklington denied it.

"Happy Harold has obviously lost all his marbles," said the Oilers owner. "He belongs to me and I expect he always will. It's absolute rubbish."

Again the story went away.

Every once in a while a story would surface and then disappear. It had the effect of the boy who yelled wolf.

But the number always stayed the same. The number, in every substantiated report and in most of the unsubstantiated reports, was $18 million.

The last time the story was emphatically denied was under my by-line on Aug. 4, 1988.

"The rumour has been running rampant for days: Wayne Gretzky to the Los Angeles Kings for $18 million."

That was my first paragraph.

It was followed by the denial paragraphs.

"There's nothing to it," said Glen Sather. "Every summer it's a differ-

Oilers owner Peter Pocklington managed to put on a happy face on a sad day in Edmonton's hockey history.

ent rumour. This one goes in the same bin as all the other ones. Put it in with the ones about him going to the New York Rangers, the Vancouver Canucks and the Calgary Flames. I don't even know where Wayne and Janet are. If there were anything like that I assume Peter would let me know. There is nothing to it."

Five days later ...

Most Canadians remember where they were when they heard. Like most people remember where they were when John F. Kennedy was as-

sassinated or when man landed on the moon.

On Aug. 9, 1988, Wayne Douglas Gretzky was sold to the Los Angeles Kings for $18 million Cdn.

I remember where I was. I wasn't there. After covering most of the magic memory-making moments of Gretzky's career, that was the one I missed.

I was in the Ozark Mountains. I'd taken Sather's emphatic denial at face value and taken my son Shane on a holiday en route to Kansas City for a homestand of his favourite baseball team, the Kansas City Royals.

It was a combination birthday and high school graduation present. I don't know why, maybe I had a premonition. I wasn't listening to the radio as I drove out of the Ozarks in the general direction of Kansas City. But when we stopped for soft drinks in a tiny town called Aurora, Missouri, and my son wanted to play a video game, for no real reason I called the office. The people at *The Sun* informed me they were in the process of trying to find me in hotels in six different states when I called. I checked into a hotel in Joplin, Missouri, and wrote the following while my son listened to the Royals game on the car radio.

"Shock. Outrage. Anger. None of those emotions quite cover it, do they? The emotions we're dealing with here are not unlike those of a death in the family. A death not by natural causes.

"Wayne Gretzky is more than the greatest player in the history of hockey. He is more than the most dominant team-sport athlete in history. He's that to the world. But to Edmonton, Wayne Gretzky was our mark on the map. This morning our city can only be in a state of mourning.

"Babe Ruth was once traded from the Boston Braves to the New York Yankees. I can't think of anything else that can compare. And, really, even that doesn't do it. Babe Ruth wasn't Babe Ruth then. He hadn't put up the numbers that, to this day, separate him from everybody else who has played the game. He hadn't won the World Series four times yet. He wasn't in his prime, at the very peak of his career.

"This, unquestionably, is the biggest deal in hockey history. This, arguably, is the biggest deal in the history of professional sport.

"Was it for love? Or money?

"How did it happen?

"You can believe what you want. I know what I believe. With every bone in my body, I know what I believe.

"I know the first reaction is to finger the blushing bride. She stole our Wayne away. You can believe, if you wish, all the white-knight stuff about doing what Wayne wanted. I don't buy it. I believe the suggestion that the whole thing was Wayne Gretzky's idea was quite likely a crock."

I fingered Peter Pocklington.

The Edmonton Sun's coverage was incredible the next day. And the front-page headline, written by sports editor Phil Rivers, will be remembered almost as long as the day will be remembered: "99 Tears."

On the cover of the collectors' item which was the Aug. 10, 1988 edition of *The Sun* there was the picture of Gretzky dabbing his tears. The only other words on the front page were these: "Pages 2, 3, 4, 5, 6, 10, 11, 18, 19, 23, 30, 36, 37, 38, 39, 40, 41, 42, 43, 46 and 47."

Peter Pocklington had finally done the dirty deed. He sold Gretzky to Bruce McNall of the Los Angeles Kings.

Only 14 months earlier the Oilers had signed Gretzky to a new contract.

"Today, Wayne Gretzky is the highest-paid player in hockey," his new Edmonton-based financial adviser Ian Barrigan had announced then.

For the first time Gretzky was making more than a million dollars. That contract wiped out the one he'd signed on his 18th birthday. The one that expired in 1999. The one that he started to sign "Bob Smith" on the advice of a teammate but changed in mid-B to make a W.

It had been ridiculous for a few years with Gretzky making a lot less than a lot of players. But when they ripped up the old deal and did the new one, everybody was happy. And the phrase "depreciating asset"

A teary Wayne Gretzky manages a choked up thumbs-up.

The front page of *The Edmonton Sun* after the unthinkable happened.

wouldn't even be mentioned for more than a year.

In the end, other than the 18 big ones, Peter Pocklington ended up using that as the business reason behind his "bad deal."

At the press conference at Molson House in Edmonton, they were calling it a trade. For years afterward Glen Sather, who usually changed the subject when it all came up, called it a trade. But when Pocklington ceased being the Oilers owner, Sather spit it out.

"It was not a trade. It was a sale. It was all about money."

Ten years after the fact, with Pocklington out of the picture, on the anniversary of the "trade" Sather finally spilled the whole story from his side.

"I took Wayne into a room with just the two of us at Molson House," he said. "I talked to him for a few minutes. I told him I'd stop the deal. I told him I'd tell Peter I'd resign if he didn't stop the deal. But Wayne decided not to because he felt it was all beyond repair at that point.

"I was the last to know," swore Sather 10 years after the fact. "We went to the Arctic fishing. I think everybody on the Arctic trip knew about the deal except for me. When that was over Peter invited me to President Ford's golf tournament in Beaver Creek, Colorado. That's when he told me. I got on the phone to Bruce McNall from there. That's when I began to understand that the deal was already done.

"Peter was afraid to tell me. And I don't blame him. Mike Krushelnyski and Marty McSorley were already part of the deal. Gretzky had made sure he made them part of the package. By the time I got involved, I got Martin Gelinas and Jimmy Carson and the draft picks out of McNall by convincing him I'd queer the deal. But to me it didn't matter. It didn't make any difference. It would still be the same."

That there were other people involved in the Gretzky sale didn't change the impact in Edmonton, or anywhere else in the hockey world.

"Thank God I believe in life after death. Are the police on call out there?" John Mucker told *The Sun*'s Dick Chubey from his off-season home in Providence, Rhode Island, that day.

"It's like ripping the heart out of the city," said then Edmonton mayor Laurence Decore.

A Detroit newspaper ran an editorial page cartoon depicting a solitary skater on the ice. On the jersey was No. 99. In the background a Canadian flag flew at half-mast. And right in the middle of the red Maple Leaf, a heart had been carved out. Look closer and the heart was actually a puck on the end of a stick.

KING OF KINGS: Wayne Gretzky smiles for the cameras with his new owner, Bruce McNall of the Los Angeles Kings.

"I'd like to say I saw it coming," said Don Cherry. "But I must admit it. I thought Wayne Gretzky would never leave Edmonton. It's very hard for me to believe."

The headline on Graham Hicks' column was "Jezebel Janet!"

Everybody was a story. McSorley and Krushelnyski. Jimmy Carson and Martin Gelinas, the two Kings who became Oilers.

The Sun's Ottawa bureau filed a story on NDP House leader Nelson Riis "demanding the Mulroney government immediately block the Gretzky trade."

There was even a story on Joey Moss, the mentally disabled brother of Gretzky's old girlfriend Vikki Moss, for whom Wayne found work in the Oilers dressing room.

BACK IN BLACK: Gretzky's return to Edmonton as The Opposition proved highly emotional for him, his former teammates and thousands of loyal fans.

Obviously this wasn't anything on the order of your usual news story which has a "here it comes, here it is, there it goes" lifespan.

The next day Pocklington went on record as saying he didn't think Gretzky's tears at the press conference were real.

"Wayne has an ego the size of Manhattan," said Pocklington. "He's a great actor."

Best man Mio went on the record as saying there was no way Gretzky had asked for the trade.

"Gretzky never initiated any deal. Wayne loves Edmonton. He never wanted to leave. It's really important people know this wasn't Wayne and Janet's idea."

Paul Coffey seconded that motion.

"I talked with Wayne after the Stanley Cup and he said, 'I'm happy. I'll play here forever.' "

Sather had very little to say. Gretzky was refusing to say anything.

But Janet Jones-Gretzky, fuming about the way it was being perceived in places, phoned me in Kansas City and said there was no way she was going to let her husband sit silent and go down in hockey history as an egomaniac and a Canadian treasure-turned-traitor.

"Peter Pocklington is the reason Wayne Gretzky is no longer an Edmonton Oiler," she began.

"The key to everything that happened was an event five days after our wedding. Pocklington gave Bruce Mc-Nall permission to take Wayne if he could do it. And that did it!

"I never intended to talk. But let's talk. The story of the trade as presented by Peter Pocklington is false. Pocklington is the reason Wayne is gone. I know the real story. I know the whole story. I know Wayne

didn't deserve any of this. He wouldn't let Edmonton fans, Canada and, most important, his teammates down without good reason.

"Wayne speaks from the heart. People who aren't good at lying aren't good at lying. The tears that came out were not all an act. To see Wayne hurt like this hurts me. That's why I'm making the call to you.

"This is what happened. The day after the Stanley Cup, Pocklington told Wayne about an offer from Vancouver. Wayne said to Pocklington: 'I can't believe you coming to me with this the day after we win the Stanley Cup.' It was obvious Peter did not have Wayne's backing and he backed out of the Vancouver deal.

"Before the wedding, Wayne had heard so many rumours about being traded and sold he asked Pocklington about them. Pocklington suggested Wayne come to his office and talk about it. He told Wayne there was nothing to them. Wayne told me, 'Janet, all the rumours are false.' This was the day before our wedding. I brought my car to Edmonton. We had every intention of living the rest of our lives in Edmonton.

"Five days after the wedding, Wayne got a call from Bruce McNall. He told Wayne that he had talked to Pocklington and Peter had told him, 'If you can swing him over, you've got him.' "

Ten years later, on the anniversary, Gretzky looked back.

"It's the hardest thing I've ever been through. I think about it a lot still. I don't think there's an Aug. 9 that's gone by when I haven't thought about it. It still seems like yesterday, not like 10 years. And it was something I thought would never end.

"At the time we were the cream of the crop. We'd just won

GONE, BUT NOT FORGOTTEN: The Gretzkys take in an Eskimos CFL game during a return visit to Edmonton (above). Top right, Mike Barnett, Joey Moss and Walter Gretzky enjoy a tribute night at the Coliseum, where Wayne received a mini-version of his statue (below) and showed off his daughter, Paulina (right).

our fourth Stanley Cup. And I played as well as I ever played in that final. Then, all of a sudden, things happen. And, unfortunately, it all ended a little too quick.

"I've said it many times in private but not in public until now," he said in our interview on the anniversary. "But because of that day, playing in Edmonton has never been a good feeling for me. I look in the crowd and I see all the faces. The fans felt like my friends. I skate on the ice in Edmonton and still see those faces and it's difficult to this day for me to play in Edmonton.

"I'll tell you one thing I'll go to my grave believing: There may have been better teams that have won the Stanley Cup, but those Edmonton teams were the most exciting teams ever to win it. That team had so much emotion, energy and excitement."

Ten years later and he was still having trouble talking about it. That day, despite the way he publicly appeared to stand in support of his owner, Glen Sather was working the other way behind the scenes.

"Glen really wanted me to stay," he said. "It became an even bigger decision."

Sather said it didn't have to happen in 1988. Or 1989. Or 1990. Or maybe even 1991.

"If the team had been a separate entity, if Peter was not involved in the other businesses, I think we could have kept that team together for quite a while longer.

"It was so close-knit. And they could all see the things they could accomplish together historically.

"I know we would have won more than one more Stanley

Cup. Probably two or three. We were too good at that point. I think, financially, we would have been able to keep that team together another three or four years."

Sather isn't saying what the dollars would have been like in the game today. Gretzky going to L.A. was the upward spiral that started it all.

"McNall was giving money away as if it didn't mean anything," said Sather. "Because it didn't mean anything."

After scoring 583 goals and 1,086 assists for 1,669 points in 696 regular-season games, adding 81 goals and 171 assists for 252 points in 120 playoff games, setting 43 NHL records, winning eight Hart Trophies, seven Art Ross Trophies, four Stanley Cups and two Conn Smythes in nine NHL seasons and one WHA season in Edmonton, Wayne Gretzky was gone.

The memories would stay, of course, but unlike many memories which grow with time, these memories would not grow greater with time because this was one case where that was not possible.

In a year there'd be a statue outside the Coliseum, now Skyreach Centre, of Gretzky holding the Stanley Cup over his head – a reminder to Edmontonians every time they attended an Oilers game that they had watched the greatest player in the history of hockey when he was at his best.

It is only now, after his retirement, that it has become possible to celebrate Wayne Gretzky's greatness in Edmonton as if he'd never gone away.

It's like he put it in our interview on the 10th anniversary of "99 Tears."

"Somehow, some way, I can see myself being connected with the Oilers when it's done.

"I'll always be an Oiler when it's done."

BACK IN BLACK ... AND BLUE

Long before the first snow fell in Edmonton the joke had made the rounds.

Q. What's the temperature in Edmonton?

A. Minus 99.

The 1988-89 hockey season and the foreseeable future, with Wayne Gretzky wearing a Los Angeles Kings uniform, was going to be excruciating for Edmonton and for The Great One.

Both the city and the world's greatest hockey player knew the relationship couldn't be changed by one game or one season. To complicate matters, the 40th NHL All-Star Game had been scheduled for Edmonton that year and Gretzky would come back, sit in his same stall in the dressing room and play on a line with his former teammates. And then there was the matter of the statue ...

Edmonton couldn't just wave goodbye to Gretzky. The city had to do something.

Hanging a banner with his number from the ceiling was out of the question for now and in great doubt for the future.

"Wayne will never agree to having his number retired by the Oilers as long as Peter Pocklington owns the team," Walter Gretzky said that summer.

MEMORABLE MILESTONE: Wayne Gretzky breaks Gordie Howe's record for career points with No. 1,851 in Edmonton on Oct. 15, 1989.

Through my column, in an interview in the summer, Gretzky told Edmonton what he considered the acceptable parameters for a tribute to him. He said he understood, and appreciated, the movement led by former alderman Olivia Butti. But he wanted Edmonton to know how tough this was going to be for him.

He said he didn't want a banner, didn't want the Coliseum named after him, didn't want 99 Street named after him and didn't want a Wayne Gretzky Day. Maybe at the end of his career, something like that ... but definitely not now.

Gretzky said whatever tribute the City of Edmonton had in mind, he was horrified that they thought of doing it on his first game back in town as a member of the Kings.

"I'm honoured ... extremely honoured. I think it's great and I don't want to throw any monkey wrenches into it. But it is all kind of awkward because of the timing. I feel very uncomfortable with any of that because I'm still playing. And the first game would be real tough."

Gretzky's agent Mike Barnett framed it.

"Obviously the city wants to do something to say thanks, and Wayne appreciates that. But the people organizing things shouldn't lose sight of the fact this should be something from the city and from the fans. It has nothing to do with the Oilers and the NHL. Wayne is no longer an Oiler. He's a member of another NHL club."

I told Gretzky most people seemed to think the best idea would be a statue like the one of Roger Bannister in Vancouver or the one of Stan Musial in St. Louis.

"Something like that," said No. 99, "would be fine."

Wife Janet, Gordie Howe and Mark Messier (below, left) congratulate Wayne on setting the record for most career points.

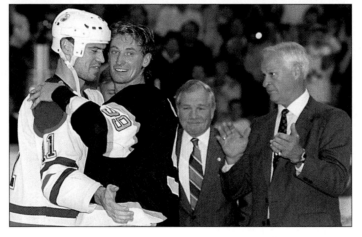

Gretzky's Edmonton tribute and the unveiling of his statue would, it was finally decided, happen the next off-season. But there was oh-so-much for everybody to go through before they got to that point.

First, Gretzky had to move. It was the week before the Kings opened training camp in Victoria that he returned to Edmonton. Wayne didn't allow any photographs to be taken as he packed boxes and removed the pictures from the walls of his penthouse apartment. He figured any pictures of him moving would probably rub salt in the wounds of Edmonton fans, and he was probably right.

Gretzky then went to a rink to skate with his old Oilers teammates and other Edmonton-based NHLers who got together every year to get into skating shape before they headed to training camp.

Soon enough the season would start and Gretzky would be skating in another uniform.

The introductions at Gretzky's first Los Angeles game, by Kings play-by-play man Bob Miller, provided a memorable moment.

Gretzky was the last King introduced.

"Acquired August 9th in the trade of the century ..." was about all anyone heard as a crowd of 16,005 rose to give Gretzky a one-minute standing ovation.

The town that used to chant "Gretzky sucks!" was now chanting "Gretzky! Gretzky! Gretzky!"

Meanwhile, back in Edmonton, the Stanley Cup banner was being raised.

"I'm sure there wasn't a person in the building who wasn't thinking about him as it was being raised," said new Oilers captain Mark Messier.

"I think it was the first time in this kind of ceremony that I've got choked up," said Kevin Lowe. "It went through my mind that he'd be watching on TV."

Gretzky, who before the season started signed an eight-year contract for $15 million US, scored his first goal as a Los Angeles King in his first shot on goal in his first game. And just to juice up the story a bit, the goal came against the Detroit Red Wings' Greg Stefan, the kid who'd been his goalie on that Nadrofsky Steelers team when he was a kid in Brantford.

Gretzky's first game in a Los Angeles Kings uniform, however, was not the media event circled on most calendars. The one that drew the crowd was the home-and-home date the Oilers and Kings were scheduled to play, beginning in Edmonton on Oct. 19.

The media mob met Gretzky in Calgary where he played two nights earlier. And No. 99 made it perfectly clear then and there that while he wasn't looking forward to playing the Edmonton Oilers, he couldn't wait to wear the Los Angeles Kings uniform in Edmonton in front of Peter Pocklington, the owner who'd sold him, accused him of shedding phoney tears, and said he had an ego the size of Manhattan.

"For 10 years the organization was really nice to me. At times, when I needed help it was there. What spoiled it was the final day," said Gretzky. "The way it was handled ... some of the things that were said ... it left a sour taste in my mouth. I'm sure it'll inspire me. I don't get mad, I get even.

"But I'm not looking forward to it. I'm not looking forward to it at all. I have a lot of friends there. That city was great for me for 10 years. I always enjoyed the building, the ice surface, the people and the atmosphere. So, no. I'm not looking forward to it. It's going to seem strange. But I'm going to have to put my head down and go. It'll be tough, but once the puck is dropped we're just playing hockey again."

Only months earlier *The Sun* headline was "99 Tears."

If there was any question of whether Gretzky should be met with cheers or jeers, there was very little doubt left by the time the game started.

"If it feels good, do it" was the advice of the Oilers who, clearly, didn't want Gretzky to return to town and be booed. The Oilers were cheering for cheers.

"I hope they do (cheer)," said Craig MacTavish. "He deserves it. He's done a lot. This is a night for memories and he's been part of them all."

Kevin Lowe agreed.

"If the fans cheer for him and not us, I don't think the players will take it personally," he said.

Mark Messier wouldn't go that far.

"We expect everybody to cheer for him, but I'd be disappointed if they cheered for Los Angeles."

It would be the first time in hockey history, perhaps, that 234 media representatives would come to cover a crowd.

What would the Edmonton fans do? How would they react? Would they bring down the building for him? Or would they restrain themselves because that was then and now he's them? That was the story.

"This isn't like any other game for any of us, the players or the fans," said Lowe. "There's so much emotion involved. All the hype is deserved. I know Wayne is dreading this, but I find it kind of exciting. This is great for the game. This is the first time I've really seen an NHL game promoted like this. The TV commercials are like for the World Series or the Super Bowl."

Messier said this one game couldn't compare with the other 839 NHL games that season.

"Everybody's emotions are the biggest thing. The fans have to have a great deal of emotion. There's sorrow. There's every emotion. He's Wayne Gretzky. He's the greatest player who ever played the game. And he's a friend.

"It's definitely a big day for hockey and a big day for Edmonton. He gave Edmonton 10 pretty awesome years. It's going to be pretty hard not to make a fuss over him. He was instrumental in us winning four Stanley Cups. He put Edmonton on the map."

When he arrived in Edmonton with the Kings, the media contingent was so large Gretzky was forced to hold a pre-game press conference.

"This one is going to be pretty hard on me, pretty hard on the Oilers and pretty hard on the Oiler fans," he said.

"There are a lot of emotions involved here. The things you think about now that this game is here are all the memories and all the fun. We had something that very few teams ever had. We were the Green Bay Packers of our time. We were in a small city and we grew up together and we had a great relationship with each other and the city. Those are the things I'm thinking about. Every other game I've ever gone into, I've disliked the other team because I've wanted to win so badly. This one will be different."

Before the game Gretzky visited Joey Moss. He took the Oilers locker-room attendant out and bought him a bacon-cheeseburger at a local sports bar called Bleachers.

"I don't think he'll ever understand," said Wayne.

"Down the drain without Wayne," read one of the signs in the Coliseum that night.

"I'm mad as hell and I'm not going to ticket any more," read another.

"The tears have dried but your magic and Peter Pocklington's betrayal will never be forgotten," read yet another.

There were signs with half a Kings logo and half an Oilers logo, a caricature of Peter Pocklington as "The grinch who stole No. 99." And there were dozens of simple ones with messages like "We love you."

The people that never had a chance to say goodbye tried to pay Wayne Gretzky off for a million memories as they rode an emotional roller coaster

Gretzky's first game as a King, vs. Vancouver.

King Gretzky acknowledges cheers from his faithful Edmonton fans.

to nowhere that night.

When he stepped on the ice for the pre-game warmup, several hundred fans crowded behind the L.A. bench. They applauded him when he appeared. They applauded him again when he left.

Gretzky kept peeking at the Oilers as he skated during the warmup.

Was he "looking back to see if they were looking back at me?"

They weren't. The Oilers went out of their way to not sneak a peek, it seemed.

"I didn't talk to anybody and nobody talked to me," he said.

The minute the Kings started to file onto the ice for the game, the ovation began. The Oilers organization played canned music dialled to the limit but when Gretzky appeared the fans drowned it out. The PA announcer fought to introduce anthem singer Tim Feehan as early as possible and finally succeeded after four minutes.

"To come to that ovation ... it was a great feeling," said Gretzky. "Words can not describe it."

When Gretzky stepped over the boards for his first shift, he was given another 30-second standing ovation. The first time he touched the puck, they let loose again.

You could feel the crowd wanted to explode just once for a Great Gretzky goal when, late in the second period, he slid one through the crease and again in the final minute when he hit the post.

In the end, the Oilers had an 8-6 win and Gretzky had a goal-less and, for him, very quiet game.

"In fairness to Wayne, maybe this was too much for him emotionally," said Lowe.

Breaking up is hard to do and Gretzky didn't make it any easier when the two teams travelled to Los Angeles a few days later to do it all over again.

He invited the entire team to his $2.7-million house three doors down from Michael Jackson's place, before the second game of the Homecoming and Home Series.

His wife Janet told me, after the team had left, that her husband hadn't left his last tear in Edmonton.

"He was teary-eyed when we drove up to our house and all the other guys were standing there," Mrs. 99 reported.

"He loves those guys so much you can just see it pulling his heartstrings when they're around.

"It was a great night. He really enjoyed having them all over. You could just see that it's going to be a long, long time before he doesn't have a soft spot for all those guys. Wayne wants very much for them to still be friends off the ice."

This game wasn't going to be as difficult but it was still an event.

"It's the first time we've ever come here and the players haven't had enough tickets to go around," said MacTavish.

One tour group from Edmonton bought 500 tickets.

"What we're going through here is really a divorce," said co-coach John

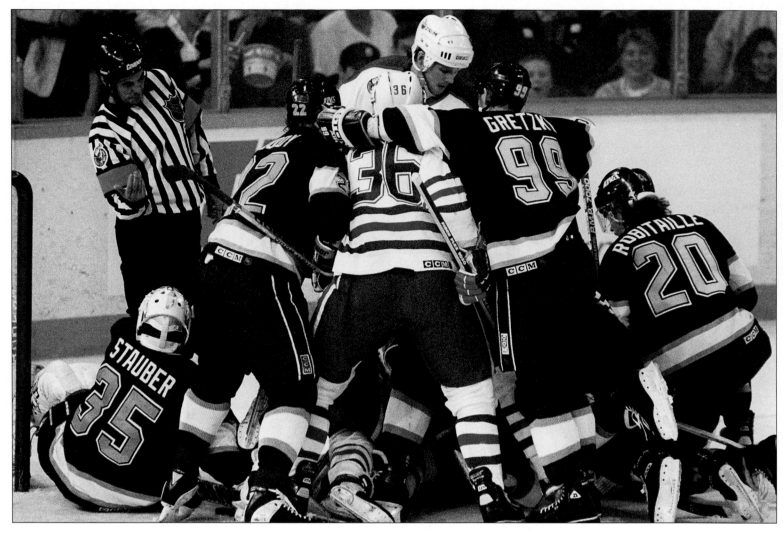

KINGS-SIZED PILEUP: Gretzky and Los Angeles teammates tangle with the Oilers. Below, No. 99 visits with Joey Moss.

Muckler. "Sooner or later you put your life together and go on. Time heals all wounds."

Again, Gretzky didn't get a goal. But Game 2 of the Back-to-Back Back-in-Black Series, as I called it, was much easier.

"No comparison," said Gretzky. "I don't think it's ever going to feel normal. But this was nothing compared to going back there for the first time."

Again the Oilers won, the time 5-4, and it was Jimmy Carson, who came to Edmonton in the Gretzky deal, who scored the prettiest goal of the game.

The Oilers were able to get on with it for a while. But then there was the all-star game in Edmonton in February 1989, arguably the most special all-star game Gretzky ever played (see Chapter 18).

And then came the playoffs.

It was Gretzky again.

Edmonton vs. Los Angeles.

Gretzky scored 54 goals and added 114 assists for 168 points to win the Hart Trophy in his first season with the Kings and led the club from the depths of the league to finish with a 42-31-7 record, second in the Smythe Division and ahead of the Oilers.

The series was compelling in Canada. But in the beginning, L.A. took no notice.

For the first time in the 21 years of the franchise the Kings were opening the playoffs at home and the *Los Angeles Times* didn't have one word on the series the day the Oilers arrived.

It was the middle of a heat wave. The temperature was 104 F (40 C) the day the series opened.

The series was tied 1-1 when it returned to much cooler Edmonton. And it was on that Coliseum ice surface where Gretzky had woven his greatest magic when it happened: the freeze-frame of the Oilers' playoff year.

Midway through the second period, Mark Messier ran over Gretzky and left his old friend a perplexed pretzel on the ice.

"Obviously we're going to have to put our friendship aside," said Messier.

"They definitely cut the cord tonight and it was great to see," said Sather.

The Oilers won Game 4 and headed back to Los Angeles one win from putting Gretzky and his new playmates away.

At poolside of the Airport Marriott before Game 5, Messier and I talked at length. In what should have been an upbeat, positive time, I didn't have to possess special powers to see that it wasn't. Not for Messier. While he'd hit Gretzky hard in Game 3, it was quite clear that it was Messier who was hurting on the inside. And sitting there, waiting for Game 5 and a chance to put Gretzky out of play, he poured his heart out.

"This is no damn fun," he said.

"It just doesn't seem right.

"Obviously, I have responsibilities to the guys on my team now and to the Oilers organization. But I can honestly say it hasn't been real enjoyable.

"I just want to get this series over with. I've played with this guy so long. We've been so close. I'm godfather to his daughter Paulina. To go out there and slam his head through the boards isn't easy. It's the most difficult thing I've ever had to do."

Somewhere between the series starting and then coming back to the Fabulous Forum, something had happened.

Suddenly, Hollywood had discovered the Kings. Tom Hanks was at the game. Dudley Moore. Mary Fran. Larry Mann. John Candy.

The Kings won, went back to Edmonton and won again, and came home and won Game 7 to become only the sixth team in Stanley Cup playoff history to come from behind three games to one and win a series.

Gretzky the L.A. King vowed he'd never forget Edmonton.

"I feel deeply sorry for the Edmonton players, especially Mark and Kevin," said Gretzky. "I wanted to talk to them, but I couldn't. No one takes losing as hard as those two guys. We beat the best playoff team in the league."

The Calgary Flames, the NHL's best team that regular season with 117 points, dispatched Gretzky and his new gang in four straight games, then went on to be part of the seventh straight final on Alberta ice, defeating Montreal in six games for the Stanley Cup.

Gretzky had five goals, 17 assists and 22 points in his first 11 playoff games as a King.

The unveiling of the Gretzky statue was scheduled for the Coliseum in late August 1989. The Oilers refused to participate in any way. Glen Sather and Peter Pocklington did not attend, nor did anyone in the organization.

More than 14,000 people were on hand and Gretzky had no better idea than any of them what his statue was going to look like.

"I have no clue," he said. "All I can tell you is that I was very happy when I heard that it was going to be a pose with the Stanley Cup, because that's what this team was all about."

Gretzky said his agent, Mike Barnett, was involved with the Edmonton people in the planning.

"The theory was that if they got the nose right and the number right, they couldn't miss," said Barnett. "I haven't had a great deal of experience assessing an 18-foot-high statue. All I know is whether it's bang on or not, it isn't going to score 1,852 points."

Gretzky said he was a mess when he woke up that day.

"When I got up this morning I was honestly more nervous that I've ever been in my life. I've never been that nervous for anything. I wasn't that nervous when I got married. I wasn't that nervous for a Stanley Cup final. I wasn't that nervous for *Saturday Night Live*. Man, I was a nervous wreck."

He had trouble explaining it, except to point out that he was still alive, he was only 28 years old and there was about to be a statue unveiled of him. Even for the most honoured player in hockey history, it was something that didn't compute.

"I don't think I'd be lying if I said I was a little embarrassed, too," is how he put it.

Gretzky was brought into the Coliseum for a tour of the

building in a convertible and rode around waving under the spotlights.

He took the same tour with his daughter Paulina in his arms at the end of the affair.

Then mayor Terry Cavanagh declared it Wayne Gretzky Day with eight hours and 32 minutes left in the day.

Gretzky received a 99-page photo album and an oil painting titled "The Parting" by artist Joan Healy. Molson gave him the Molson Cup he'd won for nine straight seasons. No. 99 also received an 18-inch replica statue. Another three versions of the replica statue became trophies for Edmonton's minor hockey association.

Speaking to the crowd after the unveiling, Gretzky struggled to find the right words.

"I was very proud. I was thrilled. It felt wonderful," he said.

"I'll never forget Edmonton. It will always be part of my life. It's going to be hard to come in here to play now. Harder."

It wasn't until the crowd had cleared that he really had a handle on how he felt.

He said he purposely avoided reminiscing so as to not get mushy and gushy.

"I tried not to reflect. It would have been too emotional."

He looked up at the statue behind him.

"I think it looks pretty close. I think it's wonderful."

The statue was placed in front of the Coliseum.

So now Gretzky was gone and life could go on, right?

Not so fast.

Gretzky had one more game to play before he could really begin to go away.

Again, that sense of stage that existed throughout Gretzky's career was in play. And you just knew how it was going to work out.

Gretzky was on the verge of breaking Gordie Howe's record of 1,850 career points. And one look at the schedule and you knew where and when it was going to happen.

Edmonton. Oct. 15, 1989.

The buildup began five days earlier in Los Angeles.

It was 11:30 a.m. and Gretzky and Howe sat side-by-side at a huge press conference to discuss the fall of one of North America's most remarkable sports records.

Gretzky, in his 11th season, was headed into his next game, against the New York Islanders, eight points away from breaking Howe's 26-years-in-the-making record of 1,850.

"It's basically down to where I thought it would be," said Gretzky. "Here, Vancouver on Friday and Edmonton on Sunday."

Gretzky, having scored 1,669 of his points for the Oilers, admitted the thought of doing it in Edmonton added drama and spice. Pressure, too.

"I think going back for that game in Edmonton, with the chance of him breaking the record there, is really playing on his mind," said teammate Larry Robinson. "He wouldn't be human if it wasn't."

Howe said he'd travel to Vancouver and Edmonton and back to Los Angeles. He'd stick with Gretzky until No. 99 put his record away.

Gretzky said other than the Edmonton part of

it, he expected the countdown to be much the same as when Phil Esposito was following him around for the breaking of Espo's record.

"I know the point will come, so there's no pressure in that regard," said Wayne.

"I'll get the points but having Gordie and the media following me around, I'd like to get it done so they can get on with their lives."

Howe, during the game in Los Angeles, looked up at the roof.

"I just wanted to see if there were any up there," he said.

"Any what?"

"Balloons," said No. 9.

"What?" I asked.

"I was a little slow getting it. Real slow. I was in no hurry at all," Howe said as he started to tell the story.

"Up in the rafters of the Detroit Olympia they had a whole bunch of balloons they were going to release when I broke the record. They must have been up there for a couple of weeks. When I finally did it, most of the air had gone out of them. They came down like a bunch of blobs."

Gretzky had a goal and two assists to bring the number down to five. It still looked like Edmonton.

"More and more," said Gretzky.

Gretzky needed one to tie and two to break after the game in Vancouver.

I returned from covering the World Series for one day, a one-day road trip to Edmonton, along with a Los Angeles-area sports columnist.

The crowd had come to cheer for Gretzky yet again. The agony of anticipation built all night. There was exquisite split-personality tension involved. The hoping that it would happen in Edmonton. The hoping it wouldn't cost the Oilers a hockey game. And then you could see the crowd say the heck with it as time ticked away and they were left with a last-minute hope that maybe one last time they'd sit in on Wayne Gretzky making hockey history in the Coliseum.

It wasn't enough for The Great One to break Howe's record on the ice he used to own. He waited until 5.3 seconds remained in the game to get a goal to send it to overtime. Then he scored the winner in overtime!

"I don't know who writes his scripts," said Howe.

"There is no end to his brilliance."

Gretzky assisted on a goal by Bernie Nicholls early in the first period to get within one.

Gretzky had his bell rung after firing four shots on goal in the first period.

"I almost didn't play the third period," he said.

The Kings didn't get much going until Los Angeles pulled netminder Mario Gosselin in the final minute.

"Everybody's been guessing how it would happen, whether it would be

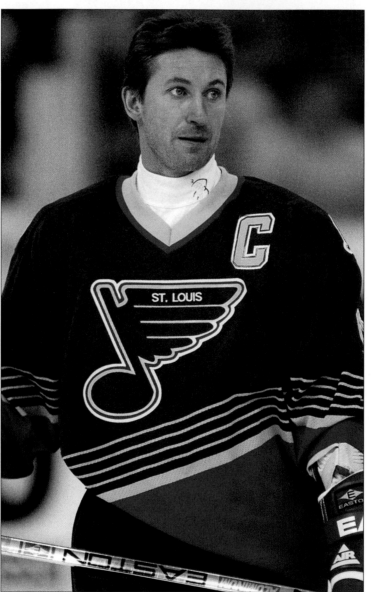

Gretzky's days in St. Louis were short-lived. He only played 18 regular-season games with the Blues.

a goal or an assist," said Gretzky. "I kinda figured it would be a goal. I kinda figured it would be on a backhand. I've scored an awful lot of goals on the backhand ... and here's two more.

"I usually don't go out front. Something told me to get out there.

"It was fitting that I did it here. It was only fitting that the Edmonton fans, who were so great to me, were able to see it."

Gretzky was amazed the way it went with the Edmonton fans. With 1:46 left to go, they decided they cared more about history than the win and began the chant, starting in the upper deck and moving around the building.

"Gretzky! Gretzky! Gretzky!"

Howe, sitting with L.A. Kings owner Bruce McNall, was with the crowd.

"When we got to the last minute, Gordie said, 'Watch this. Watch this last minute because Wayne has that extra gear he gets into. He's going to do it.' "

And then it happened. Gretzky! Alone in front! Backhand! He scores!

No. 99 jumped into the arms of Larry Robinson.

For five minutes the fans stood and saluted the man who had put them on the map.

Finally, Coliseum announcer Mark Lewis interrupted to announce the obvious.

"Ladies and gentlemen, we have just witnessed a piece of sports history ... Wayne Gretzky has become the greatest scorer in the 73-year history of the NHL."

The crowd was with Gretzky in overtime and watched him score another one. The winner. In overtime.

"He kept us up late," laughed Howe.

"I think I'm as excited as Wayne's family.

"I thought I knew Wayne pretty well, but he just grew an inch taller. It's really nice to be able to share this honour with him. I have more a sense of something gained than something lost with this record. And with him breaking the record in the style he broke it ... I feel sorry for people who couldn't get tickets to watch this."

Howe was a part of the presentation on the ice. The Kings presented 99 with a crystal hologram engraved with the image of Gretzky. And the Oilers gave him a diamond bracelet with the inscription: "A great man is made up of qualities that meet or make great occasions. Presented in friendship by the Edmonton Oilers Hockey Club, 1989-90."

It was after the record in Edmonton that Oilers fans began to let go ... well, as much as they ever would.

The Oilers themselves had decided to get over it and make another run at the Stanley Cup. And Gretzky was obviously doing something that would have a long-range effect, as the ambassador for the game based out of L.A.

Gretzky, it was clear in his second year, had managed to turn Los Angeles into a hockey town. And Gretzky, it was also clear, was going to benefit greatly from playing in a major U.S. market. He'd already signed big deals with Coca-Cola and Nike and the biggest of the big corporations in America were lining up for him.

"I knew he was like God in Edmonton but I never realized how big he was going to be in the States," said Kings VP Rogie Vachon. "I didn't think he'd compare with the Magic Johnsons, Kareem Abdul-Jabbars or the Michael Jordans of the world, but he fit right in."

Only once in history has a team been last in NHL road attendance one season and first the next season. In 1987-88 the Los Angeles Kings were last with an average road capacity of 77 per cent. The next season, with Gretzky in the lineup, the Kings became the league's best draw at 98 per cent of capacity.

"Every time I walk by a tennis court and see a sign that says 'no ball hockey allowed' it puts a smile on my face," Gretzky would say years later.

Gretzky, in his second season as a Los Angeles King, watched his goals

spect for feeling that way, but that's the emotions of the game.

"Having to adjust to facing Gretzky as an opponent was devastating. It took a year and a half to get back to playing the way you have to play against him. You can't be a spectator. You can't give him room. You have to be physical.

"That first year we didn't do it at all. We had a 3-1 lead and I think we thought, 'Oh, good, we'll be able to win this series without really having any incidents.'

"He came back and basically stuck it down our throats. Scored some big goals and I'll never forget Game 7 in L.A. He had a couple of big plays and the empty-netter at the end, and he did a little celebratory dance down centre ice.

"When we got back in the dressing room, before everyone took all their stuff off, Muckler said, 'Guys, I want you to remember that moment of Wayne dancing in the middle of the Forum. He basically said it's over, he just stuck it down your throats, he embarrassed you and you have to keep that memory in your mind.' "

Wayne Gretzky lies unconscious on the ice after being hammered by former Oilers teammate Kelly Buchberger.

total drop to 40. But his 102 assists, the 10th straight season he'd hit the century mark with helpers, led the league, as did his 142 points. He won another Art Ross Trophy but it was his old buddy Mark Messier who won the Hart.

In the spring of 1990 the Kings won the first-round playoff series against Calgary in six games, two of them without Gretzky. Then, again, they met the Oilers.

Messier swore the feelings that tore at him and his teammates the previous year had evaporated.

"I don't think they enter into it," he said. "All the emotional ties are gone now. It doesn't have anything to do with Wayne now. All that's involved now is to win the series and move another round closer to winning the Stanley Cup. It's the Oilers versus the Kings now, not the Oilers versus Wayne Gretzky."

Gretzky, who had nine points in the four games against the Flames, agreed: "For the first time in two years, I really think it's changed that way."

Years later, Craig Simpson looked back on that.

"The worst moment of my career with him was in the '90 playoffs. We ended up playing against them again. We hit him. We played him physically. He was behind our net, he took a pass, and I ran him. Consciously, I thought, 'I have to play physical on him. I have to hit him.' I hit him pretty hard and I'll never forget, he chased me down the ice, calling me names. He called me a so-and-so and I got back to the bench and just felt devastated.

"I remember talking to Craig MacTavish after and said, 'Oh, man, that was the hardest thing.' You don't ever want a guy you have so much re-

Just in case anybody managed to forget that, Muckler threw out a quote before the series started:

"I'll never forget the enjoyment Wayne Gretzky got last year," Muck said. "It sticks in my mind."

The Oilers won 7-0 and 6-1 at home and, with Gretzky unable to play because of his back, finished off the Kings in L.A. to sweep the series.

The ghost of Gretzky had been exorcised and No. 99 predicted a fifth Stanley Cup for Edmonton.

"They could be pretty much unstoppable," he said.

And they were.

When the Oilers carried the Cup on a foreign ice surface for the first time and returned to the visitors dressing room in the Boston Garden to celebrate, a lot of people expected them to be pounding their chests over winning one without Wayne.

That's not how it was.

"This one is for the G-man," said Kevin Lowe in the dressing room.

"This afternoon Mark and I were in our hotel room and saying, 'Let's win this one for Wayne.' He was a big part of our lives. He was a big part of this whole thing. We followed on his coattails and developed our pride, our abilities and our winning attitude."

Voted top player of the '80s, Gretzky went into the '90s and in October made it, as one headline writer put it, "Into the 21st Century."

He registered his 2,000th point on a long pass to Tony Granato against Winnipeg.

Gretzky, whose own rookie card was getting to be worth a lot of money, joined Kings owner Bruce McNall in the purchase of a Honus Wagner baseball card for $451,000. During the 1990-91 season Gretzky broke his

own NHL record with a 23-game assist streak. He managed at least one point in 73 of the 78 games he played and won yet another scoring title, registering 41 goals, 122 assists and 163 points.

And guess who he met in the playoffs again?

Correct. The Edmonton Oilers.

This time Gretzky was physically healthy. But it didn't matter. The Oilers had become masters of overtime, winning the final two games of a seven-game series against Calgary in overtime and then taking the first three against the Kings to OT, winning two. The Oilers also put away the series with an overtime win in Game 6.

The Kings were forced to play most of one game without Gretzky, who left late in the first period after he was hit on the ear and cut for 25 stitches on a shot by teammate Steve Duchesne. And Esa Tikkanen did a masterful job of shadowing his old teammate in the series, leaving him without a goal for the series.

"There's no better playoff team than Edmonton," said No. 99. "It's disappointing we lost three games in overtime."

Gretzky had 15 more points in the playoffs, including four goals. With Jari Kurri spending a year in Europe, the goals allowed Gretzky to pass his old linemate as the all-time Stanley Cup-playoff goal-scoring leader with 93.

Not long later the big news in hockey was that Kurri was headed to the Kings to ride with Gretzky again.

"We haven't played together for three years but I think we can pick it up quickly," said No. 99 when the deal was announced. "I'm pretty excited."

But the season had barely begun with the two skating together when Gretzky received some bad news. His father, Walter, had a brain aneurism. He spent most of the year unable to recognize people or remember much about Gretzky's career. Wayne was a mess.

"I've got to get my act together," he said in late November. "I haven't played well at all."

He wasn't in the top 50 of point-getters.

As the year wore on and his father's condition began to improve, so did Gretzky's play.

"It'll be a long process, kind of one day at a time," Gretzky final spoke of it. "He's out of danger as far as it being life-threatening. It's a matter of getting his thoughts and memory back. He doesn't know what's going on."

Gretzky had something to cheer about when he showed up in Winnipeg for the 1991 Grey Cup game. A part-owner of the Toronto Argos with John Candy and Bruce McNall, Gretzky's Argos won the Grey Cup.

"A Grey Cup, and our horse won today," said Gretzky of the thoroughbred he and McNall purchased together which had won the $1.2-million Japan Cup.

"I think I may hold Wayne's Grey Cup ring until May," said McNall. "Maybe we can make it a double ring ceremony."

It didn't work that way.

Gretzky, who moved into second place all-time on the goal-scoring charts behind Gordie Howe, ended up with 31 goals, 90 assists and 121 points. It was his 13th consecutive 100-point season. And the 90 assists led the league.

For his fourth straight season in Los Angeles, it was the Oilers again in the playoffs. And Kings coach Tom Webster couldn't resist when he penciled in his starting lineup. Wayne Gretzky. Jari Kurri. Marty McSorley. Paul Coffey. Charlie Huddy. And Edmonton native Kelly Hrudey in goal.

The Oilers won the first game but "The Fab Five," as Webster called his ex-Oilers Gretzky, Kurri, Mc-

Sorley, Coffey and Huddy, were flying in Game 2.

The "Oil Kings" won it 8-5.

"Paul got those first two power-play goals and Gretzky fought through that checking all night. Kurri scored a very big goal. I believe they brought a great deal of pride to the rink tonight," said Webster.

Gretzky had four assists to bring his playoff total to 303.

In Game 5, he finally scored a playoff goal against Edmonton.

It had been 752 minutes and 58 seconds. Including overtime, it had been 41 playoff periods. And when he got one, he got another. L.A. won 5-2 and made it a 3-2 series.

But the Oilers won Game 6, booting the team which had come to be known as Edmonton West out of the playoffs in six games. They headed to the final four for the final time before missing the playoffs for four straight years.

When the 1992-93 season started, Gretzky was watching.

He was stuck at 999 games played and there was real concern he might not play 1,000.

Dr. Robert Watkins, at a press conference in Los Angeles, told the hockey world that Gretzky had a herniated disc and that "this injury has the chance of being a career-ending injury."

Finally, in early January, he was back.

The night before his first game of the season and 1,000th of his career, we talked long-distance via telephone.

"It's not like people think it might have been," said Gretzky. "I went through a few stages. The first stage, when everyone was asking me if I'd ever play again, was actually calm and mellow. I wasn't thinking a lot about hockey. I just wanted to get pain-free.

"When it got tough, when it got really frustrating was when I realized I was on the road to recovery. That's when it was the worst for me, when I was getting ready to play and couldn't.

"Then I hit the stage when I really perked up. That was when it was just a matter of time. That's when I really got excited.

"I've always loved to play. Three months ago they told me I might never play again. Now I can play."

Gretzky missed the first 39 games of the season with the herniated disc. During the year he endured a 16-game run without a goal and ended up with 16 goals, 49 assists and 65 points.

This time the Oilers weren't around for the playoffs. And Gretzky, having played only half a season, was on a tear.

"This is the best hockey I've played in a long time. I've played very well the last four or five games," he said after scoring goals in four consecutive playoff games to lead the Kings past Calgary and Vancouver and win the Smythe Division banner.

Against the Canucks he became the first player to register 100 (and 101) playoff goals.

"It's different for me now because everybody thought I'd died and left the game," Gretzky explained as the Kings opened the Campbell Conference final against the Toronto Maple Leafs.

"This is exciting for me, just like the first time we went to the Stanley Cup in Edmonton."

The Maple Leafs were one win away from making the matchup of all matchups against the Montreal Canadiens the ultimate celebration of the Stanley Cup's anniversary party when Gretzky read somewhere that he looked like he was skating with a piano tied to his back.

But the piano man was still playing and the fat lady wasn't going to sing for a while, either.

It was only seconds after Gretzky had put the puck in the net in overtime to win Game 6 for the Kings by a 5-4 score that Gretzky remembered.

It was that goal that broke Gordie Howe's record for most goals, regular season and playoff combined.

"I have to admit I thought about it," said Gretzky, who answered the "Where's Wayne?" question that had become the series storyline after the first five games.

"I yelled, 'Grab the puck!'

"Jari Kurri was telling me, 'Grab the net!' "

What Gretzky grabbed was a one-game, sudden-death shot at getting back to the Stanley Cup final for the first time since he was an Oiler.

"I couldn't have picked a much bigger goal at a much bigger time," said Gretzky. "I just wanted to make sure when I did something it was big and it was important. I'll take that tonight."

Coach Barry Melrose was happy on a lot of levels, but when it came to his star, he said, "I'm glad for him because people in Toronto, the press there, have been ripping him."

That reference in the *Toronto Star* about Gretzky looking like he was carrying a piano on his back? In Game 7 he played that piano. He played it like he'd never played it before.

It was Gretzky's greatest game.

A 5-4 victory over Toronto in Maple Leaf Gardens, the second straight game where Gretzky scored the winner.

"In my mind, that was maybe the best game I ever played," Gretzky said when it was all over.

"We were an underdog, we were playing on the road and we were playing against not only a team but an entire country. The Montreal Canadiens had already qualified for the Stanley Cup and all of Canada wanted to see the Leafs and Montreal in the finals, and I couldn't blame them."

At the time he was saying, "Not bad for a guy with a piano on his back, eh?"

The line had been written by Bob McKenzie and he became the most recent writer to fire up No. 99.

"The last thing he told me before he went to the rink tonight was, 'The piano man has a tune to play,' " said Mike Barnett.

Gretzky had a hat trick in the game and added an assist.

"I don't think I've ever had this much personal satisfaction," he said in the post-game dressing room.

"I took the lead and I answered the bell. After 14 years in this league, I didn't want to be remembered as the guy who didn't play well in the Stanley Cup semifinal.

"This took five hard years of work," he said of getting back to the Stanley Cup final. "In Edmonton, it took us five years to win a Stanley Cup. This is my fifth year here. Maybe it's our time.

"I think it really helped this team to have all this Edmonton experience around here. It really calmed everybody down."

"I love Game 7. That's what it's all about. There isn't any pressure in Game 7. It's fun. Every kid dreams of Game 7.

"This is the sweetest moment of my hockey career. To win the seventh game in the other team's building is just so sweet I can't describe it."

Kurri watched Gretzky from a seat on a trunk in the equipment room.

"All I can say is Wayne Gretzky is unbelievable," he said. "He showed that he's still the No. 1 player in the world. He just stepped out tonight and won it."

It was a one-hour flight to the Stanley Cup final in Montreal. And it took Gretzky back years.

"I remember my first playoff game at the Montreal Forum," Gretzky said at the press conference prior to the final.

"I had five hotdogs right before the game. Mustard and onions, too. I used to do that before every game. I was a real regular at the concession stands. I had pizza in Chicago and hotdogs in Montreal and Quebec."

Gretzky said he wasn't going to assume, the way he did way back then, that he'd be in Stanley Cup final after Stanley Cup final.

"I know we would have won seven or eight Stanley Cups in Edmonton. It would have been disappointing for me never to get back to another final. People say it's maybe my last time in a final and I think you always have to look at it as your last time in a final. Every time you get there, you better enjoy it.

"All those years in Edmonton we used to tell people we were the underdogs. Nobody bought it. In this series we're *definitely* the underdogs."

Gretzky, who had 16 goals in the regular season, scored his 14th of the playoffs and added three assists to lead the Kings to a 4-1 win over the Canadiens in Game 1.

But the truth was, he actually scored two. One was a Steve Smith. An own goal. On his own net. He scored the Canadiens' only goal.

"Nice shot," said Kelly Hrudey to Gretzky.

" 'Nice shot.' That's what he said to me," said Gretzky.

"If he has nights like that he can score on his own goal any time," said Hrudey.

"When I scored on my own goal, I kind of wanted to redeem myself," said No. 99.

In Game 2 the Habs called for a measurement on Marty McSorley's stick. It was illegal, and it won the Canadiens a hockey game. It broke the back of the Kings.

"People say it cost the Stanley Cup," said Gretzky years later. "I never said that. But it did cause a huge shifting of momentum in that series."

The Kings didn't win another game, and when it was over and Gretzky had come and gone from the interview room, people were wondering if he'd just announced his retirement.

To some it sure sounded that way. To others, including his agent, it sounded like disappointment doing the talking.

"I'm not sure," said Gretzky. "I'm not trying to create a bunch of controversy. But I said to my wife before the playoffs that I wanted to go out on a high. I think I played as well as I can these playoffs. I'm going to sit back with my wife over the next few days and decide what my future is."

Gretzky, who was criticized for taking much of the focus off the Canadiens on the night they won the Cup, never got back to a Stanley Cup final.

But he had plenty of reasons to get back on the ice. One of them was Gordie Howe's goal-scoring record.

By early February people were circling dates on their calendars and coming up with March 25, Game 74 of the season, at Northlands Coliseum in Edmonton.

Gretzky had been scoring one goal every two games in the 1993-94 season. He needed 12 more. That would be 24 games. And that would be Los Angeles at Edmonton on March 25.

The countdown was under way. Sports sections had charts with Howe's 801, and Gretzky at 789 and counting.

"It's really getting kind of exciting," he said. "This one I'm definitely going to enjoy. This is a different kind of record. This one I didn't think I'd get close to ... I always believed 801 was the one I wasn't going to get. As long as I don't have a 15-game drought with everybody following me around."

I joined the tour, still on schedule for it happening again, storybook fashion in Edmonton, when Gretzky made it 799 in Los Angeles.

Two goals to Gordie.

It was in San Jose that Gretzky scored the goal that should have a name but only had a number – 801.

Gretzky doesn't just paint them, he puts frames around them. It's not enough to just break one of the greatest records in the game, but he has to mount them in your memory. And that's what he did as he equalled Howe's mark.

"It was picture-perfect," said setup man Alex Zhitnik.

Gretzky opened the game with No. 800. No. 801 came with 43 seconds to play.

As with No. 1,851 to break Howe's points record in Edmonton five years

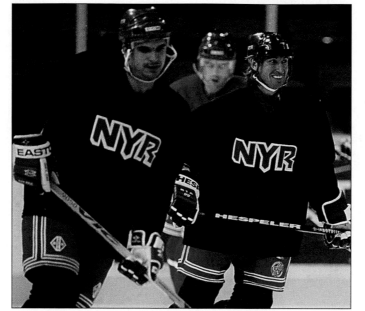

BIG STAR IN THE BIG APPLE: Gretzky, right, is all smiles during practice with the New York Rangers.

earlier, it was one that mattered. It gave the Kings a 6-6 tie and kept them in the playoff hunt. And, like the one in Edmonton, it came late.

"We all said that, sitting together in the stands," said wife Janet. "It looked exactly like the record he broke in Edmonton."

There was one game to go before Gretzky could head to Edmonton to break it there. A home game in Vancouver. And this time he cheated the City of Champions.

He scored the great goal – Gr802. Hockey history. March 23, 1994. Second period. Gretzky from Marty McSorley and Luc Robitaille at 14:47. Power play. Juri Slegr in the penalty box.

Back in Edmonton, the Oilers were home to the New York Rangers. With about 10 minutes to play, Mark Messier was about to move into the faceoff circle for the draw when he knew just from the sound what had happened. He backed away from the faceoff circle and allowed the crowd to give Gretzky a standing ovation for his accomplishment even if it hadn't been accomplished in front of them.

"I think everybody felt a little something when they announced it," said Messier. "The people here have witnessed a lot of his special moments, and stepping back from the faceoff was just my way of acknowledging it myself."

They stopped the game for more than 10 minutes. Gretzky's mother, father and wife were brought to centre ice with commissioner Gary Bettman. A three-minute video was shown on the scoreboard.

"You've always been The Great One but tonight you've become The Greatest," said Bettman.

Gretzky told the world he hadn't run out of goals.

"I'd like to get 1,852 assists," he said of the idea of accumulating more assists than Howe had points.

Gretzky won his 10th and last scoring title with 130 points (38 goals) to become, at age 33, the oldest player ever to win the Art Ross Trophy. But for the first time in his career, Wayne Gretzky missed the playoffs.

In the lockout season of 1994-95 Gretzky registered his 2,500th point with an assist April 17 against Calgary. But again he missed the playoffs.

Owner Bruce McNall was headed to jail and Wayne's World was full of rumours throughout the front end of the 1995-96 season.

"There are rumours he's going everywhere but the Soviet Red Army team," cracked Kevin Lowe at one point.

He ended up going to St. Louis.

The Blues were on the road at the time with a game in Vancouver and then a game in Edmonton before they'd head home. The media converged on a practice rink in Burnaby, B.C.

If nothing else, the scene made for a wonderful practical joke. At the Vancouver airport two Edmonton scribes, me and Jim Matheson of the *Journal*, rented a stretch limo. We had the driver wheel slowly around the complex in Burnaby so that photographers and fans could keep up, running after us, figuring this was the arrival of Gretzky.

Gretzky showed up a little later riding in the St. Louis team bus.

Brett Hull surveyed the scene and said it was about right.

"The greatest player in the world just got traded. That doesn't happen every day," he said.

"I knew four or five weeks ago that I was going to be moved," said Gretzky at a press conference. "This is easier than it was leaving Edmonton. I was leaving a winning team, not a floundering team. This is the opposite situation. This is a chance to play for a championship again. This is what it's all about. That's what I'm excited about."

Gretzky scored a breakaway goal in his first game as a Blue.

Back in Edmonton, drinking a Diet Coke in the lounge of the Hotel Macdonald, Gretzky poured his heart out in a one-on-one interview.

For the past weeks he'd heard himself being called "The Grey One" and in the past days read a lot of negative coverage about his move to St. Louis.

"Gretzky Bad News For Blues" was one of them.

"It hurts," he said. "I wouldn't be telling the truth if I tried to pretend it didn't hurt."

Kelly Buchberger clobbered Gretzky in his game in Edmonton. He stuck an elbow in Gretzky's ear and No. 99 lay on the ice for the longest time without moving. It was a wobbly, woozy Wayne who was finally helped off the ice.

"He was out cold," reported coach Mike Keenan. "He told me only twice in his career had he been knocked out. And both times it was on the same spot on the ice in the same building."

Early in Gretzky's career Bill McCreary (no relation to the referee) of the Toronto Maple Leafs turned out his lights. Gretzky was only out a second or two as a result of that hit. Play continued while Gretzky crawled to the bench.

This time he didn't return.

"Kelly Buchberger gets picked the first star and he's minus-one?" was the only post-game quote Gretzky offered that night.

Between the two teams Gretzky had his 15th consecutive 100-point season (102 with a career-low 23 goals, to be exact). Gretzky and the Blues went two rounds in the playoffs. He scored two goals and added 14 assists in the playoffs.

There were plenty of rumours and reports indicating Gretzky was just visiting St. Louis. And they turned out to be true.

Wayne Douglas Gretzky would join Mark Douglas Messier with the New York Rangers.

GM Neil Smith introduced No. 99 at the press conference as "simply the greatest hockey player ever to play."

Smith said he couldn't resist.

"I just thought it over and this is the perfect place for Gretzky. Without question, the chance to play with Mark again will be very exciting."

Gretzky made some fun of the moment.

"I'm probably the first free agent to come to New York for less money," he said.

Messier would make more.

Gretzky and Messier warmed up for the season together playing for Canada in the World Cup of Hockey. And, as the season began in New York, Gretzky said he felt a freedom he'd never felt before.

He didn't have to save a franchise or sell hockey. All he had to do was play – and he was playing with Mark Messier.

"I don't care if I'm 1, 1A or 3D," said Gretzky. "I plan on playing hard and helping Mark."

And that he did.

Gretzky played all 82 games for the seventh time in his career, led the league with 72 assists and finished with 97 points.

But it was the playoffs that people remember from his first season with the Rangers. It was the last time he played in Lord Stanley's tournament, and he and Messier made it memorable by making it to the final four.

Gretzky beat Florida 3-2 in one game. He scored all three Ranger goals, his ninth career playoff hat trick.

He scored his second hat trick of the playoff year in a 5-4 win over Philadelphia, playing right-wing on a line with Messier and Esa Tikkanen.

With 10 goals and 10 assists for 20 points, the last playoff of Gretzky's career turned out to be terrific.

In the off-season Messier and the Rangers had a major falling-out which resulted in No. 11 breaking up with No. 99 again and heading to Vancouver.

Gretzky registered his 50th regular-season hat trick to open the 1997-98 season in an Oct. 11 game against Vancouver.

He accomplished his private goal of reaching 1,851 assists – more assists than any player had ever accumulated points – in an Oct. 26 game against Anaheim.

As he entered what turned out to be his final season, Gretzky wanted one more record for sure.

Again, it belonged to Gordie Howe.

Howe, in the NHL and WHA, playoffs and regular season, had scored 1,071 professional goals.

Gretzky came to Edmonton in February 1999 for what turned out to be his last game in what was now Skyreach Centre, with a chance to break the goals record in front of Oilers fans.

"It would be nice to get it here," he said. "Most of it comes from being here. It includes the WHA. This would be the perfect place. Any record is special. But this is a unique record."

Gretzky, suffering from a neck injury, didn't get it that night. He ended up missing a dozen games and it was a while before he recorded it.

Roy Mlakar, former president of the Los Angeles Kings, put it as well as anyone as he watched the sun set on Gretzky's amazing career.

"If this league doesn't have Wayne Gretzky, there is no Dallas, no San Jose, no Anaheim, no Miami and no Tampa Bay," he said before franchises in Nashville, Carolina, Atlanta, Columbus and the like were added to that list.

"We had so many good things for this league because of Wayne Gretzky. He's done so much for this game."

That was certainly the theme as the curtain came down and Gretzky stood at his press conference, in front of all those pictures of himself in other uniforms, and waved goodbye to the game that April afternoon in Madison Square Garden.

A lot of things were written and said that weekend but one of the most memorable came from Gretzky's old Oilers roommate, Kevin Lowe.

On the last day of Gretzky's career, Lowe finally 'fessed up: he had not scored the first goal in Edmonton Oilers history.

During TV commercial breaks in Wayne Gretzky's last game, several people from No. 99's life who couldn't be there appeared in video messages on the Madison Square Garden scoreboard. There was one from Howe. And Michael Jordan. But it was Lowe's message that made news.

It was a true confession.

"I have to come clean," said Lowe.

"It was you," he said of the player who really scored the first goal in Oilers history in old Chicago Stadium.

"So you really didn't have to score that last goal the other night to break Gordie's record."

Gretzky scored 1,072 goals, regular season and playoffs, in the NHL and WHA. He broke Howe's record by one. With Gretzky failing to score a goal in his last game, it was his last one.

Gretzky watched his old friend Kevin Lowe, whose assistant coaching duties with the Edmonton Oilers prevented him from being there, and he laughed.

"I told him for years that I tipped that shot," said Gretzky. "He wouldn't give it to me."

Lowe's final statement in his video message was emotional, and he said it for everybody in Edmonton and everywhere else in the hockey world:

"I feel so strongly there will never be another one like you."

TRUE COLOURS: Fans show their allegiance to No. 99.

Chapter 16

THE ULTIMATE AWARD

an anonymous sports poet once wrote a few lines about sports Halls of Fame:

> *The Halls of Fame are open wide.*
> *And they are always full;*
> *Some go in the door marked "push."*
> *And some by the door marked "pull."*

Wayne Gretkzy pushed open the front door of the Hockey Hall of Fame like no one has done before.

But when he was a kid, he used to sneak in the back door.

"As a kid, when I was 12 and 13 years old, I used to sneak down to the Hockey Hall of Fame," Gretzky said before his final game in New York. "There used to be a guy who let me go in. I used to just stand there for hours and stare. Obviously if they want my skates or anything else for the Hall of Fame, that's where everything will go."

And that, Gretzky knew, was where he'd go. Directly.

"I've never really been controversial or egotistical, but I guess it's safe to say I'm probably going to go there. Now that I'm retired, I can say that."

The first day after Gretzky's last game in the NHL, the process began. He was nominated for membership in the Hockey Hall of Fame, bypassing the customary three-year waiting period.

CUP CRAZY: Wayne Gretzky and Lyle (Sparky) Kulchisky have some fun with the Campbell bowl.

"Wayne's achievements, both on and off the ice, are unparalleled in the sport of hockey," said Jim Gregory. "Wayne obviously exemplifies all aspects of the election criteria which include playing ability, sportsmanship, character and contributions to his teams and to the game of hockey in general."

The same day in Ottawa, the House of Commons unanimously approved a motion to create a Wayne Gretzky stamp. And No. 99 was named the NHL's player of the week for the 44th and final time.

The Hall of Fame had asked for several items of memorabilia from Gretzky's final game and he said they could have anything they wanted.

Already there were seven Gretzky jerseys, nine sticks, his 802-goal puck, helmet, gloves, pants and socks. Also the first award he'd ever received, the Wally Bauer Trophy he won in 1968-69 as the most improved player in novice hockey.

But nothing compares with getting in yourself and, while there was hardly an element of doubt involved, it became official on June 23.

Wayne Douglas Gretzky had become the 10th player to be approved for induction without the customary three-year waiting period, joining Dit Clapper (1947), Rocket Richard (1961), Ted Lindsay (1966), Red Kelly (1969), Terry Sawchuk (1971), Jean Beliveau (1972), Gordie Howe (1972), Bobby Orr (1979) and Mario Lemieux (1997) in the exclusive category.

At the NHL awards night Gretzky – who had won nine Hart Trophies, eight of them as an Edmonton Oiler – along with his wife Janet, presented the award for the 1998-99 season to the player he'd thrown the torch to, as he put it, in his final game, Jaromir Jagr.

"Wayne, thanks for everything you did for hockey," said Jagr at the awards banquet held in the Air Canada Centre in Toronto.

Gretzky won his final NHL award that night, his fifth Lady Byng.

"I didn't expect this," he said after receiving a standing ovation from the 6,000 people in attendance.

"This is a tremendous way to finish my career, getting the Hall of Fame announcement and now this trophy."

In the beginning, Gretzky struggled at awards. Ever so briefly.

In the end he set records for awards just as with anything else. But when you look at his complete collection, you could make a case that he was jobbed out of a couple.

Gretzky poses with the Conn Smythe Trophy in 1985.

The NHL ruled he wasn't eligible for the Calder Trophy as the top first-year player in the NHL because he'd played in the WHA the year before. The NHL refused to concede the WHA was a major league – except when it deemed Gretzky ineligible for the Calder.

And then he didn't get a share of the Art Ross Trophy because there was a clause where, in the event of a tie, the award would go to the player with the most goals (Marcel Dionne).

Then *The Sporting News* announced Gretzky had been beaten out by one vote for Player of the Year honours.

"That really bothers me," said Oilers original NHL GM Larry Gordon at the time. "It just doesn't make any sense. He lost two trophies, the Calder and the Art Ross, on technicalities. When you stop to consider what he's accomplished, there's no way he shouldn't be the winner."

The Hockey News MVP was out next.

Gretzky was in Hawaii when he was informed of the vote.

"Really? You gotta be kidding. You mean I finally won something? It was beginning to hurt."

But all of the above was turned into nitpicking when the NHL awards were announced.

"Byng-O! The Kid Has Hart" was the head on my column the next day.

You could have called it a day like no other day in hockey history. On the same day No. 9 officially retired from hockey, No. 99 officially ascended his throne.

Following the most spectacular first-year performance in NHL history, Gretzky was informed he'd won both the Hart Trophy as the most valuable player and the Lady Byng Trophy as the player combining ability and sportsmanship.

At 19, he was the youngest player to win either award.

Only four times had a player been honoured with both awards in the same year, the most recent having been Stan Mikita in 1968.

If Gretzky had felt stung by not winning those other awards, getting the Hart and being named the MVP in his first year in the league made up for it.

"I remember when I was in Montreal at the award ceremonies last year

Gretzky got lots of practice making acceptance speeches over the years. Above right, he tackles the phone lines after being named *Sports Illustrated's* top athlete in '83.

Wayne Gretzky accepts the Art Ross Trophy from his idol, Gordie Howe, in 1985 and (below) kisses the Hart Trophy in '89.

and I saw those trophies," he said. "There were a lot of people kidding me when I looked at them. But I made up my mind when I looked at the Hart that someday I'd have my name on that one. I felt then, if I tried as hard as I could, I'd be able to do it. I've always thought there is no use shooting for a medium goal. You have to shoot for the highest goal. And other than the Stanley Cup, that's the greatest trophy there is to win in the NHL. When a 15- or 16-year-old kid like Tracy Austin can win the world tennis championship, I didn't think it was impossible for an 18-year-old to win one of those trophies.

"I have mixed emotions about the two trophies I didn't win. I understand that when the Art Ross Trophy was awarded, it was stipulated by the Ross family that they wanted one winner. But when Bobby Hull and Andy Bathgate tied, the owners should have had a vote. I hear they are still talking about splitting the trophy in the event of a tie for the future, and I think they should. I don't think it's right the way it is. I have younger brothers and they have a lot of friends and they've been brought up

to believe an assist is as important as a goal. They don't believe that any more."

Gretzky suggested they create the Gordie Howe trophy for most goals scored during a season. The year he retired, they did. They named it the Rocket Richard Trophy.

"As for the Calder, I was disappointed about that. But I have to admit that I did know when I signed with the WHA, that it would be that way."

Gretzky knew he'd won something.

"I was told by Ron Andrews of the NHL I had to be in Montreal by the 10th or 11th of June for the NHL awards banquet. So I figured I'd maybe won something. I've been on edge for the last couple of weeks waiting to find out. People were telling me I had to be here and I had to be there. Now that I know I've won this kind of makes me pinch myself just a little bit. Sometimes I don't believe all this has happened to me."

Gretzky identified the time and place he figured he had a shot at the Hart in his first year in the league. It was the night he scored his 48th and 49th goals and added four assists during the *Hockey Night In Canada* telecast. That was the performance that convinced every observer, in Canada at least, that he was for real.

"They'd just had a Wayne Gretzky Night in my home town of Brantford. There was an unbelievable amount of publicity in Toronto that week. And a lot of pressure had built up on me. My parents and friends and my agent, Gus Badali, were all there and they were pretty nervous because a lot of people were expecting quite a bit from me that night. After that game I knew I had a chance to win the Hart."

The Lady Byng was a bonus. A lot of voters who first look at the penalty minutes, noticed he had 32 minutes and even one fight (if you could call it that). Guy Lafleur had only 12 minutes of penalties. Mike Bossy had 12. Mike Rogers had 10.

"The Lady Byng Trophy is a little special because it's for the player who combines ability with sportsmanship. I know I'll always cherish that one. I've always tried to be that kind of hockey player and I'll always try to be that kind of hockey player."

After that it was one award after another for his entire career.

Another one came out of nowhere for him the next day when he found out he'd won the Charlie Conacher Award for his work off the ice. He reacted to it like he'd reacted to the Byng.

"To me, the Conacher award is special because it's given for something you do as a person, not as a hockey player."

Before the calendar year was out, Gretzky would win his first award as Canadian male athlete of the year. In the annual year-end poll conducted by The Canadian Press, sportswriters and broadcasters made Gretzky the overwhelming choice for 1980, beating out Terry Puhl of Melville, Sask., an outfielder with the Houston Astros. In third place was Terry Fox, who showed his disregard for physical limitations by running 5,000 km from St. John's, Nfld., to Thunder Bay, Ont., on one good leg and an artificial limb, in what became known as the Marathon of Hope for cancer research. It was the first of six occasions Gretzky was named Canada's male athlete of the year.

In February, he was named winner of the Vanier Award, becoming the first hockey player in history to win it. The award, named after Gov. Gen. Georges Vanier, is given to outstanding young Canadians. CFL quarterback Russ Jackson, figure skater Karen Magnussen, ballerina Karen Kain and singers Anne Murray and Gordon Lightfoot had been previous winners.

Gretzky won his second straight Hart Trophy in his second season on the same day Alberta resident Jeff Landry of Morinville was putting his new licence plates on his 1961 Cadillac.

In Edmonton, this was a story.

His licence plate number was MVP 099.

Landry spent three years reconditioning the car, the exact same

Gretzky accepts an Emery Edge award in 1985 (above) and the president's trophy in 1986.

amount of time Gretzky had been in Edmonton. Only a couple of weeks earlier, he'd registered the car. And finally he was putting his licence plates on it, the same day Gretzky was named MVP.

"Somebody in my shop brought it to my attention," he said of the plates, which were regular issue.

He hadn't noticed.

"I didn't even know what I had," he said.

"I think it looks pretty good on the car. After all, 1961 was the year Wayne was born. And he most certainly is a Cadillac."

When he was told that story, Walter Gretzky laughed.

"I know you are going to think I'm crazy, but I'm convinced Wayne's life was planned a long time ago. The things that have happened ...

"A guy in Edmonton draws an MVP 099 licence plate number and puts it on his car, a Cadillac from the same year Wayne was born, the same day Wayne wins the MVP. It's like when Wayne tied Phil Esposito's record at 1:52 of the period and it was exactly 1:52 p.m. in Edmonton when he did it. I'm not surprised at any of that stuff any more. I really am convinced his life was planned a long time ago."

And if The Sporting News had snubbed him as NHL player of the year in his first season, they more than made up for it by making him man of the year for 1981.

"They're all an honour, but I have to look at this one as the biggest," said Gretzky. "I have to look at who I'm up against.

"When I win over John McEnroe, Fernando Valenzuela, George Brett and Bear Bryant, well, what can I say? It's really shocking that I won."

Big as The Sporting News man of the year award was, Sports Illustrated's sportsman of the year award was bigger.

"Every award is an honour, but I feel this one is a little bit more prestigious from an individual point of view," said Gretzky, suddenly having to compare it to The Sporting News award.

"This one has more of an American influence than any other award. For myself or any other Canadian hockey player to win, this can do nothing but help promote our game in the United States."

Gretzky became the first player on a Canadian-based team, the second Canadian citizen and only the third hockey selection in the then 29-year history of the magazine's highest honour. Bobby Orr was named SI's sportsman of the year in 1970 after becoming the first defenceman ever to lead the NHL in scoring. The other hockey award went to the American "Miracle On Ice" team that won the Olympic gold medal at Lake Placid.

Just winning the Hart was no longer news for Gretzky as he made his third straight trip to the NHL awards in '82.

But it was news this time because, for the first time, it was unanimous.

Bobby Hull made the presentation of the Art Ross Trophy, Gretzky's second straight, at the ceremony.

"Wayne has done more for the sport of hockey than any other person who has ever played the game and likely ever will," said Hull, whose own son, Brett, would end up winning it one day.

"The game required a shot in the arm when he came along and made a positive impact – the greatest impact I've ever seen in any sport."

He was the first unanimous winner and joined Orr as the only other player to win it for three consecutive seasons.

Phil Esposito made the Hart presentation.

"The fact Wayne won it unanimously says it right there," said Espo. "Here's a young man who has done more for hockey than anyone can imagine. He's a Canadian living in Edmonton and sells the game not only in his own country but in the U.S. as well. When he comes to New York or any other U.S. town, it's excitement."

Suddenly the question was: how many Harts will this kid win?

"Gee, I dunno," Gretzky said. "I guess as long as the team is winning, I've got a chance. But it'll get harder every year because people are looking for a change."

Nobody, of course, had won four straight Harts. But as the next season came to a conclusion, Edmonton native Pete Peeters was putting down the idea he might be the guy to stop the Gretzky streak.

"Are you kidding me?" he said for the record as he went to the ceremony to find out how the voting members of the Professional Hockey Writers Association had filled in their ballots.

"I'm being realistic. There is no way I'm going to win that trophy."

He was right.

Gretzky became the first player in the 66-year history of the NHL to be named MVP for four straight seasons.

Peeters received 16 Hart votes. He'd had a 2.36 goals-against average and eight shutouts to win the Vezina Trophy.

"He had 196 points and I only had one," laughed the goaltender when

Gretzky accepts the Molson Cup in 1981.

Gretzky got used to hauling in lots of league hardware.

the results were announced.

Gretzky made it five Harts in a row the following year.

Rod Langway finished second.

"Even I would not have voted for me," said Langway.

It was now getting as hard to keep track of Gretzky's awards as his records.

No award surprised him any more. He'd taken trips to Las Vegas to receive the Victor Award and many other prestigious honours. But the one he received on June 27, 1984 caught his attention.

He was voted into the Newspaper Carrier Hall of Fame. Growing up in Brantford, he had delivered the *Toronto Telegram*, the paper that had folded and been re-created by Doug Creighton and staff members as *The Toronto Sun*, the paper that, in turn, had given birth to *The Edmonton Sun*.

Willie Mayes, Jack Dempsey, Julius Erving and Canadian prime ministers Lester Pearson and John Diefenbaker were previous winners.

A few days later, along came another slightly more prestigious honour.

Wayne Gretzky, at age 23, headed the list of Canadians to be named to the Order of Canada. It was some years later when he actually had it presented to him in Ottawa. Fourteen years later, to be exact. The Order of Canada is never presented in summer and it took Gretzky all that time for the presentations not to conflict with the NHL hockey schedule. Once it was scheduled to work out but was called off when then Gov. Gen. Ray Hnatyshyn's mother died.

Gretzky and the Oilers won their first Stanley Cup in 1984. And most people figured when Gretzky won his first Stanley Cup, he'd win the Conn Smythe Award as the MVP of the playoffs along with it. Didn't work that way. Mark Messier had a brilliant Stanley Cup final and it was no contest.

One year later, when the Oilers won their second straight Cup, it was a contest. It was such a contest that *Hockey Night In Canada* and *The Edmonton Sun* teamed up to conduct a poll to find out from fans who should win it.

The fans chose Paul Coffey with 3,667 votes or 47.1 per cent. Grant Fuhr finished second in the poll with

Walter Gretzky was on hand as son Wayne received a 'great role model' award from Esso.

The year before, when the Oilers won their third Stanley Cup, the playoff MVP award had gone to Philadelphia Flyers netminder Ron Hextall in a losing cause in a seven-game Stanley Cup Final.

Before he carried his fourth Stanley Cup, Gretzky had been only the third player to be presented with his second Conn Smythe. Only Bobby Orr (1970 and '72) and Bernie Parent (1974 and '75) had ever won the award twice in the 23-year history of the playoff MVP award to that point.

"What can you say about him that hasn't been said before?" said coach Terry O'Reilly of the Stanley Cup-finalist Boston Bruins.

"OK. He's a bum. That hasn't been said before," he laughed.

"We got great playoffs from Glenn Anderson and Jari Kurri and I thought Mark Messier and Grant Fuhr were outstanding," said Gretzky. "Actually, I feel kind of bad I won again."

Gretzky, who had been injured during the season, had failed to win the Art Ross for the scoring title that year, finishing second to Mario Lemieux. And finally, in 1988, in what turned out to be Gretzky's final year as an Oiler, his streak was stopped.

Gretzky, in '88, in fact, finished third. Lemieux garnered 292 votes, Fuhr 108 and Gretzky 73.

Lemieux was gracious. In accepting the award, he said Gretzky was still No. 1. And he went on record as saying Gretzky gave him the assist to

2,625 votes and 33.7 per cent. Gretzky was third with 1,494 votes and 19.2 per cent.

Gretzky, the night the Oilers carried the Cup, was given the nod by the people in the press box.

"That was probably the toughest one ever picked," said No. 99.

"It's a great thrill to win it, but I wish Paul and Grant could have their names on it with me. I feel bad for those guys. They would have been worthy winners. I'm more disappointed they can't put their names on that trophy than I am thrilled that my name is going on. But we all get our names on the Stanley Cup and that's the only one that really counts."

Gretzky won his sixth Hart to tie Gordie Howe; the only difference was Gretzky's six were all in a row. And him winning his seventh didn't even rate the biggest headlines in Edmonton because Paul Coffey had won his first Norris Trophy as the league's top defenceman.

The Oilers' biggest haul at the awards night was in '86, when Gretzky took the Hart and Art Ross trophies as usual, Glen Sather won the Jack Adams as coach of the year, and Coffey won his second straight Norris Trophy.

"I've won it so many times in the past, I thought this was the year for it to end," said Gretzky of his eighth straight Hart in 1987. Mario Lemieux had surfaced to become his main competition.

"The King Of Harts" was the headline in *The Edmonton Sun.*
And he won his second Conn Smythe.

It took him several years to actually collect it, but the Order of Canada was Gretzky's most prestigious non-hockey honour.

be able to win it when the two were teamed together and combined together on that never-to-be-forgotten goal to win the Canada Cup.

"That's where it all started, playing with Gretzky," he said.

"The only reason Gretzky didn't win the Hart is because he was hurt," added Lemieux. "I was fortunate to take advantage of that."

When it was all over and Gretzky had worn the Edmonton Oilers uniform for the last time, he'd won four Stanley Cups, eight Harts, seven Art Rosses, three Lester B. Pearson Awards as most outstanding, four Lady Byngs, four Emery Edges (plus-minus), three Dodge Chryslers (performer of the year) and two Conn Smythes – and those were just the ones from the NHL.

He won the Hart one last time in his first year with the Los Angeles Kings, and three more Art Ross Trophies as the scoring champion. The Americans couldn't wait to make him eligible and present him with the Lester Patrick Award for service to hockey in the United States, bestowing it on him in 1994.

Just when it looked like they were running out of awards for Gretzky, they invented a new one.

Gretzky had an interesting trip to the Hockey Hall of Fame in Toronto the year before his ultimate trip to the place where he's now enshrined.

That was in 1998 when he was invited there by *The Hockey News* to celebrate the publication's all-time top 50 NHL players on the occasion of its 50th anniversary.

As if being named the greatest player in hockey history while standing in front of all those faces in the Hall of Fame by the bible of the sport wasn't enough, Gretzky's agent Michael Barnett made it even better with a special presentation. He gave Gretzky the set of skates he wore for his first game

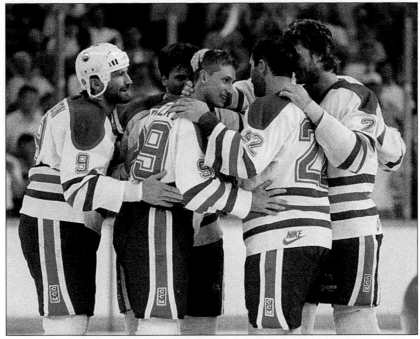

The Oilers congratulate Gretzky on winning the Conn Smythe Trophy after their 1988 playoff triumph over Boston.

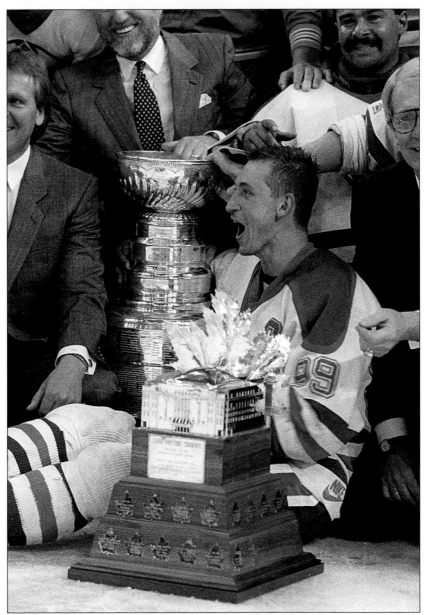

Gretz sits contentedly between Stanley and the Conn Smythe after his fourth and final Cup win with the Oilers in 1988.

as an Edmonton Oiler in the NHL in 1979. Barnett had them silver plated and encased in glass.

"Those are pretty cool," said Gretzky of the skates, which rank right up there with any treasure in the building.

"I'm a little bit embarrassed to be standing here," he told the invited guests. "If I was voting, I'd vote for Gordie Howe and Bobby Orr and be happy to be third."

Orr was voted second and Howe third. Howe helped make the moment.

"I'm in the money," he said. "Win. Place. I'm show.

"I'm almost as proud of Wayne as Phyllis and Wally. I'm proud of the fact that many years ago I shook the hand of this young man in Brantford and had the opportunity to play with him in that WHA all-star game in Edmonton. I'm proud of the fact I was there when the young man started. If anyone thinks I'm jealous, please don't. And I called it. This is how I would have voted."

Gretzky said the best thing about it was that the top 50 included four Edmonton Oilers.

Indeed, one look at the list and it really hit home what we'd watched in Edmonton. Mark Messier was No. 12, Paul Coffey No. 28. And Jari Kurri, No. 50.

There was also Jacques Plante (No. 13) who finished up his career with the Oilers in the WHA, former Edmonton Flyer Glenn Hall (No. 16), Eddie Shore, (the Edmonton Express, No. 10), and former Edmonton Oil King Johnny Bucyk (No. 45).

There are longtime Edmonton hockey fans who should will their eyes to the Hockey Hall of Fame.

But No. 1 will always be No. 99.

And now you can go to the Hockey Hall of Fame and see not just his memorabilia but see Gretzky up there where he belongs between Green and Griffis.

OH, CANADA

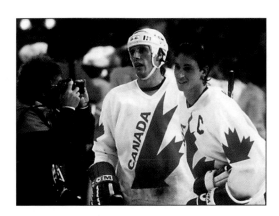

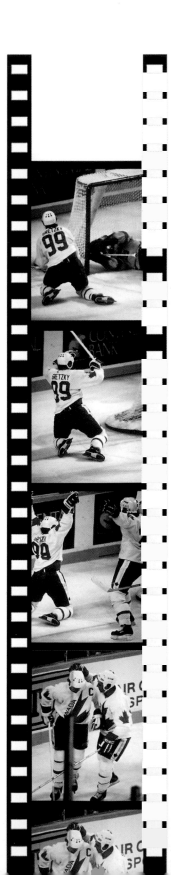

When Brian Adams sang his version of the national anthem, "O Canada, we stand on guard for thee – we're going to miss you, Wayne Gretzky," at Madison Square Garden before Gretzky's final game, it could be heard in every arena, especially the international arena. Gretzky wore the red Maple Leaf and carried Canada's colours as well as anybody in history.

He was the leading scorer in six of the eight international competitions in which he played, not including Rendez-Vous '87, and yet the final freeze-frame will be the greatest player, the greatest goal scorer in hockey history, being frozen out of a chance to make a difference for Canada on the ultimate international stage. Why didn't they pick him for the shootout in Nagano? Why?

Funny. The Olympic dream was the one Gretzky didn't dream. His dream was always another '72 Canada-Russia summit series.

Gretzky was 11 when they held the original and that was the dream he voiced again and again and again.

It never happened. And now, with the NHL full of Russians and players from every other hockey-playing nation in the world, no Canadians will ever get the chance again. If he'd only been able to talk hockey into it, how wonderful that would have been. Oh, how he tried.

Team captains Wayne Gretzky and Larry Robinson savour the Canada Cup in 1984.

Not that No. 99, otherwise, didn't have the full meal deal in terms of international experience.

He was a 16-year-old kid who was famous in southern Ontario, known to some extent elsewhere in Canada, and mostly unheard of on the other side of the world when he received his first international invitation and made it his first validation.

Gretzky became the youngest player to compete in the World Junior Hockey Championships at the 1978 tournament in Montreal. Playing against players ranging in age from 18 to 20, the Sault Ste. Marie Greyhounds junior star proved to be the tournament's top scorer with eight goals, nine assists and 17 points in six games.

Muzz MacPherson, the man who convinced Gretzky to wear No. 99 for the first time in the Soo, said his favourite on-ice memory of the Soo season was Gretzky at the world junior tournament.

"I saw him score a lot of beautiful goals but he scored one, making a move on a Soviet defenceman, that I can't even describe," MacPherson said way back when.

Gretzky made a believer out of Team Canada co-coach Orval Tessier then and there.

"I was skeptical about Gretzky, not having seen him play except once in his own league," said Tessier. "But he's certainly convinced me and everyone else now. He's very intelligent. He has a tremendous amount of puck sense. He's a pleasant surprise."

Gus Bodnar, who took his turn behind the bench, needed no convincing.

"Gretzky's always played two years above his class," he said. "He's just amazing."

Gretzky, who played with the likes of Bobby Smith, Mike Gartner and Craig Hartsburg on that team, was voted to the tournament all-star team at centre.

Several years later, after he'd won his third Hart Trophy, Gretzky said it was nice, but ...

"This may be the biggest honour, but the one I cherish the most – the one which will never be overtaken – is the first team centre nomination at the world junior," he said.

The other members of that first all-star team?

Alexander Tychnykh of the U.S.S.R. in goal.

Slava Fetisov of the U.S.S.R. on defence.

Risto Siltanen of Finland on defence.

Mats Naslund of Sweden at forward.

Anton Stastny of Czechoslovakia at forward.

The world junior was one thing. With two years as an NHL pro behind him, Gretzky suddenly found himself in the Canada Cup.

Speculation all summer was along the lines of who might end up on

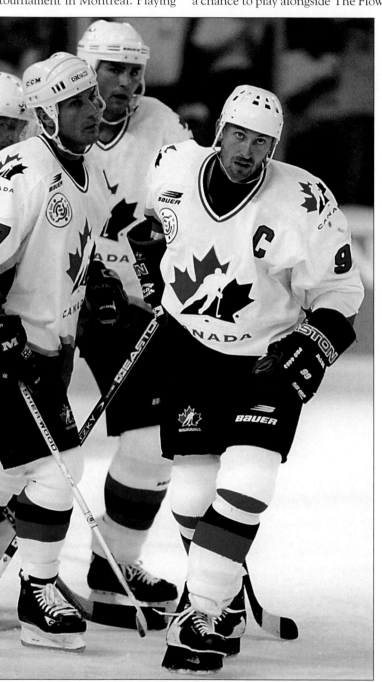

Team Canada stalwarts Paul Coffey, left, Eric Lindros and Wayne Gretzky.

the same line with No. 99. At the WHA all-star scenario, Gordie Howe was perfect, in terms of the promotion, etc. But this was the Canada Cup. This mattered.

Still, fans were hoping he'd find himself on the same line as Guy Lafleur.

Gretzky was trying to play it down.

"Um, oh ... it really doesn't matter," he said. "I'd be honoured if I got a chance to play alongside The Flower. I guess I'd love to play with Guy Lafleur. It would be a little like playing with Gordie Howe against the Soviets, but ..."

Coach Scotty Bowman could never be accused of being a PR man, but he liked the combination from every angle.

On Aug. 10, as Team Canada went to camp, Gretzky and Lafleur were on the same line.

At the end of the session, Bowman made it official.

"Gretzky will play with Lafleur and Steve Shutt," he said.

Lafleur, who used to sign sticks for Gretzky, was delighted.

"It will be a lot easier to play with him than against him," he said.

"I think he's a great hockey player. It will be great to have a chance to play with him."

When Team Canada arrived in Edmonton for the final pre-tournament game, after a bit of line-juggling along the way, Gretzky was with Lafleur and Gil Perreault. And the scene was something special in Northlands Coliseum.

Gretzky's new linemate Lafleur was welcomed like never before in Edmonton, welcomed in a way he never expected and welcomed as he would be with just about every game he ever played in Edmonton after that.

All night long, the fans who had occasionally booed Lafleur in the past – as fans have been known to do with players such as Bobby Orr, during visiting games – chanted, "Guy! Guy! Guy!"

"I didn't expect that," said Lafleur. "Maybe it's Edmonton fans' way of saying 'thank you' for what happened last spring," said The Flower of when the Oilers shocked the hockey world by sweeping the Canadiens in the first round of the Stanley Cup playoffs.

Gretzky with Lafleur was wonderful.

"Wayne was doing everything," said Lafleur after Canada won the game, 3-2.

"Gilbert and I are still rushing things. We don't have good timing yet. Tonight, with the right timing, I could have had three goals set up by Wayne. I've never played with anybody who can do what he can do. When he's behind the net, it has to be tough on the Russians. They've never played against anybody who plays the game like he does behind the net."

A more-than-interested observer of the scene was Oilers general manager and coach Glen Sather. And he was willing to produce a prediction on the spot.

"I think I wondered if he'd find his level in the Canada Cup," said Slats. "Everybody saw it tonight. He was head and shoulders above anybody else on the ice. After watching him tonight, I don't think I have any doubt about him finding his level now. I think it's going to be his show."

Gretzky was the poster boy for the event. He was on every magazine cover. It was his Canada Cup, from that point of view, no matter what happened.

For the most part, he lived up to the hype. But in the end it was, as he put it himself, the first major setback of his career.

Gretzky was the top point-getter in the entire tournament. He won the Labatt soapstone carvings as Canada's most valuable player against both Sweden and the U.S.S.R.

In the end it was, as all Canadians wanted it to be, a Canada-Russia final. But the Russians won it. And they didn't just win it, they won it big. They won it 8-1.

Gretzky, like most of his teammates, didn't play well. But he was Gretzky. And, in the end, that made him the Canada Cup goat.

He wasn't there when it mattered most. And the most vivid Gretzky memory from the game was when he gave the puck away at the Soviet blueline and the Soviets had a clear path to the net and a 5-1 lead.

"It was a strange feeling," Gretzky said later. "You wanted to look at it as just another hockey game. But there was no way to rationalize the feeling that you let the whole country down. I just went and hid for five days. My parents didn't even know where I went."

Scenes from the 1981 Canada Cup.

No. 99 decided the experience would be good for him.

"It was the first real setback of my career. Everything in my lifetime has gone my way. Everything has gone well. It proved I had a lot to learn. But I'm only 20 and I'm sure I'll have another Canada Cup."

Not before he'd have a world championship.

When your team makes an early exit in the playoffs, the better players have the pleasure (although it is not always seen as such at the time) of playing for Canada in the world championship.

It was the longest season for Gretzky – or at least the longest season without a Stanley Cup final at the end of it. He had played in seven Canada Cup games, six pre-season games for the Oilers, all 80 regular-season games, the all-star game and the Miracle on Manchester five-game series loss to the Los Angeles Kings in the Stanley Cup playoffs when ... Canada came calling!

When Gretzky and Kevin Lowe returned to their apartment after the loss to Los Angeles, they received a phone call from Alan Eagleson inviting them both to join Team Canada at the world championships as last-minute additions.

Former Canadian Olympic team coach Dave King remembers.

"I was with him when he made his first and only appearance at the world championships in 1982 in Finland. He came to Finland and it was like he was a rock star."

Canada lost twice to the Soviets in the tournament and ended up playing against Sweden in the bronze-medal game.

"We should have won the first game with the Soviets. We had three situations and didn't score on any of them," said Gretzky.

"That was the turning point. Then I lost that crucial faceoff in the second game against the Soviets and that cost us the hockey game."

"I guess if I proved anything over there, I proved it in that last game against Sweden," he said of his two-goal, three-assist, 6-0 win which gave the Canadians a bronze medal to take home.

"For everybody who was saying I was exhausted, tired and worn down, I think I proved something by playing the best hockey game I played all year in the last game I played."

Gretzky wasn't really thrilled with his play on that team, which included Bobby Clarke and Bob Gainey, but he led the tournament in scoring with six goals and 18 assists for 14 points, and joined Bill Barber on the world championship all-star team.

The bottom line was that nobody was going to remember that his last game was great. What would be remembered was that his fabulous season, scoring 50 goals in 39 games and breaking record after record after record had been framed by international failures.

When he returned home he had plenty to analyse.

"I guess one of the things I'm going to remember most was after the second game against the Soviets," Gretzky said when he returned home. "Kevin and I couldn't get to sleep. We stayed up all night. Kevin is a good fundamentalist and analyst of hockey. He's going to be a coach someday. But I've got my own ideas, too. We sat in our hotel room for four or five hours, until 4 or 5 a.m., arguing. He had his reasons why we got beat again and I had mine. When he finally turned out the lights and went to bed, we hadn't settled anything. I guess my argument was politics. And Kevin's was hockey.

"I'm going over to the Soviet Union this summer and old-time Russian coach Anatoly Tarasov has invited me to attend a couple of Red Army practices as his guest. It's amazing. On June 27, the Russian hockey team is going to be right back at it, practising. Are they crazy? My argument is how can we beat that? Their players have no choice. Nine out of 10 of our players would say, 'No way!' They have 300 million people and we have 25 million. They should be better. Kevin argued that we should have the discipline to work just as hard. He says we can do it if we want to do it. I say it's impossible in our system. He says it's not. We just sat up and argued, like a couple of hockey fans, for hours."

Although the Soviets spoiled Gretzky's greatest season to that point, they kind of made up for it with the invitation for Wayne and his entire family to visit Moscow in the summer.

"Wayne and Vladislav Tretiak signed autographs together at the Kremlin," Walter Gretzky raved when they returned to Canadian soil.

"I couldn't believe how much Tretiak enjoyed signing autographs. The people knew who Wayne was. Some of the people would go to Wayne for an autograph first and others to Tretiak. There's no question Tretiak is well known over there. And boy, is his wife proud of him. They showed Wayne Tretiak's collection of medals; it was a collection Wayne just couldn't believe.

"We went to the famous circus on ice and that was a big thrill. They introduced Wayne and Tretiak in the crowd and I couldn't believe the response. I expected them to applaud politely. They cheered and cheered. It was real noisy. It was something that I'm sure Wayne will remember probably better than anything from all of this. Heck, I'm sure Wayne will remember every moment. After all, who else has it ever happened to?"

The Ice Cold War resumed in 1984. And a few things had changed. That spring, Wayne Gretzky and the Edmonton Oilers had just stopped the four-in-a-row Stanley Cup streak of the New York Islanders.

It was perfectly predictable that the players from the two teams that dominated this Team Canada lineup might not be happy campers.

There were six Islanders and eight Oilers on that team and the rivalry didn't disappear because they were suddenly wearing the same sweaters.

Finally, Glen Sather convinced Gretzky and Larry Robinson to buy a bunch of beer and call a meeting and get it worked out.

Bob Bourne of the Islanders is said to have stood up during that meeting and said, "We just don't like you guys."

Understandable. The Oilers had just taken "their" Stanley Cup away from them.

Gretzky always maintained it was just the opposite with the Oilers. They'd used the Islanders as their model, their target and eventually their trophy and had put them on a pedestal until the time came to knock them off.

Canada Cup action in Vancouver.

Gretzky went into the tournament figuring that Canada had learned a lesson from being sandbagged by the Soviets when the Canadians went through the 1981 Canada Cup unbeaten, only to get clobbered 8-1 in the final.

"Since '72, we've been told we have to put together a program that matches the Soviet and European style of hockey," said Gretzky as he headed to camp in Montreal.

"From '72 to '84, through minor hockey and professional and junior programs, we've put together a system where the NHL has more skating

and puck-handling – a style similar to the Europeans and Russians.

"I think since '72 this is what Canada has built and trained for. On this team we have guys like Paul Coffey, Mark Messier, Glenn Anderson and Ray Bourque who have been training the closest thing to a European style. And that's what I think will make this team different.

"This is a completely different team than '81. Basically the difference is that the '81 team was still a version of the NHL's old style of hockey. It was more a grinding team. This team will rely on speed."

Speed indeed. The Oilers proved that speed kills. And there were eight Oilers on this team.

"Skating will be one of the strengths of this team," added No. 99. "The team we had in '81 isn't a skating team compared to this. The speed on this team should be something else. There's no question the Oilers are going to be a big influence on Team Canada. Most of the guys selected play a similar way. I also believe the guys from the other teams are going to learn some things our team uses that'll benefit their game as well. Glen Sather lets you play an offensive game. He reminds you of defence, but doesn't take anything away from offence. I think you'll see guys like Michel Goulet perform very well in this tournament playing for Sather and John Muckler."

Sather put Gretzky on a line with Mike Bossy for the first game in the tournament against West Germany. Gretzky scored three, getting goals on his first two shots, and set up Bossy for his first of two in a 7-2 win.

Gretzky, however, had a bad lobster in Montreal and ended up with food poisoning.

After a game against Sweden in Vancouver, Sather said he'd never seen Gretzky look so bad.

"He looks like a wreck," said Slats.

The Canadians also beat the Czechs 7-2. But a 6-3 loss to the Soviets in front of all those Oilers fans in Northlands Coliseum left Team Canada fourth after the round-robin and facing the Soviets in a one-game semifinal in the brand-new Calgary Saddledome.

Alan Eagleson had changed the tournament format so there would be no 8-1 loss in a Canada-Russia sudden-death final involving Team Canada this time. And Canada ended up against Russia in the sudden-death semifinal.

"It's ironic that we changed the tournament final to a best-of-three so we didn't have to play them in a one-game situation, and now we have to play them in a one-game situation and we think it might be better for us," said Gretzky after practice the next morning.

What happened next might have been the greatest game ever played. I was there for that New Year's Eve game in Montreal between the Canadians and the Red Army and at two memorable Canada Cup games against the Soviets in Hamilton, and I'm not sure any of those beat what we watched that night in Calgary.

It was Canada-Russia as it was supposed to be – The Bear vs. The Beaver with all the fur flying.

Every Canadian with a pulse still remembers what happened that night.

Mike Bossy scored the winner for Canada. But it was Paul Coffey who put his name on the game with a great defensive play to break up a two-on-one Soviet break and then put the puck on the stick for Bossy for one of those few shots in sport which really could be heard around the world.

"Tonight is the best I've felt in my life," said Coffey. "I won a Stanley Cup, but there's no feeling like this."

Captain Canada vs. Sweden in 1984.

Gretzky was over the moon himself.

"Without question that is the greatest hockey game in which I've ever played," he said. "Without question it's the most gratifying. I've never played in a hockey game in my life like that one. Now I think I know the feeling those guys in '72 had."

Gretzky had told a French-language reporter before the game about the two factions tearing the team apart. When it was over he was telling everybody about how Russia-Canada brought them all together and brought out the best in all of them.

"It was just meant to be," said Gretzky.

"It was more guts than anything. We have more guts than they do. We have more emotion. But we didn't prove tonight that we are better than they are," warned No. 99. "They'll have their wins and we'll have ours. What it proved is that we have to keep playing them."

Canada avoided the obvious pitfalls involved and took care of Sweden in the best-of-three series and Gretzky carried the Canada Cup onto Northlands Coliseum ice just the way he'd carried the Stanley Cup on the same surface the year before.

Canada vs. Sweden just didn't have the sizzle for a final of a Canada vs. Russia. So Canada-Russia it would be the next time out in the spring of 1987 in Quebec City, instead of an all-star game.

Rendez-Vous '87 was something to behold. It was an event like none other in hockey history. It was the centre ring of the circus, but there were some interesting acts going on around it which sometimes made it seem, in the beginning at least, like a sideshow.

I came to Rendez-Vous '87 from Europe where I'd been covering winter sports events to set up the 1988 Calgary Winter Olympics. On my flight from Paris were 19 journalists from all over the world who had been invited to Rendez-Vous '87 by the Quebec government. They had little interest in hockey.

There were 185 singers, dancers and musicians from the Red Army Chorus, Soviet gymnastics stars, the Bolshoi ballet and the Soviet rock

group Autograph. There was a $350-a-plate, 12-course gourmet dinner featuring Soviet, American and Canadian chefs. There was lunch with Lee Iacocca of Chrysler and brunch with Mila Mulroney and designer Pierre Cardin, followed by a Cardin fashion show.

There was an opening variety show featuring Quebec entertainers Yvon Deschamps and Jean Lapointe playing host to more than a dozen entertainers from Canada, France and the Soviet Union. There was an international gala featuring Alan Thicke and a collection of stars including Paul Anka, Gordon Lightfoot, David Foster and Crystal Gayle.

And there was hockey.

There were three parades featuring floats from all the NHL teams and 4,000 pieces of memorabilia – virtually the entire Hockey Hall of Fame collection – in the Menage Milirare on Grande Allee. All sorts of hockey greats, including Gordie Howe and Rocket Richard, plus greats from other sports such as Pele, Joe DiMaggio, Wilt Chamberlain, Gary Carter, Ken Read and Nancy Greene were also invited.

The price tag was guestimated between $8 million and $14 million for the event, timed to coincide with the annual Quebec Winter Carnival where Gretzky had played as a peewee.

Seven Oilers were picked for the team and Gretzky had the unique opportunity to play with his regular linemates Jari Kurri and Esa Tikkanen.

It was a two-game "series" and Team NHL won the first game 4-3.

"That was the fastest-paced game I've ever played in," said Gretzky, who set up Kurri for the first goal of the game.

"In the NHL we're not used to that kind of play except when the Oilers play," said Team NHL coach Jean Perron.

There seemed to be almost a relief in not losing for the quickly thrown together all-star team which considered itself a massive underdog.

"It's not over yet, but we can't lose," said Gretzky, who played remarkable two-way hockey in the first game.

The NHL all-stars lost the second game 5-3 (with Gretzky assisting on all three NHL goals) and everybody left Quebec City agreeing it was a wonderful event.

"It was a great spectacle," said No. 99. "I wish we could play another game. I think it was great hockey."

Gretzky was singing a different tune a few months later after having won his third Stanley Cup and having to contemplate going right back at it in August with a training camp for yet another Canada Cup.

He was saying enough, already. He was suggesting he had nothing left to give Canada this time and guessing that he might not play.

"If my dad says 'play' then I'll play," said Gretzky in the middle of June. "If he says 'don't play,' then I won't play. But I know which way I'm leaning."

Agent Mike Barnett was saying "don't play."

"Wayne may be 26 years of age but with all the exhibition games, all the playoff games, the previous Canada Cups, all-star games, Rendez-Vous

'87 and a world championship, he's played what amounts to a dozen, not nine."

Gretzky said it wasn't that he didn't want to play for Canada.

"I'm concerned we play the Canada Cup series too often," he said. "I think it should be held once every six years. Then everybody would look forward to it as a once- or twice-a-career event, and everyone would look forward to it as a great thrill."

Gretzky said he knew the dangers of such loose talk.

"I've already had people tell me it wouldn't be patriotic if I didn't play." On July 16 the exclusive story ran in *The Edmonton Sun.*

"He'll Play!" screamed the headline.

Gretzky told me he'd made a deal with Alan Eagleson. He'd play if the Eagle gave him his word that there would not be another Canada Cup until 1992.

"I was probably the first guy ever to take a stand on the Canada Cup," said Gretzky. "I stood up for the 30 guys who play these games. We didn't want to play them every second season. It was time for somebody to take a stand that we were playing these games too often."

Gretzky also made his first of many pitches for the series he said they all really wanted to play.

"It would be different if it were a Canada-Russia series like 1972," he said. "It has always been my dream to play in a series like they had in 1972."

Gretzky knew he had to play well in this series after having threatened to not play in it in the first place. And Mario Lemieux was in a similar boat, having re-

Gretzky sticks it to the Russians.

fused to answer Canada's call to play in the previous two world championships.

Ask not what your country can do for you but what you can do for your country was not a philosophy Lemieux had embraced in the past.

But he embraced the idea of playing with Gretzky and scored all three goals, with No. 99 setting up two of them, as Canada beat the U.S. 3-2 in Hamilton.

Canada rolled through the tournament much like the team did in 1981 when it was shocked 8-1 in the end. In fact, after the round-robin, there were a lot of comparisons to 1981. Canada had no losses and a tie in '81, and the tie was a 4-4 game against the Czechs. Same story in 1987, right down to the 4-4 tie with the Czechs.

Canada met Czechoslovakia in the sudden-death semifinal in Montreal and won 5-3. Gretzky and Lemieux dominated. And Gretzky, for one, was quite happy he'd decided to play. Lemieux, too.

"This has turned out to be the biggest thing since '72," said Gretzky. "Think about it. Most of the other times we just had to beat them once. There were two games in Rendez-Vous, but we had to win just one to get a tie.

"I'm not saying I want to settle for this series. I want to play in an eight-game series with four in Russia and four games in Canada. But I do think this has become the most meaningful series we've had since 1972," he said as the Russians and Canadians prepared for the best-of-three final.

The Russians won the first one 6-5 in overtime in Montreal. But the Canadians didn't seem to be rattled other than, well, maybe No. 99.

Canada won the next one in a game which will be remembered as one

of the greatest games ever played. It was also one of the greatest games Gretzky ever played, and he didn't get a goal in his greatest game.

"It was the second game of the 1987 Canada Cup series," he said, looking back years later.

"That was the best game I ever played in my life. We'd lost the first game and after the game my dad was really mad. He said, 'Don't you ever do that again!' That's really something when you've just lost a game and your dad is blaming you for it. He said I had stayed on the ice too long in overtime and I was on the ice when they scored the winner."

Gretzky had five points in the game.

In the opening game Gretzky and Lemieux had a two-on-one and Lemieux passed the puck to Gretzky for the shot.

"You're a better scorer than I am. But I'm a better passer than you are. I'll make the passes, you take the shots," Wayne told Mario.

"We won on desire and hard work," said Gretzky after that game, after he set up Lemieux for the winner at 10:07 of the second overtime.

"It's easy to score when you are playing with the greatest hockey player in the world," said Lemieux.

"We play a lot alike," said Gretzky. "It's like Jari Kurri and I play. We play on instinct and go to the holes."

"Double Trouble" was the headline on *The Edmonton Sun*'s first sports page that day.

"66 And 99 So Fine" was the subhead.

It was written that no human being could do more to win a hockey game than Gretzky did that night. As I phrased it: "It was the best versus the best and the best of the best played his best game ever."

"I've seen him play for 10 years and I've never seen him play a better game," said Paul Coffey.

"He was scary," said Doug Crossman. "What he did tonight was unbelievable. He played the game better than anyone has ever played it and he played it for 4½ periods."

Gretzky said he kept reminding himself that he was at the centre of the controversy about not playing.

"My dad sat me down and reminded me. He told me I'd put pressure on myself," said Gretzky.

Gretzky used oxygen on the bench during the game.

"With all the double-shifting, I had to go to the oxygen tank," he said.

And it wasn't just Gretzky. It was the game. This game, along with the New Year's Eve game in Montreal and the Canada Cup semifinal in Calgary, completed the hat trick of the three greatest hockey games ever played.

"Tonight was something special," admitted No. 99.

"Not only was this one of the greatest games in Canadian history but in Soviet history, too," said Russian coach Igor Dmitriev.

And it was definitely the greatest thing ever to happen to Lemieux.

"Mario has made the most of it," said Perron as the teams prepared for the third and deciding game of the series. "He will not be the same after this. He now wants to win at all costs."

Mario could hear the cheers.

"That's the loudest I've ever heard a crowd cheer for me," he said after his overtime winner.

Canada won Game 3 by the now familiar 6-5 score. There was 1:26 remaining in the game.

On the magic play, Gretzky cruised down the left wing, drawing one defenceman across while Larry Murphy drove to the net, taking the other. That left Lemieux in the slot. After 215 minutes and 40 seconds of unbelievable hockey it was over.

"No. 66 was going to get it no matter what," said Gretzky of the pass.

"This is much more special than 1984," said Gretzky. "It's so much more special because of the way we did it. We were down 3-0! When you are down 3-0 you are out of the game!"

Indeed.

Gretzky and the other Oilers had a moment together in that dressing room to toast themselves.

"We won the Stanley Cup and Canada Cup in 1984 and now we've done it again in 1987," said Mark Messier.

"I think everybody feels the same," said 1984 hero Coffey. "The feeling right here, right now, is, 'Geez! I played in that!' This is one for everybody to tell their kids about."

But the biggest grin in the room belonged to Lemieux.

"Everyone dreams of a moment like this," said Lemieux. "This is the most beautiful moment of my life."

Glen Sather was on the Team Canada management team that year.

"At that time Mario had been in the league for a couple of years but hadn't really taken off. He hadn't done an awful lot yet. He hadn't become Mario Lemieux yet. I think Wayne and Mark and the players on that team really taught Mario what it takes to be a great player in the NHL. He learned that from those guys. And that's the way it should be. The great players should teach the new guys what it takes to win.

"That was the first real opportunity Mario had to be exposed to those guys. He learned a lot from them. His career took off after that series in '87. He became Mario Lemieux."

Sather said he'll take Lemieux's famous goal over Paul Henderson's.

"I know Henderson's goal was a very unique situation. But when you think about how that goal was scored ...

"Just the purity of those two goals, well, there was no comparison. Henderson's goal was kind of scored on a scramble from in front of the net. I don't want to say a fluke play. But it wasn't a real play. It was a scramble.

"Wayne's setting up of that play was a real play. It was off a faceoff. Down the boards. Into the corner. Drop it back. Great shot. It was an executed, highly skilled play.

"The Gretzky play described the way hockey was in the '80s while Henderson's goal described the way it was in the '70s. That's the way it was. They were both great goals in great situations and they both won great tournaments."

When Gretzky retired in New York, Lemieux was there to say what he needed to say.

"There's never going to be another Gretzky. He was the greatest player

Gretz takes a Coffey break.

of all time and he taught me a lot. I think back in 1987, playing with him in the Canada Cup and having a chance to practise with him for six weeks, he really showed me how to be a winner, how to win, how hard you have to work every day to become the No. 1 player in the world. It doesn't come easy. Just his work ethic. It was a great experience for me."

Gretzky had made a deal with Alan Eagleson that there wouldn't be another Canada Cup until 1992. They were back at it in 1991.

And when they went to camp on Aug. 7 without Mario Lemieux or Mark Messier on board, the question was what player would be the wind beneath Gretzky's wings this time?

"In 1987, from my vantage point, Wayne told Mario everything he knew about how to win," said Team Canada coach Mike Keenan. "It's like he said, 'Mario, here's everything you need to know, but you're still not going to become a better player than me.' Wayne needs the stimulus of having other people push him. He needs that leadership role. You see it on any championship team. Players develop an unselfish attitude and develop a positive rivalry."

No. 99 had been the top scorer in all three Canada Cups in which he'd played to that point, but he was missing a lot of familiar faces from other Canada Cups. There was a changing of the guard going on. And with Lemieux out with an injury, and Messier recuperating from a year of injuries and about to tell the world he'd played his last game as an Edmonton Oiler, Gretzky was looking at a lot of new faces.

The Messier problem was rectified before the end of camp. Gretzky had been working on him by phone for days.

"I don't think I'd be here if Wayne hadn't kept phoning," said Messier.

It was Gretzky and Eric Lindros who made the match to replace the missing Lemieux and beat the Americans and move into first place in the tournament.

"Gretzky played one of his greatest-hockey-player-in-the-world games," said Keenan of Wayne's goal and three assists in a 6-3 win. But Lindros was on the same line and "was a physical force as well as an offensive threat," said the coach.

In a big game against Sweden it was Gretzky and Oilers goaltender Bill Ranford in a 4-1 win.

"Ranford was almost flawless. And what do you say about Wayne? He was a magician," said Keenan. "He showed it again tonight. He showed a lot of leadership. Our best player was best."

Gretzky made brilliant pass-play setups to Steve Larmer, Paul Coffey and Dirk Graham to win that one.

Against the Czechs in Montreal, for the third straight game, Gretzky turned the Canada Cup into his own personal production. For the third straight game he was the Labatt Player of the Game for Canada.

Gretzky scored a goal three minutes and four seconds into the game to prevent the Czechs from getting any crazy ideas. And then, at the start of the second period, he scored a goal that was a carbon copy of the one he scored over Mike Vernon's left shoulder during the 1988 Stanley Cup playoffs against Calgary. Canada won 6-2.

"I haven't seen him play this possessed since 1987," said Messier. "And

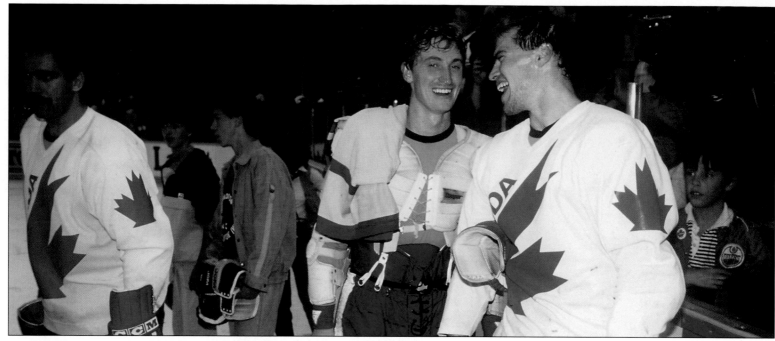

OIL FRIENDS: Gretzky and Mark Messier share a Canada Cup laugh.

if he was possessed in '87 he's triple-possessed now. I don't think I've ever seen him play better."

Al MacInnis, who also scored two goals, said he was in awe.

"He's just been putting on a clinic since Day 1. I've played against him for eight years. I know what he can do. But every time he makes a play, I'm saying, 'Holy cow, look at that!' But it doesn't seem to faze the Oilers guys any more."

The next day at practice, Keenan said, "Gretzky has renewed life," and No. 99 confessed that he'd hired a personal trainer, Jim Zimmerman, to work with him in the summer to get ready.

"It's what you have to do if you're going to play in 1999," said No. 99.

"You can't reach 39 years old and say, 'I better start getting in shape.' You have to go do it now. Besides, I don't want somebody coming up to me in three years and saying it's time to quit. I want to walk away with people saying I could play another three years.

"And I really want to win this," Gretzky continued. "When I was sold, I went from a Stanley Cup-champion team to a team that was 17th overall. If you're realistic, it's pretty tough to win a Stanley Cup on a team that's 17th overall."

Gretzky's Canada Cup came to a crashing conclusion when Gary Suter of the U.S. sent him face-first into the boards in Game 1 of the best-of-three final.

Mark Messier took over that night and led Canada to a 4-1 win.

"His friend and former teammate went down and Mark Messier was the man who was responsible for picking this team up tonight," said Keenan. "He felt a great deal of compassion for Wayne. He knows how much Wayne wants to be in this tournament, to be on this ice."

There was justice at Hamilton's Copps Coliseum – where signs such as "Neuter Suter" were everywhere – when the guy who took Gretzky out of the Canada Cup became the goat in a 4-2 empty-net Canadian triumph as Steve Larmer scored the winning goal on a breakaway at Suter's expense.

And there was Gretzky, who led all Team Canada players with 12 points and who was about to miss a significant part of the coming hockey season, at centre ice accepting the trophy.

"It was very difficult not to play in that game," he said. "I've never had to go through this situation before. But I knew we would win. Every year I've been here I've said, 'This is the best Canada Cup team I've played for,' and this was the best Canada Cup team I've played for. This was better than the '87 team."

The next time Gretzky played internationally, winning and losing wasn't a big deal. During the lockout year of 1994, Gretzky put his own team together. The Ninety-Nines played six games in Europe.

The Wayne Gretzky Travelling All-Stars & Road Kings tour of Europe included ex-Oilers Messier, Coffey, McSorley, Huddy, Lowe, Fuhr and even Pat Conacher and Edmonton native Kelly Hrudey.

Gretzky's best man, Eddie Mio, was the travelling secretary for the group which was coached by Doug Wilson, with Messier's dad Doug and Gretzky's dad Walter along as assistant coaches. McSorley's dad Bill and Coffey's dad Jack were also part of the tour team.

The tour opened in Helsinki against Jari Kurri's team Jokerit, where officials reported they could have sold 50,000 tickets easy. They sold out Jaahalli arena in an hour.

After much debate about which team Kurri would play for, Gretzky offered him a spot on a line with himself and Messier to swing the deal.

Everybody had a terrific time.

"We had a million laughs," said Conacher.

Wilson, he reported, ran it like a regular team, complete with 1 a.m. room checks. Players not in the room by 1 a.m. were fined. The room in question, however, he pointed out, was the hotel bar.

Gretzky's Ninety-Nines ought to have held training camp in Whistler, B.C. That's where Team Canada gathered next for the inaugural World Cup of Hockey. To get there, Gretzky had to drive up Highway 99 and past all the signs that said "99 Watch" – and even past the Ninety-Niner Restaurant, where he stopped for a hotdog that got a less-than-ringing endorsement from No. 99.

And was I the only one to notice that each new phase of

Gretzky's hockey life began in British Columbia? He signed his World Hockey Association contract in Nelson Skalbania's jet somewhere over B.C. His first on-ice experience as a Los Angeles King was at training camp in Victoria. His first game as a St. Louis Blue was in Vancouver. And now he was in Whistler getting ready to play with Messier as a New York Ranger.

And the road to Whistler for Gretzky and a significant number of players from Team '96 was one last time down the road for old times' sake.

Glen Sather was coaching the team. He'd picked Gretzky, Messier, Coffey, Billy Ranford, Curtis Joseph, Adam Graves and Vincent Damphousse from the Oilers alumni plus the entire Oilers training, equipment and PR staff for the project.

"I had to laugh when I saw all those 99 signs coming up here," said trainer Barry Stafford. "And I couldn't help but think about what this one means to a lot of guys. This one is special for a lot of guys. There's no question it's probably the last hurrah. How many more years can they play?" he asked of Gretzky, Messier and Coffey.

"They're the core group from one of the best groups of players ever to play together, and every time they get together with a Team Canada it's still an extension of it for them. Part of my job is to talk to all the players before they get here, and these guys are excited to be coming here and to be back playing together in one of these again. They've had that ever since they left Edmonton."

Sather gave Team Canada a short speech at the start of camp, which he ended with: "And by the way, Wayne Gretzky is captain. Anybody got a problem with that?"

Nobody stuck up their hand. A few players looked over at Messier, but he had a great grin on his face.

"Slats just threw it out," said Messier. "Guys kind of looked at each other as if to say, 'No, I don't think anybody is going to have a problem with that.' Wayne has been the Canada Cup captain since 1984."

The interesting twist was that Messier remained captain with the Rangers when Gretzky joined him in New York.

"In New York, definitely Mark," said Gretzky. "He's the captain of that team."

Wayne Gretzky's dreams of a gold medal were dashed at the 1998 Nagano Olympics.

Sather scheduled a pre-tournament game in Edmonton and when Team Canada walked into the Oilers dressing room he made sure all the ex-Oilers on the team, including Gretzky and Messier, had the same stalls they'd had when they played in Edmonton.

Then, just before game time, he announced his starting lineup.

Wayne Gretzky. Mark Messier. Paul Coffey. Adam Graves. Curtis Joseph. Lyle Odelein.

"Maybe he thought I was Selmar," said Odelein of his brother, a former Oilers draft choice.

"I wanted to put them together," said Sather. "I figured it would be the last time they'd play together on this ice in front of this crowd. I felt emotional about it. It was fun."

It was also worthy of a standing ovation.

The Edmonton fans insisted on yelling "Moooooooose," when Messier touched the puck. Where that came from, nobody knew. They never used to do that when he was an Oiler.

"I thought they were booing me at first," said Messier. "I never heard that here before. That was weird. It sure was nice of Slats to do it. We can't help but come back here and have memories flood through our minds."

Gretzky had three assists in that game against Slovakia to bring his pre-tournament-leading points total to eight.

"Gretzky looked great, didn't he?" said Sather. "He was really dancing. You could see the gleam in his eye."

Gretzky was delighted with the night. "I was really tickled by it," he said. "It was really special. Just to be in this building and back on that bench ..."

As the tournament began, Gretzky was still looking reborn. He'd been called "The Grey One" by some scribes because of his recent regular-season struggles in Los Angeles and St. Louis. But he had jump.

"Look at him," said Sather after the tournament was under way. "Look at the legs. Look at the eyes. He's laughing. He's having fun."

The World Cup of Hockey was a struggle for Sather's Team Canada. It narrowly averted the national embarrassment of missing the playoffs when Steve Larmer saved the Canadian bacon with less than four minutes to go for a 3-2 win over Slovakia.

Gretzky, for the second game in a row, was voted Canada's best player.

"The one guy who doesn't look tired, amazingly, is Gretzky," said Slats.

Canada made it to the best-of-three final against the U.S. and won Game 1 in Philadelphia with a goal in overtime that was clearly offside.

In Montreal between games, Walter Gretzky mentioned the O-word for the first time.

"I heard Wayne say the other day that he'd like to be in the Olympics in Japan," Walter said. It was the first public mention that No. 99 was having such thoughts.

Sather said he thought Gretzky and Messier should do that.

"Wouldn't it be neat to play in the Olympics together? You win it and you walk away and throw your skates in the Sea of Japan."

Gretzky laughed when I passed on that quote to him.

"And the medal, too?" he asked.

Then he confirmed it.

"I think I'd like to play in the Olympics now," said the 35-year-old of an event still 18 months away. "I'd like to do it. It would be pretty special."

The World Cup had been pretty special until the Americans came back to win games 2 and 3.

"Devastating," said Gretzky after one of the most excruciating evenings in Canadian hockey history.

Canada, winner of the last three Canada Cups, lost the first World Cup of Hockey – and all of a sudden Gretzky wasn't thinking about winning a medal in Japan.

"This is a crushed locker room right now and probably a crushed country," he said.

Indeed it was. But 18 months later Canada was sky-high again as Gretzky was named to the Canadian Olympic team.

It wasn't quite the same scenario as with Sather's World Cup of Hockey team. In fact, they went out of their way at a lot of turns to make sure Gretzky knew that the NHL was using this showcase to promote a new era of stars, and that he wasn't one of them.

They named Eric Lindros captain, inviting a tonne of controversy. And they didn't even give Gretzky an "A."

But if there were many members of the media giving the Canadian Olympic team brain trust a tough time before the team left for Japan, Gretzky wasn't one of them. He made it quite clear he was thrilled just to be on the team and that he'd play whatever role they had in mind and be the best team-guy on the team.

The all-star game was in Vancouver that year, and the Canadian Olympic team used it as staging for Nagano. Mock rooms from the Olympic Village were made up to show the NHLers used to plush major-league hotels what their accommodations would be like.

"Whatever it is is OK with me," said Gretzky. "I don't care if I'm rooming with four or six other guys, that's where I want to be. Part of being in the Olympics is staying in the Olympic village. I want to enjoy every part of that. I think it's important that we all fit in and be a part of the entire Canadian Olympic team. It's part of being an Olympian. But I don't think it's going to seem real to me until I walk into that room with four other guys."

If there was some doubt about the World Cup of Hockey, there was no doubt about Gretzky saying "Sayonara" internationally at the ultimate show in sport, the five-ring circus that few players wanting to play pro hockey ever made part of their childhood dreams.

"I never thought this would happen to me," said Gretzky.

What happened next wasn't something anybody expected.

When Team Canada arrived at the Nagano train station, there was such a crush of Japanese fans wanting to get a look at Wayne Gretzky in the flesh, there was serious concern for his safety.

It was like the Beatles, and Gretzky was John, Paul, George and Ringo rolled into one. Finally the police had to move in to clear a path so Gretzky could get from the train to the team bus.

The Great One celebrates another great goal.

Wayne Douglas Gretzky had lived his life as a hockey icon and he wasn't ready for the Great Train Throbbery. It didn't compute.

The frightening scene of 2,000 Japanese appearing out of nowhere for the arrival of his hockey highness was followed by a crunch of almost the same magnitude at the first Team Canada press conference.

"That was one of the few times in my life that I've been a little nervous," said Gretzky, who then told everybody about Cam Cole, then of the *Edmonton Journal*, who got caught in the middle of the mob and was carried away on a wave.

"I saw Cam go by me and he looked like a cartoon character," said Gretzky.

At the press conference, Canadian Olympic team officials, still trying to devalue Gretzky's position on the team, put Lindros, Patrick Roy and Ray Bourque on the stage behind microphones. The media became a mob and ignored everybody else and surrounded Gretzky at the back of the stage. Gretzky was the story and they couldn't stop that.

Gretzky adapted to the role on the ice as well.

"Wayne is a very committed player," said coach Marc Crawford. "He's taken a real lead role. To see a player of Wayne's stature adhering to the system that we're playing, to see him playing as hard in the defensive zone as the offensive zone is something that the other players on this team can really look at and get positive reinforcement from."

Canada made up for the loss to the Americans in the World Cup of Hockey with a 3-2 win over the U.S. and finished in top spot in its pool. Gretzky was clearly having the time of his life.

"I'm really enjoying myself," he said as the team prepared for medal-round play.

"It's as much fun as I've ever had in hockey. We've got a good group here and it's a whole different game. There's so much more ice. There's no room to clutch and grab. You can see finesse is an important part of the game. It's up and down all night. And there are no four-minute commercial breaks."

And Gretzky had no complaints about the perceived snubs the media were mentioning from start to finish of these Olympics.

"My role is different than in 1987 or 1991," said Gretzky of the Canada Cups. "But it's not that much different from the World Cup team.

Gretzky takes a breather during 1984 Canada Cup play.

You get into a team concept. For me that's enjoyable. That's the idea. Talented players fitting into a team concept. I've learned over the years that for a team to be successful, talented players have to check their egos at the door. And, let's face it, I'm probably not going to be around for 2002 so I have to make the most of this."

Canada drew the Czech Republic in the semifinal. When the game went to a shootout, Gretzky wasn't chosen to participate.

Backstopped by Dominik Hasek, the Czechs won and went on to win the gold medal in the final. Canada lost the bronze-medal game to the Finns.

"It's devastating," Gretzky said, using the same word he'd used after the World Cup of Hockey loss to the Americans.

"It's tough to swallow. We hadn't lost a game. Then we lost in a shootout. We didn't get beat. Normally when you lose you can say you didn't do things right, you didn't play well. But that didn't happen here. You knew when I lost my first Stanley Cup in Edmonton I thought it was the end of the world. But I knew I'd get another shot at it. I don't want to be nostalgic, but this is my last international competition as a player. This is it for me.

"The Olympics were a great experience. We all fit in nicely. That was the best part. The other part was that the guys were all great guys, very unselfish and very focused. But we came here with one goal and that was gold, and we didn't get that."

Coach Crawford said they gave the Olympics a game never to be forgotten.

"History will say this was a great hockey game between two great hockey teams."

Wrong, I wrote in my column that day from Nagano.

"History will say that he blew it for not allowing Wayne Gretzky, the greatest goal scorer and point-getter of all time, to take a shot for Canada in the shootout. History will remember that the player with the greatest sense of stage in hockey history had to watch Canada get removed from the greatest stage in sport without having a chance to do anything about it."

STARRY, STARRY NIGHTS

Star light, star bright, where was Wayne Gretzky tonight?

That was the usual storyline of No. 99 at the NHL All-Star Game. Gretzky treated the annual showcase game like public skating and made no bones about it. It was the only game all season Gretzky felt he didn't have to take seriously. With only a few exceptions, including the one in Edmonton in 1989 and the last one of his career, Gretzky was almost religious about that. Still, he managed to break all the all-star records and manufacture major memories wearing all those different sweaters. He played with incredible-sized Oiler delegations and then enjoyed the mid-season reunions with ex-Oilers in the second half of his career.

Gretzky's first and his last all-star experiences he'll remember forever.

For his first all-star game, he had yet to turn 18. And his right-winger just had his 50th birthday.

It was the final WHA all-star event. Wayne played with Gordie Howe.

Everybody else, including the Moscow Dynamo team that was contracted to supply the opposition, were extras on the set.

No. 9, the oldest player in hockey, and No. 99, the youngest, were the story. Even Gordie's son Mark played on the same line with Gramps and The Kid, and didn't get much notice.

"I'm playing with a 17-year-old and my son and still we're the oldest line on the ice," laughed Gordie.

10-GALLON HAT TRICK: Gretzky donned a Stetson for all-star game festivities in Cowtown in 1985.

Wayne Gretzky has an all-star hug for Joey Moss during the 1989 showcase in Edmonton.

Wayne Gretzky fraternizes with all-star opponents Ray Bourque and Paul Coffey.

Gretzky may have been a pro player already making more money than Gordie made most years in his career. But he was still a 17-year-old kid. And Gordie was his idol.

"I'll be on such a cloud for my first shift with Gordie, it'll be unreal," he said when the WHA Stars gathered in Edmonton for the event.

"It'll be a dream when they drop the puck. I was happy just to play on the same team with Gordie. But on the same line! Me centring Gordie Howe! I think I might pass him the puck."

When Father Time, as Gordie was being called back then, skated on the ice, the old man looked at the kid and made a statement Gretzky would remember forever.

He told Wayne he was nervous.

Howe said Gretzky gave him a look he'd never seen on the young man's face before or since.

"He looked at me like I was crazy," remembers Howe.

"I remember leaning over to Gordie on the bench before the game started and telling him, 'I'm so nervous,' " Gretzky recalls today.

"He looked back at me and said, 'So am I.'

"I didn't believe him then. I thought he was kidding. But then I became the old guy playing with the young kids. They tell me they're nervous. And I tell them, 'I'm nervous too.' And I'm not kidding. Now I know Gordie wasn't kidding."

The all-star experience with Howe remains Gretzky's favourite moment

Campbell Conference all-stars Grant Fuhr and Wayne Gretzky.

of his year in the WHA.

"At the time that was the highlight of my life," No. 99 says today.

Actually, that was already about the ninth time that Gordie was involved in what was, for the moment, the highlight of Gretzky's life.

Howe delighted in telling stories about the previous occasions when the two had met.

"I sort of took him under my wing in New York at the meetings this year," said Howe as he held court before the game. "We had a super day. He met Debby Boone and he really got a charge out of that. I told him he was a real rookie because he didn't even ask her out. We met Muhammad Ali and Bobby Hull and Wayne told me, 'I'll never forget this day.' "

Gretzky had played with Howe's young son Murray when he left Brantford to go to Toronto so Gordie was around a lot then. But that wasn't the first time he met the then greatest player in hockey history.

"I was 10 years old," Gretzky told that story on the other side of the dressing room at the WHA all-star practice.

"I was at a banquet and I had to speak and I didn't know what to say. Gordie helped me out."

That was when they took the famous picture with Howe hooking Gretzky around the neck with a hockey stick.

Howe said there had been one other occasion when the two had crossed paths.

"I dropped the puck to him at a bantam tournament once," he said.

Gretzky was asked about that.

"I can't remember that one," he finally chose the right words. "But if Mr. Howe said he did, then he did."

Gretzky said prior to the all-star game with Howe, the Debby Boone-Muhammad Ali-Bobby Hull day "was the greatest day in my life."

Gordie today tells of one other experience which certainly didn't start as the best day of No. 99's life. Howe told of playing with Gretzky and Sam Snead in the Greater Hartford Open pro-am golf tournament.

"Wayne's first shot almost hit five people," remembers Howe. "Sam said, 'Wayne, you're gonna kill people. Do you mind if I talk to you for a minute?' Wayne said,

Larry Robinson (19) and Wayne Gretzky take the ceremonial face-off to start the 1989 all-star game in Edmonton.

'God, no.' Sam went with him over on the side and showed Wayne a few things. How you hold the club. Something with his stance. And damn if Wayne didn't get it right away. He birdied the third hole, a par five."

But this was hockey. And the WHA all-star show was a night for the aged and for the ages.

Gordie was playing what many expected would be his last all-star appearance and Gretzky his first.

Wayne remembers the first shift best.

"Gordie told me just to get the puck to him and he'd get it in," said Gretzky. "And on our first shift that's what happened."

Actually it was 35 seconds into the game.

Gretzky, in addition to the assist, scored two goals in the game and was named player of the game.

"That was tops," he said when he came off the ice.

Even Pops said it was tops.

"This is what keeps me going. It's fun," said Howe.

"He's an amazing man," said Gretzky with a giant grin as he looked at Howe peeling his equipment off after the game.

"He'll never make it," said Gordie.

Gordie Howe signs autographs in the crowd during the '89 all-star proceedings.

Howe looks back now and marvels as much as he did then.

"He was one of those kids who really catch your attention. He was polite and he asked a million great questions. Not just dumb questions, but really great questions. And what really amazed me was that he really listened to everything that you said. What a kid."

Gretzky would later look back on that all-star event and be thankful.

"I didn't know for sure I would even make the team," he said. "It was a tremendous thrill that I not only made the team but that Jacques Demers put me on the line with Gordie and Mark. I'm grateful to Jacques Demers."

As it turned out, Gretzky would play another all-star game with Howe. The NHL and WHA merged that summer and Howe, a Hartford

Whaler, decided to return for yet another season, his 26th in the NHL.

Gretzky was off to the game, with linemate Blair MacDonald.

"I remember they had just finished building Joe Louis Arena," said MacDonald. "It was so new the goal judges had to wave a towel because the goal lights weren't working yet."

As a 19-year-old, Gretzky was the youngest player ever to play in an all-star game to that point.

He didn't get a point.

The following year Gretzky went to the all-star game after scoring 50 goals in 39 games. He was having the greatest season in the history of hockey. But any comparison between that Wayne Gretzky and the Wayne Gretzky of the Campbell Conference team was purely coincidental.

But he did get a point, his first as an NHL all-star, combining with Mike Bossy to set up a goal by Behn Wilson in the game held in Los Angeles.

Washington played host to the next one. And for the third straight year Gretzky didn't wow anybody at the starry show.

Grant Fuhr, Mark Messier and Paul Coffey were also picked to the Campbell Conference "Soups" as they were being called, making it the youngest all-star team ever, featuring 25 first-timers.

Gretzky scored his first all-star goal that year with Paul Coffey and Dino Ciccarelli assisting. But he found himself having to explain how a guy who was putting up so many points was accomplishing so little surrounded by so many stars.

"I'm always in a fog at the all-star game," Gretzky laughed.

By now, we were getting the idea. Gretzky wasn't going to the all-star game to play hockey so much as to enjoy himself and to skate out in the spotlight when it was his turn at the introductions.

"The idea is to have fun," he said, and confessed that the night before the game he stayed up past midnight. Way past midnight.

"For the other 80 games of the year, I've got pressure to produce. I decided I don't need to put that kind of pressure on myself for the all-star game, too. This is the one game of the year where I can forget about the pressure, where I can forget about the shouting and the screaming, and just be one of the guys and go out and enjoy. This is the No. 1 fun game of the year and I come here to have fun.

"Don't get me wrong. I care. We all care. It's a showcase game so you want to look good and hope everybody looks good. But you don't have the proper sleep or the proper routine. The way I look at it, the all-star game is a reward. It's a chance to get to know all the other top players in the league and to have an experience you're going to remember. I'll never forget the WHA All-Star Game because of what a thrill it was to play on the same line as Gordie Howe. And I'll never forget my first NHL All-Star Game because it was my first chance to get to know players like Guy Lafleur."

In his fourth all-star game, in Long Island, New York, Gretzky got them off his back. After what he did in that game – in one period in that game – they wouldn't have Wayne Gretzky to kick around at the all-star game any more.

Four goals! In one period!

Nobody in NHL all-star history had accomplished that before. Gretzky had only done it once before in a regular-season game.

The four goals in one game gave Gretzky a share of Ted Lindsay's all-star record from 1950 when he turned the trick.

Howe previously held the record for most points in an all-star game period with three.

Howe was the current all-star game record-holder with 10 goals in 23 games. Gretzky now had half that in four and had essentially had one good period. He moved into a tie for fourth place on the all-star goal-scoring list with Bobby Hull and Lindsay. Hull had played in 12 all-star games and Lindsay, 11.

"I just got tired of everybody saying how poorly I played at the all-star game," said Gretzky.

"After the all-star dinner on Sunday night I hit the sack early and I went to bed fairly early on Monday night, too," he said after the Tuesday night game. "I promised myself I'd prepare for this one. I'd received so much criticism that it started to bother me. Trouble was, I really felt lousy when I got to the rink."

He obviously felt terrific by the start of the third period when he grabbed the game by the throat and provided a 9-3 Campbell Conference win.

Gretzky said playing on the same line as Mark Messier and Jari Kurri made it special and made it work.

"I think it's a great advantage to play on the same line as your teammates at the all-star game. There's no doubt that the three of us were pressing a little bit at the start of the game and that we really didn't start playing well together until the third period. But it certainly wasn't Jari's fault. This was his first all-star game. He just went out and had a lot of fun and played a fabulous hockey game."

Messier and Kurri each had two assists and the other Oilers all-star, Paul Coffey, registered his first all-star game point, assisting on a Gretzky goal.

Gretzky won a $14,000 car and claimed there might be a lesson to be learned here.

"What was wrong with me at the first three all-star games was that I wanted to have fun," he said. "Well, this is kinda fun."

Gretzky obviously decided one goal per all-star game would keep everybody happy for the next few years.

His point proved, he went back to having fun at the all-star game.

Gretzky is reunited with several former Oilers teammates on the 1989 Campbell Conference squad, including Jari Kurri (below).

He managed to score one goal a year later in a 7-6 loss – playing for coach Glen Sather with Oiler teammates Kurri, Coffey, Fuhr, Messier, Anderson and Lowe – in New Jersey.

In 1985 the all-star game was in Calgary and Gretzky scored another one to tie Rocket Richard for third on the all-time all-star list. The Rocket had seven goals in 13 games; it was Gretzky's sixth game. Mike Krushelnyski was added to the list of Oilers returning from the all-star game the year before, making it, including coach Sather, a record nine Oilers.

The next year, in Hartford, No. 99 added another to tie Frank Mahovlich for second with eight. And this time there were 10 Oilers in the game, with Andy Moog and Lee Fogolin joining Sather, Anderson, Coffey, Fuhr, Kurri, Lowe, Messier and Gretzky.

In 1988 Gretzky went to the game in St. Louis with a mere six teammates and scored one more to trail only Howe in the all-star record books.

That would turn out to be Gretzky's last all-star game as an Oiler. But that set up Edmonton's all-time favourite Gretzky all-star game the following year.

As his dad, Walter, always said, Wayne's life seemed to be planned out for him. And it just happened that Edmonton had been awarded the 1989 all-star game before Gretzky was sold to the Los Angeles Kings.

It was one last time for old times' sake.

Peter Pocklington may have robbed Edmonton fans of watching Gretzky for the second half of his career but there was no way they would rob the Oilers faithful of watching Gretzky and Jari Kurri play together again on Edmonton ice.

"Never," said Campbell Conference co-coach John Muckler.

"You can bet Gretzky and Kurri will be on the same line again for this game. And, you know what? We'll even let Wayne take penalty shots in overtime," Muckler added in reference to the fact that Kings coach Robbie Ftorek chose Luc Robitaille to take an overtime penalty shot a few nights earlier.

The hype began early for this all-star game.

The normally unexcitable Kurri started talking about it days earlier.

"I'm going to be so excited about this that I hope I can be relaxed and not be too nervous, like I was the first time I played on the same line as Wayne," he said.

"This is special. There are so many good memories playing with Wayne. We've played together so many times in front of this crowd. I know I have forgotten a lot of those games. But I don't think I'll forget this one last time in the all-star game where we had so many good times."

Kurri said it didn't even cross his mind that Campbell co-coach Glen Sather would have it any other way.

"I know Slats. I knew it wasn't going to be

CENTRES OF ATTENTION: Mario Lemieux and Wayne Gretzky face off against each other at the 1989 all-star game in Edmonton.

a problem. Hey, I knew we'd have to do it for at least one shift. We're both on the starting team."

Fuhr, Lowe and Mark Messier were also on the team and they all understood what the game meant to the Edmonton fans.

"There are a lot of people who have watched hockey for a long time in this city and if you told most of them, 10, 15, 20 and 30 years ago that they'd be watching an NHL All-Star Game here one day ..." Messier, a born-and-raised Edmontonian, didn't have to finish the thought.

"And with Gretz coming back ...

"One year we had eight Oilers in the all-star game. This year we have seven. Of course, that's counting Gretzky and Paul Coffey."

Coffey would be on the other squad but he said he felt the same as the Oilers.

"I had a lot of fun in Edmonton. It's going to feel funny skating around in the warm-up in this one. The last time I played here, I looked up at those 17 pennants hanging from the ceiling and I couldn't help thinking I put 14 of them up there.

"I couldn't be happier for Wayne and Jari. This is going to make this all-star game a lot more special than most. They had a lot of magic there. I know how Jari feels. One more time. It's going to be great."

Gretzky said he wouldn't be treating this one like most of the others.

"I've made no bones about it, I haven't put any preparation into all-star games. To me they have always been a bit of a break and a time for a little enjoyment. I think a great deal of the success I've had in my career comes from preparation and being ready to play. I haven't put any preparation into all-star games. But this is the last game when I'll be on the team Edmonton fans are cheering for. It would be nice for us to have a great game. It would be nice to win."

This would be Gretzky's ninth all-star game, not including the Rendez-Vous in '87 which was an international summit series in every way. And here was a guy who had registered more assists than any player in NHL history and who, in all-star games, had but one single, solitary assist. He also had nine goals, but four of them had come in one period.

Gretzky said he and his former teammates were in the business of Stanley Cups, not all-star games, and the record showed that. He had only been on the winning team twice. Fuhr had been in five and lost them all. Lowe had played in four and lost them all. Both Messier and Kurri had played in five and had one win, the one where Gretzky got serious for that third period on Long Island and scored four goals to break Ted Lindsay's record for both a period and a game in 1983.

Wayne and daughter Paulina say hello to Uncle Gordie.

There was another angle to the game and Lowe made sure it was addressed. The Mario Lemieux Factor.

"It's sort of Gretzky vs. Lemieux," he said.

Lemieux was the MVP the year before and had been poaching on Gretzky's spotlight all season.

"Of all of them, I know I'll be more pumped and more prepared to play than I've ever been in an all-star game," Gretzky promised.

No. 99 delivered. He scored a goal to tie Gordie Howe as the all-time all-star game goal scorer and added two assists to capture his second MVP award.

It was magic.

From the moment he stepped on the ice until he stepped off to accept his car, it was wonderful.

Wayne and Janet on the way to the all-star banquet.

"I had a great time," said Gretzky. "I couldn't stop smiling all night. I was tickled by everything. The ovation was something I'll never forget.

"What happened to me earlier this year (breaking Howe's all-time points record against the Oilers in Edmonton) was something very special. And this was extra special. I can't wait to watch the tape."

For five magical minutes at the start of the 40th NHL All-Star Game it was Gretzky waving his wand in concert with Kurri. Together again, they put on a two-goal show that was more than enough to remind every Edmonton fan of the way it was and the way it would still be if …

Muckler looked down the bench midway through the second period and said it.

"God, it's nice to have you two guys together again."

Sather said it was terrific.

"It was great to see Wayne having such a good time. It was nice to see him smile. He was enjoying the game tonight. It was a lot of fun to see them play like that because everybody was anticipating something like that from them."

Gretzky bubbled after the game.

"We were giving and going, weren't we?

"What a lot of people don't realize other than the people who watched us play all those years in Edmonton, is that Jari and I, the less we handled the puck the better we went."

Somebody asked No. 99 how many cars he had won.

Gretzky looked at *The Sun*'s Dick Chubey.

"How many, Chubes?"

"Thirteen or fourteen," said the hockey writer.

"Fourteen," said Gretzky.

He'd given all of them away.

Who gets this one?

"I think I'm going to give this one to a guy who didn't get a lot of recognition for what he did for me in my career. I'm going to give this car to Dave Semenko. If he wants to take it, I'll give it to him."

Semenko took the black Dodge Spirit.

"Good car," says Semenko all these years later. "I had it for six years.

Gretzky said if his daughter was 16, she'd get it. But she was 6½ weeks old.

Gretzky's daughter made a first-period appearance that sent the crowd buzzing and had fans surrounding the seats between periods trying to get a glimpse of Paulina and mom Janet.

You couldn't have picked worse seats in the house to sit with a month-old baby. It was right in slapshot alley behind the net.

"I wasn't too thrilled to see that," said Kings owner Bruce McNall.

"If Wayne had seen her there, he wouldn't have been too thrilled, either."

Gretzky said he had heard.

"Larry Robinson told me," he said.

"I thought there was a fight up there," he added of all the people milling around.

Before the game Gretzky speculated, "This will be the last time Edmonton fans cheer for me."

If that were true, and it wasn't, the cheers would've rung in his ears for the rest of his career.

The fans were fabulous for all the Oilers and even more for ex-Oiler Paul Coffey to make him feel at home, too. But it was Gretzky's introduction that rattled the rafters.

When he played his first game as a Los Angeles King in Edmonton the fans stood for four minutes before the Oilers forced the national anthem on them. This night, after more than a minute of standing ovation, Oilers play-by-play man Rod Phillips attempted, with the help of a spotlight, to introduce the Campbell Conference coaches. The fans just turned up the dial on the din.

The last time was a great time.

"I just couldn't stop smiling," said Gretzky. "People talk about things you'll remember when you retire and I'll remember this forever."

The following year in Pittsburgh, Mario Lemieux decided to put his

Wayne Gretzky tells the media how it feels to be back in Edmonton for the all-star festivities.

name on his home all-star game as he equalled Gretzky's record of four goals in a game. And No. 99 didn't get a sniff. Only three Oilers – Kurri, Messier and Lowe – went to that all-star game to keep him company.

And he wasn't very good company.

Gretzky failed to show for the all-star practice where fans had paid $5 each to see the stars in the flesh. And he was booed big time by the Pittsburgh crowd in the game.

"I've been booed before," said Gretzky. "Back when I was a kid I went to Maple Leaf Gardens and the fans booed Bobby Orr. I couldn't understand why but my dad told me they were booing more out of respect than anything."

A year later in Chicago and Gretzky made news by suggesting they scrap the game. Call it off. Not play it.

The Gulf War had just begun. And Gretzky, a conscientious objector, showed up wearing 'KH' on his sweater. Kevin Hopper, the son of his father's sister, was a U.S. marine pilot stationed in the Gulf region where 1,850 Canadian Armed Forces personal had been sent.

LEAN TIMES: The all-star introductions.

"I didn't mean to upset people," said Gretzky of his statements. "I just thought with what's going on in the world that maybe it would have been better to all go home for a few days and think about it, reflect on it."

Gretzky scored another goal in the game. That made him the all-time all-star game goals record-holder.

In 1992, the game was in Philadelphia and Gretzky decided Brett Hull could use a new vehicle.

Gretzky set up Hull with a couple of key passes which helped him win the MVP award.

"With the kind of year Brett's having, I just wanted to get him the puck," said Gretzky.

Gretzky went back to having very quiet all-star games in Montreal, New York and Boston, but started to get his crank turned for the game again as the calendars moved toward the end of the century and the end of his career.

In San Jose in 1997, Gretzky – now a New York Ranger – played with Mario Lemieux for the first time in the all-star game. He set a record just by stepping on the ice, passing Frank Mahovlich's mark of 15 consecutive all-star games. And he set up a Lemieux goal.

It had been 10 years since Gretzky fed Lemieux that unforgettable pass to win the Canada Cup.

The next year, at the all-star game and Olympic staging event in Vancouver, Gretzky added two more assists to his total and set up Messier for the winner, the first time the two had combined on an all-star goal since 1983.

"Something magic happens between players and we worked at it to make that magic happen over the years," said Messier after the game. "It seemed like yesterday. We seemed to be on the same tune right from the get-go."

If Gretzky was scattering hints that 1999 was going to be his last season, the 1999 all-star game should have been a big enough clue.

The first paragraph on my dispatch from Tampa Bay the next day:

"When Wayne Gretzky drives off into the hockey sunset, it will be in a 1999 Dodge Durango."

This one was a keeper. In his incredible career Gretzky had won enough cars to open his own dealership. And he'd given them all away. Every last one.

"I'm going to keep this one. It's like a trophy to me," said the greatest player in the history of hockey who got to be the star of stars one last time in the all-star game.

"I've won a lot of cars and I've never kept one. I'm going to keep this one. It's like a memento to me. I want to keep this to be a reminder of this game. I had a wonderful weekend. It was a fun game. After 21 years of professional hockey, 20 in the NHL, I just feel like this is the one to keep. I don't want to forget it."

Gretzky had done so much and won so much, you wouldn't think a goal and a couple of assists in an all-star game, or even being named MVP for a fourth time, would turn his crank that much at this stage of his career. But it did. Oh, how it did. He was thrilled.

He was asked which was the greater thrill, hanging in with the old guys in his first all-star game or being the old guy who hung in with the young guys in this one.

"I'm more proud of today than when I was 20," he said. "I'm really excited about it. I was really excited at the age of 19 and 20. But there's something about being two days away from being 38.

"The difference between my first all-star game and this all-star game is that when I look over and see No. 9, it's Paul Kariya, not Gordie Howe."

Gretzky gave his first MVP car to his dad, although giving it wasn't quite the way he remembered it.

"My dad took it. Are you kidding? I didn't get near it. Those were the days when he just grabbed everything. Yeah, my dad took the first one. My sister has it now, I think."

ALL-STAR STUNT: Anders Hedberg (15) catches No. 99 giving Mario Lemieux a playful pinch.

The last one he'd won, in Edmonton, he'd given to Dave Semenko. He brought that up again this night.

"It was a different era back then. It was a kind of an era where there was a tier system. The top players made a lot of money, then the middle guys made OK money and then there was a tier of guys who didn't make a lot of money," he said of the group where Semenko, his personal protector, resided.

"I felt that the bottom guys in the salary category were very, very important to my success and the success of the hockey team. I don't believe I would have had the same success without Dave Semenko. It was just my way of thanking him for what he had done for my career and the careers of a lot of guys on that team," he said of the Oilers.

"The other side of it was that I had a lot of great years in Edmonton and I wanted that vehicle to stay in that city."

The goal and two assists led the North American All-Stars to an 8-6 win over the World All-Stars and left Gretzky with a record 13 goals and a record 25 points for his all-star play.

Gretzky always had a sense of moment. He certainly did after the game. But he also did before the game. He spent a lot of time talking to Rocket Richard, chosen to perform the ceremonial opening faceoff to celebrate the unveiling of the new Richard Trophy for the top goal scorer.

"One of the greatest parts of our game is the history," said Gretzky. "And I mean the Stanley Cup itself, the original six teams and the star players who created the NHL.

"Sometimes there are some guys who don't get as much recogition as they deserve for getting the game to the level it is today. And I was just telling Rocket at centre ice that the NHL was lucky to have him in the game and that it was an honour for any player who gets an opportunity to win his trophy. I was thinking that I wished they had that trophy when I came into the league so I would have got my name on it."

North American coach Ken Hitchcock, who was coaching midget hockey in Sherwood Park and sharpening skates at Alberta Cycle when he was watching Gretzky with the Oilers, said this all-star game was a treat for himself and everybody involved.

"You know, it's not just his game. For me, it's watching him and the professionalism that he exhibits."

It was at the press conference after he waved goodbye that night of April 15, 1999 in Ottawa, that Gretzky suggested one of the things that had been pulling at him to come back was a chance to be in the NHL 2000 all-star game in Toronto.

"I never played in the new building," he said of the Air Canada Centre.

"I happen to know a pretty good restaurant there," he added, referring to Wayne Gretzky's.

"And the all-star game is my game!"

He was asked if he'd accept it if the NHL made a special exemption for him to play in the Toronto all-star game.

"No," he said. "If you are not playing, you can't be there."

I took the floor mike and informed him there is another all-star game at the all-star game, the Heroes of Hockey old-timers game.

"I will not be in that game!" laughed Gretzky. "I know I'm not going to be in that."

One day he will. Gordie played in it in 1999. One last chance to play with Gordie again. He won't be able to resist for long.

BOYS ON THE BUS – THE REUNION

It was Black Friday in New York, at least from John Muckler's perspective, when he lost his battle to talk No. 99 out of retirement and stood at the press conference looking more depressed than anyone in the place.

All of a sudden, he smiled. A strange thought had popped into his head.

"You know, pretty soon the reunions will start. I can hardly wait for that."

It wouldn't be a long wait. Weeks earlier Dave Hunter had convinced Gretzky to attend the Oilumni annual golf tournament in August. It turned into the Boys on the Bus Reunion with No. 99 the guest of honour.

While plans were being put in place for that, the City of Edmonton went to work trying to figure out how to best honour Gretzky.

A Civic Recognition of Wayne Gretzky selection committee was put together to make recommendations as to how to honour No. 99.

Wayne Gretzky speaks at the Oilumni reunion in August, 1999.

Chaired by Coun. Terry Cavanagh, it included Al Hamilton from the Oilers Alumni, Bill Tuele from the Oilers, Lyle Best representing season ticket-holders, myself representing the media and Darwin Daviduk, winner of a random draw.

Joey Moss poses with Wayne Gretzky's eldest son Ty, right, and Craig MacTavish's son, Nathan, left.

Ideas came in by letter, e-mail, phone and in special Gretzky suggestion boxes.

When Jenelle Turpin of the City of Edmonton communications office sent me and the other members of the committee a list of some of the ideas that were sent in by Edmontonians, it made for great reading.

One citizen wanted Edmonton to be renamed "Gretzkyton." Another wanted the Oilers to be renamed the "Gretzkys."

The Gretzkyton Gretzkys was not seriously considered.

Nor, to tell the truth, were most of the ideas.

One suggestion was for lower property taxes for homeowners who placed ceramic Wayne Gretzky statues in their yards.

Another was for Edmonton to buy a hot air balloon in the shape of Gretzky holding the Stanley Cup.

"No homework on Wayne Gretzky's birthday," was another.

I'd say you get the idea, but you don't. Even in a book there isn't room for the entire list of ideas. But here's a portion of the list, from the desk of Ms. Turpin, just to give you an idea:

• Build an Edmonton Sports Hall of Fame and call it the Wayne Gretzky Hall of Champions.
• Rename an arena.
• Rename Skyreach Centre.
• Put Gretzky's name on the City Hall skating rink.
• Build a new pyramid at Muttart Conservatory in Gretzky's honour, and have it contain only Canadian plants.
• Rename the International airport Wayne Gretzky International Airport.

• Rename 99 Street.
• Rename 99 Street Wayne and 99 Avenue Gretzky.
• Rename Capilano Drive Wayne Gretzky Way.
• Change the address of Skyreach Centre to 99 Wayne Gretzky Way.
• Rename Jasper Avenue.
• Create "Great One Boulevard."
• Create a flowerbed in the shape of the number 99 in a new park named after Gretzky.
• Plant 99 trees in a park in Gretzky's name.
• Plant a grove of trees in the shape of 99 in Hawrelak Park.
• Build a playground called "Gretzky's Play."
• Start a "thank-you" book for people to sign and present to Wayne.
• Have Wayne Gretzky day on 9/9/99.
• Hold a parade of past Oilers players.
• A Gretzky Gala at Winspear.
• A lunch program in Gretzky's name.
• Create a massive mural of Gretzky in downtown Edmonton.
• Engrave his record in cement at Sir Winston Churchill Square.
• Rename the Molson Cup the Gretzky Cup.
• Create a silhouette of Gretzky on the side of Skyreach Centre.
• Put the number 99 on top of Skyreach Centre.
• Make Wayne the parade marshal for Klondike Days.
• Paint "99" on the ice behind the nets.
• Award a Wayne Gretzky medal to the most sportsmanlike player on each team in Edmonton minor sports.
• Hold "Wayne Gretzky Minor Hockey Week."

- Give Gretzky an honourary doctorate from the University of Alberta.
- Lower the High Level Bridge waterfall to 99 feet.
- Erect a 99-foot statue of Wayne so it would be bigger than the 75-foot one the Alberta government built of a dinosaur in Drumheller.
- Build statues of children looking up at the statue of Gretzky in front of Skyreach Centre.
- Rename City Hall "Gretzky Hall."
- Rename the LRT "Wayne's Express."
- Rename West Edmonton Mall after Gretzky.
- Let Mark Messier wear No. 99.
- Put a speed limit of 99 kmh on the new ring road.
- Have a 99-cent coin created.
- Name a Rocky Mountain after Gretzky.
- Have a birthday party every year for Wayne.

And everybody's favourite, from a very young fan who figured it was the very best gift anybody could possibly receive:

- Give Gretzky a monster truck.

In all, there were 5,000 submissions from the public that we had to deal with. But it was no problem choosing one.

"Wayne Gretzky Way," we decided.

The 4.5-km Capilano Drive, which delivered the majority of Edmonton hockey fans to Skyreach Centre, would be renamed in honour of No. 99.

City council approved the spending of $40,500 for sign changes and the cost for 25 private businesses to change their addresses.

"It was by far the best choice," said Al Hamilton. "When you go to a hockey game and you see Wayne Gretzky Way, it'll bring back a lot of good memories. Everything Wayne did was centred around that building, all the records he set there and all the great times he had with the Oilers."

Gretzky was thrilled.

"It was very special to live and play in Edmonton all those years, and it's beyond anything I ever dreamed to have a freeway named after me.

"It's an award I'll have a little trouble putting in my office," he laughed.

One of the ideas that was also seriously considered was renaming Edmonton International Airport after Gretzky.

"No one should forget that during all my years in Edmonton I was a very bad flyer," said Gretzky of the runner-up idea.

Agent Mike Barnett said Wayne Gretzky Way was perfect.

"It's a very appreciated honour. It's very meaningful to Wayne. I think it was very thoughtful. That's the road that takes you to the building where so many of Wayne's memories are housed," he said of Skyreach Centre.

"It's very meaningful and appropriate."

The decision was popular. But a *Sun* poll said 55 per cent of the readers didn't believe Edmonton was doing enough for Gretzky by just changing the name of Capilano Drive to Wayne Gretzky Way.

The city then changed the name to Wayne Gretzky Drive because of a technicality that drives were major roadways and ways were three- and four-block affairs.

Two councillors, Jim Taylor and Robert Noce, agreed.

"This is the greatest hockey player probably who ever lived and renaming a street is OK, but it doesn't excite me," said Noce.

Mayor Bill Smith announced that a book would also be created into which fans could sign special messages for No. 99.

And he hinted he'd have a surprise or two, as well, to add on Oct. 1.

The combination of the retirement, the Oilers reunion and the Oct. 1 jersey retirement ceremony resulted in Gretzky's former teammates spending most of the summer spinning stories of their many memories of No. 99.

Steve Smith, who within weeks would be named captain of the Flames, spoke of how he would always treasure the moment when Gretzky handed the Stanley Cup to him first the year after he scored his famous "own goal" against Calgary.

But the story he really enjoyed telling was of when he was a kid heading off to Fort Lauderdale, Florida, with a bunch of friends during spring break.

"On the way, we stopped at some roadside greasy spoon outside of Atlanta," he reminisced.

"I went into the bathroom. Carved into the wall were the words, 'Jesus Saves!' Right beside it, someone had added, 'But Gretzky scores on the rebound!'

"This is Atlanta, remember. They had no team then. That stayed with me. I thought about it the first time I walked into a dressing room with the man. I was in awe. I'm still in awe."

Smith talked about meeting Gretzky for the first time as a rookie.

"I expected him to be seven feet tall and full of muscle."

He said he was seven feet tall

ALL ABOARD: Oilers alumni relive old times. Below, former defencemen Randy Gregg (21) and Kevin Lowe are tight-lipped as they prepare to board the reunion bus.

when he introduced Gretzky to his parents.

"One of the fondest memories I have is how gracious he was the first time I had an opportunity to introduce him to my parents. They were obviously very intimidated by the idea of meeting Wayne Gretzky. I'll always remember how humble and human he was. It really shocked them. My mom still remembers the day like it was yesterday. She even told me what kind of chocolate bar he was eating and what kind of soda he was drinking."

Kelly Buchberger said it was great being a new Oiler because Gretzky adopted you.

"At first you were in awe," said Buchberger. "But he wanted to be treated like one of the boys."

"My first year I lived with Kevin Lowe and every game day I used to eat at Gretz's house. He looked after the young guys very well. I felt so lucky to have had the chance to play with him and win a Stanley Cup with him. Even though I only played a few games in the playoffs that year, he made me feel like I was one of the team and that's what makes him so special to me."

Goalie Grant Fuhr, who like Steve Smith headed into the 1999-2000 season as a Flame, said it was strange to wear the Calgary uniform after all the times he'd had with Gretzky in an Edmonton uniform. He suggested he was a Flame for now but, like the rest of the Boys on the Bus, would be an Oiler forever.

"Just playing with Wayne Gretzky is memory enough for everybody," he said of that dream team. "To experience the feeling of winning that we had – to watch Gretz surpass the 200-point plateau, the 50 goals in 39 games, those are the kind of things that are going to stand for a long time. To have been a part of that is always going to be special."

Fuhr said knowing Gretzky was even better than playing with him.

"He had a way with the guys that was great. He always treated everybody with the utmost respect. At the rink and away from the rink."

Craig Simpson said most of the ex-Oilers, when they sit down over a beer and talk about their old teammates, usually tell more off-the-ice stories than on-the-ice stories. Sometimes, however, an on-the-ice story becomes an off-the-ice story.

"We all talk about that big goal in Game 2 in Calgary in '88," Simpson recalled.

"The slapper. I remember just how euphoric everybody was and going crazy at the moment and just how exciting that goal (of Gretzky's) was. But what happened after it was something extra special. What he did after it made a real lasting impression on me.

"I couldn't believe, in the midst of all that emotion and enthusiasm, Wayne had the presence of mind to think of someone else and go give a little kid his stick before he left the ice.

"He went down the bench, tapped the glass and gave a little guy wearing an Oilers jersey, sitting next to his dad who was wearing a Flames jersey, his stick.

"I can remember talking with my father. You always want to think that you would have the presence of mind to be thinking thoughts of someone other than yourself at that kind of moment. But not many of us would. I think for me it solidified his level of awareness of everything around him."

Former Oilers backup goaltender Daryl Reaugh told a story from a dozen years ago.

"We were playing a game at the Montreal Forum in 1987 and they had just installed the new Plexiglas, the kind that didn't scratch, so the fans could actually see through it," Reaugh remembered.

"He had the puck at the blueline and the defence was closing in on him. He dropped a pass to Jari Kurri and there was just no way in the world he could have known Jari was there. But he'd never looked. Jari scored. I asked Wayne after the game how he knew Jari was there for the pass. He said he saw his reflection in the glass."

Several players told the story of a time in the old Calgary Corral where there were two levels to the players box. Gretzky returned to the bench and Semenko yelled, "Hey, Gretz, come up here, quick."

Gretzky climbed up.

"What is it, Sammy?" he said.

"Nothing," said Semenko. "I just wanted you to have to make this climb for once."

Cam Connor told a tale.

"I remember that first year," he said. "We had strength tests with 32 guys and Wayne finished 32nd. He didn't have any muscles.

"Wayne got a car every year as part of his contract, and I remember that first summer Wayne asked if I would mind looking after it for a few weeks when he went home to Brantford," Connor continued.

"I said sure. I told him I'd park the car, a big Lincoln, in my garage. When the neighbour kids found out that I had Wayne's car in my garage, every morning at 8:30 the doorbell would ring and there'd be a bunch of kids standing there asking if I'd mind if they sat in Wayne Gretzky's car.

"My wife would go out, roll the windows in the car down, and there would be six to eight kids sitting in there for two to three hours."

For Kevin Lowe, Gretzky's roommate for most of his career in Edmonton, Gretzky was always a study.

"I still drive by our old place once in a while," said Lowe of 5125 Riverbend Rd. where the two shared apartment No. 426 for three years.

"I think the same manager lives there. I remember we always used to forget our keys and we'd have to buzz him all the time to let us in. I remember there was a pretty fair-sized storage room. Wayne had that thing filled with Mr. Big chocolate bars, Bic shavers and all the other stuff he was endorsing. We had a washer and dryer on the same floor. We were forever

Little boys and big boys, including Marty McSorley (bottom pic, left) ride the 99 reunion bus.

forgetting stuff down there. We'd be gone on a two-week road trip and there'd be a load of our clothes sitting on the dryer.

"Before he moved in with me, Wayne used to live with Ray and Wendy Bodnar, so Wendy sort of took care of everything for us. She found the apartment for us and made sure there were pots and pans in there. Former *Sun* sports editor Kaye Corbett's wife used to send over perogies and cabbage rolls."

Lowe said two by two, it seemed that half the team moved into the place. Doug Hicks and Dave Lumley were next. Then Paul Coffey and Jari Kurri.

"We used to cook for Hicks and Lummer more than they would cook

MAKE SURE YOU GET US ALL IN: The Great One choreographs an informal alumni team photo.

for us. They were always at our place."

Lowe said the thing he always marvelled at most about Gretzky was the way he worked his way through all levels of society.

"One minute he could be mingling with the prime minister or a president of companies, and the next minute grabbing Joey Moss and taking him for a hamburger and watching WWF.

"He recognized that he was an ambassador for the game and accepted that responsibility. But he still loved to have fun and play the game like any other kid would."

Jari Kurri remembered the first day he met The Great One.

"I had heard the name, but never saw him play. For me it was more like, 'That's the guy! That's the guy!'"

Kurri agreed the eyes Gretzky was accused of having in the back of his head had to be there somewhere.

"His vision was unbelievable. What a great opportunity I had. I was the guy who got to play with the greatest player. I can say that for sure."

Mark Messier said that's what really hits home in the end.

"We're talking about someone who's in the Top 10 athletes of the century. Maybe the Top 5."

Even Oilers who weren't around when Gretzky was an Oiler, guys who were there when Teddy Green was left with a shell of a team to coach, have one favourite Gretzky story to contribute.

Shaun Van Allen was an Oiler then, and on one occasion was knocked unconscious.

"Is he all right?" Green shouted at the trainer.

"He doesn't know who he is!" the trainer shouted back.

"Tell him he's Wayne Gretzky," said Green.

Gretzky steps off the bus ... and into the official ranks of Edmonton Oilers alumni.

Van Allen has his own story.

"I remember when I was with Anaheim, and one day we were getting set to play the Kings," he remembers. "The president of the Ducks said he didn't think Gretzky had it any more, that he was too old, that he had lost a step. The next night, five Gretzky points later, we lost the game. Never challenge the guy."

Esa Tikkanen said he'll always cherish the days when he played with Gretzky but his favourite story might come from one of the occasions when he played against him.

"When they traded him to L.A., I had the job of checking him. I'll never forget that. One day we were in L.A. and he hit his stick into my head and said, 'That's it. I don't want to listen to you any more,'" said the speaker of the strange language that became known around the league as Tikk Talk.

Almost everybody in the league viewed Gretzky as a teammate because at Canada Cups, World Cups and all-star games, he'd been one. And if they had never played *with* him, they knew they'd all be telling their grandchildren about playing against him.

"Playing with him was the highlight of my career," said Shayne Corson.

"He's somebody who will be remembered as a legend, like Rocket Richard, and I'll be able to tell my kids that I played on the same line with Wayne Gretzky.

"He made the people he played with better. On Team Canada I played on a line with Wayne and Steve Larmer. I played with him in St. Louis and again at the Olympics. The one thing that always struck me about him was that he was always so modest about his achievements. He was a superstar, but he was also just one of the guys."

Wayne Gretzky with his former Oilers coach Glen Sather.

Toronto Maple Leaf Mats Sundin said meeting the man in the flesh the first time was an experience.

"You were curious to see this guy and then you found out he was human, with two arms and two legs like everybody else. I played with Guy Lafleur in Quebec, but you couldn't believe Gretzky had done all these things, scored 215 points in a season and all that. You thought the goalies must have let him score."

It was as if everybody expected Gretzky to be so much different away from the ice than they were.

Like Daniel Alfredsson, who played with Gretzky in his rookie all-star appearance.

"After the game we sat around in the trainer's room and had a couple of beers. He was telling stories and laughing. Just a regular guy."

That's not even a good story. But because he's Gretzky, it's the kind of story you tell.

Goalie Curtis Joseph played with him and against him. He's not sure which was more memorable.

"I remember the first time I

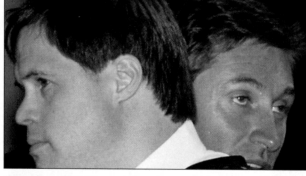

Wayne and Joey.

Gretzky tries to accommodate autograph seekers.

played against him. He came at me and wound up for the big shot and I thought, 'Oh, God, I've seen this on TV 100 times.' One save against him was worth 30 against anybody else."

Theo Fleury had been keeping it quiet but decided to tell the hockey world that he'd been quietly putting together a collection of Gretzky memorabilia for several seasons. He said the thing that shocked him was how Wayne managed to find out about it.

"After he played in Calgary the last time, he gave me the jersey he wore for that game. That was something special that I didn't expect," said Fleury, who thought Gretzky was thinking not about retirement, but about trying to recruit him to join him as a free agent in New York.

John Davidson became a good friend to Gretzky and acted as emcee for his New York press conference.

"I think I played him only three times. I remember one game in Edmonton. I had a personal 10-game winning streak going and he scored the winner to end that."

Jacques Demers, a coach who goes back to the WHA with Gretzky, says he still doesn't know how a get well card and autographed picture wound up in his son's hospital room, or how it was that Gretzky even knew his son was there.

Demers tells of how he told close friends about the accident, how a car hit seven-year-old Jason and left him with a broken leg and a collapsed lung. It wasn't public knowledge.

But Gretzky found out and sent the card and the picture.

Brendan Shanahan played with Gretzky on several Team Canada and all-star squads.

"He would seek out the younger guys. He could tell when the younger guys were excited or nervous. And he'd come up and sit beside you and ask about your family. I can't say enough about the guy."

Even his enemies confessed in the summer of '99 how they loved him.

Neil Sheehy proudly owns and displays a photo showing Gretzky angrily cuffing him.

"Wayne not only had an amazing ability but he was the ultimate competitor," said Sheehy, a former Calgary Flame. "Each and every time he went on the ice, he drove himself and his teammates to become better.

"The only conversation I ever had with Wayne was when we were walking out of Northlands Coliseum in Edmonton after beating them out of the playoffs the year of the Steve Smith scenario, and he said to me: 'Neil. Great series. Great job. Keep the Cup in Alberta.' I'll always remember that because he was not only a great champion but a gracious man in defeat. It just showed me what an outstanding athlete and sportsman he truly is."

Bob Probert has a treasured photo, too.

"I have a picture of a hit I put on Wayne when he was kind of up in the air. And he signed the picture! I thought that was really classy."

Probert played on the same team with Gretzky once, in the 1983 all-star game.

"I assisted on one of his goals. That was a big deal for me. I was 23 years old. I just tossed it to him at the blueline. He walked in and scored. It's like a fish story I'm going to tell my grandkids."

Remember Jack Carlson, the former WHA Oiler who ended up much more famous as one of the Hansen brothers in the movie *Slapshot*?

"You would hit Gretzky, if you could, in the playoffs. But you didn't play goon hockey against Gretzky. The only guy who ever gooned Gretzky was Neal Broten. It reminded me of midget wrestling. There was room

Wayne chats with former teammate Kelly Buchberger ...

for 15 guys to fight in between them."

Everybody he played against has a memory of Gretzky they'll take to their grave. It was a privilege to be on the same ice. But it is the Boys on the Bus who have the greatest memories of all and every last one of them will last a lifetime.

And in August, in Edmonton, they were back together again.

What had up till then been a low-profile event that put old Oilers together with new Oilers on the golf course to raise a little money for charity became a monster event in August 1999.

"Dave Hunter gave me a call and said Wayne had agreed to come to the golf tournament," said organizer Lyle Best. "That was before he retired.

"The golf tournament is a pretty private affair. So we went back to wait and asked if we could sell 999 tickets for an affair the night before at $399 a ticket. We sold those in a day and a half. Then I talked to Mike Barnett and said we may have to make it 2,999.

"Wayne agreed, with one reservation. He said it couldn't be all about him. He didn't want it to be strictly a Wayne Gretzky tribute. We agreed. We decided to make it a reunion. Don Metz's working title for the video was the *Boys on the Bus Reunion*, so we took that title for the whole deal.

"It kind of grew into something quite massive, step by step by step. None of us ever envisioned it being the affair or the success it turned out to be.

"Al Hamilton and I phoned all over North America and Europe getting players to come back for the event.

"And Gretzky was amazing. We set it up so he wouldn't have to sign autographs, but he signed hundreds. We had everybody back on the bus ready to roll out of there and he was still signing autographs. He said he'd take a cab. But we'd set up for a lot of fireworks to go off when we put the bus in reverse, so we couldn't go until he got back on the bus. So we just put some more beer on the bus and let him sign as long as he wanted to keep signing."

The entire affair raised a quarter of a million dollars for 13 charities.

... and shares a laugh with radio play-by-play man Rod Phillips.

"It was perfect. It was so Edmonton," said former Oilers goalie and longtime Oilers radio broadcast colourman Ken Brown, currently the advertising director for The *Edmonton Sun* and the Oilumni golf tournament chairman.

"It was the people we see every day. When you go to an event it's the people you see all the time. But they were all in a higher gear. You can't

Gretzky waves to the AgriCom crowd gathered at the Oilers reunion 99 event after being presented with his alumni jersey.

imagine the electricity with 3,000 people in that room. It was awesome.

"Wayne was just taken aback. I think he had a ball."

The highlight for the players was sitting together on the bus.

"It was so much fun," Gretzky told me later.

"We all sat on the same seats on the bus and I think Semenk saved up for two months for all the one-liners he threw out," he said.

"I'm still laughing about one he delivered. Dave Lumley was talking about the year he scored 32 goals and said that would be worth about $3 million today. Semenk looked at me and said, 'You got nine goals last year and you got $7 million.'

"Just getting on that bus together was great. Everybody went straight to their own seats. I was teasing Kevin and MacT that it would be the last time they'd be sitting at the back of the bus," he said of the new Oilers head and assistant coaches.

The highlight for the 3,000 people who paid $99 each to be part of the occasion was Gretzky pulling an Oilers sweater over his head again.

Every other player on the bus was wearing one, but Gretzky stepped off the bus sans sweater. Alumni president Al Hamilton was there to make the presentation of an Oilers sweater to him and make him an official member of the Oilers Alumni Association.

Each member of the Oilers who played on a Stanley Cup-winning team was on the bus and was introduced individually as he stepped off the bus, led by longtime locker-room attendant Joey Moss. Gretzky, of course, was last.

He gave a short speech.

"It's such an emotional night and great evening, I don't know how to wrap it up in just a couple of words.

"It's almost 11 years to the day that I was, as Glen Sather says, sold. Well, it's really nice to put this sweater back on," Gretzky told the crowd.

"I was a 17-year-old kid when I got off an airplane with a couple of teammates who told me this would be a great place to play. We were a bunch of brash kids who everyone thought couldn't make it, from a little city that everyone thought wouldn't have a chance to compete against the New Yorks and L.A.s of this world.

"For every guy I ever played with, I want them to know how important the team was to the city and to

Mike Barnett (above, with Joey Moss) and Wayne Gretzky had a smokin' good time at the Oilumni golf tourney.

me as a player. Every guy had the responsibility for wearing the sweater with pride."

And that they did again that night.

"We were saying in the bus that Edmonton is such a tremendous community that Oiler players spend their summers here and when they quit playing they retire here," said Gretzky.

He went out of his way to say thank-you to Bill Hunter, the man who created the Oilers and the World Hockey Association, who was in attendance.

"We wouldn't be here without this man, without his vision," he said.

One of the more prominent figures at the event, Hunter proudly took part in the event despite battling cancer.

"A wonderful, wonderful evening," he told Mario Annicchiarico of The Sun. "Great for Edmonton. Great for the players. Great for all of us because it really is a reunion. A lot of us haven't seen each other in 25 years.

"I've seen Wayne Gretzky quite often, though. I just received a beautiful letter from him in my sickness."

Bernie Ferbey, who owns Popeye's Fitness Shop, and Brian Wilder, owner of a well-servicing firm in Drayton Valley, bid for the right to play golf with Gretzky during a live auction at the Boys on the Bus reunion. Wilder paid $11,500 and Ferbey $11,000 for the pleasure. Ferbey also spent $5,000 so his six-year-old son Jake could be Gretzky's caddy.

"I've been a fan of his since I was 16 and if there was one person I wanted to spend a day with, it was him," said Ferbey. "He's my idol, so who can put a dollar value on that? It was the chance of a lifetime."

While there will be many more reunions to come, there was only one honouring Wayne Gretzky on the occasion of his retirement.

"It was such a great night," said agent Mike Barnett. "The Oilers should package that video presentation Don Metz put together and make a tape of it for all their draft choices so that they can see what they should be striving for.

"For every young boy who becomes a member of the Edmonton Oilers by way of the entry draft, if they could have attended this event they would understand what it's about being a member of the Oiler family.

"The bonding that occurred and took place during all those years, learning to win and then winning, is something that will last them a lifetime and beyond."

Indeed.

The coaching tandem of Kevin Lowe and Craig MacTavish wanted the 1999-2000 Edmonton Oilers to absorb every aspect of it all.

"I think it establishes a real strong tradition here, and the tradition is winning," said MacTavish. "I really believe that the players want to carry on that tradition, especially the young players. I think our young guys want to carry on the tradition that was started by guys like Gretz."

The head coach said there's an atmosphere in Edmonton you just don't find anywhere else in the NHL.

"This stuff doesn't happen in Tampa, I'll tell you that much," he said. "Edmonton is a great hockey town and let's hope the hockey team can keep up the tradition."

It wasn't lost on the players.

"You could see how emotional Wayne was," said Boyd Devereaux.

"When he was talking about all the parts that make up a Stanley Cup experience, right down to the trainers and the guys in ticketing, you could see him giving off his memories and it checks things off in your mind, too. You could tell it was close to his heart and just how emotional he was about it was incredible."

Ryan Smyth knew Gretzky from being a stick boy at a Team Canada training camp in his home town of Banff.

"He's such a classy guy on and off the ice. He touches a lot of people's lives."

Paul Comrie used to be picked up at his house and taken to the Oilers practices, where he skated on the same ice with Gretzky afterwards.

"It was a thrill to grow up and not only watch Gretzky but to know him and do that special stuff with him, too," he said.

GM Glen Sather said it was terrific for everybody, and for Gretzky most of all.

"The players really seemed to appreciate it. A lot of them, I think, were humbled by the re-

Wayne receives a gift box made out of hockey sticks from former teammates ...

... he shares a moment with publisher Craig Martin, left, and retail advertising manager John Caputo of *The Edmonton Sun* ...

... and is all smiles on the bus to the reunion.

ception they got. There aren't many cities in the world where you could put something like that on that was that exciting. I thought it was very exciting.

"Wayne said that of all the places he'd been and all the franchises he'd seen, this was probably the most special night he'd been around in a long time. I think it meant a lot to him and the rest of the players," said Slats.

"Wayne was stunned by the reaction he was getting from the crowd and, to look at the video of the *Boys on the Bus*, he was getting a little teary."

Gretzky said it was great that the current Oilers team could be part of the reunion.

"Maybe some of the young guys on today's Oilers team might see just how great of a situation they are in and how much fun they can have playing and living in this city," said No. 99 at the 16th hole at the Derrick Golf and Winter Club the next day.

"It was a wonderful time. I had a chance to reminisce. It was a great crowd.

"It's hard to compare any team to the tradition of the Original Six, but this team, in a short period of time, built up such a tradition by just being a hard-working championship organization. When you become champions, people want to wear your jersey and that means a lot. It was nice to put the jersey back on."

It was all just a warmup for what was to come, for everybody involved.

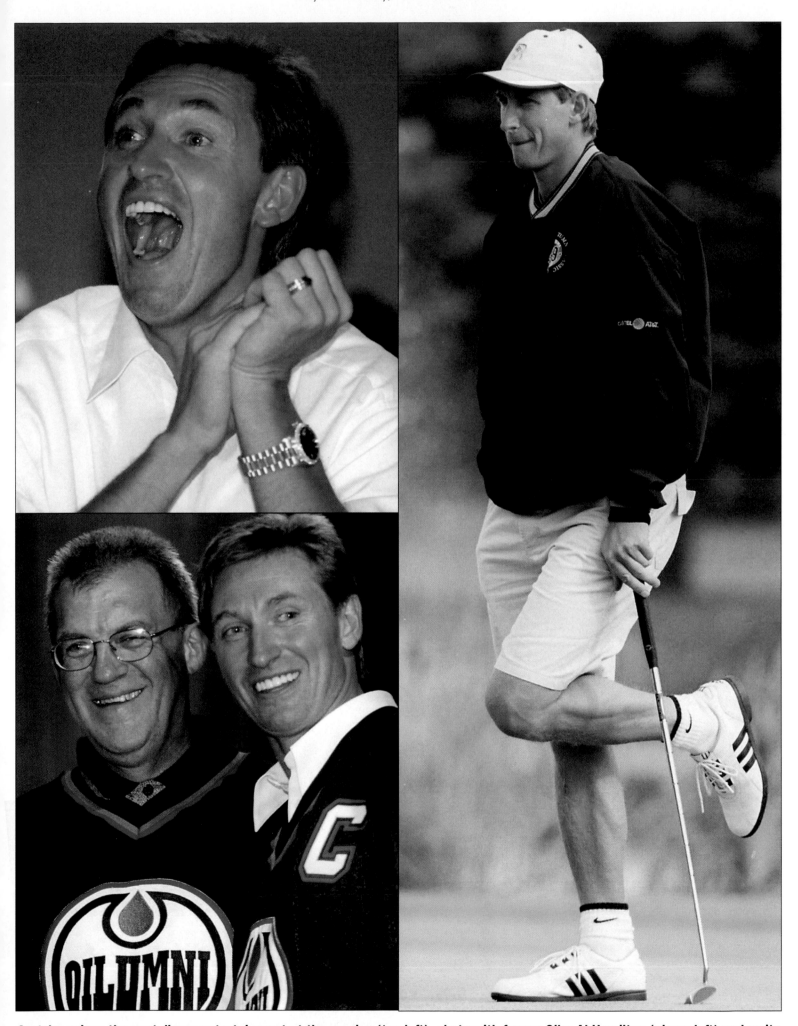

Gretzky enjoys the post-dinner entertainment at the reunion (top left), chats with former Oiler Al Hamilton (above left) and waits for his turn to putt during the Oilumni golf tournament (right).

THE GRETZTRAVAGANZA

there had been some talk about naming Edmonton's airport after Wayne Gretzky. The International airport. Now if it had been the downtown, formerly Municipal airport ...

Gretzky landed there with Nelson Skalbania to announce he'd signed a WHA contract with the Indianapolis Racers somewhere over the Rocky Mountains. He'd landed there with Eddie Mio and Peter Driscoll when he was sold to the Oilers. He'd flown out of there to Los Angeles when he was sold by Peter Pocklington. And he flew back to there for Wayne Gretzky Day, his arrival televised live on local TV stations.

Private planes were used for all of Gretzky's previous flights, including the one that Eddie Mio had to put on his credit card because all Gretzky had in his jeans was about $100. The only difference was, this time Gretzky owned the plane.

When Wayne and family arrived in Edmonton for the Gretztravaganza, it was a scoop, it was news, that he flew in his own personal, private plane.

This, I wrote, is what is known in the business as a "Man Bites Dog" story. Gretzky, the most fearful flyer in the history of hockey, owning his own plane is the equivalent of Callista Flockhart buying a restaurant, or Alberta Premier Ralph Klein bringing in Prohibition.

"It's true," confessed agent Mike Barnett.

"It's a Hawker nine-passenger jet.

Joey Moss presents Wayne Gretzky with a replica of the '99' banner raised at Skyreach Centre on Oct. 1, 1999.

"There was a pretty proud smile on his face when we took the first flight. There was a real sense of accomplishment.

"The first time we took a trip on it, I said, 'This is a great inspiration for a kid to get up in the morning and skate around frozen Javex bottles.' At the same time, when we went up to Edmonton for the Boys on the Bus night, Wayne intentionally tried to sneak the plane in and out of Edmonton so nobody knew he owned his own plane. It's his style. He's a lot better flyer now. The pilot of Bruce McNall's plane spent a lot of time with Wayne. And he's a lot more secure in a plane this size."

Barnett, who was a passenger on the plane, said he'd be experiencing the same emotions as Gretzky would here in Edmonton. He'd taken the entire ride on the inside.

It began when Barnett used to be in the bar business in Edmonton and Calgary. He promoted an NHL softball tournament in both cities.

"Wayne flew for 17 straight hours from northern Sweden to get to Edmonton for the first inning. Literally. He arrived during the first inning. He was determined to fulfil the commitment he made to me to be there. He was a really young guy then. That spoke volumes right there."

Gretzky and Barnett had a partnership and a friendship different than just about any other in sport.

"The intention in 1981 when we started together was to end together," he says.

"Being an Albertan, I'm like everybody else. He and the Edmonton Oilers as a group put northern Alberta on the global map. Everybody in Alberta should be thankful for that. For a serious string of years, a small city in northern Alberta had the best hockey team in the world and the best player and players in the world. And what is not to be forgotten is the fans in Edmonton then realized that. They knew what they were witnessing.

"They were Wayne's favourite days. They're still my favourite days."

Gretzky, in a one-on-one interview we did over the phone a few hours before he took the flight from Los Angeles, said he couldn't wait for his kids to experience Edmonton, the hockey city.

On the night we'd all be watching Wayne Gretzky's face for every trace of emotion while his No. 99 was raised to the rafters with the Oilers' Stanley Cup banners, Gretzky said he'd be watching his kids.

"The questions they always ask me are always about Edmonton and the Oilers," he said. "It's going to be great for them to see what it's like in that building, see all the banners and get a real feel for the place where I played."

Wife Janet says it's natural that the questions from Paulina, Ty and Trevor are always about Edmonton.

"I believe they are fascinated with the Edmonton years because Ed-

Wayne Gretzky greets fans at Edmonton's City Hall.

monton is what Wayne talks about more than anywhere else he's played. It's where we got married. It's where our lives together started. It's going to be fun to show them the church where we got married."

Besides, she suggests, this is where all their uncles played. Uncle Mess. Uncle Kevin. Uncle Jari. Uncle Coff. Uncle Fuhrsie. Uncle Mork. Uncle MacT. Uncle Tik.

"They know them all," said Janet. "And when they're together, they all talk about Edmonton."

Gretzky's boys came up with their dad for the Oilumni Boys on the Bus reunion event in August, 1999, staying at Craig MacTavish's place and playing with his kids, who were their friends from New York.

"The city itself, the hockey, the people ... when everything reflects something very good in your life, you can't help that it exudes from you when you are talking to the children. This is where their dad cemented his friendships. This is where they all started. We go to Paul Coffey's cabin every year for five or six days. Kevin Lowe, Craig MacTavish, Charlie Huddy, Mark Messier ... our kids grew up knowing all those guys. It's nice for our kids to see where it all started. Our boys are into hockey and they know. The kids are old enough now. They're seven, nine and almost 11.

"In New York it was a highly emotional thing. They were just getting it. This is a fun thing. We're all going to be happy," Janet said.

Gretzky said he wanted to drive them down Wayne Gretzky Drive, see his statue, the whole bit. Maybe even show them the apartment he and Kevin Lowe first shared on the city's south side, the highrise penthouse where he later lived, Ross Sheppard high school where he went to school, the pay phone where he proposed to their mom, and Earl's Tin Palace where he announced their engagement to his teammates.

But mostly, he said, he wanted his children to see and feel the building and the fans who saw him at his greatest with the greatest group of guys playing the greatest, most exciting hockey that's ever been played.

"They were the best years," said Wayne prior to boarding the plane.

Thousands of Edmontonians turned out for the official unveiling of the Wayne Gretzky Drive sign.

"They were special for me. We grew up together. We treated each other the same. Nobody looked at each other as superstars. You can only get that when you grow up together. And as a group we didn't treat anybody in town different than each other. We treated the Zamboni driver the same way we treated each other and he treated us the same way back. That was one of the greatest things about playing in Edmonton. People always treated me as an Edmontonian."

Gretzky said he told his kids what the night was going to mean to him.

"I had so many great years and so many great years in Edmonton, I told them how difficult it was to come back and see those faces in the crowd.

"I told my kids this is really special, that I consider this, not what hap-

IT'S A DRIVE, HE SAID: Mayor Bill Smith presents Wayne with his own framed version of his street sign.

pened in New York, to be the official end of my hockey life. Once they hang up your sweater, you're totally finished."

The Oilers had all summer to plan the event. And they decided early what they wanted.

"We want to do it in a sincere, emotional, classy way so that everybody could understand how the fans here feel about Wayne," said Glen Sather. "We wanted to make it special. We don't want it to be about dragging out a television and giving him a car and a bunch of other gifts. Those things don't mean anything. What we want to do is get across the emotion and the relationship that Wayne had with the fans all those years. We want the real sincerity that they shared. We wanted to keep things sophisticated and classy because that's the way Wayne was for his whole career."

The Oilers picked local TV producer Don Metz to design the show that was seen live on *Hockey Night In Canada* and live on ESPN in the United States to open the NHL season.

For Metz it was about more than just being a hired gun wanting to say thank you to Gretzky for the 17,099 fans at Skyreach Centre and the millions who would watch around the hockey world. This was personal.

"I consider this to be an absolutely awesome privilege," he said. "The two most special moments of my career involved Wayne Gretzky. One was being given the opportunity to shoot his wedding. The other was being asked to put together the tribute video for the Great Goodbye in New York last year.

"Hopefully they'll rank No. 2 and No. 3 by Friday night," he said.

"The three most important people in my career have been Wayne

Gretzky, Glen Sather and John Shannon," he said, including the executive producer of *Hockey Night In Canada* in his three-star selection.

"This is about paying homage to a guy who has been around my life for 20 years and a guy I've been very close to for the last 12."

Metz became a big-league TV producer and remained in Edmonton by choice. His Aquila Productions started in his garage when he was a cameraman for CBC and then TSN. At the same time he was producing the show, he was also producing the highly acclaimed *100 Years Of Canadian Sport*, the Be A Player series. He has four Olympic credits, was Clint Eastwood's personal cameraman for *Unforgiven* and was hired to do Eastwood's video autobiography on the set of *Midnight in the Garden of Good and Evil*.

The Gretzky wedding was a big break.

Metz, as a result of his work on the wedding, was hired by Coca-Cola to film 28 commercials at Gretzky's house. He's done several Gretzky videos, and was in the process of packaging an audio CD of Gretzky's 25 Greatest Moments while he was producing the show as well.

The call from Shannon to produce the tribute video for The Great Goodbye in New York was one of the most emotional experiences of his life, says Metz of his work, which was incorporated into the Madison Square Garden show.

"First of all it was so hard to believe it had happened. I worked around the clock for 72 hours with a lump in my throat, wishing it wasn't true."

The tribute was commissioned by *Hockey Night In Canada* and was first shown at the Edmonton-Calgary game which ended the Oilers' regular season. Metz's tribute won the Golden Matrix Award as the best special-occasion video for in-arena presentation, the first time hockey has ever won the award.

Metz said he wasn't trying to meet or beat the New York show. That wasn't the idea.

"Not at all. New York did a fantastic, fabulous job. I have a lot of respect for what the guys did and what they pulled off there. He played a game in New York. Our show is pre-game. I'm trying to take off on what they did. I want people to remember his face, his warmth. Wayne touched a lot of people here. If there's anything I want to come through, it's that."

Metz knew a lot about having been touched by Wayne Gretzky. So did everybody touched by him. And anybody who was ever part of Gretzky's life and times in Edmonton was asked to dive into their memory banks for the occasion.

Amid the outpouring of Gretzky memories, some of the most touching testimonials came from the fans.

Believing this was every bit as much about the Edmonton fans as Gretzky himself, sports editor Phil Rivers ran a short invitation for *Edmonton Sun* readers to respond with their brushes with greatness. The response was phenomenal.

It set the tone for the entire buildup to the event and the day itself. Edmonton chose to celebrate Gretzky the person ahead of Gretzky the hockey player.

And what a buildup there was. *The Sun* produced a 28-page "A Banner Night" special tribute to No. 99, entitled "Still The One." If anybody knew how the city felt about Gretzky it was my newspaper. Nine of the 10 top-selling *Sun* papers of all time featured Gretzky on the cover. Only the 1987 tornado prevented him from making a Top 10 sweep.

When it came to being news, Gretzky seldom was one-angle news.

Whenever anything happened in Gretzky's career there always seemed to be subplots galore. And for his final time on the best ice surface in the NHL, Kevin Lowe was the best subplot of all.

Gretzky's final, official goodbye would be on the same night as his former roommate's first game as head coach of the Oilers.

"It will be very easy for me to remember coaching my first game," said Lowe.

"A big thrill about what's going to happen is that my number is going to go up there the same night Kevin coaches his first NHL regular-season game," said Gretzky.

"I lived with him when I was 18. I could tell then he was going to be a coach. He's going to be a great coach. And I'm

Calgary Sun cartoonist Dave Elston had some fun with the events of the day.

happy Craig MacTavish is here with him."

Gretzky, just before he caught his flight to Edmonton to watch his No. 99 go up, talked about not being able to wait to come back to experience similar shows for No. 11, No. 4, No. 17, No. 31, No. 7 and No. 9.

"That's going to be fun. They all deserve to be up there," he said.

"Where do you draw the line? I wouldn't want to be the guy making the decision. It's a really special group of guys.

"A lot of them have a chance to be Hall of Famers."

In there may be the answer.

Sather promised the Gretzky banner wouldn't be gaudy.

"It isn't going to be 40 feet by 40 feet. It'll fit in with the decor. We're leaving room for the others."

As the day approached some interesting people started showing up at Skyreach Centre in addition to the media.

Like Vegard Dahl-Olsen.

From Sauda, Norway, the 30-year-old fan bought a 21-game Oilers mini-pack season ticket to be assured of a seat among the crowd of 17,099.

"Most people in Norway want to go somewhere hot for holidays, but I like the cold and the ice and I love hockey," said the big Gretzky fan.

And like Todd McFarlane, the Edmonton-born creator of *Spawn* comic books who paid $3.5 million US for 10 home-run baseballs hit by Mark McGwire and Sammy Sosa and in 1998, became one of the 37 Oilers owners.

"These are the most expensive seats I've ever bought," he laughed of the tickets for Gretzky's farewell night. "All I had to do to get them was buy a piece of the Edmonton Oilers."

Finally the day arrived. And it was winter. The temperature was –1 C. And it was snowing.

"This is what Canada is all about," said Gretzky as he stepped off his plane the night before the ceremony, while his kids cavorted in the background trying to get snowflakes to land on their tongues.

"This is hockey weather."

There have been slicker ceremonies than the one unveiling "Wayn ky Dr." But it was a delightful down-home scene as 12,000 people jammed in front of Edmonton's City Hall and cotton-ball-sized snowflakes floated like Gretzky saucer passes to the stick of Jari Kurri in a *Mystery, Alberta,* kind of atmosphere.

A professional events co-ordinator would have found fault with the noon-hour event. There was a great deal of controversy over the site, which was deemed too small for the

crowd; and about holding a contest to select nine school classes to bus to the event, with one student from each asking Gretzky a question. The planning appeared a little country-fairish. But it turned out to be wonderful.

It was a home-spun thanksgiving day which Mayor Bill Smith declared "Wayne Gretzky Day" on Oct. 1, 1999 and every Oct. 1 in the new millennium.

The cover on the "Wayne Gretzky Dr." sign didn't come off like it was supposed to but the noon show, with its winter wonderland backdrop, came off with the world's No. 1 hockey hero himself.

The highlight was nine kids each asking Gretzky one question.

One, Jayson Vavrek, a Grade 2 student from John Paul I elementary, asked him, if he wasn't a famous professional hockey player, what would he do for a living?

"Right now I'd probably clean my highway," said Gretzky of the snow.

Another, Andrew Kucy of St. Joseph's high school, asked what was Wayne's favourite Edmonton memory.

"By far, the very first Stanley Cup we won," he said, then looked over the crowd and talked about the scene that followed the 1984 parade that ended up at the same spot in front of City Hall.

"It was a day kind of like this, where everyone rallied around and we came out and the whole city seemed to be there that day."

Another student, Dean Halliday from St. Pius X elementary, asked Gretzky to name the best thing that happened during his career.

"I came to Edmonton and played for the Oilers," was Gretzky's answer.

It was great heartland-of-hockey stuff. Having a contest for nine kids to ask Wayne Gretzky a question isn't New York, New York stuff. But it fit the scene and made the day.

As for the City Hall site, the way it worked out with the weather and with every TV station in town covering the event live, even that turned out to be terrific. It ended up being the perfect location. It had a charm and it went like a charm, despite the snag with the uncovering of the sign.

"I love my sign," said No. 99, who was also informed that the LRT track to Skyreach Centre would be named "Route 99."

Mayor Smith also presented Gretzky with a book of messages and signatures from fans.

The snow and cold, though it eventually chased Gretzky's wife and kids inside, made the moment.

Twelve thousand people standing out in the snow and cold for the salute to Gretzky said something in itself.

"I think this is why this is the greatest hockey town in the world," said Glen Sather in introducing Gretzky.

"Wayne gave us something to brag about," he added. "He belongs to all of us.

"He's agreed to come back for one more year and play for the Oilers. And he said, 'No charge.' Which fits into our budget," laughed Sather, who spoke without a prepared speech.

"I've always said he was the greatest player and even a better person. If you cheer him a little bit I'm sure he'll play tonight against the New York Rangers."

Oct. 1, 1999 was truly a night to remember as Gretzky's No. 99 lit up Skyreach Centre.

Sather then introduced Gary Bettman.

The crowd booed Bettman because the NHL commissioner didn't give Edmonton the stand-alone NHL game they wanted to say farewell to No. 99. The Oilers had asked for the Gretzky night game to be the first game on the NHL schedule with no other game to be played anywhere else in the league that night. The league scheduled a game in Dallas to parade the Stars' Stanley Cup at the request of U.S. television. Then, ESPN decided it should show the Gretzky night in the U.S. as well, so the league moved the start time of the Gretzky jersey-retirement ceremony ahead to 5:30 p.m.

Bettman was on the stage of the noon event at City Hall, although he was not originally part of the program and had no part to play.

Sather, having fun with the whole event, turned the crowd around.

"This man has done more for Edmonton ... I was going to say than Wayne Gretzky, but that's not true ... to keep this team in the NHL and he is going to continue to help us," said Sather of Bettman.

"All the cheers should go to Gary."

And then Sather led the crowd, which had been chanting 'Gretzky! Gretzky! Gretzky!' to chant 'Gary! Gary! Gary!' much to the amazement and the amusement of Bettman.

"I didn't think it would be this big," he confessed of the scene with 12,000 fans.

Bettman handled it well.

"We had to go a little out of our way to be here today but I'm glad we were here. It was a special day," he said of his NHL contingent.

Bettman said he thought the best part of it was simply "Wayne's emotion for Edmonton."

Bettman then flew immediately to Texas for the unveiling of the Dallas Stars' Stanley Cup banner.

Gretzky told the crowd, "I loved every minute of being an Edmonton Oiler."

He then held a short press conference at City Hall and the atmosphere outside moved inside.

Gretzky's family, meanwhile, went up to the mayor's office to get warm. In a city where Gretzky played for a decade without much more than a scratch until his final season, his youngest kid was hurt on his second day in town.

Fell off the mayor's couch.

Bonked his head on the mayor's desk.

Trevor Gretzky ended up with a large welt on his forehead.

"He was jumping up and down on and off the couch and he kind of got his foot caught up and went head-first into the table," reported Mayor Smith. "Felt sorry for the little guy.

"But he was pretty brave about it."

"He's a maniac," said Gretzky of his son.

Gretzky had plenty of time for everybody, as always, at the press conference.

But, as was the case outside in the snow, the best question came from a kid.

A cub reporter for *Nickelodeon* asked Gretzky how many miles he figured he'd skated in his career.

"I don't know how many miles. But I went *that* way harder than I went *that* way, he said, pointing forward, then backward.

One questioner noted there were hundreds of Oilers sweaters with No. 99 on the back and a significant number of New York Rangers sweaters, but no Los Angeles Kings sweaters.

"Have you seen their new sweaters? I wouldn't buy one of them either," Gretzky laughed. "Smart kids up here."

But mostly Gretzky talked about Edmonton.

"The thing about Edmonton is how much it rallies around," he said to out-of-town media members, trying to explain what makes the place tick.

"I can remember getting involved when we built the home for the mentally retarded and the Down's syndrome kids. I remember I made five phone calls and I

Family and former teammates watch as the '99' banner is raised to the Skyreach rafters (above). Below, Wayne receives a Wei Luan painting from his former Oiler teammates.

pictured on the radio.

"We built our history here. Years from now people will talk about the Oilers and about Edmonton. I think it remains imperative that history remain a part of our game and this city, especially, has become a big part of the history of the NHL."

It's also, he conceded, the biggest part of Wayne Gretzky's history.

"People are always going to look at me as an Oiler," he said.

Gretzky said he loved his nooner.

"I was overwhelmed by it," he said.

He called it "a very special day" and a "unique day."

He said, "I never played the game to have streets named after me. This was a day which makes me very proud."

Gretzky also tipped his emotion for the evening ahead.

"Tonight will be the first time I'm watching a game saying 'I wish I was out there.' Tonight will be the first time in 21 years I'm not part of the league any more, and that will be tough.

"I still wish I could play. I still wish I could be out there. I never hide that fact. I loved it.

"Tonight is going to be very special," he said, explaining how he told his kids that this, not what they had watched in New York, was the official end.

"That was a celebration," he said of the way he asked everybody to treat The Great Goodbye in Madison Square Garden.

"That was a celebration in Ottawa and New York. Tonight it will be difficult. There will be a little bit of sadness. Tonight I'll probably be sentimental about it. It kills me that I can't play. I wish I was out there and still playing. I miss it so much.

"Tonight will be very emotional for me.

"It's going to be hard out there. Tonight there's going to be sadness that it's over. I still wish I could play. Tonight will be tough. Once that sweater goes up, it's the end."

Leaving City Hall, Gretzky went back to his suite at the Hotel Macdonald, grabbed a bite, took a hot shower to take the bite out of the winter weather he'd shivered through, changed clothes and headed straight for the rink up Wayne Gretzky Drive.

He visited the Rangers in their dressing room and the Oilers in their dressing room and then headed for the back of the Oilers room to have a little fun with his old friends.

They were all there.

Mark Messier. Jari Kurri. Dave Semenko. Kevin Lowe. Craig MacTavish. Ted Green. Glen Sather. And Wayne Gretzky.

"Gretz came back and Mess came in and it was like old times, kibitzing over the same things we used to kibitz over. It was a special time. We

seemed to have about 200 volunteers. It's a small community where everybody pitches in and helps out. It's a real special community and Edmontonians are very proud of the community."

Gretzky also aimed a few words at Bettman & Co., encouraging the NHL to work toward preserving the Oilers.

"One of the great things about sport is history," he said. "We really need to have history.

"Years from now people are going to look at the Edmonton Oilers and say, 'That was a team of great players and a team of champions.'

"When we were playing here, a lot of people who lived here and were watching us had grown up listening to the radio and watching TV and the Montreal Canadiens and the Toronto Maple Leafs. When we won our first Stanley Cup, I can remember taking the Stanley Cup and showing it to people. They just stared at it and they said it was just like they had a lot of laughs. I wish you guys could have been there," said Lowe.

"We had a lot of laughs for a short period of time. It was great," said MacTavish.

"We told old tales for about 20 minutes," said Green.

Finally, it was showtime.

Gretzky watched the early part of the ceremonies, the early fanfare and the special video package of his career as an Oiler, on a TV monitor in a green room, his face inset into the corner of the TV set.

When he was presented to the already teary-eyed crowd, Gretzky came onto the ice in the back of a black pickup truck. As he made his last lap of Skyreach Centre ice, he picked out those familiar faces in the crowd that had made it so tough for him to come back to town in other uniforms. Now it was great to find their faces again. He had a great grin on his face all the way around, waving and pointing at people he recognized.

The entire crowd gave him a standing ovation for the duration as he passed both benches, where players from both teams also stood and applauded. They kept it going until he'd taken his tour and had been driven to centre ice for the ceremony.

FAMILY AFFAIR: Wayne was accompanied by his wife Janet and their children, Trevor (left), Paulina and Ty.

"Wayne, Welcome Home" flashed across the new concourse-level message boards as his wife Janet and children Paulina, Ty and Trevor, along with his mom and dad, Phyllis and Walter, were introduced and brought to centre ice.

"This would be a lot easier if I was in the dressing room, believe me," began Glen Sather.

"This is a special night, just as Wayne was a very special hockey player. It is fitting that this game features the Edmonton Oilers against the New York Rangers. The Rangers should be saluted for their co-operation and insistence that New York and Edmonton should be the teams facing off tonight. I'd like to especially salute my friend Neil Smith and my partner for a lot of years, coach John Muckler.

"There are two guys who are standing behind our bench who are proud to be here to enjoy this night, Kevin Lowe and Craig MacTavish. They were not only teammates of Wayne's, but Edmonton Oiler captains, and along with coach Ted Green they will continue to nurture our proud Oilers tradition.

"I've so many things I could say about Wayne. It's important to touch on a lot of memories. Wayne's contributions to the Edmonton Oilers, the city of Edmonton and the province of Alberta have been remarkable. I have absolutely no doubt that Wayne's accomplishments on this ice surface did more to insure that Edmonton would be regarded as a major-league city than any other event in the history of our community.

"It didn't take him long, with his spectacular ability, to become not just a hockey star but a Canadian hero. He lived up to that status every day. He never disappointed this team, the league, the city or this country. We were lucky. We always think of Wayne as ours. We may never know how fortunate we are to have Wayne as an Oiler hero.

"His accomplishments were unbelievable. And this was the place where it all began. It seems like a short time ago when you consider the records, the awards and the achievements he packed into one career, and the term 'greatest' really seems to be the perfect fit.

"I'm proud of the fact this is where it all began. I'm proud of the fact it was in a Canadian city. I'm proud that he had such an impact on Canadian citizens and the great Canadian game.

"It was such an unbelievable, unforgettable time in our lives and it was an unforgettable team," said Sather, his voice beginning to break.

"I don't think the love affair hockey fans have had with Wayne will ever die and I'll tell you why. In this building a boy arrived with his teammates. They changed the way the game was played. He then took his efforts to an international stage and had the same impact. The boy became a man. And then became a legend. I've been very proud to have been associated with all three of them. The boy. The man. And the legend."

The ovation, at that point, was huge.

"It is especially rewarding to know that he hasn't lost any of the qualities that he brought to the rink. He continues to be the greatest ambassador for our game. He continues to hold his heart in a special place for all of Canada. He continues to excel as a husband and a father and he now seems to be driven to become a tremendous citizen during the next part of his life.

"Wayne, I was going to thank you for all the things we got to enjoy together. But then I really thought I needed to say thanks on behalf of everyone in this building, everyone who has ever watched you in this building, and for the millions who enjoyed your play on radio and on television. You brought joy to our lives on so many cold winter nights. For that, on behalf of your teammates, your fans and your friends in Edmonton, I say thank you, Wayne."

Gretzky was then presented with a painting commissioned by the Oilers by internationally renowned artist Wei Luan, a native of China who moved to Edmonton in 1990 and has done portraits of actors Charlton Heston and Bob Newhart, broadcaster Larry King, former first lady Barbara Bush and former Israeli prime minister Shimon Peres. A cropped version of the painting was the program cover for the occasion.

The presentation of the painting was made by former Oilers teammates Mark Messier, Jari Kurri and Dave Semenko.

Before the banner was unveiled, a replica banner was delivered to Gretzky at centre ice by his special friend Joey Moss.

It was perfect, in its own way, that Moss delivered the banner to Gretzky upside-down.

Gretzky turned the banner right side up, had Joey grab a corner and help him show it off to the fans in all directions, and asked Joey to wave to the fans with him.

Parts of the retirement ceremony were a little overwhelming for Wayne's three children.

It was great stuff.

The banner was simplicity itself. The exact same size as the Stanley Cup banners. Last name, number and Oilers logo. Blue background. Orange jersey stripe on the bottom.

Also unfurled were four picture banners of Gretzky hoisting the 1984, '85, '87 and '88 Stanley Cups.

The most emotional moment by far was when Rod Phillips, the Oilers' radio play-by-play man, introduced Gretzky.

"Ladies and gentlemen, we'll now say these words for the last time ever in this building," Phillips said evenly.

Then he broke down.

"Hockey fans ...

"Tonight's first star ...

"No. 99 ...

"Wayne Gretzky."

Phillips hugged Gretzky and said softly, "I'm sorry" for getting all choked up.

The banner was raised to the roof and No. 99's eyes were wet as he watched it make the trip to the rafters at the opposite end of the arena from where the Stanley Cup banners hang.

"It's hard to put 21 years into a few minutes, so I'll try to do the best I can," Gretzky began after the crowd finished cheering.

"First and foremost I want to thank, as Glen said, my old teammates and a great organization, the New York Rangers. This is the third game in a row they've had to go through a Wayne Gretzky ceremony. I'm sure they'll be happy to get back to normal circumstances. But I wish Neil Smith and John Muckler and my Ranger teammates the best this season, and I'm glad they're playing this game here in Edmonton.

"We used to kid a little bit when we were younger that Joey would still be in the locker room when we weren't going to be here, but that's the truth. Joey is still here. It's great that Joey came out. And it's great that the whole city embraces Joey.

"I don't know where to begin with the years I had here. They were nothing but wonderful and nothing but great. We were a group of kids ... some of us bigger kids than others, right, Semenk?" he laughed, looking at Semenko.

"We were just a group of guys who loved coming to this rink and absolutely loved getting on this ice and playing. We just came out here and did our business because of the passion we had, and were embraced by a community we all fell in love with. And that's why anyone who was an Oiler always calls Edmonton home."

Gretzky spoke briefly of Kurri, Semenko and Messier, more to give them their own introductions so the fans could cheer them separately. He also thanked his Edmonton coaches, Sather, Muckler and Green, and

wished Lowe and MacTavish good luck. And he thanked his mom and dad and wife and children.

"In closing, I'd like to thank the National Hockey League," he said. "It's the greatest game in the world and the greatest life in the world.

"I wish I could have played one more year. It wasn't meant to be. But I guess it's only fitting that they are parking me right behind that net. Thank you all very much."

Gretzky managed to get through all of it without a tear. He left his last tear in Edmonton 11 years ago. There were no tears left for his final official goodbye to the game and the city where he was greatest.

It was sad. It was final. But the greatest player in the history of hockey handled it like he handled the puck in Edmonton for 10 years.

He handled it when Sather, struggling with emotion, talked about the boy, the man and the legend.

Janet Gretzky waves to the crowd.

He came closest to losing it when Phillips broke down.

"He said to me, 'You were the guy responsible for making me scared of flying. Now I'm going to start crying because of you,'" said Phillips.

Gretzky's eyes were wet when the banner went up but he thought of the location, directly above his office, behind the net he used to fill in the first and third periods, and smiled.

He had a lump in his throat when Joey Moss delivered his replica banner to centre ice, upside-down. But he smiled thinking how wonderful it was for his most special friend to have a moment like that himself.

The Great Gretzky said it was great. He thought nothing but good thoughts of the good old days, the great old days, of where it all began.

"As emotional as it was, I couldn't help but stand there the whole time and smile the whole time because I was thinking over all the wonderful times that I had living here," he said after it was over and he'd waved goodbye to let a new season and the rest of hockey history go on without him.

"It was tough when Rod broke down. With my fear of flying, it was Rod who used to sit beside me," he said of his fellow white-knuckle flyer.

"The saddest I felt was when the banner went up. That's the one time in this scenario since April that I felt the saddest. Yet I felt the most proud at that point, too. I felt very proud of what I did and how hard I worked and ... I just felt proud. As I said on the ice, it was raised near the back of that goal where I spent so many hours, so many games – right above where I used to stand."

Gretzky also spoke of the finality of the moment.

"It was my life," he said of the game. "It was my love. The fact I can't

Gretzky rides onto the Skyreach ice in the back of a pickup truck.

HI FIVE: Wayne waves to the crowd at Edmonton's City Hall before heading to Skyreach Centre for his jersey-retirement ceremony.

do it now ... it kills me."

Sather's speech, he said, was also moving.

Sather's voice cracked with emotion and Gretzky said it was tough to control his own emotions as his old coach spoke.

Lowe said it was quite a night considering everything it involved for him.

"I got a little teary-eyed for 2½ seconds. Well, a couple of times, actually. When Joey Moss came out with the banner, and then again when the banner went up."

Lowe said he marvelled at his old roommate.

"It's incredible how he's always got a smile on his face," he said of Gretzky getting through the night without letting the emotion spill over.

Sather, however, said it was Gretzky and Messier who made him almost lose it during his speech.

"I made the mistake of looking at Wayne when he was losing things," said Slats.

"Then I looked at Mark and he was worse."

Lowe said he was disappointed

Wayne Gretzky and Don Metz stroll through Skyreach Centre.

that Semenko, Kurri and Messier were introduced all at once.

"I wanted to hear the ovations for each of them one at a time. But Wayne was on top of that and introduced them separately."

The 0-0-1 Oilers coach said he thought the night was great for his hockey team.

"It was great for a local boy like Paul Comrie, and (newly re-signed) Roman Hamrlik desperately wanted to play in the game and be a part of it."

MacTavish said the team couldn't help but benefit from the tradition that oozed out everywhere. "To watch the highlights and see the memories while they were wearing the same uniforms ... that can't help but rub off. I think it was special for everybody involved.

"Kevin was amazing. He's been so composed from the get-go. He was a lot more calm than the players and at least one of the assistant coaches," he said, referring to himself. "He was enjoying the ceremonies as well as understanding what effect it was going to have on the team."

MacTavish said you couldn't compare it to the ceremony in New York back in April.

"They were different entities," he said. "I couldn't pick a favourite.

"I liked the simplicity of it. And I liked Wayne being brought out in the back of a pickup truck. Was that rural Alberta or what? It was great."

Ted Green said he was proud of everybody.

"I was proud of the city. I was proud of the organization. I think it was a first-class job. I found it was real emotional to be part of it. The thing I liked best, other than the banner going up, was just to see Wayne and his family on the ice like that."

Messier left immediately after the ceremony to head back to Vancouver, where his Canucks played the Rangers the next night.

"It was so emotional," said Messier.

Jari Kurri stayed around for the entire game and was in the dressing room area afterwards.

"It was very touching for me," said Kurri.

Wayne wipes away a tear as he addresses the media in a post-retirement ceremony press conference.

"It was a lot of emotion for me. A lot of memories came back for me of the good old days. It was a good feeling out there.

"I wouldn't have missed this for the world. It was very easy to decide to come. Hopefully we'll see more sweaters go up there."

John Muckler, Keith Acton and Charlie Huddy weren't invited to the Oilers room before the game for the obvious reason that they were coaching the Rangers.

The Rangers ended up 0-for-Gretzky goodbyes. They tied in Ottawa in his last game on Canadian ice; lost to the Pittsburgh Penguins in The Great Goodbye, his final game as a Ranger at Madison Square Garden; and tied the Oct. 1 league lid-lifter against the Oilers.

Muckler said he loved Don Metz's video show as much as anything.

"It was great to see that and reminisce, with all those shots up on the board," he said. "It was great to relive old times.

"And when Wayne was brought out in the back of the truck, I thought that was great, too."

Huddy said he spent the whole ceremony thinking how fortunate he was to have played with Gretzky in Edmonton, to have won the Stanley Cups with him and then "to be at the little one in Ottawa, the big one in New York and this special one here. It was great just to be a part of it."

Unlike commissioner Gary Bettman, NHLPA boss Bob Goodenow did attend the ceremony at Skyreach.

"Just to see Wayne stand out there on that ice surface one last time and to hear the 'Once an Oiler, always an Oiler'... it was outstanding," Goodenow said.

Wayne's father Walter said he got caught up in it all.

"What was best of all was that the people were so sincere. They were so genuine. You knew it was coming from their hearts.

"I couldn't help but think of how fitting it was that where it all started, it ends.

"Edmonton has always been so special to him."

Eddie Mio, best man at Gretzky's wedding, agreed.

"I think it was a heck of a tribute and something we knew Edmonton was going to do. Wayne made a comment, 'Once an Oiler, always an Oiler. I can't tell you how true that is. I was here from '78 to '81 and I still kinda feel I'm an Oiler.

"I know Wayne was very, very impressed and flattered. I've seen that face since 1978. I know when it's genuine. It was honestly genuine and he was definitely happy."

Mike Barnett kept it short and sweet, but he said it best.

"Overwhelming," he said. "Typical Oilers class."

Parts of the production were judged underwhelming, particularly the selection of a group called the Moffatts to sing to Gretzky, but on the whole it was the simple, classy ceremony the Oilers wanted with not too many dry eyes in any house in Canada.

Everyone went away with their memories. But one, more than any other, would be most special to No. 99.

Gretzky said the banner, as delivered by Joey Moss, brought on the most touching moment.

Gretzky told of what the crowd didn't hear in his press conference after the first period.

"We had a saying in the locker room that Lyle Kulchisky started with Joey," Gretzky informed the media later.

"We'd tell Joey, 'Gimme one!'

"I asked Joey to gimme one. He said, like he always does, 'I love you, I love you.'"

It wasn't just Joey. All of Edmonton gave him one.

"I don't think I dreamed of this kind of a day. My dreams were to make it and to have my name on the Stanley Cup. I never really thought of my sweater being hung or going into the Hall of Fame. Obviously, now that has happened, I'm thrilled to death.

"It was a wonderful night," said Gretzky. "Tonight was special. I was an Oiler again."

An Oiler forever.

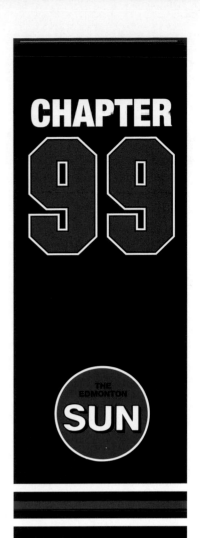

NUMBERS STAY IF MEMORIES FADE

no matter how many teams a superstar might play for during in his Hall of Fame career, there is always one uniform he'll wear for eternity.

Wayne Gretzky will always wear No. 99 with the Edmonton Oilers.

For a decade it hurt Edmonton fans to watch the greatest player in the history of hockey play in those other cities in those other uniforms.

Wayne Gretzky put Edmonton on the map. Thousands felt like they knew him because they did, they actually did. When he was an Oiler, so many people were able to get up close and personal, when he left it was like the loss of a member of the family.

But with his retirement and the ceremonies which opened the 1999-2000 NHL season Oct. 1 in Edmonton, he went back to being an Edmonton Oiler again. For the ages.

Now that he's called it a career, now that the great scorekeeper has come to write against his name, he must write that it was with the Oilers where Gretzky won lasting fame.

It was in Edmonton where we watched The Greatest at his greatest.

It was in Edmonton where he won his four Stanley Cups, where he broke most of his 61 records, and all but one of the 34 single-season, single-game or single-series records.

OPPOSITE: Wayne Gretzky displays the puck with which he scored his record-breaking 1,851st point.

Wayne Gretzky, An Oiler Forever

It was in Edmonton where he scored 583 of his 894 goals, 1,086 of his 1,963 assists and 1,669 of his 2,857 points. It was in Edmonton where he scored 81 of his 122 playoff goals, 171 of his 260 playoff assists and 252 of his 382 playoff points.

It's now you realize that it'll be as an Edmonton Oiler that Wayne Gretzky will live forever.

Fifty years from now, it'll be a trivia question that he once played for the St. Louis Blues. It'll be a footnote that he finished with the New York Rangers. It'll be a testimonial that it was as a Los Angeles King that he sold the sport to so many corners of the United States where it hadn't been before. But when it comes to the essence of who he was and what he accomplished, most of the major memories – the moments which will live forever – were made in Edmonton.

It was in Edmonton where he won eight of his nine Hart Trophies as the most valuable player in the NHL and both of his Conn Smythe Trophies as the most valuable player in the Stanley Cup playoffs. It was in Edmonton where he won seven of his 10 Art Ross Trophies as the league's scoring leader.

As time goes by, the legend of Wayne Gretzky will, as impossible as it sounds, grow and grow like the legend of Babe Ruth. That's who he was in hockey. Or, as NHL commissioner Gary Bettman put it when Gretzky retired, maybe even Babe Ruth doesn't cover it.

"I don't think any player has had the impact on any sport the way Wayne Gretzky has had on hockey. I think Wayne Gretzky is Babe Ruth, Muhammad Ali and Michael Jordan all rolled into one. And he is The Greatest."

Indeed.

Gretzky's 894 goals are 12 per cent more than the 801 scored by second-place Gordie Howe.

His 1,963 assists are 78 per cent more than Paul Coffey's. His ex-Oilers teammate had 1,102 at the end of the 1998-99 season.

His points total of 2,857 is 54 per cent higher than second-place Howe. Compare that with numbers in other sports.

Hank Aaron's 755 home runs are six per cent more than runner-up Babe Ruth's 714.

Pete Rose's record for career hits with 4,256 ended up two per cent better than second-place Ty Cobb and his total of 4,191.

In basketball, Kareem Abdul-Jabbar ended up with a record 38,387 points, 22 per cent more than Wilt Chamberlain's 31,419.

In the National Football League, Walter Payton's record of 16,726 yards rushing is nine per cent better than Barry Sanders' runner-up total of 15,269, and Dan Marino's record of 58,913 yards passing is 14 per cent better than John Elway's 51,475.

You get the picture.

"The game will go on. All games do. Wayne himself said that," said Bettman. "No one person is bigger than the game. But there will never be another Wayne Gretzky."

He transcended the game.

Gretzky's retirement inspired the most eloquent testimonials.

A small sampling:

"Watching his career was like reading a great book. You don't want to put it down. You want to keep going, you don't want it to finish. He was a phenomenon. A talent like that comes along once a century."

Igor Larionov

"He's like Edmund Hillary, the man who cimbed Mount Everest. He brought attention to the mountain. Gretzky did something extraordinary by showing how artistic our game was. He showed people how excited he was to be a hockey player and he made everyone else excited. He used skill to intimidate."

Ken Hitchcock

"He put hockey on the map."

Patrick Ewing

"There is one record book for Wayne and one for everybody else in the league."

Marcel Dionne

"What he did best was make you look bad."

Richard Brodeur

"I'm not going to miss him putting the puck between my stick and my skates. You only find guys like him once in a lifetime. Nobody will replace him."

Ken Daneyko

"We don't have royalty in Canada. He's it."

Daryl Reaugh

"When you skated alongside him, he was so quiet. Like a deer."

Randy Carlyle

"He had the greatest impact in the world. Nobody has ever done the things he's done; I don't think ever will."

Phil Esposito

"I think Wayne, in the long term, is going to be considered the greatest athlete of all time, transcending all sports."

Andy Moog

"He became the greatest player of all time, then he became the greatest playmaker of all time."

Luc Robitaille

"It's the end of a great era."

Grant Fuhr

"Gretzky is the best thing to ever happen to hockey. There are always going to be those who argue Howe or Orr or some other personal opinion. But there's no doubt about who did the most for the game."

Bob Clarke

"There's nobody who has done close to what Wayne has done in his career. You'd have to add career stats of two or three guys just to get close to what he did."

Lee Fogolin

"I sometimes think if you part Wayne's hair, you'll find another eye."

Gordie Howe

"What I'd like to know is how did he always know what the toughest play would be for the goalie to make?"

Chico Resch

Edmonton sports legend Cecil (Tiger) Goldstick, left, umpires a charity slowpitch game featuring Wayne Gretzky and Kevin Lowe.

"People today talk about athletes who don't play hard because of all the money they're making. Do you think Wayne Gretzky played for money? He played because he loved the game. And that's what we need more of. He thought the game like nobody else. He didn't do it with strength. He didn't do it with speed. He did it with his head. He didn't think, he knew. I don't know if any player has been able to read the ice like him. The numbers speak for themselves. They are numbers I don't think will ever be touched."

Bobby Orr

"What amazed me most is that he never stopped amazing me."

Mark Messier

"What Gretz has done is the most unheard-of thing I have ever heard of."

Glen Sonmor

If those words and the memories fade over time, the numbers won't.

Ten years, 20 years, 30 years from now this is going to look like fiction, like some sort of fairy tale. It does now.

Go through Gretzky's games as an Oiler one by one. And don't just look at his number. Look at the scores of those games. One after the other. They don't compute today.

Will there ever be another Gretzky? Forget that. Will there ever be another player who would be declared ineligible in most office hockey pools?

Goalies were not his greatest fans. But one, Jim Lorenz, once fished the puck out of the net after a Gretzky goal and kept it for himself as a souvenir.

In the end, long after Wayne Gretzky is gone and the game goes on, the numbers will seem more and more incredible, especially the numbers Gretzky assembled in his one WHL and nine NHL seasons in Edmonton.

Bettman offered an interesting quote at the '99 Stanley Cup Finals.

"The only regret I have about Gretzky's retirement is when I look at what he did in the '80s," said Bettman. "His performance in Edmonton was probably the equivalent of Mark McGwire hitting 100 home runs a year for four consecutive seasons. But Gretzky was doing it in relative anonymity. That was an opportunity lost for this sport."

Folks in Edmonton were left wondering quite how to take that, but in there, either way, is the point. Even if the NHL failed to make the most of it as it was happening or where it was happening, there's no escaping the idea that the most fortunate fans in the history of hockey arguably were those who watched the very best of the very best in the Wayne Gretzky Edmonton Era.

No. 99 put it best himself.

"I don't know if we were the greatest team in the history of hockey," he once said. "But I'm pretty sure we were the most exciting."

As time goes by and the memories fade, the freeze-frame for the ages will be Wayne Gretzky, in an Oilers uniform, holding the Stanley Cup over his head.

They can drape 99s from every ceiling in the league and retire his number everywhere forever. But the indelible image will always be of that statue which stands in front of Skyreach Centre in Edmonton.

And, in the NHL record books, most of them possibly forever, there will always be Wayne Gretzky's numbers ...

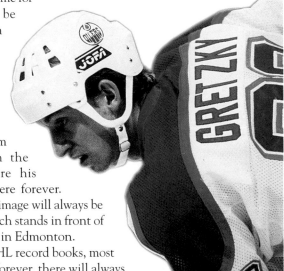

Career Statistics

REGULAR SEASON

Season	Team	GP	G	A	TP	PIM	+/-	PP	SH	GW	GT	S	Pct
1979-1980	Edmonton	79	51	86	137	21	0	13	1	6	4	284	17.96
1980-1981	Edmonton	80	55	109	164	28	41	15	4	3	2	261	21.07
1981-1982	Edmonton	80	92	120	212	26	81	18	6	12	3	369	24.93
1982-1983	Edmonton	80	71	125	196	59	60	18	6	9	0	348	20.40
1983-1984	Edmonton	74	87	118	205	39	76	20	12	11	0	324	26.85
1984-1985	Edmonton	80	73	135	208	52	98	8	11	7	2	358	20.39
1985-1986	Edmonton	80	52	163	215	46	71	11	3	6	1	350	14.86
1986-1987	Edmonton	79	62	121	183	28	70	13	7	4	0	288	21.53
1987-1988	Edmonton	64	40	109	149	24	39	9	5	3	0	211	18.96
1988-1989	Los Angeles	78	54	114	168	26	15	11	5	5	2	303	17.82
1989-1990	Los Angeles	73	40	102	142	42	8	10	4	4	1	236	16.95
1990-1991	Los Angeles	78	41	122	163	16	30	8	0	5	2	212	19.34
1991-1992	Los Angeles	74	31	90	121	34	-12	12	2	2	1	215	14.42
1992-1993	Los Angeles	45	16	49	65	6	6	0	2	1	0	141	11.35
1993-1994	Los Angeles	81	38	92	130	20	-25	14	4	0	1	233	16.31
1994-1995	Los Angeles	48	11	37	48	6	-20	3	0	1	0	142	7.75
1995-1996	Los Angeles	62	15	66	81	32	-7	5	0	2	1	144	10.42
1995-1996	St. Louis	18	8	13	21	2	-6	1	1	1	0	51	15.69
1996-1997	N.Y. Rangers	82	25	72	97	28	12	6	0	2	1	286	8.74
1997-1998	N.Y. Rangers	82	23	67	90	28	-11	6	0	4	2	201	11.44
1998-1999	N.Y. Rangers	70	9	53	62	14	-23	3	0	3	1	132	6.92
NHL TOTALS		1487	894	1963	2857	577	503	204	73	91	24	5089	17.57

PLAYOFFS

Season	Team	GP	G	A	TP	PIM
1979-1980	Edmonton	3	2	1	3	0
1980-1981	Edmonton	9	7	14	21	4
1981-1982	Edmonton	5	5	7	12	8
1982-1983	Edmonton	16	12	26	38	4
1983-1984	Edmonton	19	13	22	35	12
1984-1985	Edmonton	18	17	30	47	4
1985-1986	Edmonton	10	8	11	19	2
1986-1987	Edmonton	21	5	29	34	6
1987-1988	Edmonton	19	12	31	43	16
1988-1989	Los Angeles	11	5	17	22	0
1989-1990	Los Angeles	7	3	7	10	0
1990-1991	Los Angeles	12	4	11	15	2
1991-1992	Los Angeles	6	2	5	7	2
1992-1993	Los Angeles	24	15	25	40	4
1993-1994	Los Angeles	--	--	--	--	--
1994-1995	Los Angeles	--	--	--	--	--
1995-1996	St. Louis	13	2	14	16	0
1996-1997	NY Rangers	15	10	10	20	2
1997-1998	NY Rangers	--	--	--	--	--
1998-1999	NY Rangers	--	--	--	--	--
NHL TOTALS		208	122	260	382	66

● Signed as an underage free agent by the World Hockey Association Indianapolis Racers on June 12, 1978. Traded to Edmonton (WHA) with Eddie Mio and Peter Driscoll for cash, November 1978. Reclaimed by Edmonton as an underage junior prior to the National Hockey League expansion draft, June 9, 1979. Claimed as a priority selection, June 9, 1979.

● Traded to Los Angeles with Mike Krushelnyski and Marty McSorley for Jimmy Carson, Martin Gelinas and Los Angeles' first-round choices in 1989 (acquired by New Jersey, which selected Jason Miller), 1991 (Martin Rucinsky) and 1993 (Nick Stadjuhar), entry drafts and cash, Aug. 9, 1988.

● Traded to St. Louis for Craig Johnson, Patrice Tardiff, Roman Vopat, St. Louis' fifth-round choice (Peter Hogan) in 1996 entry draft and first-round choice (Matt Sultek) in 1997 entry draft, Feb. 27, 1996.

● Signed as a free agent by New York Rangers, July 21, 1996.

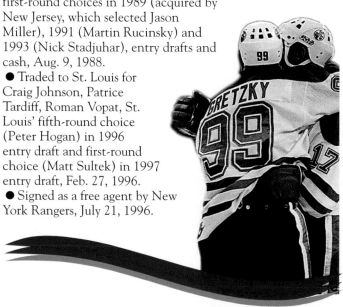

Team-By-Team Statistics

REGULAR SEASON

Team	GP	G	A	TP	PIM
Edmonton	696	583	1086	1669	323
Los Angeles	539	246	672	918	182
St. Louis	18	8	13	21	2
N.Y. Rangers	234	57	192	249	70

PLAYOFFS

GP	G	A	TP	PIM
120	81	171	252	56
60	29	65	94	8
13	2	14	16	0
15	10	10	20	2

Before & After Statistics

Team	GP	G	A	TP	PIM		GP	G	A	TP	PIM
Edmonton	696	583	1086	1669	323		120	81	171	252	56
U.S. Franchises	791	311	877	1188	254		88	41	89	130	10

Trophy Case

STANLEY CUP (4)
1984 – Edmonton
1985 – Edmonton
1987 – Edmonton
1988 – Edmonton

CONN SMYTHE (2)
MVP, PLAYOFFS
1985 – Edmonton
1988 – Edmonton

HART TROPHY (9)
MVP, SEASON
1980 – Edmonton
1981 – Edmonton
1982 – Edmonton
1983 – Edmonton
1984 – Edmonton
1985 – Edmonton
1986 – Edmonton
1987 – Edmonton
1989 – Los Angeles

ART ROSS (10)
NHL SCORING LEADER
1980 – Edmonton
1981 – Edmonton
1982 – Edmonton
1983 – Edmonton
1984 – Edmonton
1985 – Edmonton
1986 – Edmonton
1987 – Edmonton
1990 – Los Angeles
1991 – Los Angeles
1994 – Los Angeles

LADY BYNG (5)
NHL SPORTSMANSHIP
1980 – Edmonton
1991 – Los Angeles
1992 – Los Angeles
1994 – Los Angeles
1999 – New York Rangers

1ST TEAM ALL-STAR SELECTIONS(8)
1981 – Edmonton
1982 – Edmonton
1983 – Edmonton
1984 – Edmonton
1985 – Edmonton
1986 – Edmonton
1987 – Edmonton
1991 – Los Angeles

ALL-STAR GAME APPEARANCES
1980 – Edmonton
1981 – Edmonton
1982 – Edmonton
1983 – Edmonton
1984 – Edmonton
1985 – Edmonton
1986 – Edmonton
1988 – Edmonton
1989 – Los Angeles
1990 – Los Angeles
1991 – Los Angeles
1992 – Los Angeles
1993 – Los Angeles
1994 – Los Angeles
1996 – Los Angeles
1997 – New York Rangers
1998 – New York Rangers
1999 – New York Rangers

ALL-STAR GAME MVP
1983 – Edmonton
1989 – Los Angeles
1999 – New York Rangers

Wayne Gretzky with one of the few awards he didn't win: the CFL's Grey Cup Trophy.

PERFORMER OF THE YEAR (3)
1985 – Edmonton
1986 – Edmonton
1987 – Edmonton

LESTER PEARSON AWARD (1)
OUTSTANDING SERVICE TO HOCKEY (U.S.A.)
1994 – Los Angeles

CANADA CUPS (3)
1984 – Team Canada
1987 – Team Canada
1991 – Team Canada

EMERY EDGE AWARDS
BEST PLUS-MINUS RATING
1984 – Edmonton
1985 – Edmonton
1987 – Edmonton

A Record(s) Achievement

REGULAR SEASON

RECORDS (40)
GOALS (6)

MOST GOALS: 894 (1,485 games)
Second: 801 -- Gordie Howe, 26 seasons, 1,767 games
MOST GOALS, INCLUDING PLAYOFFS: 1,016 -- 894 regular season and 122 playoff
Second: 869 – Gordie Howe, 801 regular season and 68 playoff
MOST GOALS, ONE SEASON: 92 – 1981-82, 80-game schedule
Second: 87 – Wayne Gretzky, 1983-84, 80-game schedule
MOST GOALS, ONE SEASON, INCLUDING PLAYOFFS: 100 – 1983-84, 87 goals in 74 regular season games and 13 goals in 19 playoff games.
Second (tied): three players
MOST GOALS, 50 GAMES FROM START OF SEASON: 61 – 1981-82 (Oct. 7, 1981 to Jan. 22, 1982, 80-game schedule); 1983-84 (Oct. 5, 1983 to Jan. 25,1984, 80-game schedule
Next (third): 54 – Mario Lemieux, 1988-89 (Oct. 7, 1988 – Jan. 31, 1989, 80-game schedule)
MOST GOALS, ONE PERIOD: 4 – (Tied with 10 other players) Feb. 18, 1981, at Edmonton, third period (Edmonton 9, St. Louis 2)

ASSISTS (6)

MOST ASSISTS: 1,962 (1,485 games)
Second: 1,102 – Paul Coffey, 19 seasons, 1,320 games
MOST ASSISTS, INCLUDING PLAYOFFS: 2,222 – 1,962 regular season and 260 playoff
Second: 1,226 – Paul Coffey, 1,090 regular season and 136 playoff
MOST ASSISTS, ONE SEASON: 163 – 1985-86, 80-game schedule
Next (eighth): 114 – Mario Lemieux and Wayne Gretzky tied, 1988-89, 80-game schedule
MOST ASSISTS, ONE SEASON, INCLUDING PLAYOFFS: 174 – 1985-86, 163 assists in 80 regular season games and 11 assists in 10 playoff games
Next (tied for 11th): 121 – Mario Lemieux 1988-89; 114 assists in 76 regular season games and seven assists in 11 playoff games
MOST ASSISTS, ONE GAME: 7 – (tied with Billy Taylor) done three times – Feb. 15, 1980 at Edmonton (Edmonton 8, Washington 2); Dec. 11, 1985 at Chicago (Edmonton 12, Chicago 9); Feb. 14, 1986 at Edmonton (Edmonton 8, Quebec 2)
Second: 6 – 23 players
MOST ASSISTS, ONE ROAD GAME: 7 (tied with Billy Taylor) – Dec. 11, 1985 at Chicago (Edmonton 12, Chicago 9)
Second: 6 – four players

POINTS (4)

MOST POINTS: 2,856 –1,485 games (894 goals, 1,962 assists)
Second: 1,850 Gordie Howe, 1,767 games (801 goals, 1,049 assists)
MOST POINTS, INCLUDING PLAYOFFS: 3,238 – 2,856 regular season and 382 playoff
Second: 2,010 – Gordie Howe, 1,850 regular season and 160 playoff
MOST POINTS, ONE SEASON: 215 – 1985-86, 80-game schedule
Next (fifth): 199 – Mario Lemieux, 1988-89, 80-game schedule
MOST POINTS, ONE SEASON, INCLUDING PLAYOFFS: 255 – 1984-85; 208 points in 80 regular season games and 47 points in 18 playoff games
Next (sixth): 218 – Mario Lemieux, 1988-89; 199 points in 76 regular season games and 19 points in 11 playoff games

OVERTIME SCORING (1)

MOST OVERTIME ASSISTS, CAREER: 15
Second: 13 – Doug Gilmour, 16 seasons

SCORING BY A CENTRE (6)

MOST GOALS BY A CENTRE, CAREER: 894
Second: 731 – Marcel Dionne, 18 seasons
MOST GOALS BY A CENTRE, ONE SEASON: 92 – 1981-82, 80-game schedule
Next (third): 85 – Mario Lemieux, 1988-89, 80-game schedule
MOST ASSISTS BY A CENTRE, CAREER: 1,962
Second: 1,040 – Marcel Dionne, 18 seasons
MOST ASSISTS BY A CENTRE, ONE SEASON: 163 – 1985-86, 80-game schedule
Next: Gretzky holds first through fifth positions
MOST POINTS BY A CENTRE, CAREER: 2,856
Second: 1,771 – Marcel Dionne, 18 seasons
MOST POINTS BY A CENTRE, ONE SEASON: 215 – 1985-86, 80-game schedule
Next (fifth): 199 – Mario Lemieux, 1988-89, 80-game schedule

SCORING BY A ROOKIE (1)

MOST ASSISTS BY A PLAYER IN HIS FIRST NHL SEASON: 7 – Feb. 15, 1980, at Edmonton (Edmonton 8, Washington 2)
Second: 6 – Gary Suter, April 4, 1986 at Calgary (Calgary 9, Edmonton 3)

PER-GAME SCORING AVERAGES (4)

HIGHEST GOALS-PER-GAME AVERAGE, ONE SEASON: 1.18 – 1983-84, 87 goals in 74 games
Second (tied): 1.15 – Mario Lemieux (1992-93, 69 goals in 60 games) and Wayne Gretzky (1981-82, 92 goals in 80 games)
HIGHEST ASSISTS-PER-GAME AVERAGE, CAREER (300 MIN.): 1.321 – 1,962 assists in 1,485 games
Second: 1.183 – Mario Lemieux, 881 assists in 745 games

HIGHEST ASSISTS-PER-GAME AVERAGE, ONE SEASON: 2.04 – 1985-86, 163 assists in 80 games
Next (eighth): 1.52 – Mario Lemieux, 1992-93, 91 assists in 60 games
HIGHEST POINTS-PER-GAME AVERAGE, ONE SEASON (AMONG PLAYERS WITH 50 OR-MORE POINTS): 2.77 – 1983-84, 205 points in 74 games
Next (third): 2.67 – Mario Lemieux, 1992-93, 160 points in 60 games

SCORING PLATEAUS (12)
MOST 40-OR-MORE GOAL SEASONS: 12 in 20 seasons
Second: 10 – Marcel Dionne in 18 seasons
MOST CONSECUTIVE 40-OR-MORE GOAL SEASONS: 12 – 1979-80 to 1990-91
Second: 9 – Mike Bossy, 1977-78 to 1985-86
MOST 50-OR-MORE GOAL SEASONS: 9 (tied with Mike Bossy) – Gretzky in 20 seasons and Bossy in 10 seasons.
Second: 6 – Guy Lafleur in 17 seasons
MOST 60-OR-MORE GOAL SEASONS: 5 (tied with Mike Bossy) – Gretzky in 20 seasons and Mike Bossy in 10 seasons
Second: 4 – Phil Esposito in 18 seasons
MOST CONSECUTIVE 60-OR-MORE GOAL SEASONS: 4 – 1981-82 to 1984-85
Second: 3 – Mike Bossy, 1980-81 to 1982-83
MOST 100-OR-MORE POINT SEASONS: 15
Second: 10 – Mario Lemieux in 12 seasons
MOST CONSECUTIVE 100-OR-MORE POINT SEASONS: 13 – 1979-80 to 1991-92
Second: 6 – six players
MOST THREE-OR-MORE GOAL GAMES, CAREER: 50 – 37 three-goal games; nine four-goal games; four five-goal games
Second: 39 – Mike Bossy in 10 seasons (30 three-goal games, nine four-goal games)
MOST THREE-GOAL-GAMES, ONE SEASON: 10 (done twice) – 1981-82 (six three-goal games; three four-goal games; one five-goal game) and 1983-84 (six three-goal games, four four-goal games)
Next (third): 9 – Mike Bossy (1980-81, six three-goal games, three four-goal games) and Mario Lemieux (seven three-goal games, one four-goal game, one five-goal game)
LONGEST CONSECUTIVE ASSIST-SCORING STREAK: 23 games – 1990-91, 48 assists
Second: 18 – Adam Oates, 1992-93, 28 assists
LONGEST CONSECUTIVE POINT-SCORING STREAK: 51 Games – 1983-84 (Oct. 5, 1983 to Jan. 28, 1984, 61goals, 92 assists for 153 points)
Second: 46 – Mario Lemieux, 1989-90 (39 goals, 64 assists)
LONGEST CONSECUTIVE POINT-SCORING STREAK FROM START OF SEASON: 51 – 1983-84; 61 goals, 92 assists for 153 points (Oct. 5, 1983 to Jan. 28, 1984)

PLAYOFFS
RECORDS (15)
INDIVIDUAL PLAYOFF RECORDS (7)
MOST PLAYOFF GOALS, CAREER: 122
Second: 109 – Mark Messier
MOST ASSISTS IN PLAYOFFS, CAREER: 260
Second: 186 – Mark Messier
MOST ASSISTS, ONE PLAYOFF YEAR: 31 – 1988 (19 games)
Next (fourth): 28 – Mario Lemieux, 1991 (23 games)
MOST ASSISTS IN ONE SERIES (OTHER THAN FINAL): 14 – (tied with Rick Middleton) 1985 Conference Finals (six games vs. Chicago)
Second: 13 – Doug Gilmour, 1994 Conference Semifinals (seven games vs. San Jose) and Wayne Gretzky, 1987 Division Semifinal (five games vs. Los Angeles)
MOST ASSISTS IN FINAL SERIES: 10 – 1988 (four games, plus suspended game vs. Boston)
Second: 9 – three players
MOST ASSISTS, ONE PLAYOFF GAME: 6 – (tied with Mikko Leinonen) April 9, 1987 at Edmonton (Edmonton 13, Los Angeles 3)
Next: 5 – 11 players
MOST ASSISTS, ONE PLAYOFF PERIOD: 3 -- Three assists by one player in one period of a playoff game has been recorded on 70 occasions. Gretzky has had three assists in one period five times. (Ray Bourque, three times; Toe Blake, Jean Beliveau, Doug Harvey and Bobby Orr, twice.)

POINTS (4)
MOST POINTS, CAREER: 382 – 122 goals and 260 assists
Second: 295 – Mark Messier, 109 goals and 186 assists
MOST POINTS, ONE PLAYOFF YEAR: 47 – 1985 (17 goals and 30 assists in 18 games)
Next: 44 – Mario Lemieux, 1991 (16 goals, 28 assists in 23 games)
MOST POINTS IN FINAL SERIES: 13 – 1988 three goals and 10 assists (four games plus suspended game vs. Boston, three goals)
Second: 12 – four players
MOST POINTS, ONE PLAYOFF PERIOD: 4 – (tied with nine other players) April 12, 1987 at LosAngeles, third period, one goal, three assists (Edmonton 6, Los Angeles 3)

An All-Star Attraction

NHL ALL-STAR GAME POINTS

YEAR	TEAM	G	A	P
1980	Edmonton	0	0	0
1981	Edmonton	0	1	1
1982	Edmonton	1	0	1
1983	Edmonton	4	0	4
1984	Edmonton	1	0	1
1985	Edmonton	1	0	1
1986	Edmonton	1	0	1
1988	Edmonton	1	0	1
1989	Los Angeles	1	2	3
1990	Los Angeles	0	0	0
1991	Los Angeles	1	0	1
1992	Los Angeles	1	2	3
1993	Los Angeles	0	0	0
1994	Los Angeles	0	2	2
1996	Los Angeles	0	0	0
1997	NY Rangers	0	1	1
1998	NY Rangers	0	2	2
1999	NY Rangers	1	2	3
TOTALS		13	12	25

NOTE: There was no All-Star game in 1987 because of Rendez-Vous '87, a two-game series between Team NHL and the Soviet Union. There was no game in 1995 due to the owners' lockout.

SHORTHAND GOALS (2)
MOST SHORTHANDED GOALS, ONE PLAYOFF YEAR: 3 – (tied with five other players) 1983 (two vs. Winnipeg in Division Semi-Finals, won by Edmonton, 3-0; one vs. Calgary in Division Finals, won by Edmonton 4-1)
MOST SHORT-HANDED GOALS, ONE PLAYOFF GAME: 2 – (tied with eight other players) April 6, 1983 at Edmonton (Edmonton 6, Winnipeg 3)

GAME-WINNING GOALS (1)
MOST GAME-WINNING GOALS IN PLAYOFFS, CAREER: 24
Second: 19 – Claude Lemieux

THREE-OR-MORE GOAL GAMES (1)
MOST THREE-OR-MORE GOAL GAMES: 10 (eight three-goal games, two four-goal games)
Second (tied): 7 – Maurice Richard (four three-goal games, two four-goal games, one five-goal game) and Jari Kurri (six three-goal games, one four-goal game)

NHL ALL-STAR GAME
RECORDS (6)

NHL ALL-STAR GAME GOALS (3)
MOST ALL-STAR GAME GOALS: 13 (in 18 games played)
Second: 11 – Mario Lemieux (in eight games played)
MOST ALL-STAR GAME GOALS, ONE GAME: 4 – (tied with three players) 1983 Campbell Conference
MOST ALL-STAR GAME GOALS, ONE PERIOD: 4 – 1983 Campbell Conference, third period

NHL ALL-STAR GAME ASSISTS (1)
MOST ALL-STAR GAME ASSISTS, CAREER: 12 – (tied with four players)
Second: 10 – Paul Coffey (in 14 games played)

NHL ALL-STAR GAME POINTS (2)
MOST ALL-STAR GAME POINTS, CAREER: 25 – (13 goals, 12 assists in 18 games)
Second: 22 – Mario Lemieux (11 goals, nine assists in eight games played)
MOST ALL-STAR GAME POINTS, ONE PERIOD: 4 – (tied with Mike Gartner and Adam Oates) 1983 Campbell Conference, third period (four goals)

Points per team

International Acclaim

Career Regular Season vs. Each Club

Opponent	GP	G	A	P
Anaheim	23	5	25	30
Boston	53	25	48	73
Buffalo	55	27	56	83
Carolina	57	36	73	109
Calgary	117	69	161	230
Chicago	60	25	77	102
Colorado	51	38	94	132
Dallas	58	44	72	116
Detroit	62	37	108	145
Edmonton	54	23	62	85
Florida	20	5	12	17
Los Angeles	69	60	119	179
Montreal	55	23	65	88
Nashville	2	1	7	8
New Jersey	67	32	91	123
NY Islanders	55	33	65	98
NY Rangers	46	34	47	81
Ottawa	17	3	25	282
Philadelphia	58	34	66	100
Phoenix	105	79	151	230
Pittsburgh	57	44	80	124
St. Louis	57	39	68	107
San Jose	32	12	39	51
Tampa Bay	20	5	19	24
Toronto	63	55	95	150
Vancouver	117	76	163	239
Washington	57	30	75	105
TOTALS	**1485**	**894**	**1962**	**2856**

Career Regular Season as an Oiler

Opponent	GP	G	A	P
Anaheim	–	–	–	–
Boston	27	12	28	40
Buffalo	29	15	35	50
Carolina (Hartford)	27	22	36	58
Calgary	62	47	92	133
Chicago	28	16	54	70
Colorado (Quebec)	28	27	57	84
Dallas (Minnesota)	29	32	48	80
Detroit	29	21	66	87
Edmonton	–	–	–	–
Florida	–	–	–	–
Los Angeles	63	58	112	170
Montreal	28	17	35	52
Nashville	–	–	–	–
New Jersey	34	18	60	78
NY Islanders	26	19	38	57
NY Rangers	29	25	32	57
Ottawa	–	–	–	–
Philadelphia	27	27	32	59
Phoenix (Winnipeg)	56	57	87	144
Pittsburgh	28	31	44	75
St. Louis	28	27	57	84
San Jose	–	–	–	–
Tampa Bay	–	–	–	–
Toronto	29	39	44	83
Vancouver	64	50	103	153
Washington	26	19	38	57
TOTALS	**696**	**583**	**1086**	**1663**

Year	Team	Event	GP	G	A	P
1978	Canada	World Junior	6	8	9	17
1981	Canada	Canada Cup	7	5	7	12
1982	Canada	World Championship	10	6	8	14
1984	Canada	Canada Cup	8	5	7	12
1987	Team NHL	Rendez-Vous '87	2	0	4	4
1987	Canada	Canada Cup	9	3	18	21
1991	Canada	Canada Cup	7	4	8	12
1996	Canada	World Cup	8	3	4	7
1998	Canada	Winter Olympics	6	0	4	4
TOTALS			**63**	**34**	**69**	**103**

Gretzky In Canada

In 635 games played in Canada, Gretzky scored 1419 points, and average of 2.2 points per game – approximately 30% higher than his 1.7 PPG in the United States. Ottawa's Corel Centre was one of two arenas in Canada in which he failed to score a goal (seven games); He was also blanked in six games at Montreal's Molson Centre, and did not play at Toronto's new Air Canada Centre.

	GP	G	A	P	PPG
Regular Season in Canada	635	480	939	1419	2.2
Regular Season in U.S.A	852	414	1024	1438	1.7
Edmonton Home Games	355	316	586	902	2.5
Visiting Player in Canada	280	164	353	517	1.9
Playoff Totals in Canada	118	79	160	239	2.0

Home-Road Breakdown

Regular Season: Does Not Include Two Neutral Site Games in 1993-94.

HOME						ROAD					
SEASON	CLUB	GP	G	A	P	SEASON	CLUB	GP	G	A	P
1979-80	EDM	40	28	49	77	1979-80	EDM	39	23	37	60
1980-81	EDM	40	29	62	91	1980-81	EDM	40	26	47	73
1981-82	EDM	40	59	64	123	1981-82	EDM	40	33	56	89
1982-83	EDM	40	31	63	94	1982-83	EDM	40	40	62	102
1983-84	EDM	39	44	66	110	1983-84	EDM	35	43	52	95
1984-85	EDM	40	34	70	104	1984-85	EDM	40	39	65	104
1985-86	EDM	40	29	82	111	1985-86	EDM	40	23	81	104
1986-87	EDM	40	36	71	107	1986-87	EDM	39	26	50	76
1987-88	EDM	36	26	59	85	1987-88	EDM	28	14	50	64
1988-89	L.A	40	33	70	103	1988-89	LA	38	21	44	65
1989-90	L.A	37	24	55	79	1989-90	LA	36	16	47	63
1990-91	L.A	40	26	65	91	1990-91	LA	38	15	57	72
1991-92	L.A	37	18	42	60	1991-92	LA	37	13	48	61
1992-93	L.A	22	6	25	31	1992-93	LA	23	10	24	34
1993-94	L.A	39	17	53	70	1993-94	LA	40	20	34	54
1994-95	L.A	24	9	19	28	1994-95	LA	24	2	18	20
1995-96	LA-STL	36	14	44	58	1995-96	LA-STL	44	9	35	44
1996-97	NYR	41	15	42	57	1996-97	NYR	41	10	30	40
1997-98	NYR	41	9	38	47	1997-98	NYR	41	14	29	43
1998-99	NYR	32	5	25	30	1998-99	NYR	38	4	28	32
Totals		745	493	1067	1560	Totals		742	401	896	1297

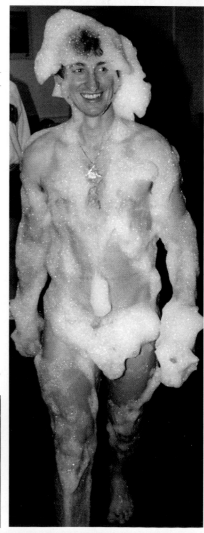

Milestones Along Highway 99

(Career game number in parentheses)

GOALS

GAME	DATE	TEAM / OPPOSITION
1	10/14/79	Edmonton vs Vancouver (3)
100	3/7/81	Edmonton at Philadelphia (145)
200	10/9/82	Edmonton at Vancouver (242)
300	12/13/83	Edmonton at NY Islanders (350)
400	1/13/85	Edmonton at Buffalo (436)
500	11/22/86	Edmonton vs Vancouver (575)
600	11/23/88	Los Angeles at Detroit (718)
700	1/3/91	Los Angeles at NY Islanders (886)
800	3/20/94	Los Angeles at San Jose (1116)
801	3/20/94	Los Angeles at San Jose (1116)
		(Ties Gordie Howe's record)
802	3/23/94	Los Angeles vs Vancouver (1117)
		(Breaks Gordie Howe's record)
894	3/29/99	NY Rangers vs NY Islanders (1479)

ASSISTS

GAME	DATE	TEAM / OPPOSITION
1	10/10/79	Edmonton at Chicago (1)
100	11/7/80	Edmonton at Winnipeg (92)
200	10/18/81	Edmonton at Chicago (165)
300	3/10/82	Edmonton at Los Angeles (229)
400	1/23/83	Edmonton vs Los Angeles (290)
500	12/17/83	Edmonton vs Quebec (352)
600	11/29/84	Edmonton at Boston (416)
700	10/20/85	Edmonton at Los Angeles (478)
800	2/6/86	Edmonton at New Jersey (527)
900	2/12/86	Edmonton vs Winnipeg (584)
1000	11/4/87	Edmonton vs NY Rangers (645)
1049	2/17/88	Edmonton vs Toronto (678)
		(Ties Gordie Howe's record)
1050	3/1/88	Edmonton vs Los Angeles (681)
		(Breaks Gordie Howe's record)
1100	10/28/88	Los Angeles at Winnipeg (706)
1200	4/1/89	Los Angeles vs Vancouver (774)
1300	3/17/90	Los Angeles at Boston (846)
1400	3/5/91	Los Angeles at Washington (913)
1500	3/4/92	Los Angeles at San Jose (986)
1600	11/30/93	Los Angeles vs Winnipeg (1068)
1700	10/20/95	Los Angeles at Washington (1179)
1800	12/13/96	NY Rangers at Buffalo (1286)
1900	3/21/98	NY Rangers vs Detroit (1404)
1962	4/12/99	NY Rangers vs Tampa Bay (1485)

POINTS

GAME	DATE	TEAM / OPPOSITION
1	10/10/79	Edmonton at Chicago (1)
100	2/24/80	Edmonton vs Boston (61)
200	1/7/81	Edmonton vs Washington (117)
300	4/4/81	Edmonton vs Winnipeg (159)
400	12/27/81	Edmonton vs Los Angeles (197)
500	3/19/82	Edmonton vs Calgary (234)
600	12/22/82	Edmonton vs Minnesota (274)
700	3/29/83	Edmonton at Vancouver (317)
800	12/17/83	Edmonton vs Quebec (352)
900	3/13/84	Edmonton at Quebec (385)
1000	12/19/84	Edmonton vs Los Angeles (424)
1100	3/17/85	Edmonton at Los Angeles (464)
1200	12/13/85	Edmonton at Winnipeg (504)
1300	3/5/86	Edmonton vs Los Angeles (539)
1400	12/5/86	Edmonton at Pittsburgh (580)
1500	3/11/87	Edmonton vs Detroit (620)
1600	12/22/87	Edmonton vs Los Angeles (667)
1700	11/6/88	Los Angeles at Chicago (711)
1800	2/18/89	Los Angeles vs Quebec (754)
1850	10/15/89	Los Angeles at Edmonton (780)
		(Ties Gordie Howe's record)
1851	10/15/89	Los Angeles at Edmonton (780)
		(Breaks Gordie Howe's record)
1900	12/10/89	Los Angeles at Quebec (803)
2000	10/26/90	Los Angeles at Winnipeg (857)
2100	2/22/91	Los Angeles at Winnipeg (908)
2200	1/10/92	Los Angeles at Washington (962)
2300	3/6/93	Los Angeles vs Edmonton (1026)
2400	1/12/94	Los Angeles vs Hartford (1086)
2500	4/17/95	Los Angeles at Calgary (1165)
2600	3/18/96	St. Louis at Los Angeles (1244)
2700	4/3/97	NY Rangers vs Boston (1331)
2800	10/17/98	NY Rangers at Pittsburgh (1422)
2856	4/12/99	NY Rangers vs Tampa Bay (1485)

An Oiler forever: Game by game

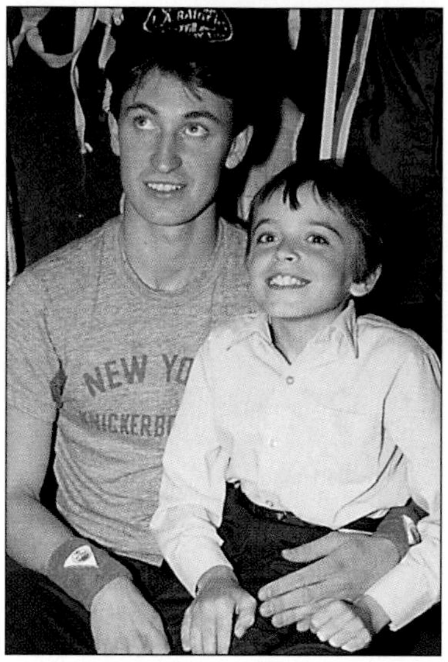

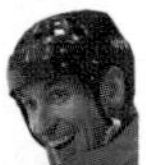

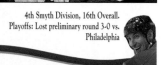

4th Smyth Division, 16th Overall.
Playoffs: Lost preliminary round 3-0 vs. Philadelphia

1979-80 SEASON

Game	Date	Team	Score	G	A	P
1	OCT. 10	CHICAGO	4-2 L	0	1	1
2	OCT. 13	DETROIT	3-3 T	0	1	1
3	OCT. 14	VANCOUVER	4-4 T	1	1	2
4	OCT. 19	QUEBEC	6-3 W	0	3	3
5	OCT. 21	MINNESOTA	5-5 T	1	1	2
6	OCT. 23	NY ISLANDERS	3-3 T	0	1	1
7	OCT. 24	NY RANGERS	10-2 L	0	0	0
8	OCT. 26	ATLANTA	7-3 L	0	0	0
9	OCT. 28	WASHINGTON	6-4 L	0	0	0
10	OCT. 30	ST. LOUIS	2-1 L	-	-	-
TOTALS				2	8	10

Game	Date	Team	Score	G	A	P
11	NOV. 2	NY ISLANDERS	3-3 T	2	1	3
12	NOV. 4	BOSTON	2-1 L	0	1	1
13	NOV. 7	DETROIT	5-3 L	1	1	2
14	NOV. 8	BOSTON	4-2 L	0	0	0
15	NOV. 11	TORONTO	6-3 L	0	2	2
16	NOV. 13	WASHINGTON	5-3 W	1	1	2
17	NOV. 15	PHILADELPHIA	5-3 L	0	2	2
18	NOV. 17	HARTFORD	4-0 L	0	0	0
19	NOV. 18	BUFFALO	9-7 L	1	2	3
20	NOV. 21	TORONTO	4-4 T	2	2	4
21	NOV. 24	PHILADELPHIA	2-2 T	0	1	1
22	NOV. 28	CHICAGO	4-2 W	0	2	2
23	NOV. 30	NY ISLANDERS	5-3 W	1	2	3
TOTALS				8	17	25

Game	Date	Team	Score	G	A	P
24	DEC. 5	MINNESOTA	6-1 L	0	0	0
25	DEC. 7	WINNIPEG	8-3 L	0	0	0
26	DEC. 9	HARTFORD	3-0 W	1	1	2
27	DEC. 12	ATLANTA	5-5 T	0	1	1
28	DEC. 14	MONTREAL	5-3 W	1	1	2
29	DEC. 16	WINNIPEG	4-3 L	1	1	2
30	DEC. 19	DETROIT	6-4 L	2	1	3
31	DEC. 21	COLORADO	5-4 L	0	1	1
32	DEC. 22	LOS ANGELES	9-3 L	2	1	3
33	DEC. 26	COLORADO	4-3 W	1	1	2
34	DEC. 28	VANCOUVER	5-3 W	1	0	1
35	DEC. 30	QUEBEC	2-1 L	0	1	1
TOTALS				9	9	18

Game	Date	Team	Score	G	A	P
36	JAN. 2	HARTFORD	3-3 T	0	1	1
37	JAN. 5	LOS ANGELES	3-3 T	2	0	2
38	JAN. 7	MONTREAL	3-3 T	0	0	0
39	JAN. 9	QUEBEC	6-2 L	1	0	1
40	JAN. 11	NY RANGERS	6-2 L	0	1	1
41	JAN. 13	BUFFALO	6-5 W	0	2	2
42	JAN. 16	WASHINGTON	5-2 W	1	1	2
43	JAN. 17	BOSTON	7-1 L	0	0	0
44	JAN. 19	PITTSBURGH	5-2 W	2	2	4
45	JAN. 20	BUFFALO	4-4 T	0	1	1
46	JAN. 23	PITTSBURGH	4-3 W	1	1	2
47	JAN. 26	TORONTO	8-3 W	0	2	2
48	JAN. 27	PHILADELPHIA	5-3 L	1	1	2
49	JAN. 29	ST. LOUIS	3-2 L	0	0	0
50	JAN. 30	LOS ANGELES	8-1 W	1	4	5
TOTALS			3	9	16	25

Game	Date	Team	Score	G	A	P
51	FEB. 1	WINNIPEG	9-2 W	3	1	4
52	FEB. 3	LOS ANGELES	8-1 W	1	1	2
53	FEB. 6	ST. LOUIS	6-3 L	1	2	3
54	FEB. 8	ATLANTA	4-2 W	1	0	1
55	FEB. 10	WINNIPEG	2-2 T	0	0	0
56	FEB. 13	MINNESOTA	5-3 W	0	1	1
57	FEB. 15	WASHINGTON	8-2 W	0	7	7
58	FEB. 17	ST. LOUIS	5-5 T	1	2	3
59	FEB. 19	HARTFORD	6-2 L	0	0	0
60	FEB. 20	NY RANGERS	4-1 L	0	0	0
61	FEB. 22	COLORADO	3-1 L	0	0	0
62	FEB. 24	BOSTON	4-2 L	0	1	1
63	FEB. 27	CHICAGO	5-2 W	0	2	2
64	FEB. 29	BUFFALO	4-2 L	0	1	1
TOTALS				7	18	25

Game	Date	Team	Score	G	A	P
65	MARCH 1	VANCOUVER	5-2 L	0	0	0
66	MARCH 4	NY ISLANDERS	6-4 L	2	2	4
67	MARCH 6	MONTREAL	5-4 L	1	2	3
68	MARCH 8	PITTSBURGH	5-4 L	1	1	2
69	MARCH 9	PHILADELPHIA	5-3 L	0	1	1
70	MARCH 12	QUEBEC	6-3 W	2	0	2
71	MARCH 14	CHICAGO	6-4W	0	0	0
72	MARCH 15	MONTREAL	7-3 W	1	0	1
73	MARCH 19	NY RANGERS	4-2 W	0	1	1
74	MARCH 21	PITTSBURGH	9-2 W	3	1	4
75	MARCH 25	ATLANTA	5-4 W	2	2	4
76	MARCH 26	DETROIT	5-2 W	0	2	2
77	MARCH 29	TORONTO	8-5 W	2	4	6
TOTALS				14	16	30

Game	Date	Team	Score	G	A	P
78	APRIL 1	VANCOUVER	5-0 L	0	0	0
79	APRIL 2	MINNESOTA	1-1 T	1	0	1
80	APRIL 4	COLORADO	6-2 W	1	2	3
TOTALS				2	2	4

'79-80 TOTALS				51	86	137

1979-1980 Leading Scorers

Player	Team	GP	G	A	P
Dionne, Marcel	Los Angeles	80	53	84	137
Gretzky, Wayne	**Edmonton**	**79**	**51**	**86**	**137**
Lafleur, Guy	Montreal	74	50	75	125
Perrault, Gilbert	Buffalo	80	40	66	106
Rogers, Mike	Hartford	80	44	61	105
Trottier, Bryan	NY Islanders	78	42	62	104
Simmer, Charlie	Los Angeles	64	56	45	101
Stoughton, Blaine	Hartford	80	56	44	100
Sittler, Darryl	Toronto	73	40	57	97
MacDonald, Blair	Edmonton	80	46	48	94
Federko, Bernie	St. Louis	79	38	56	94

1979-80 PLAYOFFS

Game	Date	Team	Score	G	A	P
1	APRIL 8	PHILADELPHIA	4-3 L	1	1	2
2	APRIL 9	PHILADELPHIA	5-1 L	0	0	0
3	APRIL 11	PHILADELPHIA	3-2 L	1	0	1
TOTALS				2	1	3

1979-80 Playoff Leaders

Player	Team	GP	G	A	P
Brian Trottier	NY Islanders		12	17	29
Mike Bossy	NY Islanders		10	13	23
Ken Linseman	Philadelphia		4	18	22
Bill Barber	Philadelphia		12	9	21
Gilbert Perrault	Buffalo		10	11	21
Bob Bourne	NY Islanders		10	10	20
Paul Holmgren	Philadelphia		10	10	20
Bob Clarke	Philadelphia		8	12	20

1980-81 SEASON

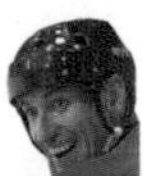

4th Smythe Division, 14th Overall.
Playoffs: Won Preliminary Round 3-0 vs. Montreal;
Lost Quarter-final 4-0 vs. NY Islanders

Game	Date	Team	Score	G	A	P
1	OCT. 10	QUEBEC	7-4 L	2	1	3
2	OCT. 13	COLORADO	3-2 L	0	2	2
3	OCT. 15	BUFFALO	2-0 L	0	0	0
4	OCT. 18	NY ISLANDERS	5-5 T	2	1	3
5	OCT. 19	NY RANGERS	4-2 W	1	3	4
6	OCT. 22	CALGARY	5-3 W	0	2	2
7	OCT. 24	MINNESOTA	4-2 L	0	0	0
8	OCT. 26	LOS ANGELES	4-4 T	0	0	0
9	OCT. 29	TORONTO	4-4 T	0	2	2
TOTALS				5	11	16

Game	Date	Team	Score	G	A	P
10	NOV. 1	WASHINGTON	2-2 T	0	0	0
11	NOV. 3	PITTSBURGH	4-4 T	2	0	2
12	NOV. 5	VANCOUVER	4-3 L	0	2	2
13	NOV. 7	WINNIPEG	4-2 W	0	1	1
14	NOV. 9	ST. LOUIS	6-4 L	0	2	2
15	NOV. 13	PHILADELPHIA	8-1 L	0	0	0
16	NOV. 15	TORONTO	4-2 L	1	0	1
17	NOV. 16	CHICAGO	5-4 W	1	2	3
18	NOV. 19	VANCOUVER	6-4 L	0	2	2
19	NOV. 23	BUFFALO	6-3 W	0	1	1
20	NOV. 25	COLORADO	4-3 L	0	1	1
21	NOV. 26	CHICAGO	10-3 W	1	4	5
22	NOV. 28	HARTFORD	6-4 L	0	2	2
23	NOV. 29	BOSTON	6-3 L	1	0	1
TOTALS				6	17	23

Game	Date	Team	Score	G	A	P
24	DEC. 5	NY RANGERS	3-2 L	1	0	1
25	DEC. 7	HARTFORD	6-4 W	1	2	3
26	DEC. 10	NY ISLANDERS	3-2 L	0	0	0
27	DEC. 13	MONTREAL	4-1 L	0	1	1
28	DEC. 14	QUEBEC	6-5 L	0	1	1
29	DEC. 16	DETROIT	4-3 L	0	2	2
30	DEC. 17	WASHINGTON	5-2 L	0	0	0
31	DEC. 20	MONTREAL	4-3 W	0	1	1
32	DEC. 23	LOS ANGELES	7-4 L	3	0	3
33	DEC. 27	DETROIT	4-4 T	0	3	3
34	DEC. 28	PHILADELPHIA	2-1 L	0	0	0
35	DEC. 30	CALGARY	5-3 L	1	1	2
TOTALS				6	11	17

Game	Date	Team	Score	G	A	P
36	JAN. 2	BOSTON	7-5 W	0	1	1
37	JAN. 3	TORONTO	4-1 W	1	2	3
38	JAN. 7	WASHINGTON	6-3 W	2	2	4
39	JAN. 9	HARTFORD	6-6 T	0	1	1
40	JAN. 11	QUEBEC	6-3 W	1	4	5
41	JAN. 12	MONTREAL	5-0 L	0	0	0
42	JAN. 14	TORONTO	7-4 W	2	1	3
43	JAN. 16	BUFFALO	5-5 T	0	0	0
44	JAN. 17	ST. LOUIS	7-6 L	1	3	4
45	JAN. 21	VANCOUVER	5-1 W	1	2	3
46	JAN. 23	NY RANGERS	7-4 L	0	2	2
47	JAN. 24	MINNESOTA	6-1 L	0	1	1
48	JAN. 28	MONTREAL	9-1 W	1	4	5
49	JAN. 30	CHICAGO	4-2 W	1	2	3
TOTALS				10	25	35

Game	Date	Team	Score	G	A	P
50	FEB. 1	WASHINGTON	7-4 L	0	2	2
51	FEB. 3	ST. LOUIS	3-3 T	0	0	0
52	FEB. 4	CHICAGO	6-3 L	1	0	1
53	FEB. 6	WINNIPEG	10-4 W	3	3	6
54	FEB. 8	CALGARY	10-4 W	1	2	3
55	FEB. 13	QUEBEC	4-2 L	1	0	1
56	FEB. 14	BUFFALO	2-2 T	0	1	1
57	FEB. 17	ST. LOUIS	9-2 W	5	2	7
58	FEB. 19	BOSTON	5-1 L	0	0	0
59	FEB. 21	WINNIPEG	5-1 W	0	1	1
60	FEB. 24	LOS ANGELES	5-2 L	1	0	1
61	FEB. 25	PHILADELPHIA	6-2 W	2	2	4
62	FEB. 27	DETROIT	5-2 W	1	1	2
63	FEB. 28	COLORADO	3-1 L	0	1	1
TOTALS				15	15	30

Game	Date	Team	Score	G	A	P
64	MARCH 3	NY ISLANDERS	8-8 T	2	2	4
65	MARCH 4	NY RANGERS	5-5 T	1	0	1
66	MARCH 7	PHILADELPHIA	5-3 W	4	0	4
67	MARCH 8	PITTSBURGH	6-4 L	0	1	1
68	MARCH 12	NY ISLANDERS	5-0 L	0	0	0
69	MARCH 15	CALGARY	3-3 T	1	0	1
70	MARCH 16	PITTSBURGH	7-6 W	0	3	3
71	MARCH 18	MINNESOTA	5-3 W	0	4	4
72	MARCH 20	MINNESOTA	1-1 T	1	0	1
73	MARCH 21	LOS ANGELES	6-6 T	1	4	5
74	MARCH 23	BOSTON	7-2 W	0	2	2
75	MARCH 25	HARTFORD	7-2 W	1	3	4
76	MARCH 28	DETROIT	4-2 W	0	1	1
77	MARCH 29	PITTSBURGH	5-2 W	0	3	3
TOTALS				11	23	34

Game	Date	Team	Score	G	A	P
78	APRIL 1	COLORADO	4-4 T	0	2	2
79	APRIL 3	VANCOUVER	7-2 W	1	1	2
80	APRIL 4	WINNIPEG	7-2 W	1	4	5
TOTALS				2	7	9

'80-81 TOTALS				55	109	164

1980-1981 Leading Scorers

Player	Team	GP	G	A	Pts.
Gretzky, Wayne	**Edmonton**	**80**	**55**	**109**	**164**
Dionne, Marcel	Los Angeles	80	58	77	135
Nilsson, Kent	Calgary	80	49	82	131
Bossy, Mike	NY Islanders	79	68	51	119
Taylor, Dave	Los Angeles	72	47	65	112
Stastny, Peter	Quebec	77	39	70	109
Simmer, Charlie	Los Angeles	65	56	49	105
Rogers, Mike	Hartford	80	40	65	105
Federko, Bernie	St. Louis	78	31	73	104
Richard, Jacques	Quebec	78	52	51	103
Middleton, Rick	Boston	80	44	59	103
Trottier, Bryan	NY Islanders	73	31	72	103

1980-81 PLAYOFFS

Game	Date	Team	Score	G	A	P
1	APRIL 8	MONTREAL	6-3 W	0	5	5
2	APRIL 9	MONTREAL	6-2 W	3	1	4
3	APRIL 11	MONTREAL	3-1 W	0	2	2
TOTALS				3	8	11

Game	Date	Team	Score	G	A	P
1	APRIL 16	NY ISLANDERS	8-2 L	1	0	1
2	APRIL 17	NY ISLANDERS	6-3 L	0	1	1
3	APRIL 19	NY ISLANDERS	5-2 W	3	0	3
4	APRIL 20	NY ISLANDERS	5-4 L	0	2	2
5	APRIL 22	NY ISLANDERS	4-3 W	0	2	2
6	APRIL 24	NY ISLANDERS	5-2 L	0	1	1
TOTALS				4	6	10

'80-81 PLAYOFF TOTALS				7	14	21

1980-81 Playoff Leaders

Player	Team	GP	G	A	P
Brian Trottier	NY Islanders		6	23	29
Mike Bossy	NY Islanders		17	10	27
Denis Potvin	NY Islanders		5	16	21
Tomas Gradin	Vancouver		9	10	19
Dennis Savard	Chicago		11	7	18
Stan Smyl	Vancouver		9	9	18
Joe Mullen	St. Louis		7	11	18
Peter Stastny	Quebec		7	11	18
Bernie Federko	St. Louis		3	15	18

1981-82 SEASON

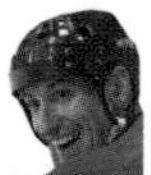

1st Smythe Division, 2nd Overall.
Playoffs: Lost Smythe Division Final 3-2 vs. Los Angeles

Game	Date	Team	Score	G	A	P
1	OCT. 7	COLORADO	7-4 W	0	1	1
2	OCT. 9	VANCOUVER	6-2 L	0	0	0
3	OCT. 10	LOS ANGELES	7-4 W	1	1	2
4	OCT. 14	WINNIPEG	4-2 L	1	0	1
5	OCT. 16	CALGARY	8-4 W	1	2	3
6	OCT. 18	CHICAGO	7-5 L	1	3	4
7	OCT. 20	CALGARY	5-4 W	1	1	2
8	OCT. 21	HARTFORD	5-2 W	0	0	0
9	OCT. 23	PITTSBURGH	8-3 W	1	1	2
10	OCT. 24	COLORADO	3-1 W	1	0	1
11	OCT. 27	NY ISLANDERS	4-3 L	0	1	1
12	OCT. 28	NY RANAGERS	5-3 W	2	2	4
13	OCT. 21	QUEBEC	11-4 W	4	1	5
TOTALS				13	14	27

Game	Date	Team	Score	G	A	P
14	NOV. 4	TORONTO	6-4 W	2	0	2

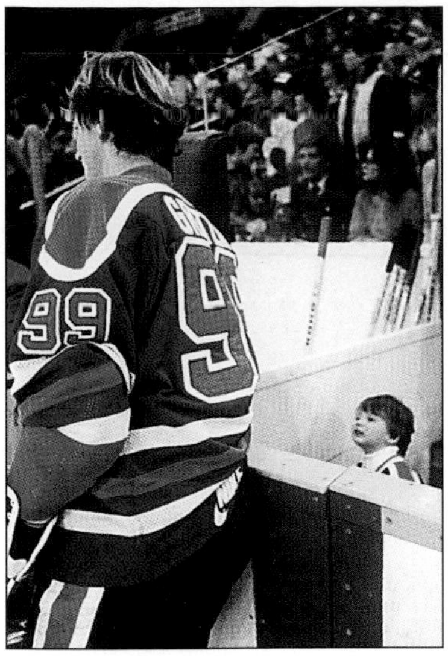

15	NOV. 7	COLORADO	5-4 L	0	0	0
16	NOV. 11	HARTFORD	4-4 T	2	1	3
17	NOV. 12	BOSTON	5-2 L	0	2	2
18	NOV. 14	NY ISLANDERS	5-5 T	1	3	4
19	NOV. 15	NY RANGERS	5-3 W	1	2	3
20	NOV. 17	ST. LOUIS	5-1 W	2	1	3
21	NOV. 19	MINNESOTA	2-2 T	0	0	0
22	NOV. 21	VANCOUVER	8-3 W	2	2	4
23	NOV. 23	DETROIT	8-4 W	1	1	2
24	NOV. 25	LOS ANGELES	11-4 W	4	1	5
25	NOV. 27	CHICAGO	8-1 W	2	3	5
26	NOV. 29	WINNIPEG	10-2 W	1	3	4
TOTALS				18	19	37

Game	Date	Team	Score	G	A	P
27	DEC. 1	MONTREAL	3-3 T	0	3	3
28	DEC. 2	QUEBEC	9-8 L	0	2	2
29	DEC. 4	VANCOUVER	7-3 W	0	3	3
30	DEC. 5	VANCOUVER	3-3 T	0	2	2
31	DEC. 9	LOS ANGELES	5-5 T	1	0	1
32	DEC. 13	NY ISLANDERS	4-3 W	1	3	4
33	DEC. 16	COLORADO	7-4 W	1	2	3
34	DEC. 17	CALGARY	5-4 W	1	0	1
35	DEC. 19	MINNESOTA	9-6 W	3	4	7
36	DEC. 20	CALGARY	7-5 L	2	1	3
38	DEC. 23	VANCOUVER	6-1 W	1	3	4
39	DEC. 27	LOS ANGELES	10-3 W	4	1	5
39	DEC. 30	PHILADELPHIA	7-5 W	5	1	6
40	DEC. 31	VANCOUVER	3-1 L	0	0	0
TOTALS				19	25	44

Game	Date	Team	Score	G	A	P
41	JAN. 2	BOSTON	4-4 T	1	1	2
42	JAN. 6	COLORADO	5-3 W	2	2	4
43	JAN. 9	CALGARY	7-2 W	1	4	5
44	JAN. 10	CALGARY	5-1 L	0	0	0
45	JAN. 13	WASHINGTON	6-6 T	1	2	3
46	JAN. 14	PHILADELPHIA	8-2 L	1	0	1
47	JAN. 16	TORONTO	7-1 L	1	0	1
48	JAN. 17	DETROIT	4-4 T	0	2	2
49	JAN. 20	ST. LOUIS	8-6 W	3	2	5
50	JAN. 22	VANCOUVER	4-3 W	1	1	2
51	JAN. 24	COLORADO	7-4 W	0	3	3
52	JAN. 26	ST. LOUIS	6-4 W	1	1	2
53	JAN. 27	CHICAGO	3-3 T	1	1	2
54	JAN. 29	BUFFALO	3-1 W	1	0	1
55	JAN 31	PHILADELPHIA	7-4 W	3	2	5
TOTALS				17	21	38

Game	Date	Team	Score	G	A	P
56	FEB. 3	MONTREAL	6-3 L	1	1	2
57	FEB. 6	TORONTO	5-1 W	0	2	2
58	FEB. 7	NY RANGERS	8-4 W	1	1	2
59	FEB. 12	WASHINGTON	5-3 W	1	2	3
60	FEB. 14	BOSTON	2-2 T	0	1	1
61	FEB. 17	MINNESOTA	7-4 W	2	3	5
62	FEB. 19	HARTFORD	7-4 W	3	2	5
63	FEB. 21	DETROIT	7-3 W	1	4	5
64	FEB. 24	BUFFALO	6-3 W	3	2	5
65	FEB. 27	PITTSBURGH	4-1 W	1	0	1
66	FEB. 28	WASHINGTON	4-1 W	2	1	3
TOTALS				15	20	35

Game	Date	Team	Score	G	A	P
67	MARCH 2	MONTREAL	3-3 T	0	2	2
68	MARCH 3	QUEBEC	6-4 L	0	2	2
69	MARCH 6	COLORADO	5-2 L	0	0	0
70	MARCH 10	LOS ANGELES	3-2 L	0	2	2
71	MARCH 12	BUFFALO	3-2 L	0	0	0
72	MARCH 13	VANCOUVER	5-3 W	0	3	3
73	MARCH 15	LOS ANGELES	3-3 T	2	0	2
74	MARCH 17	PITTSBURGH	10-4 W	3	2	5
75	MARCH 19	CALGARY	3-3 T	1	1	2
76	MARCH 25	CALGARY	7-2 W	2	2	4
77	MARCH 26	COLORADO	6-6 T	1	2	3
78	MARCH 28	LOS ANGELES	6-2 W	1	1	2
79	MARCH 31	LOS ANGELES	7-3 W	0	3	3
TOTALS				10	20	30

Game	Date	Team	Score	G	A	P
80	APRIL 4	WINNIPEG	2-1 W	0	1	1
TOTALS				0	1	1
'81-82 TOTALS				92	120	212

1981-1982 Leading Scorers

Player	Club	GP	G	A	Pts.
Gretzky, Wayne	**Edmonton**	**80**	**92**	**120**	**212**
Bossy, Mike	NY Islanders	80	64	83	147
Stastny, Peter	Quebec	80	46	93	139
Maruk, Dennis	Washington	80	60	76	136
Trottier, Bryan	NY Islanders	80	50	79	129
Savard, Denis	Chicago	50	32	87	119
Dionne, Marcel	Los Angeles	78	50	67	117
Smith, Bobby	Minnesota	80	43	71	114
Ciccarelli, Dino	Minnesota	76	55	51	106
Taylor, Dave	Los Angeles	78	39	67	106

1981-82 PLAYOFFS

Game	Date	Team	Score	G	A	P
1	APRIL 7	LOS ANGELES	10-8 L	1	3	4
2	APRIL 8	LOS ANGELES	3-2 W	1	1	2
3	APRIL 10	LOS ANGELES	6-5 L	2	2	4
4	APRIL 12	LOS ANGELES	3-2 W	0	1	1
5	APRIL 13	LOS ANGELES	7-4 L	1	0	1
'81-82 PLAYOFF TOTALS				5	7	12

1981-82 Playoff leaders

Player	Team	GP	G	A	P
Mike Bossy	NY Islanders	18	17	18	35
Steve Payne	Minnesota	18	17	12	29
Brian Trottier	NY Islandera	18	11	18	29
Denis Potvin	NY Islanders	18	8	17	25
Bobby Smith	Minnesota	19	8	17	25
Dino Ciccarelli	Minnesota	19	14	7	21
Wayne Gretzky	**Edmonton**	**9**	**7**	**14**	**21**
Butch Goring	NY Islander	18	10	10	20

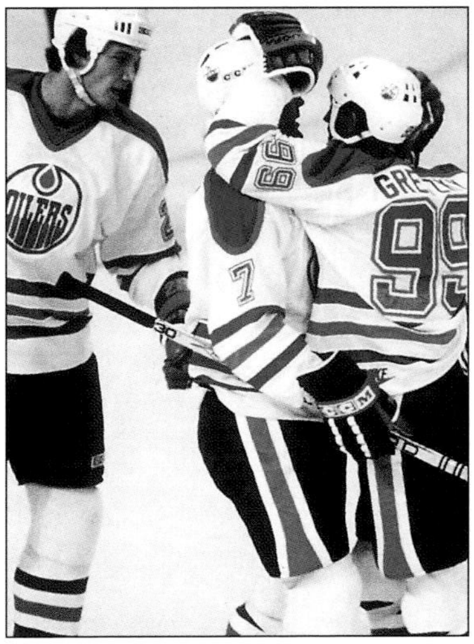

1st Smythe 3rd Overall. Playoffs: Stanley Cup Finalists; Won Smythe Division Semifinal 3-0 vs. Winnipeg; Won Smythe Division Final 4-1 vs. Calgary; Won Campbell Conference Final 4-0 vs. Chicago; Lost Stanley Cup Final 4-0 vs. NY Islanders

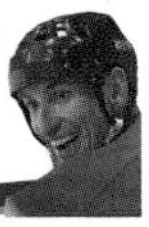

1982-83 SEASON

Game	Date	Team	Score	G	A	P
1	OCT. 5	CALGARY	7-5 W	0	1	1
2	OCT. 8	NY ISLANDERS	6-4 L	1	1	2
3	OCT. 9	VANCOUVER	6-3 W	2	1	3
4	OCT. 12	CALGARY	9-4 L	1	2	3
5	OCT. 14	HARTFORD	4-4 T	1	2	3
6	OCT. 16	BOSTON	6-6 T	0	2	2
7	OCT. 17	BUFFALO	6-4 L	1	2	3
8	OCT. 20	HARTFORD	4-2 W	0	1	1
9	OCT. 21	BOSTON	5-3 L	0	1	1
10	OCT. 24	WINNIPEG	9-5 L	0	3	3
11	OCT. 27	CHICAGO	4-4 T	0	2	2
12	OCT. 29	LOS ANGELES	6-3 W	1	2	3
13	OCT. 31	VANCOUVER	3-2 L	1	0	1
TOTALS				8	20	28

Game	Date	Team	Score	G	A	P
14	NOV. 3	WINNIPEG	7-2 W	1	1	2
15	NOV. 5	NY RANGERS	5-1 W	1	1	2
16	NOV. 8	QUEBEC	5-5 T	0	4	4
17	NOV. 10	PITTSBURGH	5 4 L	0	3	3
18	NOV. 11	NEW JERSEY	5-1 W	1	0	1
19	NOV. 13	PHILADELPHIA	4-3 W	1	0	1
20	NOV. 14	NY RANGERS	7-2 W	2	2	4
21	NOV. 16	NY ISLANDERS	4-2 L	0	1	1
22	NOV. 20	VANCOUVER	3-3 T	0	1	1
23	NOV. 21	QUEBEC	9-7 L	3	3	6
24	NOV. 24	WASHINGTON	3-3 T	1	1	2
25	NOV. 26	WINNIPEG	6-5 W	2	2	4
26	NOV. 28	DETROIT	7-5 W	0	4	4
TOTALS				12	23	35

Game	Date	Team	Score	G	A	P
27	DEC. 1	PHILADELPHIA	4-2 L	0	2	2
28	DEC. 4	CALGARY	7-5 W	1	3	4
29	DEC. 5	LOS ANGELES	7-3 W	1	4	5
30	DEC. 7	ST. LOUIS	3-2 W	2	0	2
31	DEC. 9	LOS ANGELES	3-3 T	0	0	0
32	DEC. 11	MINNESOTA	5-4 L	1	2	3
33	DEC. 17	NEW JERSEY	10-4 W	1	3	4
34	DEC. 19	MONTREAL	5-2 W	0	1	1
35	DEC. 22	MINNESOTA	8-2 W	1	2	3
36	DEC. 23	LOS ANGELES	6-2 W	1	0	1
37	DEC. 26	CALGARY	4-4 T	0	2	2
38	DEC. 29	CHICAGO	8-6 L	0	2	2
39	DEC. 31	VANCOUVER	8-1 W	2	1	3
TOTALS				10	22	32

Game	Date	Team	Score	G	A	P
40	JAN. 1	WINNIPEG	5-3 W	0	0	0
41	JAN. 4	CALGARY	6-3 W	1	0	1
42	JAN. 5	WINNIPEG	8-3 W	2	3	5
43	JAN. 7	PITTSBURGH	7-2 W	2	0	2
44	JAN. 9	DETROIT	4-3 L	0	2	2
45	JAN. 11	ST. LOUIS	7-5 W	0	2	2
46	JAN. 12	CHICAGO	10-4 W	2	1	3
47	JAN. 15	MINNESOTA	10-4 W	1	5	6
48	JAN. 18	LOS ANGELES	3-3 T	1	1	2
49	JAN. 19	VANCOUVER	9-4 W	1	3	4
50	JAN. 22	VANCOUVER	4-3 L	1	0	1
51	JAN. 23	LOS ANGELES	8-6 W	1	3	4
52	JAN. 28	TORONTO	6-6 T	2	1	3
53	JAN. 29	CALGARY	5-4 W	0	0	0
54	JAN. 30	NY ISLANDERS	7-4 L	0	1	1
TOTALS				14	22	36

Game	Date	Team	Score	G	A	P
55	FEB. 3	LOS ANGELES	7-4 L	0	1	1
56	FEB. 4	MONTREAL	7-3 W	1	4	5
57	FEB. 11	QUEBEC	7-3 W	1	2	3
58	FEB. 14	MONTREAL	4-2 L	2	0	2
59	FEB. 17	PHILADELPHIA	7-3 L	0	2	2
60	FEB. 19	PITTSBURGH	10-7 W	2	1	3
61	FEB. 20	BUFFALO	5-4 W	0	1	1
62	FEB. 22	CALGARY	4-1 L	1	0	1
63	FEB. 23	WASHINGTON	6-3 W	2	1	3
64	FEB. 25	ST. LOUIS	5-5 T	1	0	1
65	FEB. 27	WINNIPEG	3-0 W	0	1	1
TOTALS				10	13	23

Game	Date	Team	Score	G	A	P
66	MARCH 1	NEW JERSEY	4-3 W	1	1	2
67	MARCH 2	WASHINGTON	5-3 W	1	1	2
68	MARCH 5	TORONTO	6-3 W	2	3	5
69	MARCH 6	BOSTON	5-2 W	1	0	1
70	MARCH 8	HARTFORD	9-4 W	3	1	4
71	MARCH 11	NY RANGERS	3-1 W	0	0	0
72	MARCH 13	BUFFALO	6-2 W	1	2	3
73	MARCH 16	VANCOUVER	4-3 W	1	2	3
74	MARCH 19	PITTSBURGH	9-7 W	1	4	5
75	MARCH 21	TORONTO	4-1 W	1	2	3
76	MARCH 23	WINNIPEG	7-4 L	0	1	1
77	MARCH 26	LOS ANGELES	9-3 W	2	1	3
78	MARCH 29	VANCOUVER	7-4 W	1	3	4
TOTALS				15	21	36

Game	Date	Team	Score	G	A	P
79	APRIL 1	WINNIPEG	7-4 L	1	3	4
80	APRIL 3	CALGARY	3-3 T	1	1	2
TOTALS				2	4	6
82-83 TOTALS				71	125	196

1982-1983 Leading Scorers

Player	Team	GP	G	A	Pts.
Gretzky, Wayne	**Edmonton**	**80**	**71**	**125**	**196**
Stastny, Peter	Quebec	75	47	77	124
Savard, Denis	Chicago	78	33	86	121
Bossy, Mike	NY Islanders	79	60	58	118
Dionne, Marcel	Los Angeles	80	56	51	107
Pederson, Barry	Boston	77	46	61	107
Messier, Mark	Edmonton	77	48	58	106
Goulet, Michel	Quebec	80	57	48	105
Anderson, Glenn	Edmonton	72	48	56	104
Nilsson, Kent	Calgary	80	46	58	104
Kurri, Jari	Edmonton	80	45	59	104

1982-83 PLAYOFFS

Game	Date	Team	Score	G	A	P
1	APRIL 6	WINNIPEG	6-3 W	4	1	5
2	APRIL 7	WINNIPEG	4-3 W	0	2	2
3	APRIL 9	WINNIPEG	1-0 W	0	1	1

Game	Date	Team	Score	G	A	P
4	APRIL 14	CALGARY	6-3 W	0	0	0
5	APRIL 15	CALGARY	5-1 W	0	2	2
6	APRIL 17	CALGARY	10-2 W	4	3	7
7	APRIL 18	CALGARY	6-5 L	1	1	2
8	APRIL 20	CALGARY	9-1 W	1	2	3

Game	Date	Team	Score	G	A	P
9	APRIL 24	CHICAGO	8-4 W	1	4	5
10	APRIL 26	CHICAGO	8-2 W	0	2	2
11	MAY 1	CHICAGO	3-2 W	0	2	2
12	MAY 3	CHICAGO	6-3 W	1	2	3

Game	Date	Team	Score	G	A	P
13	MAY 10	NY ISLANDERS	2-0 L	0	0	0
14	MAY 12	NY ISLANDERS	6-3 L	0	2	2
15	MAY 14	NY ISLANDERS	5-1 L	0	1	1
16	MAY 17	NY ISLANDERS	4-2 L	0	1	1
'82-83 PLAYOFF TOTALS				12	26	38

1982-83 Playoff lears

Player	Team	GP	G	A	P
Wayne Gretzky	**Edmonton**	**16**	**12**	**26**	**38**
Rick Middleton	Boston	17	11	22	33
Barry Pederson	Boston	17	14	18	32
Bob Bourne	NY Islanders	20	8	20	28
Mike Bossy	NY Islanders	19	17	9	26
Jari Kurri	Edmonton	16	8	15	23
Ray Bourque	Boston	17	8	15	23
Mark Messier	Edmonton	15	15	6	21
Brent Sutter	NY Islanders	20	10	11	21
Duane Sutter	NY Islanders	20	9	12	21

1983-84 SEASON

STANLEY CUP CHAMPIONS, 1st Smythe Division, 1st Overall. Playoffs: Won Smythe Division Semifinal 3-0 vs. Winnipeg; Won Smythe Division Final 4-3 vs. Calgary; Won Campbell Conference Final 4-0 vs. Minnesota; Won Stanley Cup Final 4-1 vs. NY Islanders.

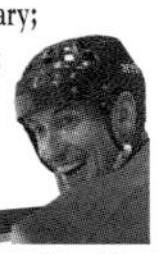

Game	Date	Team	Score	G	A	P
1	OCT. 5	TORONTO	5-4 W	1	1	2
2	OCT. 7	WINNIPEG	8-6 W	2	1	3
3	OCT. 9	MINNESOTA	4-3 W	1	2	3
4	OCT. 12	DETROIT	8-3 W	2	3	5
5	OCT. 15	CALGARY	4-3 W	1	1	2
6	OCT. 16	CALGARY	5-1 W	1	2	3
7	OCT. 19	VANCOUVER	10-7 W	2	0	2
8	OCT. 20	LOS ANGELES	7-2 L	1	0	1
9	OCT. 22	VANCOUVER	5-5 T	0	3	3
10	OCT. 26	TORONTO	8-3 W	1	0	1
11	OCT. 29	MONTREAL	2-1 W	0	1	1
12	OCT. 30	NY RANGERS	5-4 W	1	0	1
TOTALS				13	14	27

Game	Date	Team	Score	G	A	P
13	NOV. 2	WASHINGTON	11-3 W	2	3	5
14	NOV. 5	PITTSBURGH	7-3 W	0	3	3
15	NOV. 6	WINNIPEG	8-5 W	4	3	7
16	NOV. 8	QUEBEC	7-4 W	1	1	2
17	NOV. 9	WASHINGTON	7-4 W	1	3	4
18	NOV. 12	DETROIT	7-3 W	3	2	5
19	NOV. 13	CHICAGO	5-3 L	0	1	1
20	NOV. 18	BUFFALO	7-0 W	0	3	3
21	NOV. 19	NEW JERSEY	13-4 W	3	5	8
22	NOV. 21	WINNIPEG	7-6 W	1	0	1
23	NOV. 23	LOS ANGELES	7-3 W	0	2	2
24	NOV. 25	MINNESOTA	2-2 T	1	0	1
25	NOV. 26	ST. LOUIS	8-6 L	0	5	5
26	NOV. 30	PHILADELPHIA	3-3 T	1	1	2
TOTALS				17	32	49

Game	Date	Team	Score	G	A	P
27	DEC. 3	LOS ANGELES	7-3 W	0	3	3
28	DEC. 4	NY ISLANDERS	4-2 L	0	1	1
29	DEC. 7	VANCOUVER	5-4 W	0	2	2
30	DEC. 10	VANCOUVER	3-2 W	0	1	1
31	DEC. 13	NY ISLANDERS	8-5 L	1	1	2
32	DEC. 14	NY RANGERS	9-4 W	3	2	5
33	DEC. 17	QUEBEC	8-1 W	1	5	6
34	DEC. 18	WINNIPEG	7-5 W	2	2	4
35	DEC. 21	WINNIPEG	7-4 W	3	2	5
36	DEC. 23	CALGARY	5-5 T	1	1	2
37	DEC. 26	CALGARY	6-3 W	1	2	3
38	DEC. 28	VANCOUVER	4-2 W	0	2	2
39	DEC. 30	BOSTON	2-0 W	0	1	1
TOTALS				12	25	37

Game	Date	Team	Score	G	A	P
40	JAN. 3	CALGARY	9-6 W	1	3	4
41	JAN. 4	MINNESOTA	12-8 W	4	4	8
42	JAN. 7	HARTFORD	5-3 W	3	0	3
43	JAN. 9	DETROIT	7-3 W	2	1	3
44	JAN. 11	CHICAGO	5-3 W	1	0	1
45	JAN. 13	BUFFALO	3-1 L	0	1	1
46	JAN. 15	NEW JERSEY	5-4 W	0	3	3
47	JAN. 18	VANCOUVER	7-5 W	3	2	5
48	JAN. 20	LOS ANGELES	7-5 W	2	3	5
49	JAN. 21	LOS ANGELES	6-3 W	0	2	2
50	JAN. 25	VANCOUVER	6-4 W	2	2	4
51	JAN. 27	NEW JERSEY	3-3 T	1	0	1
52	JAN. 28	LOS ANGELES	4-2 L	0	0	0
TOTALS				19	21	40

Game	Date	Team	Score	G	A	P
53	FEB. 3	CALGARY	10-5 W	-	-	-
54	FEB. 5	WASHINGTON	9-2 L	-	-	-
55	FEB. 7	NY ISLANDERS	5-3 L	-	-	-
56	FEB. 9	PHILADELPHIA	4-3 L	-	-	-
57	FEB. 11	BOSTON	4-1 L	-	-	-
58	FEB. 12	HARTFORD	11-0 L	-	-	-
59	FEB. 15	WINNIPEG	5-2 W	2	2	4
60	FEB. 17	BOSTON	5-2 W	0	1	1
61	FEB. 19	PITTSBURGH	7-3 W	2	1	3
62	FEB. 21	ST. LOUIS	6-5 W	4	1	5
63	FEB. 22	PITTSBURGH	9-2 W	4	1	5
64	FEB. 24	CALGARY	5-3 W	0	0	0
65	FEB. 25	TORONTO	8-3 W	2	0	2
66	FEB. 27	WINNIPEG	6-5 W	1	1	2
67	FEB. 29	PHILADELPHIA	5-3 L	0	2	2
TOTALS				15	9	24

Game	Date	Team	Score	G	A	P
68	MARCH 4	MONTREAL	6-1 W	2	1	3
69	MARCH 7	CHICAGO	7-4 W	0	3	3
70	MARCH 10	NY RANGERS	3-2 L	1	0	1
71	MARCH 11	VANCOUVER	12-2 W	2	3	5
72	MARCH 13	QUEBEC	6-5 W	1	1	2
73	MARCH 15	MONTREAL	3-2 L	0	1	1
74	MARCH 17	LOS ANGELES	9-1 W	1	2	3
75	MARCH 18	BUFFALO	4-3 W	0	0	0
76	MARCH 21	HARTFORD	5-3 W	0	1	1
77	MARCH 24	ST. LOUIS	7-1 L	1	0	1
78	MARCH 25	WINNIPEG	3-2 W	1	0	1
79	MARCH 27	CALGARY	9-2 W	2	2	4
80	MARCH 31	LOS ANGELES	4-3 W	0	3	3
TOTALS				11	17	28

'83-84 TOTALS				87	118	205

1983-1984 Leading Scorers

Player	Team	GP	G	A	Pts.
Gretzky, Wayne	**Edmonton**	**74**	**87**	**118**	**205**
Coffey, Paul	Edmonton	80	40	86	126
Goulet, Michel	Quebec	75	56	65	121
Stastny, Peter	Quebec	80	46	73	119
Bossy, Mike	NY Islanders	67	51	67	118
Pederson, Barry	Boston	80	39	77	116
Kurri, Jari	Edmonton	64	52	61	113
Trottier, Bryan	NY Islanders	68	40	71	111
Federko, Bernie	St. Louis	79	41	66	107
Middleton, Rick	Boston	80	47	58	105

1983-84 PLAYOFFS

Game	Date	Team	Score	G	A	P
1	APRIL 4	WINNIPEG	9-2 W	0	3	3
2	APRIL 5	WINNIPEG	5-4 W	1	1	2
3	APRIL 7	WINNIPEG	4-1 W	0	0	0
TOTALS				1	4	5

Game	Date	Team	Score	G	A	P
4	APRIL 12	CALGARY	5-2 W	2	2	4
5	APRIL 13	CALGARY	6-5 L	1	1	2
6	APRIL 15	CALGARY	3-2 W	0	1	1
7	APRIL 16	CALGARY	5-3 W	0	1	1
8	APRIL 18	CALGARY	5-4 L	0	0	0
9	APRIL 20	CALGARY	5-4 L	0	2	2
10	APRIL 22	CALGARY	7-4 W	1	2	3
TOTALS				4	9	13

Game	Date	Team	Score	G	A	P
11	APRIL 24	MINNESOTA	7-1 W	1	3	4
12	APRIL 26	MINNESOTA	4-3 W	1	1	2
13	APRIL 28	MINNESOTA	8-5 W	2	1	3
14	MAY 1	MINNESOTA	3-1 W	0	1	1
TOTALS				4	6	10

Game	Date	Team	Score	G	A	P
15	MAY 10	NY ISLANDERS	1-0 W	0	0	0
16	MAY 12	NY ISLANDERS	6-1 L	0	0	0
17	MAY 15	NY ISLANDERS	7-2 W	0	2	2
18	MAY 17	NY ISLANDERS	5-2 W	2	0	2
19	MAY 19	NY ISLANDERS	5-2 W	2	1	3
TOTALS				4	3	7

1983-84 Playoff Leaders

Player	Team	GP	G	A	P
Wayne Gretzky	**Edmonton**	**19**	**13**	**22**	**35**
Jari Kurri	Edmonton	19	14	14	28
Mark Messier	Edmonton	19	8	18	26
Paul Coffey	Edmonton	19	8	14	22
Clark Gillies	NYI		12	7	19
Mike Bossy	NYI		8	10	18
Paul Reinhart	Cal		16	11	17
Glenn Anderson	Edm	19	6	11	17
Pat Flatley	NYI		9	6	15
Ken Linseman	Edm	19	10	4	14

1984-85 SEASON

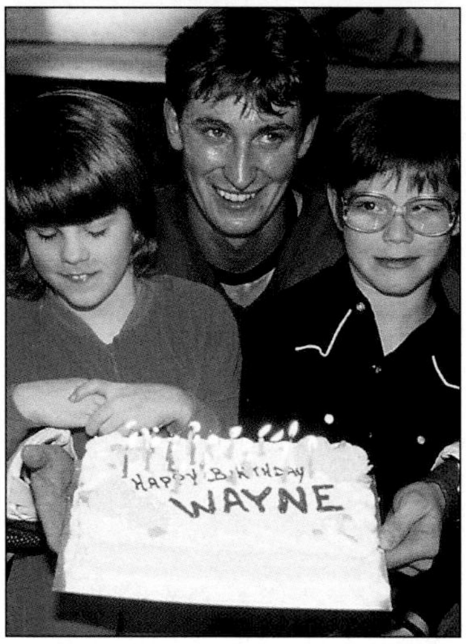

STANLEY CUP CHAMPIONS, 1st Smythe Division, 2nd Overall. Playoffs: Won Smythe Division Semifinal 3-0 vs. Los Angeles; Won Smythe Division Final 4-0 vs. Winnipeg; Won Campbell Conference Final 4-2 vs. Chicago; Won Stanley Cup Final 4-1 vs. NY Islanders.

Game	Date	Team	Score	G	A	P
1	OCT. 11	LOS ANGELES	2-2 T	0	1	1
2	OCT. 12	ST. LOUIS	5-1 W	0	1	1
3	OCT. 14	WINNIPEG	9-2 W	1	3	4
4	OCT. 16	BOSTON	7-2 W	2	1	3
5	OCT. 18	MINNESOTA	7-5 W	3	0	3
6	OCT. 19	WINNIPEG	7-4 W	2	3	5
7	OCT. 21	CALGARY	6-4 W	2	2	4
8	OCT. 24	WASHINGTON	3-3 T	0	2	2
9	OCT. 26	LOS ANGELES	8-2 W	0	4	4
10	OCT. 30	VANCOUVER	7-0 W	1	2	3
TOTALS				11	19	30

Game	Date	Team	Score	G	A	P
11	NOV. 2	CHICAGO	4-2 W	0	1	1
12	NOV. 4	WINNIPEG	2-1 W	1	1	2
13	NOV. 6	PITTSBURGH	3-3 T	1	0	1
14	NOV. 8	NEW JERSEY	3-2 W	0	3	3
15	NOV. 9	WASHINGTON	8-5 W	2	4	6
16	NOV. 11	PHILADELPHIA	7-5 L	2	2	4
17	NOV. 14	MONTREAL	4-2 L	0	0	0
18	NOV. 15	CALGARY	6-2 L	1	0	1
19	NOV. 17	VANCOUVER	7-0 W	0	3	3
20	NOV. 21	WINNIPEG	7-5 W	1	2	3
21	NOV. 24	ST. LOUIS	7-6 W	2	3	5
22	NOV. 27	TORONTO	7-1 W	3	2	5
23	NOV. 29	BOSTON	4-2 W	0	2	2
24	NOV. 30	HARTFORD	4-2 W	0	2	2
TOTALS				13	25	38

Game	Date	Team	Score	G	A	P
25	DEC. 5	NY ISLANDERS	6-4 W	1	4	5
26	DEC. 7	MINNESOTA	6-4 W	1	2	3
27	DEC. 8	VANCOUVER	3-2 L	0	0	0
28	DEC. 13	LOS ANGELES	7-2 L	1	1	2
29	DEC. 15	ST. LOUIS	8-2 W	5	1	6
30	DEC. 17	NEW JERSEY	5-2 L	0	1	1
31	DEC. 19	LOS ANGELES	7-3 W	2	4	6
32	DEC. 21	VANCOUVER	3-1 L	0	0	0
33	DEC. 22	CALGARY	7-1 W	2	2	4
34	DEC. 26	CALGARY	6-5 W	0	4	4
35	DEC. 29	DETROIT	6-3 W	3	3	6
36	DEC. 30	VANCOUVER	7-7 T	1	2	3
TOTALS				16	24	40

Game	Date	Team	Score	G	A	P
37	JAN. 2	PHILADELPHIA	5-2 L	0	0	0
38	JAN. 4	WINNIPEG	7-4 W	0	3	3
39	JAN. 6	WINNIPEG	7-2 W	1	0	1
40	JAN. 8	QUEBEC	4-0 W	1	2	3
41	JAN. 10	MONTREAL	5-2 W	1	2	3
42	JAN. 12	PITTSBURGH	4-3 L	0	3	3
43	JAN. 13	BUFFALO	5-4 W	1	2	3
44	JAN. 16	NY ISLANDERS	3-3 T	1	1	2
45	JAN. 18	VANCOUVER	4-4 T	1	0	1
46	JAN. 19	VANCOUVER	7-5 W	1	3	4
47	JAN. 21	LOS ANGELES	8-7 W	1	1	2
48	JAN. 25	NEW JERSEY	4-2 W	1	2	3
49	JAN. 26	PITTSBURGH	6-3 W	3	1	4
50	JAN. 28	CALGARY	4-3 W	1	2	3
51	JAN. 29	CALGARY	4-2 W	0	2	2
TOTALS				13	24	37

Game	Date	Team	Score	G	A	P
52	FEB. 2	NY RANGERS	5-1 W	0	0	0
53	FEB. 3	HARTFORD	6-3 W	1	2	3
54	FEB. 6	WINNIPEG	6-2 L	0	1	1
55	FEB. 8	MINNESOTA	5-3 W	0	2	2
56	FEB. 9	DETROIT	6-5 W	0	2	2
57	FEB. 15	NY RANGERS	8-7 W	2	2	4
58	FEB. 16	PHILADELPHIA	5-4 L	0	2	2
59	FEB. 18	BUFFALO	6-4 W	2	1	3
60	FEB. 19	TORONTO	9-4 W	2	3	5
61	FEB. 22	QUEBEC	6-3 W	1	1	2
62	FEB. 23	WASHINGTON	3-3 T	0	1	1
63	FEB. 27	MONTREAL	4-1 L	1	0	1
TOTALS				9	17	26

Game	Date	Team	Score	G	A	P
64	MARCH 1	LOS ANGELES	5-4 L	0	3	3
65	MARCH 3	WINNIPEG	6-3 L	1	1	2
66	MARCH 5	CALGARY	5-3 W	0	1	1
67	MARCH 9	NY RANGERS	3-3 T	1	0	1
68	MARCH 10	VANCOUVER	6-3 L	0	1	1
69	MARCH 13	DETROIT	7-6 W	1	4	5
70	MARCH 15	BUFFALO	4-4 T	0	1	1
71	MARCH 17	LOS ANGELES	5-4 L	0	1	1
72	MARCH 20	CHICAGO	6-4 W	0	2	2
73	MARCH 22	TORONTO	3-3 T	1	0	1
74	MARCH 26	NY ISLANDERS	7-5 W	1	1	2
75	MARCH 28	BOSTON	6-3 L	0	1	1
76	MARCH 29	HARTFORD	8-7 L	1	2	3
77	MARCH 31	CHICAGO	7-3 W	1	4	5
TOTALS				7	22	29

Game	Date	Team	Score	G	A	P
78	APRIL 2	LOS ANGELES	6-4 W	3	1	4
79	APRIL 5	CALGARY	5-5 T	1	1	2
80	APRIL 6	WINNIPEG	6-5 W	0	2	2
TOTALS				4	4	8

'84-85 TOTALS				73	135	208

1984-1985 Leading Scorers

Player	Club	GP	G	A	Pts.
Gretzky, Wayne	**Edmonton**	**80**	**73**	**135**	**208**
Kurri, Jari	Edmonton	73	71	64	135
Hawerchuk, Dale	Winnipeg	80	53	77	130
Dionne, Marcel	Los Angeles	80	46	80	126
Coffey, Paul	Edmonton	80	37	84	121
Bossy, Mike	NY Islanders	76	58	59	117
Ogrodnick, John	Detroit	79	50	55	105
Savard, Denis	Chicago	79	38	67	105
Federko, Bernie	St. Louis	76	30	73	103
Gartner, Mike	Washington	80	50	52	102

1984-85 PLAYOFFS

Game	Date	Team	Score	G	A	P
1	APRIL 10	LOS ANGELES	3-2 W	0	2	2
2	APRIL 11	LOS ANGELES	4-2 W	0	1	1
3	APRIL 13	LOS ANGELES	4-3 W	0	2	2
TOTALS				0	5	5

Game	Date	Team	Score	G	A	P
1	APRIL 18	WINNIPEG	4-2 W	1	2	3
2	APRIL 20	WINNIPEG	5-2 W	1	0	1
3	APRIL 23	WINNIPEG	5-4 W	1	1	2
4	APRIL 25	WINNIPEG	8-3 W	3	4	7
TOTALS				6	7	13

Game	Date	Team	Score	G	A	P
1	MAY 1	CHICAGO	11-2 W	1	3	4
2	MAY 7	CHICAGO	7-3 W	0	3	3
3	MAY 9	CHICAGO	5-2 L	0	0	0
4	MAY 12	CHICAGO	8-6 L	1	2	3
5	MAY 14	CHICAGO	10-5 W	2	2	4
6	MAY 16	CHICAGO	8-2 W	0	4	4
TOTALS				4	14	18

Game	Date	Team	Score	G	A	P
1	MAY 21	PHILADELPHIA	4-1 L	0	0	0
2	MAY 23	PHILADELPHIA	3-1 W	1	0	1
3	MAY 25	PHILADELPHIA	4-3 W	3	1	4
4	MAY 28	PHILADELPHIA	5-3 W	2	0	2
5	MAY 30	PHILADELPHIA	8-3 W	1	3	4
TOTALS				7	4	11

'84-85 PLAYOFF TOTALS				17	30	47

1984-85 Playoff Leaders

Player	Team	GP	G	A	P
Wayne Gretzky	**Edmonton**	**18**	**17**	**30**	**47**
Paul Coffey	Edmonton	18	12	25	37
Jari Kurri	Edmonton	18	19	12	31
Denis Savard	Chicago		9	20	29
Glenn Anderson	Edmonton	18	10	16	26
Mark Messier	Edmonton	18	12	13	25
Peter Stastny	Quebec		4	19	23
Steve Larmer	Chicago		9	13	22
Michel Goulet	Quebec		11	10	21
Charlie Huddy	Edmonton	18	3	17	20

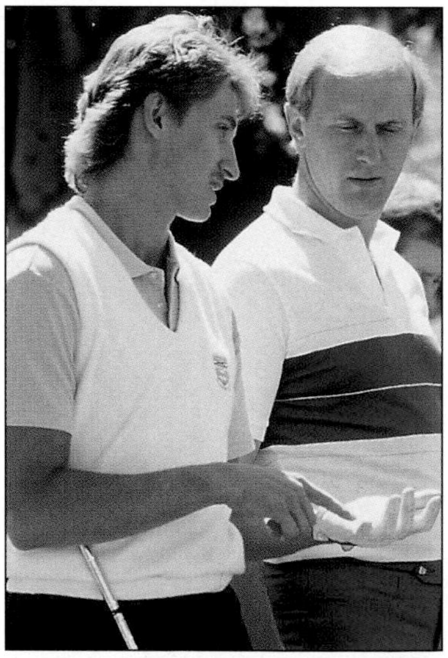

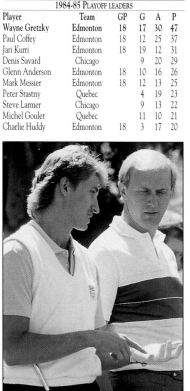

1st Smythe Division, 1st Overall. Playoffs: Won Smythe Division Semifinal 3-0 vs. Vancouver; Lost Smythe Division Final 4-3 vs. Calgary.

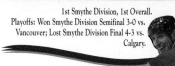

1985-86 SEASON

Game	Date	Team	Score	G	A	P
1	OCT. 10	WINNIPEG	4-3 W	2	1	3
2	OCT. 13	ST. LOUIS	6-3 W	0	2	2
3	OCT. 16	NY ISLANDERS	6-4 W	0	1	1
4	OCT. 18	BOSTON	3-2 W	0	2	2
5	OCT. 20	LOS ANGELES	8-5 W	1	2	3
6	OCT. 23	WINNIPEG	9-3 L	0	1	1
7	OCT. 25	CALGARY	5-3 W	1	2	3
8	OCT. 28	CALGARY	6-4 W	1	4	5
9	OCT. 30	WINNIPEG	7-3 W	0	4	4
TOTALS				5	19	24

Game	Date	Team	Score	G	A	P
10	NOV. 1	BUFFALO	2-0 L	0	0	0
11	NOV. 3	TORONTO	7-1 W	3	0	3
12	NOV. 5	VANCOUVER	6-4 W	2	1	3
13	NOV. 6	LOS ANGELES	4-4 T	1	1	2
14	NOV. 8	VANCOUVER	13-0 W	0	4	4
15	NOV. 12	WASHINGTON	5-2 L	1	0	1
16	NOV. 14	PHILADELPHIA	5-3 L	0	1	1
17	NOV. 16	NY ISLANDERS	4-4 T	1	0	1
18	NOV. 17	NY RANGERS	3-2 W	0	2	2
19	NOV. 19	QUEBEC	5-4 W	1	1	2
20	NOV. 20	MONTREAL	5-4 W	1	1	2
21	NOV. 23	NEW JERSEY	3-2 W	0	1	1
22	NOV. 27	VANCOUVER	5-5 T	2	0	2
23	NOV. 30	HARTFORD	8-5 W	1	3	4
TOTALS				13	15	28

Game	Date	Team	Score	G	A	P
24	DEC. 1	CALGARY	5-3 W	0	1	1
25	DEC. 3	LOS ANGELES	8-4 W	0	1	1
26	DEC. 5	LOS ANGELES	6-6 T	0	5	5
27	DEC. 7	MINNESOTA	8-4 W	1	4	5
28	DEC. 8	CHICAGO	4-3 W	0	1	1
29	DEC. 10	ST. LOUIS	7-3 W	0	2	2
30	DEC. 11	CHICAGO	12-9 W	0	7	7
31	DEC. 13	WINNIPEG	6-3 W	2	2	4
32	DEC. 15	VANCOUVER	5-3 W	0	3	3
33	DEC. 18	WASHINGTON	5-2 L	0	1	1
34	DEC. 20	LOS ANGELES	9-4 W	0	6	6
35	DEC. 22	WINNIPEG	7-5 L	2	1	3
36	DEC. 29	VANCOUVER	5-3 W	0	2	2
37	DEC. 31	PHILADELPHIA	4-3 W	3	0	3
TOTALS				8	36	44

Game	Date	Team	Score	G	A	P
38	JAN. 2	CALGARY	4-3 W	1	1	2
39	JAN. 4	WINNIPEG	4-3 W	0	2	2
40	JAN. 5	CALGARY	6-3 W	1	2	3
41	JAN. 8	TORONTO	11-9 L	3	3	6
42	JAN. 10	QUEBEC	5-3 L	0	3	3
43	JAN. 11	MONTREAL	6-3 W	1	3	4
44	JAN. 13	BOSTON	5-3 W	1	2	3
45	JAN. 15	HARTFORD	4-1 W	2	1	3
46	JAN. 18	NY RANGERS	5-4 L	0	2	2
47	JAN. 22	PITTSBURGH	7-4 L	1	1	2
48	JAN. 24	NEW JERSEY	7-6 W	1	3	4
49	JAN. 25	LOS ANGELES	5-2 W	1	1	2
50	JAN. 27	CHICAGO	4-3 W	0	0	0
51	JAN. 29	ST. LOUIS	5-5 T	0	3	3
52	JAN. 31	CALGARY	7-4 W	0	4	4
TOTALS				12	31	43

Game	Date	Team	Score	G	A	P
53	FEB. 1	CALGARY	4-4 T	0	3	3
54	FEB. 6	NEW JERSEY	6-4 W	0	3	3
55	FEB. 8	WASHINGTON	5-4 L	0	2	2
56	FEB. 9	BUFFALO	4-2 L	0	1	1
57	FEB. 11	DETROIT	3-2 W	0	1	1
58	FEB. 14	QUEBEC	8-2 W	0	7	7
59	FEB. 16	BUFFALO	7-5 W	1	3	4
60	FEB. 19	TORONTO	9-5 W	2	0	2
61	FEB. 22	BOSTON	6-5 L	1	1	2
62	FEB. 24	MONTREAL	3-2 W	1	1	2
63	FEB. 26	WINNIPEG	8-2 W	2	4	6
TOTALS				7	26	33

Game	Date	Team	Score	G	A	P
64	MARCH 2	PHILADELPHIA	2-1 W	0	1	1
65	MARCH 4	VANCOUVER	6-2 W	0	4	4
66	MARCH 5	LOS ANGELES	6-3 W	2	2	4
67	MARCH 7	PITTSBURGH	5-3 W	0	2	2
68	MARCH 9	LOS ANGELES	7-3 W	1	3	4
69	MARCH 11	MINNESOTA	4-0 L	0	0	0
70	MARCH 12	WINNIPEG	8-5 W	0	2	2
71	MARCH 14	DETROIT	12-3 W	1	4	5
72	MARCH 18	WINNIPEG	6-2 W	1	2	3
73	MARCH 21	MINNESOTA	5-4 W	0	1	1
74	MARCH 25	DETROIT	7-2 W	0	3	3
75	MARCH 26	PITTSBURGH	8-3 W	1	3	4
76	MARCH 28	NY RANGERS	4-2 L	0	1	1
77	MARCH 29	NY ISLANDERS	4-4 T	0	3	3
TOTALS				6	31	37

Game	Date	Team	Score	G	A	P
78	APRIL 2	VANCOUVER	8-4 W	1	1	2
79	APRIL 4	CALGARY	9-3 L	0	3	3
80	APRIL 6	VANCOUVER	3-2 W	0	1	1
TOTALS				1	5	6

'85-86 TOTALS 52 163 215

1985-1986 Leading Scorers

Player	Team	GP	G	A	Pts.
Gretzky, Wayne	Edmonton	80	52	163	215
Lemieux, Mario	Pittsburgh	79	48	93	141
Coffey, Paul	Edmonton	79	48	90	138
Kurri, Jari	Edmonton	78	68	63	131
Bossy, Mike	NY Islanders	80	61	62	123
Stastny, Peter	Quebec	76	41	81	122
Savard, Denis	Chicago	80	47	69	116
Naslund, Mats	Montreal	80	43	67	110
Hawerchuk, Dale	Winnipeg	80	46	59	105
Broten, Neal	Minnesota	80	29	76	105

1985-86 PLAYOFFS

Game	Date	Team	Score	G	A	P
1	APRIL 9	VANCOUVER	7-3 W	1	0	1
2	APRIL 10	VANCOUVER	5-1 W	1	1	2
3	APRIL 12	VANCOUVER	5-1 W	1	2	3
TOTALS				3	3	6

Game	Date	Team	Score	G	A	P
1	APRIL 18	CALGARY	4-1 L	0	1	1
2	APRIL 20	CALGARY	6-5 W	0	1	1
3	APRIL 22	CALGARY	3-2 L	1	1	2
4	APRIL 24	CALGARY	7-4 W	3	2	5
5	APRIL 26	CALGARY	4-1 L	1	0	1
6	APRIL 28	CALGARY	5-2 W	0	2	2
7	APRIL 30	CALGARY	3-2 L	0	1	1
TOTALS				5	8	13

'85-86 PLAYOFF TOTALS 8 11 19

1985-86 Playoff Leaders

Player	Team	GP	G	A	P
Doug Gilmour,	St. Louis	19	9	12	21
Bernie Federko,	St. Louis	19	7	14	21
Joe Mullen,	Calgary	21	12	7	19
Wayne Gretzky,	Edmonton	10	8	11	19
Mats Naslund,	Montreal	20	8	11	19
Al McInnes,	Calgary	21	4	15	19
Lanny MacDonald,	Calgary	22	11	7	18
Paul Reinhart,	Calgary	21	5	13	18
Greg Paslawski,	St. Louis	17	10	7	17
Pierre Larouche,	NY Rangers	16	8	9	17

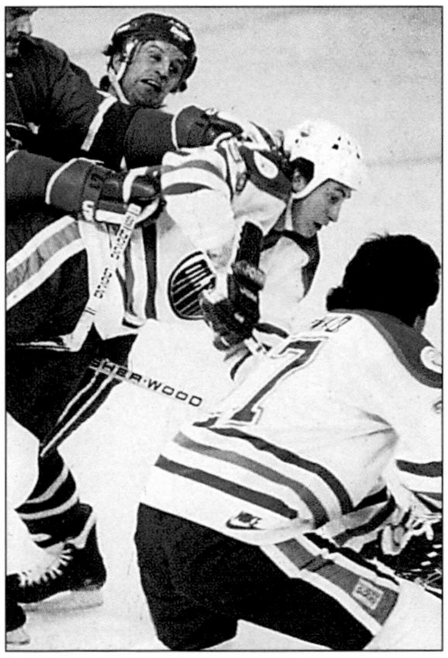

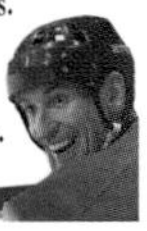

STANLEY CUP CHAMPIONS: 1st Smythe Division, 1st Overall. Playoffs: Won Smythe Division Semifinal 4-1 vs. Los Angeles; Won Symthe Division Final 4-0 vs. Winnipeg; Won Campbell Conference Final 4-1 vs. Detroit; Won Stanley Cup Final 4-3 vs. Philadelphia.

1986-87 SEASON

Game	Date	Team	Score	G	A	P
1	OCT. 9	PHILADELPHIA	2-1 W	0	0	0
2	OCT. 11	MONTREAL	5-4 W	2	2	4
3	OCT. 12	WINNIPEG	5-3 L	1	0	1
4	OCT. 15	QUEBEC	5-2 W	0	5	5
5	OCT. 17	DETROIT	4-3 W	0	4	4
6	OCT. 19	LOS ANGELES	7-6 L	0	2	2
7	OCT. 21	CHICAGO	9-1 W	2	3	5
8	OCT. 22	CALGARY	6-3 L	0	1	1
9	OCT. 24	BOSTON	6-2 W	3	1	4
10	OCT. 26	VANCOUVER	3-2 W	0	2	2
11	OCT. 29	WASHINGTON	6-3 W	1	1	2
12	OCT. 31	VANCOUVER	6-2 W	2	1	3
TOTALS				11	22	33

Game	Date	Team	Score	G	A	P
13	NOV. 2	NY ISLANDERS	3-2 W	0	3	3
14	NOV. 5	CALGARY	3-1 L	1	0	1
15	NOV. 7	CALGARY	6-4 L	1	1	2
16	NOV. 8	MONTREAL	4-3 W	0	0	0
17	NOV. 11	NY ISLANDERS	3-2 W	0	1	1
18	NOV. 13	BOSTON	4-3 L	1	0	1
19	NOV. 15	HARTFORD	6-2 L	0	1	1
20	NOV. 16	NY RANGERS	8-6 W	1	2	3
21	NOV. 19	NY RANGERS	5-4 W	1	0	1
22	NOV. 22	VANCOUVER	5-2 W	3	2	5
23	NOV. 24	CALGARY	6-5 L	1	1	2
24	NOV. 26	WINNIPEG	4-3 W	1	2	3
25	NOV. 28	CHICAGO	6-5 L	0	2	2
TOTALS				10	15	25

Game	Date	Team	Score	G	A	P
26	DEC. 3	NY ISLANDERS	7-1 W	1	2	3
27	DEC. 5	PITTSBURGH	4-2 W	0	3	3
28	DEC. 7	PHILADELPHIA	5-2 L	1	0	1
29	DEC. 9	MINNESOTA	3-2 W	1	1	2
30	DEC. 10	WINNIPEG	7-4 W	3	0	3
31	DEC. 12	WINNIPEG	6-1 W	0	3	3
32	DEC. 14	LOS ANGELES	4-2 W	0	2	2
33	DEC. 17	QUEBEC	5-2 W	4	1	5
34	DEC. 19	VANCOUVER	4-2 W	0	2	2
35	DEC. 20	LOS ANGELES	8-8 T	2	3	5
36	DEC. 23	WINNIPEG	2-1 L	0	0	0
37	DEC. 28	PHILADELPHIA	6-4 W	2	1	3
38	DEC. 30	VANCOUVER	7-3 W	2	2	4
TOTALS				18	18	36

Game	Date	Team	Score	G	A	P
39	JAN. 3	LOS ANGELES	8-1 W	1	2	3
40	JAN. 7	LOS ANGELES	6-1 L	0	1	1
41	JAN. 9	ST. LOUIS	5-1 W	0	0	0
42	JAN. 11	CALGARY	5-3 W	0	2	2
43	JAN. 13	DETROIT	5-3 L	1	2	3
44	JAN. 15	QUEBEC	4-1 W	1	1	2
45	JAN. 17	TORONTO	7-4 W	1	3	4
46	JAN. 18	BUFFALO	6-5 L	0	2	2
47	JAN. 21	WINNIPEG	5-3 W	2	1	3
48	JAN. 23	NY RANGERS	7-4 W	2	2	4
49	JAN. 24	PITTSBURGH	4-2 W	1	3	4
50	JAN. 27	VANCOUVER	4-4 T	0	2	2
51	JAN. 28	VANCOUVER	7-3 W	0	4	4
52	JAN. 30	MINNESOTA	2-2 T	1	0	1
TOTALS				10	25	35

Game	Date	Team	Score	G	A	P
53	FEB. 1	CHICAGO	6-4 L	0	2	2
54	FEB. 3	ST. LOUIS	4-2 W	0	1	1
55	FEB. 4	MINNESOTA	6-5 W	1	3	4
56	FEB. 6	NY ISLANDERS	3-3 T	0	2	2
57	FEB. 8	ST. LOUIS	6-2 W	2	2	4
58	FEB. 15	WASHINGTON	5-3 L	0	0	0
59	FEB. 18	TORONTO	9-2 W	1	4	5
60	FEB. 20	WINNIPEG	5-2 L	1	1	2
61	FEB. 24	PITTSBURGH	5-2 L	0	1	1
62	FEB. 25	NEW JERSEY	4-2 L	0	0	0
63	FEB. 27	WASHINGTON	5-2 L	0	0	0
TOTALS				5	16	21

Game	Date	Team	Score	G	A	P
63	MARCH 4	VANCOUVER	8-5 W	1	2	3
65	MARCH 6	LOS ANGELES	9-3 W	1	4	5
66	MARCH 7	MONTREAL	5-3 W	0	2	2
67	MARCH 11	DETROIT	6-3 W	1	3	4
68	MARCH 14	BUFFALO	5-3 W	2	1	3
69	MARCH 15	HARTFORD	4-1 W	1	1	2
70	MARCH 17	NEW JERSEY	7-4 W	0	3	3
71	MARCH 19	CALGARY	5-4 L	1	2	3
72	MARCH 20	CALGARY	6-3 L	0	1	1
73	MARCH 23	NEW JERSEY	7-6 W	0	3	3
74	MARCH 25	HARTFORD	5-3 W	0	2	2
75	MARCH 26	BOSTON	4-1 W	0	0	0
76	MARCH 28	TORONTO	4-2 L	0	0	0
77	MARCH 29	BUFFALO	3-2 W	0	0	0
78	MARCH 31	WINNIPEG	5-4 W	0	1	1
TOTALS				7	25	32

Game	Date	Team	Score	G	A	P
79	APRIL 2	CALGARY	4-4 T	1	0	1
80	APRIL 4	LOS ANGELES	7-3 W	-	-	-
TOTALS				1	0	1

'86-87 TOTALS 62 121 183

1986-1987 Leading Scorers

Player	Team	GP	G	A	Pts.
Gretzky, Wayne	Edmonton	79	62	121	183
Kurri, Jari	Edmonton	79	54	54	108
Lemieux, Mario	Pittsburgh	63	54	53	107
Messier, Mark	Edmonton	77	37	70	107
Gilmour, Doug	St. Louis	80	42	63	105
Ciccarelli, Dino	Minnesota	80	52	51	103
Hawerchuk, Dale	Winnipeg	80	47	53	100
Goulet, Michel	Quebec	75	49	47	96
Kerr, Tim	Philadelphia	75	58	37	95
Bourque, Ray	Boston	78	23	72	95

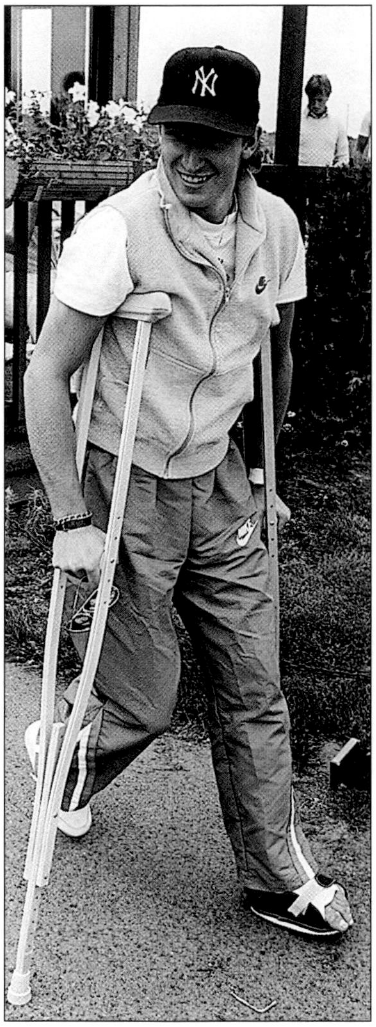

1986-87 PLAYOFFS

Game	Date	Team	Score	G	A	P
1	APRIL 8	LOS ANGELES	5-2 L	0	1	1
2	APRIL 9	LOS ANGELES	13-3 W	1	6	7
3	APRIL 11	LOS ANGELES	6-5 W	0	2	2
4	APRIL 12	LOS ANGELES	6-3 W	1	4	5
5	APRIL 14	LOS ANGELES	5-4 W	0	0	0
TOTALS				2	13	15

Game	Date	Team	Score	G	A	P
1	APRIL 21	WINNIPEG	3-2 W	0	0	0
2	APRIL 23	WINNIPEG	5-3 W	0	2	2
3	APRIL 25	WINNIPEG	5-2 W	0	3	3
4	APRIL 27	WINNIPEG	4-2 W	1	0	1
TOTALS				1	5	6

Game	Date	Team	Score	G	A	P
1	MAY 5	DETROIT	3-1 L	0	0	0
2	MAY 7	DETROIT	4-1 W	0	1	1
3	MAY 9	DETROIT	2-1 W	0	0	0
4	MAY 11	DETROIT	3-2 W	0	1	1
5	MAY 13	DETROIT	6-3 W	0	0	0
TOTALS				0	2	2

Game	Date	Team	Score	G	A	P
1	MAY 17	PHILADELPHIA	4-2 W	1	1	2
2	MAY 20	PHILADELPHIA	3-2 W	1	1	2
3	MAY 22	PHILADELPHIA	5-3 L	0	1	1
4	MAY 24	PHILADELPHIA	4-1 W	0	3	3
5	MAY 26	PHILADELPHIA	4-3 L	0	1	1
6	MAY 28	PHILADELPHIA	3-2 L	0	1	1

				G	A	P
7	MAY 31	PHILADELPHIA	3-1 W	0	1	1
TOTALS				2	9	11

86-87 PLAYOFF		**TOTALS**		5	29	34

1986-87 Playoff Leaders

Player	Team	GP	G	A	P
Wayne Gretzky	Edmonton	21	5	29	34
Mark Messier	Edmonton	21	12	16	28
Brian Propp	Philadelphia	26	12	16	28
Glenn Anderson	Edmonton	21	14	13	27
Per-Erik Eklund	Philadelphia	26	7	20	27
Jari Kurri	Edmonton	21	15	10	25
Mats Naslund	Montreal	17	7	15	22
Rick Tocchet	Philadelphia	26	11	10	21
Larry Robinson	Montreal	17	3	17	20
Ryan Walter	Montreal	17	7	12	19

1987-88 SEASON

STANLEY CUP CHAMPIONS: 2nd Smythe Division, 3rd Overall. Playoffs: Won Smythe Division Semifinal 4-1 vs. Winnipeg; Won Smythe Division Final 4-0 vs. Calgary; Won Campbell Conference Final 4-1 vs. Detroit; Won Stanley cup Final 4-0 vs. Boston.

Game	Date	Team	Score	G	A	P
1	OCT. 9	DETROIT	4-1 L	0	1	1
2	OCT. 11	LOS ANGELES	9-2 W	1	4	5
3	OCT. 14	CALGARY	5-4 L	1	1	2
4	OCT. 16	CALGARY	5-2 W	0	1	1
5	OCT. 17	BOSTON	4-3 W	1	2	3
6	OCT. 21	LOS ANGELES	6-2 W	2	1	3
7	OCT. 23	VANCOUVER	5-4 W	0	2	2
8	OCT. 24	VANCOUVER	9-5 W	2	3	5
9	OCT. 27	QUEBEC	5-0 L	0	0	0
10	OCT. 28	MONTREAL	3-1 L	0	1	1
11	OCT. 31	NEW JERSEY	6-5 L	0	3	3
TOTALS				7	19	26

Game	Date	Team	Score	G	A	P
12	NOV. 1	NY RANGERS	7-6 W	0	2	2
13	NOV. 4	NY RANGERS	7-2 W	3	2	5
14	NOV. 5	CALGARY	4-4 T	1	2	3
15	NOV. 7	BUFFALO	5-0 W	2	0	2
16	NOV. 10	LOS ANGELES	4-4 T	0	1	1
17	NOV. 14	ST. LOUIS	6-5 W	0	4	4
18	NOV. 15	CHICAGO	5-4 L	1	2	3
19	NOV.18	QUEBEC	4-1 W	0	2	2
20	NOV. 20	PITTSBURGH	4-1 W	0	2	2
21	NOV. 22	WINNIPEG	4-3 L	2	0	2
22	NOV. 25	NEW JERSEY	8-7 W	1	3	4
23	NOV. 27	CHICAGO	4-3 W	1	1	2
24	NOV. 29	BUFFALO	5-2 W	0	2	2
TOTALS				11	23	34

Game	Date	Team	Score	G	A	P
25	DEC. 1	WASHINGTON	4-2 L	0	0	0
26	DEC. 2	DETROIT	7-4 L	0	1	1
27	DEC. 5	TORONTO	5-2 W	2	0	2
28	DEC. 6	MINNESOTA	10-4 W	5	1	6
29	DEC. 9	WINNIPEG	2-0 W	0	1	1
30	DEC. 11	VANCOUVER	2-1 W	0	1	1
31	DEC. 12	VANCOUVER	6-3 W	2	1	3
32	DEC. 16	LOS ANGELES	7-5 L	1	1	2
33	DEC. 18	WINNIPEG	5-5 T	0	2	2
34	DEC. 19	HARTFORD	4-3 L	0	0	0
35	DEC. 22	LOS ANGELES	5-2 W	0	2	2
36	DEC. 26	CALGARY	5-4 W	1	0	1
37	DEC. 28	VANCOUVER	7-3 W	0	1	1
38	DEC. 30	PHILADELPHIA	6-0 W	1	3	4
TOTALS				12	14	26

Game	Date	Team	Score	G	A	P
39	JAN. 2	WASHINGTON	2-0 W	-	-	-
40	JAN. 4	BOSTON	2-2 T	-	-	-
41	JAN. 6	HARTFORD	5-1 W	-	-	-
42	JAN. 8	WINNIPEG	4-4 T	-	-	-
43	JAN. 9	NY ISLANDERS	5-1 W	-	-	-
44	JAN. 11	WASHINGTON	3-2 L	-	-	-
45	JAN. 13	CALGARY	5-3 W	-	-	-
46	JAN. 15	WINNIPEG	4-4 T	-	-	-
47	JAN. 18	MONTREAL	6-4 L	-	-	-
48	JAN. 19	QUEBEC	4-4 T	-	-	-
49	JAN. 21	PHILADELPHIA	3-1 L	-	-	-
50	JAN. 23	NY ISLANDERS	3-2 L	-	-	-
51	JAN. 25	PITTSBURGH	6-4 W	-	-	-
52	JAN. 29	CALGARY	5-4 L	0	4	4
53	JAN. 30	HARTFORD	5-2 W	1	2	3
TOTALS				1	6	7

Game	Date	Team	Score	G	A	P
54	FEB. 3	NEW JERSEY	8-5 W	1	2	3

Game	Date	Team	Score	G	A	P
55	FEB. 6	LOS ANGELES	7-2 L	1	1	2
56	FEB. 11	VANCOUVER	7-2 W	1	2	3
57	FEB. 12	BOSTON	7-4 L	0	2	2
58	FEB. 14	VANCOUVER	7-6 W	0	1	1
59	FEB. 17	TORONTO	4-4 T	0	2	2
60	FEB. 19	PITTSBURGH	7-3 W	0	0	0
61	FEB. 21	WINNIPEG	4-3 W	-	-	-
62	FEB. 23	ST. LOUIS	6-4 W	-	-	-
63	FEB. 24	CHICAGO	6-4 L	-	-	-
64	FEB. 28	CALGARY	3-2 L	1	0	1
TOTALS				4	10	14

Game	Date	Team	Score	G	A	P
65	MARCH 1	LOS ANGELES	5-3 W	1	1	2
66	MARCH 4	PHILADELPHIA	7-4 W	0	5	5
67	MARCH 5	CALGARY	7-4 L	0	3	3
68	MARCH 7	WINNIPEG	6-0 W	0	5	5
69	MARCH 9	MONTREAL	4-1 W	0	2	2
70	MARCH 12	VANCOUVER	3-3 T	0	2	2
71	MARCH 15	BUFFALO	6-4 W	0	3	3
72	MARCH 18	WINNIPEG	4-1 W	0	1	1
73	MARCH 20	MINNESOTA	5-5 T	1	2	3
74	MARCH 22	DETROIT	6-4 W	0	3	3
75	MARCH 24	NY RANGERS	6-1 L	0	0	0
76	MARCH 26	NY ISLANDERS	5-4 L	1	2	3
77	MARCH 28	TORONTO	6-4 W	1	3	4
78	MARCH 30	MINNESOTA	6-3 W	1	3	4
TOTALS				5	33	38

Game	Date	Team	Score	G	A	P
79	APRIL 1	ST. LOUIS	5-2 W	0	3	3
80	APRIL 3	LOS ANGELES	5-5 T	0	1	1
TOTALS				0	4	4

87-88	**TOTALS**			40	109	149

1987-1988 Leading Scorers

Player	Team	GP	G	A	Pts.
Lemieux, Mario	Pittsburgh	76	70	98	168
Gretzky, Wayne	Edmonton	64	40	109	149
Savard, Denis	Chicago	80	44	87	131
Hawerchuk, Dale	Winnipeg	80	44	77	121
Robitaille, Luc	Los Angeles	80	53	58	111
Stastny, Peter	Quebec	76	46	65	111
Messier, Mark	Edmonton	77	37	74	111
Carson, Jimmy	Los Angeles	80	55	52	107
Loob, Hakan	Calgary	80	50	56	106
Goulet, Michel	Quebec	80	48	58	106

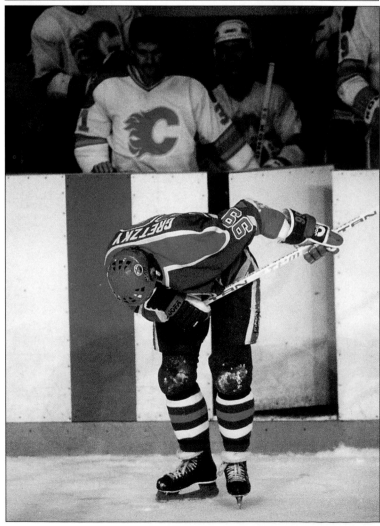

1987-88 PLAYOFFS

GAME	DATE	TEAM	SCORE	G	A	P
1	APRIL 6	WINNIPEG	7-4 W	0	2	2
2	APRIL 7	WINNIPEG	3-2 W	0	0	0
3	APRIL 9	WINNIPEG	6-4 L	0	1	1
4	APRIL 10	WINNIPEG	5-3 W	0	3	3
5	APRIL 12	WINNIPEG	6-2 W	1	4	5
TOTALS				1	10	11

GAME	DATE	TEAM	SCORE	G	A	P
1	APRIL 19	CALGARY	3-1 W	1	0	1
2	APRIL 21	CALGARY	5-4 W	2	0	2
3	APRIL 23	CALGARY	4-2 W	0	2	2
4	APRIL 25	CALGARY	6-4 W	1	0	1
TOTALS				4	2	6

GAME	DATE	TEAM	SCORE	G	A	P
1	MAY 3	DETROIT	4-1 W	0	3	3
2	MAY 5	DETROIT	5-3 W	1	2	3
3	MAY 7	DETROIT	5-2 L	2	0	2
4	MAY 9	DETROIT	4-3 W	0	2	2
5	MAY 11	DETROIT	8-4 W	1	2	3
TOTALS				4	9	13

GAME	DATE	TEAM	SCORE	G	A	P
1	MAY 18	BOSTON	2-1 W	1	0	1
2	MAY 20	BOSTON	4-2 W	1	2	3
3	MAY 22	BOSTON	6-3 W	0	4	4
4	MAY 24	BOSTON*		0	2	2
5	MAY 26	BOSTON	6-3 W	1	2	3
TOTALS				3	10	13

* Postponed due to blackout

87-88 PLAYOFF	TOTALS			12	31	43

1987-88 PLAYOFF LEADERS

Player	Team	GP	G	A	P
Wayne Gretzky	Edmonton	19	12	31	43
Mark Messier	Edmonton	19	11	23	34
Jari Kurri	Edmonton	19	14	17	31
Esa Tikkanen	Edmonton	19	10	17	27
Ken Linseman	Boston	11	14	11	25
Glenn Anderson	Edmonton	19	9	16	25
Bob Probert	Detroit	8	13	8	21
Ray Bourque	Boston	3	18	3	21
Adam Oates	Detroit	8	12	8	20
Craig Simpson	Edmonton	19	13	6	19

Regular Season Scoring By Month

	CAREER				EDMONTON			
	GP	G	A	P	GP	G	A	P
October	205	126	267	393	98	75	146	221
November	236	154	317	471	121	108	186	294
December	233	157	316	473	117	110	178	294
January	249	152	350	502	118	105	191	296
February	230	136	283	419	101	87	144	231
March	260	144	359	503	123	86	208	294
April	72	25	70	95	19	12	27	39

* Gretzky is the all-time NHL leader in goals, assists and points in every month from October through April except:
- January goals leader is Gordie Howe with 154 (Gretzky 2nd)
- February goals leader is Gordie Howe with 151 (Gretzky 2nd)

Wayne Gretzky's Teammates

A total of 354 players have lined up alongside Wayne Gretzky as teammates in his 20-year regular-season career. Following is a list of players with 200-or-more appearances:

Player	Games
Kurri, Jari	858
Messier, Mark	698
Huddy, Charlie	664
Lowe, Kevin	661
Hunter, Dave	613
Anderson, Glenn	591
Fogolin, Lee	579
McSorley, Marty	556
Coffey, Paul	546

Robitaille, Luc	491
Semenko, Dave	453
Krushelnyski, Mike	420
Lumley, Dave	379
Gregg, Randy	342
Fuhr, Grant	340
Granato, Tony	330
Taylor, Dave	327
McClelland, Kevin	316
Hrudey, Kelly	314
Hughes, Pat	294
Beukeboom, Jeff	288
Watters, Tim	287
Blake, Rob	281
Jackson, Don	262

Donnelly, Mike	257
Sydor, Darryl	244
Conacher, Pat	241
Moog, Andy	231
Leetch, Brian	228
Duchesne, Steve	226
MacTavish, Craig	226
Graves, Adam	224
Sundstrom, Niklas	221
Tikkanen, Esa	220
Tonelli, John	217
Miller, Jay	214
Kudelski, Bob	213
Siltanen, Risto	205
Samuelsson, Ulf	203

1485 Games
49 Different Sites

Arena	GP	G	A	P
Skyreach Centre	383	327	606	933
Great Western Forum	303	171	413	584
Madison Square Garden	137	46	133	179
Winnipeg Arena	50	38	70	108
Pacific Coliseum	52	30	63	93
Cdn. Airlines Saddledome	46	21	66	87
Maple Leaf Gardens	30	30	47	77
Joe Louis Arena	31	13	52	65
Civic Arena	28	21	39	60
USAir Arena	25	15	37	52
Chicago Stadium	24	14	35	49
St. Louis Arena	23	16	31	47
Colisee de Quebec	22	12	35	47
Nassau Coliseum	26	16	28	44
Hartford Civic Center	21	15	28	43
Montreal Forum	23	8	31	39
Metropolitan Sports Center	19	10	28	38
Memorial Auditorium	21	11	26	37
Continental Airlines Arena	26	8	27	35
The Spectrum	19	11	15	26
Boston Garden	19	7	17	24
McNichols Sports Arena	13	5	15	20
San Jose Arena	13	4	14	18
Stampede Corral	10	9	8	17
Arrowhead Pond of Anaheim	11	3	12	15
Kiel Center	14	5	9	14
Reunion Arena	10	3	9	12
First Union Center	8	2	8	10
Cow Palace	4	2	7	9
Miami Arena	8	3	5	8
General Motors Place	4	4	2	6
Molson Centre	6	0	6	6
MCI Center	4	2	3	5
Ice Palace	7	1	4	5
Nashville Arena	1	0	5	5
The Omni	2	2	2	4
Marine Midland Arena	6	2	2	4
Expo Hall	1	1	3	4
Ottawa Civic Centre	3	1	3	4
America West Arena	4	1	3	4
Thunderdome	2	1	2	3
Greensboro Coliseum	4	1	2	3
FleetCenter	6	1	2	3
ARCO Arena	1	0	3	3
United Center	7	0	3	3
Olympia Stadium	1	1	1	2
Corel Centre	6	0	2	2
National Car Rental Center	2	0	1	1
Springfield Civic Center	1	0	0	0

Single-Game Goals, Assists, Points Breakdown
1487 Regular Season Games Played

	Goals: 894			Assists: 1963			Points: 2857	
Goals	Career	Oilers	Assists	Career	Oilers	Points	Career	Oilers
0	849	311	0	423	149	0	266	69
1	449	249	1	489	221	1	397	155
2	139	94	2	351	183	2	365	171
3	37	27	3	148	143	3	242	143
4	9	9	4	59	39	4	121	79
5	4	4	5	13	8	5	67	57
6	–	–	6	1	1	6	20	14
7	–	–	7	3	3	7	7	6
8	–	–	8	–	–	8	2	2

Gretzky played 695 regular season games as an Edmonton Oiler

Career Goals by
Opposing Goaltender

Gretzky scored 839 regular-season goals against 155 goaltenders and added 55 empty-net goals. He scored 113 Stanley Cup play-off goals against 35 goaltenders (plus nine empty-net goals). Below are his most-frequent victims:

REGULAR SEASON GOALS
(by opposing goaltender)

Goals	Goaltender
29	Brodeur, Richard
23	Liut, Mike
21	Beaupre, Don
21	McLean, Kirk
21	Millen, Greg
18	Edwards, Don
18	Ranford, Bill
17	Lemelin, Reggie
17	Lessard, Mario
17	Vernon, Mike
15	Hayward, Brian
12	Barrasso, Tom
12	Hanlon, Glen
12	Riggin, Pat
12	Soetaert, Doug
12	Wamsley, Rick
11	Resch, Chico
10	Burke, Sean
10	Meloche, Gilles
10	Reddick, Eldon
10	Smith, Billy
10	St. Croix, Rick
10	Vanbiesbrouck, John
10	Wregget, Ken
9	Healy, Glenn
9	Herron, Denis
9	Malarchuk, Clint
9	Moog, Andy
9	Staniowski, Ed
8	Bernhardt, Tim
8	Hextall, Ron
8	Melanson, Rollie
8	Peeters, Pete
8	Sevigny, Richard
8	Stefan, Greg
7	Behrend, Marc
7	Essensa, Bob
7	Hrudey, Kelly
7	Janecyk, Bob
7	Jensen, Al
7	Keans, Doug
7	Richter, Mike
7	Romano, Roberto
7	Weeks, Steve

PLAYOFF GOALS
(by opposing goaltender)

Goals	Goaltender
12	Vernon, Mike
8	Hayward, Brian
8	Lemelin, Reggie
8	Smith, Billy
7	McLean, Kirk
5	Lessard, Mario
5	Lindbergh, Pelle
5	Potvin, Felix
4	Bannerman, Murray
4	Beaupre, Don
4	Vanbiesbrouck, John
3	Fuhr, Grant
3	Hextall, Ron
3	Ranford, Bill
3	Sevigny, Richard
3	Snow, Garth
2	Berthiaume, Daniel
2	Brodeur, Martin
2	Brodeur, Richard
2	Edwards, Don
2	Froese, Bob
2	Gamble, Troy
2	Hanlon, Glen
2	Moog, Andy
2	Osgood, Chris
1	Behrend, Marc
1	Eliot, Darren
1	Esposito, Tony
1	Myre, Phil
1	Peeters, Pete
1	Reese, Jeff
1	Roy, Patrick
1	Skorodenski, Warren
1	Wamsley, Rick
1	Young, Wendell

Gretzky Assists on Other Players' Goals

Wayne Gretzky had a total of 1963 regular-season and 260 play-off assists on goals by 141 different players during the regualr-season and another 50 during the playoffs. Below are the leaders in those categories:

REGULAR SEASON ASSISTS

Player	Assists
Kurri, Jari	364
Robitaille, Luc	115
Anderson, Glenn	106
Coffey, Paul	99
Messier, Mark	80
Granato, Tony	68
Krushelnyski, Mike	57
Sandstrom, Tomas	57
MacDonald, Blair	45
Nicholls, Bernie	40
Tikkanen, Esa	38
Huddy, Charlie	37
Callighen, Brett	36
Duchesne, Steve	35
Blake, Rob	34
Sundstrom, Niklas	34
Graves, Adam	28
Lumley, Dave	28
Semenko, Dave	27
Leetch, Brian	25
Hunter, Dave	24
McSorley, Marty	24
Kudelski, Bob	23
Hughes, Pat	20
Lowe, Kevin	19
Siltanen, Risto	17
Taylor, Dave	17
Pouzar, Jaroslav	16
Tonelli, John	16
Kovalev, Alexei	15
Donnelly, Mike	14
Stevens, Kevin	14
Gregg, Randy	13
Yachmenev, Vitali	13
Fogolin, Lee	12
Lindstrom, Willy	11
Simpson, Craig	11
Smith, Steve	10
Ashby, Don	9
Millen, Corey	9
Price, Pat	9
Tocchet, Rick	9
Allison, Mike	8
Kasper, Steve	8
Khristich, Dmitri	8
Napier, Mark	8
Summanen, Raimo	8
Benning, Brian	7
Lacroix, Eric	7
Sydor, Darryl	7
Crossman, Doug	6
Driver, Bruce	6
Harvey, Todd	6
Jackson, Don	6

Player	Assists
MacLean, John	6
MacTavish, Craig	6
Samuelsson, Ulf	6
Zhitnik, Alexei	6
Carpenter, Bob	5
Miller, Jay	5
Muni, Craig	5
Robinson, Larry	5
Schneider, Mathieu	5
Berg, Bill	4
Courtnall, Geoff	4
Cowie, Rob	4
Hicks, Doug	4
Karpovtsev, Alexander	4
LaFontaine, Pat	4
Linseman, Ken	4
Murdoch, Don	4
Roulston, Tom	4
Rychel, Warren	4
Watters, Tim	4
Ahola, Peter	3
Beukeboom, Jeff	3
Boucher, Philippe	3
Conacher, Pat	3
Druce, John	3
Hull, Brett	3
Makela, Mikko	3
Noonan, Brian	3
Petit, Michel	3
Ruotsalainen, Reijo	3
Schmautz, Bobby	3
Slaney, John	3
Wiemer, Jim	3
Chipperfield, Ron	2
Flatley, Patrick	2
Hagman, Matti	2
Knuble, Mike	2
Lavoie, Dominic	2
Liba, Igor	2
MacInnis, Al	2
McDonough, Hubie	2
Nedved, Petr	2
Prajsler, Petr	2
Quinn, Dan	2
Snell, Chris	2
Vorobiev, Vladimir	2
Weir, Stan	2
Baron, Murray	1
Brown, Kevin	1
Burridge, Randy	1
Buskas, Rod	1
Campbell, Colin	1
Corson, Shayne	1
Couturier, Sylvain	1
Creighton, Adam	1
DeGray, Dale	1
Driscoll, Peter	1
Dube, Christian	1
Dykstra, Steven	1
Elik, Todd	1
Finn, Steven	1
Forbes, Mike	1
Goneau, Daniel	1
Halkidis, Bob	1

Player	Assists
Hamilton, Al	1
Houda, Doug	1
Jones, Brad	1
Keane, Mike	1
Kontos, Chris	1
Langdon, Darren	1
Lariviere, Garry	1
Lidster, Doug	1
Lindholm, Mikael	1
Makkonen, Kari	1
Matteau, Stephane	1
McClelland, Kevin	1
McIntyre, John	1
Nilsson, Kent	1
Perreault, Yanic	1
Pronger, Chris	1
Sherven, Gord	1
Solheim, Ken	1
Sweeney, Tim	1
Thompson, Brent	1
Todd, Kevin	1
Walker, Gordon	1
Ward, Dixon	1

PLAYOFF ASSISTS

Player	Assists
Kurri, Jari	65
Anderson, Glenn	23
Coffey, Paul	16
Tikkanen, Esa	15
Robitaille, Luc	12
Sandstrom, Tomas	11
Messier, Mark	10
Corson, Shayne	8
Krushelnyski, Mike	8
Duchesne, Steve	6
Huddy, Charlie	5
Kontos, Chris	5
Nicholls, Bernie	5
Hunter, Dave	4
Rychel, Warren	4
Siltanen, Risto	4
Simpson, Craig	4
Callighen, Brett	3
Gregg, Randy	3
Hull, Brett	3
Linseman, Ken	3
Lowe, Kevin	3
Semenko, Dave	3
Blake, Rob	2
Fogolin, Lee	2
Granato, Tony	2
Laidlaw, Tom	2
Leetch, Brian	2
Lumley, Dave	2
McSorley, Marty	2
Smith, Steve	2
Taylor, Dave	2
Zhitnik, Alexei	2
Conacher, Pat	1
Courtnall, Russ	1
Hicks, Doug	1
Jones, Brad	1
Karpovtsev, Alexander	1
Kudelski, Bob	1

Player	Assists
Leach, Steve	1
MacTavish, Craig	1
McClelland, Kevin	1
Napier, Mark	1
Nilsson, Kent	1
Noonan, Brian	1
Pouzar, Jaroslav	1
Robinson, Larry	1
Ruotsalainen, Reijo	1
Summanen, Raimo	1
Sydor, Darryl	1

Players Assisting On Gretzky's Goals

A total of 143 players earned an assist on regular-season goals by Wayne Gretzky and 52 players assisted on Gretzky's playoff goals. Listed are the leaders in each category:

REGULAR SEASON

Player	Assists
Kurri, Jari	196
Coffey, Paul	116
Messier Mark	68
Anderson, Glenn	63
Huddy, Charlie	62
Robitaille, Luc	46
Krusheknyski, Mike	40
Lowe, Kevin	37
Tikkanen, Esa	33

PLAYOFFS

Player	Assists
Kurri, Jari	30
Coffey, Paul	20
Anderson, Glenn	16
Messier, Mark	13
Sandstrom, Tomas	9
Huddy, Charlie	8
Robitaille, Luc	8
Tikkanen, Esa	8
Gregg, Randy	6
Blake, Rob	4
Fuhr, Grant	4
Smith, Steve	4

Gretzky Scoring Streaks

NHL career goal-scoring streaks by Wayne Gretzky (games, dates, goals):

9 – Dec. 9, 1981 to Dec. 30, 1981 (19)
8 – Jan. 13, 1985 to Jan. 28, 1985 (10)
8 – Oct. 5, 1983 to Oct. 20, 1983 (11)
7 – Dec. 13, 1983 to Dec. 26, 1983 (12)
7 – Jan. 12, 1983 to Jan. 25, 1983 (9)
6 – March 15, 1982 to March 28, 1982 (10)
6 – Feb. 17, 1982 to Feb. 28, 1982 (12)
5 – Nov. 16, 1985 to Nov. 26, 1985 (7)
5 – Feb. 16, 1986 to Feb. 26, 1986 (7)
5 – Oct. 14, 1984 to Oct. 21, 1984 (10)
5 – Jan. 3, 1984 to Jan. 11, 1984 (11)
5 March 1, 1983 to March 8, 1983 (8)
5 – Jan. 26, 1982 to Feb. 3, 1982 (7)
5 – Nov. 21, 1981 to Nov. 29, 1981 (10)
5 – Oct. 10, 1981 to Oct. 20, 1981 (5)
5 – Jan. 30, 1980 to Feb. 8, 1980 (7)

"What amazed me most is that he never stopped amazing me."

Mark Messier